Violence and Abuse
in the Lives of
People with Disabilities

This book is printed on recycled paper.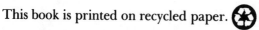

Violence and Abuse
in the Lives of
People with Disabilities

The End of Silent Acceptance?

by

Dick Sobsey, R.N., Ed.D.
Professor
Department of Educational Psychology
University of Alberta, Edmonton, Canada

·P·A·U·L·H·
BROOKES
PUBLISHING CO.

Baltimore • London • Toronto • Sydney

Paul H. Brookes Publishing Co.
P.O. Box 10624
Baltimore, Maryland 21285-0624

Typeset by Brushwood Graphics, Inc., Baltimore, Maryland.
Manufactured in the United States of America by
The Maple Press Company, York, Pennsylvania.

Library of Congress Cataloging-in-Publication Data
Sobsey, Richard.
    Violence and abuse in the lives of people with disabilities :
    the end of silent acceptance? / by Dick Sobsey.
        p.   cm.
    Includes bibliographical references and index.
    ISBN 1-55766-148-0
    1. Handicapped—Abuse of.   2. Handicapped—
Institutional care.   3. Handicapped—Abuse of—Prevention.
I. Title.
HV1568.S58   1994
362.4–dc20   93-44986
                                                         CIP

British Library Cataloguing-in-Publication data are available
from the British Library.

Contents

Foreword
A Personal Story

Note from Ruth Gerzon: *I was Mavis's social worker when she went to live with her nephew Jim about 6 years ago. I left my social work job 2 years later, but Mavis and I continue to be friends, and I sometimes act as her advocate. Mavis spends most weekends with my family. We all enjoy her company and admire her courage. The following is her story as she first shared it with me.*

In the hospitals you get abused; you get hit, and they make you a slave. When I was about 6 years old, I had to help. I never went to school. They wanted me for the work because I was so good at it.

Half the nurses wouldn't do anything at all. They'd leave it to the patients. I used to help do the dishes and look after the crippled kids in chairs. We wheeled the crippled kids with big heads and little bodies and feet onto the verandahs. Then we scrubbed the floor twice a week.

You didn't get any money, that's for sure. We didn't get any money. Staff told us when to get up and what to do. We didn't have any choices.

Some of the nurses were very strict, and we didn't get away with anything. They would hit us on the head with a wooden spoon. They are not allowed to do that now, I believe.

Some staff were nice; some were good to me. They would give me cuddles and that. When I was hit, they knew. But they wouldn't say anything. I would like the bad staff to get caught. The good staff should talk about it and put the others out.

I went to Templeton [hospital] when I was a baby in arms [in 1929]. My mother and father were fighting, and I got hit on the head with a beer bottle, and that's what damaged my brain. They said I was a normal baby when I was born.

The hardest thing for me was closed doors, locked doors. The staff had keys in their pockets on big chains. They had windows open only that much, so you couldn't climb out.

We were in the big dormitory. There were 106 in the dormitory. Some used to get favored more than others. I wasn't a favorite. I tried to be good, but they used to think I was naughty just the same.

We had a special room for when we were naughty. They called that room the naughty room. They shut us up. The door had three locks: one at the top, one in the center, one at the bottom. We had to stay there all night.

I didn't like their food. It was the same food over and over again. It wasn't fresh food. If you didn't eat it one day, you'd get it back the next day. They're not allowed to do that any more. They had big pots of food, everything done in one pot, potatoes and everything, not done nice. They used to make you eat milk puddings, force it down your throat. I can't eat milk puddings even today.

There were separate villas for the boys. We weren't allowed to mix up with the boys and men at all. Tommy was all right. He and Pat and a few of them were trusted. That's how I came to know Tommy. He was 21 when he came to Templeton. His mother and father had died.

I didn't have any clothes of my own, not even underclothes. I didn't have anything of my own. I would wear the ward stuff, the stuff from the store. Because I came as a baby in arms, I didn't have any of that. I'm glad Tommy didn't go in as a baby in arms because that wouldn't have been right for him because I love Tommy very much.

Levin [hospital] was worse. The place was dirty. It wasn't clean. The kids had cradle cap in their heads. I had it too. You get sores all over your body, little kiddies, too. One nurse came and said, "What have the kids got in their hair?" "Nits," I said. "Well, the staff can't be looking after them properly," she said. She used to trust me to lock the stores. She got me good clothes from the store; she picked out the best for me.

Before he died, my brother told my cousin Kath about me. The doctors told her I was partly handicapped, but I'm not ashamed of that. I can knit squares and other things. I can count too.

I was 26 when Kath came to get me, and I was with her going on 28 years. Tom came a long time after. Kath asked me who I would like to have living there. I said, "Tommy, I'm sure Tommy would like to come out."

We had a lot of cats and dogs, Alsatians and Siameses. Kath would breed them. We made a lot of money from that. Kath took me shopping, but she looked after my money. I wouldn't be happy unless someone looked after my money. When I went to live with Kath, I was so pleased, so happy.

I was with my cousin going on 28 years. When my cousin died, I got very upset. I didn't want to stay in Mangamuka. So Herman took us to Hamilton. Kath knew Herman, but she didn't know exactly what he was like. She was too sick to care, I think. She just wanted him to stay and keep her company.

Herman used to pinch our money for his drinking. His kids were terrible. Little devils they were. Two of them were 16 and were twins, the other one was 15, and they wouldn't let me and Tommy have a sleep. From the first night, we weren't given a fair go. Herman and the boys were cruel. We didn't know what to do to get away.

One night I was in my bedroom, and Herman said he was going to come in there. "No you're not," I said. "You're not allowed in this room. My body is my body, and no man is coming in here." I just kept banging on his face. He went and told on me, and I think that's why the cops came. I had a breakdown. They took me to Tokanui [hospital].

Then I went to IHC [residence]. Herman wanted me back, but they wouldn't let him take me. He came to see me at the hostel, and I said to Joy, "I don't want to see him." She said, "You must let us know," but I was too scared to stop him.

The lawyer and social worker found Jim, my nephew. I went to live with him on April 1, 1988. Tommy came later, and we had our own flat behind Jim's house. It was good with Jim. I loved him very much and still do. He showed me how to cook.

They told me I had another breakdown. I threw the furniture around, and I went to Ward 8 [the psychiatric ward at the local hospital]. I felt awful leaving Jim and Tommy. Jim went to see the doctor, and I went to live at the Lodge [a home for the elderly], and Tommy went to the Mary Shapley Home. I wanted to stay with Tommy.

If my cousin Kath was still alive, I wouldn't have been put away. The Lodge was like those places. The staff were nice at the Lodge, but there was no one hardly to talk to, nothing to do all day, just sitting around like some of those in the hospital who couldn't do anything for themselves. They're old people, and a lot of them don't understand. I was 63 then, but I felt young. It was boring having nothing to do all day, very boring. I wanted to help Lux the floors, do the dishes, the cooking, and things like that. I wanted to learn to read and write. Staff should have taught us, given us schooling, let us do some work, taken us for a walk down to the beach.

Now I've left the Lodge, after 18 months, and I'm glad. Jim and my friend Ruth got me out of there. I'm now in an IHC home with Paerata and Merenia. We are allowed to do what we like here. We can do dishes and Lux the floors and watch the T.V. channel we want.

I've got my own key now, to get in and out of the house when nobody's here. I have a nice bedroom, and we have a white kitten. I like to stay home by myself sometimes instead of being with the crowd.

Tommy lives nearby. He comes to see me quite a bit and sometimes stays for dinner. The staff take us out sometimes. We go to McDonald's and the beach. The staff also take me out to Ruth's farm on the weekends and to Jim's place. I am very happy here.

After listening to this book, I know the abuse is still going on. I feel terrible about that. Some places should be closed down because of the way the people get treated.

This book is good. It's trying to do something for us, to help people like me.

Mavis May
Self-advocate
Whakatane, New Zealand

Ruth Gerzon
Advocate
Whakatane, New Zealand

Foreword

Acknowledging Abuse Out Loud

This welcome and comprehensive book brings us a scholarly analysis of the causation, dynamics, and effects of abuse of people with disabilities, along with practical advice about prevention at many levels, from individual to organizational. Perhaps even more important, this book offers insights into aspects of the human condition, at times giving the reader almost unbearable pain—pain already borne by the victims of abuse.

On both sides of the Atlantic, the history of "knowing" about the physical, sexual, and emotional abuse of people with disabilities has a depressing similarity. Most individuals who have worked in day and residential services for children and adults with disabilities would know either firsthand or secondhand of incidents of abuse (although different words might have been used to describe what happened). However, despite a long series of scandals, exposés, and official inquiries into institutional "care," knowledge of abuse has largely remained at an anecdotal level. Service organization and structure did not address the issue in any systematic way. Indeed, all the ambiguities concerning societal and cultural attitudes toward people with disabilities, and toward abuse in general, continue to be played out in both institutional and community-based services.

The societal context in which abuse takes place is not a neutral one. It must be seen and understood against the background of the societal values placed on intellectual and physical ability and "wholeness" and the value (or lack thereof) accorded to those seen as impaired; of attitudes toward social and domestic violence; of the perceived sanctity and integrity of the family unit, the rights of parents, and their ownership of children; of economic and gender power imbalances; of perceptions regarding sexuality in general, and the sexuality of individuals with disabilities in particular. We live in societies in which abuse is endemic. We know, however, that risks for abuse are not of equal weight and that some sections of the population are more at risk than others. Thus, in general terms, children are more vulnerable than adults and girls are more vulnerable than boys. Where within the studies and statistics of risk do children and adults with disabilities fit in? Precision in any figures involving reporting of crime is very hard to achieve, perhaps particularly so in this area where powerful pressures exist not to report and to keep silent. Yet, overwhelmingly the evidence points to increased risk of abuse for people with disabilities in comparison with people without disabilities of the same age and gender. Why this is so is explored in depth in the pages that follow.

People with disabilities, families, human services administrators, direct service staff, legislators, law enforcement personnel, and other professionals all have parts to play in lowering the odds, but the main responsibility for safeguards against abuse must lie within service design and management. Human services providers and managers should be able to demonstrate that they have seriously considered the risks of abuse faced by users of their service. Abuse prevention strategies will take many forms, including strict screening procedures for job applicants, codes of expected staff conduct, orientation and in-service training, and working conditions that engender respect combined with a culture of empowerment of service users. When abuse is suspected, witnessed, or disclosed, there must be clearly understood policies and procedures for reporting and investigating and a climate in which reporting is rewarded, not punished. Finally, there must be support and treatment possibilities, either within the service or otherwise accessible to individuals who have been abused and all others caught up in the ripple effects of discovered abuse.

Violence and Abuse in the Lives of People with Disabilities: The End of Silent Acceptance? sends all of us two strong signals. The first is that the voices of people with disabilities, each with their own individual history and their own individual experiences powerfully articulated through the self-advocacy and disability rights movement, cannot and will not be stifled or silenced. The second is that shameful inaction on the part of service planners and providers as a response to known or suspected abuse is no longer a tenable option. Dick Sobsey's book increases our understanding and offers many ways of translating that understanding into sound practices, with, and on behalf of, children and adults with disabilities.

Ann Craft, Ph.D.
Senior Lecturer
Department of Learning Disabilities
University of Nottingham Medical School
Nottingham, England

Preface

This book is about the abuse of people with disabilities and measures that can be taken to prevent, or at least limit, the risk for abuse. It is intended for two groups of readers. First, pertinent information is presented regarding abuse and prevention for parents, professionals, administrators, and other people involved with services for people with disabilities. Second, information specific to people with disabilities is provided for the use of law enforcement officers, child protection workers, family violence counselors, and others involved in generic community services for abuse prevention and intervention. Attempting to address both of these groups in one book is indeed a challenging task, yet the establishment of communication and teamwork between these two groups is essential if progress is to be made in combating abuse of people with disabilities.

The book was written with four major goals:

1. To provide a conceptual framework for understanding abuse of people with disabilities
2. To offer strategies for abuse prevention to guide those developing specific prevention programs
3. To identify useful resources for prevention programs
4. To facilitate interaction among those concerned about abuse and how it might be controlled

Chapter 1 introduces the issue of abuse of people with disabilities and provides a brief accounting of my own personal experiences with abuse while working in an institution. Section I, Understanding Abuse, includes Chapters 2–6. These chapters present basic information about violence and abuse, discuss particular aspects of violence and abuse that affect people with disabilities, and describe a model for understanding the relationship between abuse and disability. Section II, Preventing Abuse, includes Chapters 7–13. These chapters look at how the risk of abuse can be reduced for people with disabilities by empowering them to resist it and through restructuring some of the social realities that contribute to their increased risk. The appendix to the book provides a list of useful resources of information and materials concerning abuse and disability.

In the second half of the 20th century, physical, sexual, and psychological abuse have been recognized as major social concerns for all members of society, not just for people with disabilities. Children, women, and many other members of contemporary society without disabilities are also frequently victimized, and the need for discussing abuse in relationship to disability requires some explanation. An individual with a disability is more likely to become a victim of assault or abuse than other people of similar age and gender. Furthermore, individuals with disabilities who have been victimized typically experience more prolonged and severe abuse, and evidence suggests that the harmful effects of abuse may be more serious and chronic for victims with disabilities. Ironically, people with disabilities have often been systematically excluded from programs to prevent abuse and from services that support victims. Even their basic right to personal security has often been denied through lack of access to the law enforcement and criminal justice systems that protect other members of society.

Patterns of victimization share many similarities for abused people with and without disabilities; however, there are a significant number of important differences. For example, many more people with disabilities are abused by paid caregivers entrusted with their protection and welfare. In the chapters that follow, both the similarities and differences in patterns of abuse are explored in an effort to present practical methods of risk reduction for people with disabilities. Before considering prevention methods, it is essential that these patterns of abuse be analyzed to provide a comprehensive model of abuse and disability that will serve as a foundation for risk reduction methods. The integrated ecological model presented in this book is a variation of the model that was developed by Bronfenbrenner (1977) and refined by others (e.g., Belsky, 1980; Garbarino & Stocking, 1980). This book draws upon their work and the work of many other researchers. It also utilizes the research that I have conducted with my colleagues at the University of Alberta Abuse & Disability Project in Edmonton, Alberta, Canada, and at the University of Otago in New Zealand.

NOTES FOR THE READER

The University of Alberta Abuse & Disability Project

Some of the motivation for starting the University of Alberta Abuse & Disability Project grew out of my experiences as a participating observer while working at a single institution for people with disabilities over a period of 10 years. My observations during this time of the abuse of residents (described in greater detail in Chapter 1) required validation and expansion by comparing them to other sources. I started the project in 1986, in order to develop a model for understanding abuse of people with disabilities and to devise effective ways of preventing it. A general explanation of the overall structure of the project is discussed here; specific references to work that resulted from the project are presented in various chapters of the book.

Figure 1 provides an overview of the Abuse & Disability Project. The project comprised several different components, including that of my own participant observations. The first component of the project involved a review of the relevant literature. This was designed to determine what was already known or believed about the relationship between disability and abuse (Sobsey, Gray, Wells, Pyper, & Reimer-Heck, 1991). Information from this review was organized to identify possible risk factors for abuse of people with disabilities and to determine areas of consistency, as well as gaps and areas of inconsistency within the existing literature.

The second component of the project involved developing a registry of reports by people with disabilities who had been victims of sexual

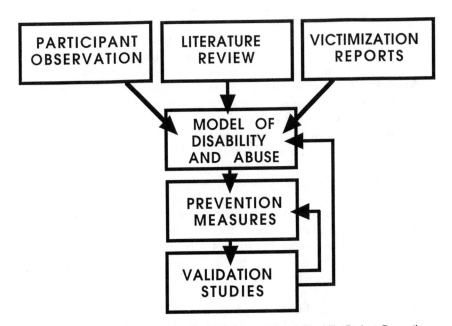

Figure 1. Components of the University of Alberta Abuse & Disability Project. Prevention measures were developed out of several sources integrated into a model of abuse and disability and were validated through expert rankings for further refinement.

abuse or assault and their advocates to determine common patterns of abuse. At the same time, a survey of sexual assault centers was conducted to determine if, and how, people with disabilities were receiving intervention and support services. The victims' report registry now includes about 220 cases and provides information about where offenses occur, who commits them, and many other offense characteristics. This information has been used to further refine our model of abuse and to provide a preliminary test of some of the hypotheses generated by the literature review. This survey is discussed in greater detail in Chapter 3.

The third component of our project involved validation of the resulting model. Aspects of a potential prevention program were ranked by people with disabilities, service providers, researchers, and several other groups to determine their perceived value in preventing sexual abuse. The rankings of these groups provided social validation for the developing model of abuse and helped to identify areas in need of further refinement. Results of this expert validation study were instrumental in the development of the various prevention measures presented in Chapters 7–13.

The Fallacies of Blaming the Victim

In discussing the relationship between disability and abuse, it is important to clarify the difference between cause and association. Recognizing that disability or any other trait of the victim of abuse is associated with increased risk must not be misinterpreted to imply that victims are partially responsible for their own abuse (Sobsey & Varnhagen, 1991; Waxman, 1991). In fact, it is society's response to disability, not the disability itself, that accounts for much of the increased risk experienced by people with disabilities. Blatant forms of blaming the victim of abuse seem absurd; however, subtler degrees of blame can be found in traditional explanations of abuse of children and of individuals with disabilities, which assert that the dependency of the victim causes stress for caregivers that subsequently leads to abuse. Although there is little empirical evidence to support this hypothesis, and much evidence to contradict it (e.g., Benedict, Wulff, & White, 1992), it has been commonly accepted as a logical explanation (Sobsey, 1989). Such a misinterpretation can have two major negative effects. First, it is unjust to blame victims, and blame often leads to the further punishment of victims who have already suffered. Second, by inappropriately blaming the victim, the actual causal and contributing factors are obscured, and the real problem cannot be corrected.

The development of the "science of victimology" (von Hentig, 1967) has facilitated victim-blaming because of its heavy focus on the attributes of the people who were offended against, rather than on those who committed the offenses. Even in von Hentig's early work in victimology, people with disabilities were recognized as common targets. However, the problem does not arise simply as result of the recognition that people's behavior and characteristics can influence their risk for victimization. The problem occurs only when too much focus on victim characteristics obscures more fundamental concerns related to the attributes of offenders and the environments that contribute to increased risk. American mass murderer Ted Bundy, for instance, typically chose victims with dark hair. Blaming these victims for their hair color would not only be illogical, it would be unlikely to help solve the problem. Understanding why Bundy chose victims with this trait, however, might prove more useful. The characteristics of crime victims are important, but only to the extent that they are understood within a complex and interactive constellation of behavioral and environmental variables associated with a particular group of offenses.

Terminology

A number of terms used in this book require some explanation. Whenever possible, terms are used in their generic sense, and reliance on highly technical terminology is avoided in order to allow readers from a variety of disciplines and backgrounds to understand the text. Although the primary focus of this book is on information relevant to people with developmental disabilities, much of the text can be generalized to people with a variety of other categories of disability. Therefore, the terms *people with disabilities* and *individual with a disability* are used unless the specific context requires a narrower focus.

The term *victim* as used in this book refers to any individual who is victimized and should not be interpreted as implying that any attribute or behavior of that individual contributed to his or her victimization. This distinction is important because the word *victim* has sometimes been associated with implicit blame. For this reason, some authors prefer alternatives such as *survivor* of a crime. Unfortunately, not all victims survive the offenses committed against them; therefore, *survivor* would not be appropriate for all the *victims* described in this book. Furthermore, a growing advocacy movement for people who have been victimized by criminal behavior asserts their right to use the word *victim* with dignity in defiance of those who have stigmatized it.

The word *treatment* is occasionally used to refer to counseling, education, and other types of support. This term is not used here in its medical sense as a "cure" for some pathological condition. The conceptualization of people who have been abused as "sick" and in need of a "cure" can add to the stigma already associated with victimization.

Where appropriate, the word *intervention* is used because of its implication that the person being supported is involved in his or her own healing, rather than being a passive recipient of that support.

The term *abuse* is frequently used in this book in its general sense of mistreatment of children or adults. *Abuse*, however, has sometimes been considered a euphemism when applied to serious crimes committed against people with disabilities. Table 1 lists some of the offenses committed against people with disabilities and the euphemisms that are at times used to decriminalize or trivialize these offenses. Crimes such as rape, murder, assault, and battery are sometimes trivialized as "abuse" or "misconduct." These euphemisms help provide a rationale for reclassifying serious crimes, especially those committed within human services, into mere "administrative infractions." As suggested by Luckasson (1992), it is essential that we classify these crimes properly and respond to them as serious offenses in order to deter their future occurrence. Furthermore, the choice of the word *abuse*, often associated with mistreatment of children, may raise issues of infantilization of adults with disabilities. Therefore, the general term *abuse* is used to span the spectrum from mild infractions to serious criminal acts against people of all ages, but the appropriate legal terms for specific offenses are used whenever they apply.

Prevention, as used here, includes all activities that are undertaken to reduce the risk of potential abuse and the harm that it inflicts. In considering prevention of abuse and other forms of violence, it is important to note that no prevention effort, no matter how large or well-designed, can ensure absolute safety for any individual. Thus, prevention implies risk management rather than invulnerability to risk.

Prevention can be accomplished on several levels. First and ideally, prevention can occur when conditions are changed to decrease the likelihood of abuse before it takes place. Second, when abuse does take place, prevention can reduce the chance of continuation or recurrence of abuse. Finally, because the real measure of abuse is its impact on the person who is victimized, prevention can be said to occur when intervention ameliorates the harm that was done.

Use of the First Person "I"

My own personal experience has played a significant part in the development of this book. For this reason, the first person "I" is occasionally used when describing my own experiences and perceptions. Any portrayal of the researcher and author as a disinterested observer would be inappropriate and misleading in this work, but such assumptions of objectivity may be inappropriate in most (possibly all) forms of scientific endeavor. The absurdity of this concept of the objective researcher who operates independent of any motivation except that of rational

Table 1. Glossary of euphemisms used to decriminalize offenses committed against people with disabilities

Generic term	Term applied to victims with disabilities
Assault	Psychological abuse, threat
Battery	Abuse, punishment procedure, aversive treatment, physical prompting, assistance, guidance
Crime	Infraction
Criminal offense	Administrative infraction, discrimination
Homicide	Euthanasia, neglect, medical discrimination
Kidnapping	Detention
Murder	Euthanasia, neglect, assisted suicide, allowing to die
Poisoning	Chemical restraint
Police (investigating unit)	Personnel relations (investigating unit)
Rape	Abuse, professional misconduct
Sexual assault	Abuse, professional misconduct
Slavery	Exploitation of labor
Torture	Treatment
Unlawful imprisonment	Detention, restraint, seclusion

discovery has been discussed in both fiction and professional literature. Kurt Vonnegut, for example, explores this idea in his novel *Cat's Cradle* (1963). Vonnegut's pure scientist investigates an interesting substance, "ice-9," a variant on the molecular structure of water that crystallizes at a higher temperature. He conducts his research with perfect objectivity, ignoring its rather obvious consequence—the total annihilation of all living things. The novel suggests that all research has social outcomes and that the pretense of science that is independent of moral values and social issues is inherently contradictory. Science is driven by its own moral value—that pure information is more important than any social outcomes that it might generate.

Jones (1992) suggests that in modern social research "the old distant voice of the objective observer/writer is seen as a fiction" (p. 19) and that truth and accuracy are best served by researchers who recognize and acknowledge their own experiences and biases. In view of my own strong feelings about the topic of this book, I have attempted to follow Jones's principles. Having worked in human services since the 1960s, I have personally witnessed hundreds of examples of abuse and heard secondhand and thirdhand accounts of a great many others. I have also seen and sometimes been a part of many well-intentioned attempts to eliminate the abuse of individuals with disabilities, and most of these efforts have made significant differences. However, sometimes the efforts to eliminate abuse left the victims in a worse situation than before. Such failures have left me skeptical about finding any easy solution to the problem.

I believe that the application of the prevention methods proposed in this book will make important differences in the lives of people with disabilities. However, I also realize that even with the best application, these methods cannot solve all the problems of abuse experienced by people with disabilities. Many of the factors that contribute to abuse are deeply embedded in our culture, and some may even be intrinsic to human nature. Such factors can only be altered through fundamental social, cultural, and psychological changes that go beyond the measures proposed here. Other causes of abuse remain unknown. It is hoped that future research may help to shed new light on approaches to prevention in the years to come.

REFERENCES

Belsky, J. (1980). Child maltreatment: An ecological integration. *American Psychologist, 35*(4), 320–335.

Benedict, M., Wulff, L.M., & White, R.B. (1992). Current parental stress in maltreating and nonmaltreating families of children with multiple disabilities. *Child Abuse & Neglect, 16,* 155–163.

Bronfenbrenner, U. (1977). Toward an experimental ecology of human development. *American Psychologist, 32,* 513–531.

Garbarino, J., & Stocking, S.H. (1980). The social context of child maltreatment. In J. Garbarino & S.H. Stocking (Eds.), *Protecting children from abuse and neglect: Developing and maintaining support systems for families* (pp. 1–14). San Francisco: Jossey-Bass.

Jones, A. (1992). Writing feminist educational research: Am "I" in the text? In S. Middleton & A. Jones (Eds.), *Women and education in Aotearoa* (Vol. 2, pp. 18–32). Wellington, New Zealand: Briget Williams, Books.

Luckasson, R. (1992). People with mental retardation as victims of crime. In R.W. Conley, R. Luckasson, & G.N. Bouthilet (Eds.), *The criminal justice system and mental retardation: Defendants and victims* (pp. 209–220). Baltimore: Paul H. Brookes Publishing Co.

Sobsey, D. (1989). Are we preventing mental retardation? *Newsletter of the American Association of Mental Retardation, 2*(2), 2, 8.

Sobsey, D., Gray, S., Wells, D., Pyper, D., & Reimer-Heck, B. (1991). *Disability, sexuality, & abuse: An annotated bibliography.* Baltimore: Paul H. Brookes Publishing Co.

Sobsey, D., & Varnhagen, C. (1991). Sexual abuse, assault, and exploitation of individuals with disabilities. In C. Bagley & R.J. Thomlinson (Eds.), *Child sexual abuse: Critical perspectives on prevention, intervention, and treatment* (pp. 203–216) Toronto, Ontario, Canada: Wall and Emerson.

von Hentig, H. (1967). *The criminal and his victims.* Hamden, CT: Archon Books.

Vonnegut, K. (1963). *Cat's cradle.* New York: Bantam Books.

Waxman, B.F. (1991). Hatred—The unacknowledged dimension in violence against disabled people. *Journal of Sexuality and Disability, 9*(3), 185–199.

Acknowledgments

Many different individuals and organizations have made important contributions to this book. Much of the book was prepared during the time that I served as a Roy McKenzie Foundation Visiting Professor at the Donald Beasley Institute in the Department of General Practice at the University of Otago Medical School, Dunedin, New Zealand. Many people at the institute offered insights and suggestions that have been incorporated. Dr. Anne Bray, Director of the institute, provided many ideas and offered much useful feedback throughout the book's development. Roz Cavanaugh organized many things during my stay in New Zealand to make writing time possible.

The remainder of the book was prepared at the University of Alberta, where, as a McCalla Research Professor, I was allowed the time to complete the work. Under its Research Program Grant 410-91-1665, the Social Sciences and Humanities Research Council of Canada provided primary funding for the research that forms the nucleus of the book. Some of the research by the University of Alberta Abuse & Disability Project was supported in part by grants from Health and Welfare Canada, and the National Health Research and Development Program. Some of the project's ongoing work in counseling reflected in Chapter 12 is funded by the Joseph P. Kennedy, Jr. Foundation. Opinions expressed in this book are solely those of the authors and are not necessarily shared by any of the funding agencies.

Many people at Paul H. Brookes Publishing Co. contributed over and above the normal requirements. I am especially thankful to Sarah Cheney for her recognition that a book on this topic was needed and for her confidence in my ability to write it. I am indebted to her for her encouragement and support throughout the development and writing of this book. I am also thankful to Melissa Behm and Paul Brookes for their support of this project and for allowing me the flexibility to focus my efforts on this project even when that meant delaying other work. Theresa Donnelly, the developmental editor, provided thoughtful editing and ideas. Amie Morrow, the production editor, helped make this book much more coherent and readable. Both Theresa and Amie contributed suggestions that helped my own conceptual understanding of abuse and disability. Roslyn Udris displayed her usual masterful skills as production manager. The entire team at Brookes deserves my gratitude for their patience.

Many others contributed to the development of this book, including Don Wells, at the University of Alberta, who provided helpful feedback and editorial assistance. I also want to extend special thanks to Dr. Fred Orelove, at the Virginia Institute for Developmental Disabilities, for teaching me the discipline of writing. Richard Lucardie and Dr. Thuppal Madhavan provided valuable help in finding reference materials. Sheila Mansell, Research Associate at the University of Alberta Abuse & Disability Project, contributed to every phase of the book. Andre Zawallich, at the University of Alberta, helped find valuable sources of information on the Nazi euthanasia and genocide programs and on a number of other topics. Dr. Anne Donnellan, at the University of Wisconsin, suggested some of the reference materials cited in the work. Dr. Stephen Trumble, at the Intellectual Disability Unit, Department of Community Medicine, Monash University, supplied useful information on the incidence and etiology of developmental disabilities. Marta Carmona, at the Alberta Association for Community Living Resource Centre, also helped locate resources. Sandra Cole, Walter Coles, Pierre Hebert, Ken Nelson, Peter Park, Ellen Shaman, Barbara Waxman, Dan Yeatman, and a great many others taught me things about the issue of abuse and disability that I hope I can pass on to others through this book.

To Louise Marie Correia

Violence and Abuse
in the Lives of
People with Disabilities

1

Perspectives on the Issue of Abuse

Michael was a psychiatric nurse, and Gary had worked as a practical nurse before finding his calling as a minister in a church serving people with developmental disabilities. Judy's son was diagnosed with mental retardation as well as physical disabilities, and Al's daughter's disability meant that she would probably never walk. Michael, Gary, Judy, and Al had two things in common. First, they were all caregivers for people with disabilities. Second, they were all brutal killers.

As a psychiatric nurse, Michael worked in psychiatric settings and residential schools. When the Third Reich transformed these schools and hospitals into euthanasia centers, Michael willingly cooperated, and his hard work and success in the euthanasia program were rewarded by selection to the team that would set up and run the larger genocidal death camps in Poland. Michael's career path was not unique. Many other health, education, and rehabilitation professionals who worked with people with developmental and mental disabilities during the Third Reich readily adapted to extermination of their clients (Sereny, 1974).

Gary believed that God had chosen him to look after people with disabilities. He befriended many and the church services that he held for his parishioners were well attended. Gary also abducted, imprisoned, raped, tortured, and murdered women. He kept his van parked on the street outside a large institution so that he could pull in women with disabilities to sexually assault them. When the church services were being conducted in Gary's living room, some of his prisoners were chained in the basement below (Englade, 1988).

Judy felt her son's disabilities made him a burden. Although his limitations were not severe, she kept him away from home in a series of residential schools. When he reached adulthood, she bought $100,000 worth of life insurance on him before feeding him a lethal dose of arsenic. Somehow he survived, but his arms and legs were paralyzed by the poison that made him seem even more of a burden to his mother. Paralyzed and wearing 60 pounds of metal arm and leg orthoses, Michael Buenoano was taken for a ride in a canoe by his mother and brother who dropped him into a Florida river. The death was never considered suspicious and was not investigated until after Judy had attempted several other murders (Anderson & McGhee, 1991).

Al was also known as the Boston Strangler. His 2-year-old daughter had an orthopedic disability, and Al felt that his wife gave the child all her attention while ignoring his needs. Al liked to remove the orthosis from his daughter's legs and massage her upper thighs so hard that she would cry intensely. Then he would put the orthosis back on and tie it with a neat little bow. He would tie that same neat little bow around the necks of the women he strangled and prop their lifeless legs into the same position that the orthosis held his daughter's legs (Blashfield, 1990).

The offenses of these four caregivers certainly were extreme. Were they unique aberrations, or can they help us to recognize that abuse and violence are realities in the lives of most people with disabilities? Abuse and violence are hidden just beneath the surface of the lives of people with disabilities where they are easily ignored. Nevertheless, much of the human devastation generated by abuse and violence could be averted. The first step toward reducing these risks for people with disabilities, however, is understanding how and why abuse and violence occur.

RIGHTS AND REALITIES FOR PEOPLE WITH DISABILITIES

Rights

According to the United Nations Convention on the Rights of the Child (1989), all children have a right to be treated with humanity and respect; every nation is responsible for protecting children from all forms of violence and abuse; and when abuse does occur, states must take appropriate measures to promote physical and psychological recovery as well as social reintegration. This Convention also declares that children with disabilities have a right to a full and decent life and to be free from all forms of discrimination. In an earlier proclamation, the United Nations Declaration on the Rights of Disabled Persons (1975) states that all people with disabilities have an inherent right to respect for their human dignity, as well as a right to protection from all degrading treatment, discrimination, and abuse.

Realities

In spite of the United Nation's noble objectives, violence, sexual abuse, and neglect of children and adults with disabilities continues throughout the world. For example, in Malaysia, adolescents with disabilities are spending their lives tied down to beds. In Africa, Eastern Europe, and Latin America, children with mental retardation are being kidnapped to sell their vital organs to affluent buyers. People who commit offenses against people with mental retardation in Germany and Spain are receiving reduced penalties because their victims are viewed as incapable of suffering, and the assailant who raped a woman with mental retardation in the United Kingdom is set free because the victim's testimony is held to be inadmissible. The United States and the United Kingdom report cases of people with disabilities being denied proper legal representation and convicted of crimes that they did not commit. Institutional abuse and neglect continues to be reported from Albania, Australia, Belgium, the Commonwealth of Independent States, Greece, Jamaica, and many others (Reid, 1992). Studies from many countries (e.g., U.S., U.K., Australia) suggest that child abuse, beatings, and rape are common occurrences in the lives of many, probably most, people with developmental disabilities.

RESEARCH TO PRACTICE

As mentioned in the preface, the primary focus of this book is to develop practical methods of preventing abuse of people with disabilities. Nevertheless, it is important to base practice on the best available information. Although much of the content of this book is based on research gathered at the Abuse and Disability Project at the University of Alberta, some of the research is based on my own experiences working in various capacities with people with disabilities and the caregiving systems that play a major role in their lives. A brief explanation of these experiences, as well as the rationale behind their inclusion here as valuable toward a better understanding of abuse of people with disabilities, is discussed below.

Ethnographic Research

Spradley (1980) provides a thorough guide for conducting ethnographic research that differs from traditional academic research in three critical dimensions. First, specific hypotheses are not set prior to beginning the study; the researcher begins with only general questions regarding the interactions, beliefs, and structures that characterize a culture. More specific questions may evolve from culture and experience as research progresses, but hypotheses cannot be externally imposed on the research. Second, there is no requirement for researcher objectivity in its classic sense (the isolation of the researcher from the phenomenon studied). Instead, the researcher must be both participant and observer because the actual experience is central to understanding the culture. Finally, attempts at experimental control are disregarded because the total understanding of natural conditions is the essence of an ethnographic investigation.

Thus, researchers in such ethnographic studies become "participant observers." They carry out a dual purpose: engaging in the activities appropriate to the culture of the particular situation being studied, while also observing the situation, explicitly aware of their role as researcher—asking questions, recording data, and comparing information from various sources and perspectives to determine validity (Spradley, 1980). The degree of participation by the researcher varies from study to study. Active participation implies that the observer participates by assuming a role similar to that of other people who are in that situation, so that the researcher can more fully comprehend the situation's rules, expectations, and, experiences. In many cases, ethnographers study situations in which they are already participants or that they participate in for reasons other than research. Riemer (1977) describes such "opportunistic" research, suggesting and that these situations often provide unique opportunities for observation. For example, it may be easier for a combat soldier, a prisoner, or a member of a secret society to become a researcher than it would be for a researcher to assume one of these roles solely for the purpose of research.

A Personal Ethnography of Abuse

I assumed the dual role of participant observer for a period of 10 years during which time I worked in a large residential institution for people with disabilities. My research skills were limited, having completed only one undergraduate sociological research methods course and one brief participant observation study. Nevertheless, much of what I learned during that time has been validated by subsequent research and contributes to the ideas presented in this book. Therefore, a brief description of these experiences is required.

In April 1968, I started work as an attendant at a large (about 5,500 residents at its peak) institution in the eastern United States. In the orientation classes where we spent half of each day for the first 2 weeks, we learned that abuse of residents by staff was rare, but that if we saw abuse occur, we must report it to our immediate supervisor. On the wards, where we spent the other half of each day, I saw residents of the institution pushed, kicked, slapped, punched, threatened, knocked over, forced to work for little or no pay, and abused in a variety of other ways by staff. I reported many abusive incidents, and several other men (in this sexually segregated institution, women were sent to different living units) in the orientation group also reported instances of abuse.

After orientation I saw many other episodes of physical and psychological abuse and again reported some of these to various supervisors. Their response was usually indifferent, and occasionally they appeared irritated by my reports. Before long, the general lack of response to these reports seemed clear, and I had seen some of the same supervisors to whom I had reported the abuse also beat residents of the institution.

The abuse that I saw was generally consistent with accounts of abuse at other institutions, such as those described in Chapter 5. The nature and severity of the abuse varied. I never saw staff sexually abusing residents, although rumors of such behavior were occasionally passed around. The variety of physical and psychological abuse was incredible. I never saw anyone killed, although on one occasion several residents provided a credible account of how an attendant had killed one of their friends. The official story indicated that he had been killed by another resident.

It would be impossible to describe the full range of offenses, but I will provide a few examples. *Strongsuits* are heavy denim coveralls that lace and tie in the back and have no openings at the end of the arms so that they restrict the use of hands and fingers. They were typically used as a form of restraint to prevent such behavior as pulling off bandages, but were often misused in other ways. On one occasion, as a punishment for yelling, a small boy was placed in a strongsuit and hung by the straps from a door hinge for about 45 minutes. On another occasion, a young man who was caught taking a shoelace out of a shoe was punished by having both arms held behind his back while his head was pushed into a wall. The resulting laceration required several stitches, but the incident report indicated that the injury occurred during a fall. The physician who sutured the laceration used no anesthetic, explaining that "severely retarded people are incapable of feeling pain."

Not all abuse occurred as punishment; sometimes it occurred as a perverse form of entertainment for the staff. One summer evening, the staff of two living units were given a cardboard box containing half a bushel of apples for "snacks" for the residents. It was a warm evening, and about 100 residents from both living units were herded into a courtyard after supper. The courtyard was surrounded on three sides by the building, and three attendants stood at the open end facing the residents in the courtyard. The three attendants took turns taking apples out of the box and throwing them as hard as they could into the crowd of residents. Some throws missed completely, some only inflicted minor injury, but other hits did more severe damage. The attendants laughed and praised each other for particularly good shots while the residents tried to take cover and scrambled to retrieve and eat the broken pieces of fruit from the dirt.

Sometimes, especially when the abuse seemed particularly violent, I attempted to intervene directly—usually by telling people to stop, occasionally by physically coming between the victim and his abuser. These attempts had some immediate repercussions, but there was no lasting impact other than my being ostracized by my fellow workers. In a few instances, I received threats; usually these were vague or anonymous, rarely were they more direct. More frequently, I failed to intervene because I was afraid, uncertain, busy, tired, or simply overwhelmed by the extent of the problem.

It would be incredibly simplistic to portray everyone else who worked in this place as the "bad guys" and portray myself as the one and only "good guy." There were some people among the staff whose behavior could only be explained by the need to inflict pain or exert control over others. These individuals committed the most severe abuse and took obvious pleasure in it. The vast majority, however, were not in this category. They were generally good people who nonetheless committed varying degrees of abuse for several reasons. First, they worked under very difficult conditions, including overwhelming overcrowding and understaffing. With few appropriate resources and little training, they were expected to manage and direct residents. Unfortunately, physical coercion often became the instrument of control. Second, some of the residents were indeed violent, and some physical force was probably required at times. However, the line between the appropriate use of minimal force and abuse was never clearly drawn, and as individuals became accustomed to using force, they tended to use it more frequently and with greater excess. Third, models of violence were all around us. As attendants saw excessive force used by other staff, they were influenced to do the same. This was further exacerbated by evident social pressures to abuse residents. Staff members who refrained from violence were viewed as outsiders and potential threats to those who abused residents. Thus, the demonstration of force against residents was required for social acceptance.

A small, but very significant number of direct care staff members showed genuine concern for residents and worked to improve conditions. They believed that some degree of force was necessary, but tried to minimize it and would take a stand against more extreme forms of abuse. This group rarely, if ever, reported abuse, but they would sometimes directly confront other staff members they thought were "over the line."

An even smaller group reported abuse to authorities within and outside the institution. These people were unpopular with other direct care staff. Usually, this meant silence and a lack of cooperation. Occasionally, it meant threats or vandalization of property. There was also a belief among this group that they were given less pleasant assignments or received harsher treatment by the administration. One of the women in this group made abuse complaints with me to the authorities. She later said that she was no longer willing to make a public statement because she had a family to consider and could not afford to lose her job "or worse." Occasionally such beliefs appeared to be substantiated by evidence of mistreatment. However, most of the time evidence of such harassment was vague or ambiguous. Nevertheless, life was typically unpleasant at the institution for people who made complaints and most left fairly quickly.

Professionals and administrators also seemed to fall into various categories. Some denied that abuse ever occurred and appeared to do everything in their power to ensure that they would remain ignorant of it so that they would not have to deal with it. For example, the director made visits to the buildings each year at Christmas, but rarely at other times and never unannounced.

Many others worked hard to make the institution a better place in a variety of ways, including fighting to eliminate abuse. Many of these people were energetic and talented, but found themselves facing an impossible situation, one where they were often constrained by a lack of resources, sabotage of their efforts by direct care staff and their superiors, bureaucratic policies and procedures, and conflicting priorities. For example, attempting to address the abuse problem could be a full-time job, and responding to it would mean less attention given to the development of training programs or the transition of residents out of the institution and into the community. Also, no real solution to the abuse problem seemed possible without admitting the scope and severity of the problem, yet any administrator making such an admission would be committing professional suicide. Thus, any administrator who admitted the extent of the problem might not be around to help solve it. Therefore, because any action powerful enough to rock the boat would not be tolerated, those trying to effect progress were limited to less sweeping measures. Individual abusers might be identified and punished, but the system that spawned abuse could not be changed.

Disillusioned with attempts at reporting abuse to my supervisor, I wrote a letter to the director of the institution explaining my concern, but there was no reply. I began to make reports to outside authorities. Several other people working there did the same, and some complaints were made collectively. Among the various people who received these reports were the state police, the local district attorney, civil liberties groups, the coordinator of a nearby community college program that trained child care workers, the community mental hygiene board of visitors, state and national developmental disabilities advocacy groups, and the organization representing families of people living in the institution.

Responses of these individuals and agencies varied. We were told that these were serious allegations and that a major investigation was being launched. However, if an investigation was launched, it was done so without interviewing any of the people who made the allegations, nor was there any other observable indication of its existence. We were also told that the state police do not enter institutions or become involved in their affairs without the "invitation" of the Commissioner of Mental Hygiene.

Some people and organizations were more helpful. The coordinator of the community college program took an active role in trying to secure help and also stopped using the institution as a training site. The local civil liberties organization also provided advice and support.

Other responses were more difficult to interpret. Advocacy organizations and public agencies for people with developmental disabilities seemed supportive, yet took little constructive action. The Executive Director of one such organization wrote, "I certainly agree with your observations and just want to assure you that many of us share your frustrations, but are trying hard to do something about it." He also sent four publications, recommended another, "Retarded Children are People," which I could purchase for 75¢, and suggested I "discuss membership" with the organization representing parents of children in the institution. Sixteen months later I wrote him again, and he replied by assuring me that "although we get many such complaints this is the first time anyone was willing to put their name down." This was surprising because my name had already been on the complaint he had responded to 16 months earlier, and other people told me that they had also made direct contact with complainants. Nevertheless, because this association was willing to "go to bat immediately with the Administration and the Department of Mental Hygiene," I traveled 100 miles to meet with him and the head of their Institutions Committee. They spoke in general terms, giving strong support for the need to solve the problem and indicating that their organization was doing important work in this area, but they were not at liberty to discuss the details at that time. Two hours after I left their office, I arrived home just as my phone was ringing. The caller never identified himself, but he let me know that he knew where I had been and what I had said. He suggested that I learn to keep quiet or I would be "very sorry." Somehow the content of that meeting was leaked back to people at the institution within 2 hours. If there was ever a more productive result from that meeting, I am unaware of it.

As an attendant, I felt powerless to change things. I went to school to become a nurse and later a certified teacher because I believed that these credentials would help me to achieve a position of authority within the institution, and thus, the power to make changes. I was wrong. In the years that followed, there were some small successes, and I would like to think that I contributed toward making a better life for the residents. I think the abuse became less frequent, but it certainly did not stop, and may have just been better hidden. I found myself tangled in the same web of constraints and compromises as other well-intentioned professionals and administrators. Most of the real progress that occurred during those years probably resulted primarily from better budgets, reductions in size, and other such factors. In 1978, having spent just over a decade working in that institution, I left believing that there was little more that I could contribute by staying.

CLOSING REMARKS

A few comments are required regarding this bleak personal account of abuse within a residential institution. Many good people continue to work to improve life in this and other institutions. Their task has been difficult, and much has been accomplished. Institutional life has improved significantly since I first became involved in 1968; hopefully, it continues to improve. Nothing said in this book detracts from their accomplishments in any way. The task faced by those working to improve institutional life has generally been thankless and this is unfair. As long as some people live their lives in institutions, it is essential that good people and adequate resources are available to make institutional life as good as it can possibly be.

The ultimate responsibility for the realities of institutional life lies within the community. The current trend toward community services has reduced the population of institutions, but it has also resulted in a greater concentration of people with the most severe needs living in institutional settings. Until and unless good alternatives can be provided for every individual in the community, institutions will continue to exist. As long as they exist, providing the best possible quality of life for the people who inhabit them is crucial. Serving every individual in the community is a desirable goal. If and when this is achieved, institutions will cease to exist because they will have become obsolete. Until this goal is reached, abandoning the efforts to improve institutional life would mean abandoning the people who continue to live in them. And unless the community changes its attitudes toward the people with disabilities who live among us, brutal killers like Michael, Gary, Judy, and Al will continue to pursue, unnoticed, the more vulnerable members of society.

I

UNDERSTANDING
ABUSE

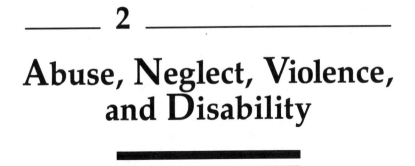

2

Abuse, Neglect, Violence, and Disability

This chapter discusses neglect, physical abuse, and psychological abuse of children with disabilities and the assault and battery of adults with disabilities. Before addressing unique aspects of these traumatic events for people with disabilities, it is important to consider what is known about these phenomena as they affect all members of society.

A BRIEF HISTORY OF THE CHILD PROTECTION MOVEMENT

There have always been people who have been interested in the welfare of children. Nevertheless, the development of organized movements to improve the lives of children has been relatively recent. The first wave of the child protection movement can be traced to the 1870s. A second wave of concern and response began in the 1960s and continues to grow. This second wave, along with the development of feminism and other significant social trends, has also been a powerful generative force in the evolution of closely related efforts to address violence against women, elder abuse, and other forms of family violence. Challenges to institutional violence, a particular concern for people with disabilities, have risen concurrently with progress in confronting family violence, and the fields have sometimes overlapped. However, the two movements have never been fully integrated. Institutional abuse is further discussed in Chapter 4.

Early Progress Toward Child Protection

In December of 1874, a group of people with a radical idea met in New York City (Bremner, 1971a). They believed that children should be fully protected by law. These "radicals" were members of the Society for the Prevention of Cruelty to Animals (SPCA) founded 6 years earlier, and they believed that if the SPCA could successfully advocate for the protection of animals, perhaps children could be provided with the same protection. They formed the Society for the Prevention of Cruelty to Children (SPCC) to advocate for children's rights. Henry Bergh, founder of the SPCA, had already taken one case to court the previous year to obtain protection for an abused 8-year-old girl. In the 1880s, shortly after the formation of the New York SPCC, word of the new society reached England, and the SPCAs in Liverpool and London gave birth to SPCC spinoff groups (Parton, 1985). Within 25 years of the founding of the New York SPCC, more than 150 organizations devoted to protecting children from abuse had become active in the United States. Bergh, who was active in the founding of both the SPCA and the SPCC, is reported in 1874 to have suggested that the emancipation of the slaves was logically followed by the emancipation of animals from mistreatment, and following that, the emancipation of children. Such a view may not seem enlightened by today's standards, but clearly represented the most progressive thinking of the day.

There are a number of reasons why the recognition of child abuse and actions against it are relatively recent. First, prior to widespread industrialization and urbanization, families were much more isolated. Events within the home were private and subjected to little external social control. The registration of births and deaths was not required until 1874 in England (Parton, 1985) and about that same time in various American states. Many children were born at home. Thus, many people were born, lived, and died with no record of their existence other than in their families' own records.

Second, prior to the modernization of sanitation and health care, the chances of survival to adulthood were much less predictable. Individual children were less valued by society. Although families typically had many more babies than most modern families, there were lower survival rates due to disease, accidents, and a variety of other causes (including infanticide and abuse).

Third, diagnostic methods were not available to identify many of the manifestations of child abuse. For example, it wasn't until the 1940s that pediatric radiologists first began to notice that many children with head injuries also had unexplained fresh, healing, and healed fractures of longbones (Caffey, 1946), and it was not until the mid-1950s that these findings were linked to child abuse (Wooley & Evans, 1955). Today, advanced diagnostic techniques such as computerized axial tomography (CAT scan) and magnetic resonance imaging (MRI) continue to clarify the diagnostic picture ("Child Abuse," 1984) and further document the physical effects of violence and abuse against children (McCelland, Rekate, Kaufman, & Persse, 1980; Sobsey, 1989b).

Fourth, the social conditions of the 1800s and early 1900s provided little basis for protecting the rights of children, and evolving social conditions since that time have led to an increasing role for society as a whole in protecting these rights. For example, the industrial revolution led to the growth in the numbers of mothers who were working outside their homes and subsequently to the use of paid child care. Child abuse by paid caregivers became the focus for child welfare intervention, at a time when intervention with abusive families was generally considered unacceptable. In England, for example, the abuse perpetrated by two childcare providers, Margaret Waters and Sarah Ellis, led to an investigation by a Parliamentary committee and the subsequent passage of England's Infant Life Protection Act in 1872 (Parton, 1985). The civil rights of many were seriously violated during this era. In 1850, slavery was still legal in much of the United States, and until 1920, in most states women were denied the right to vote. In a society with a multitude of inequalities, it is not surprising that violations of the basic rights of children were overlooked.

Finally, discipline of children by parents was highly valued, and "sparing the rod" was seen as a greater threat to the moral development of the child than excessive punishment. Bremner (1971a) cites a story from the 1874 *New York Times* suggesting that even Henry Bergh, founder of the SPCA and active force in the founding of the SPCC, "said he was in favor of a good wholesome flogging, which he often found most efficacious" (p. 191). By the mid-1850s, however, rising crime rates were being linked with child abuse and other forms of family violence. Thus, society began to recognize its interest in preventing family violence, if not to protect children from victimization, then to protect society from the violence that these children often exhibited as adolescents and adults (Parton, 1985).

The early history of the American SPCC is a study in "good intentions." The organization represented high ideals and advocated for many important reforms, but it was often deficient in technical skills and resisted external control of its own activities, which members of the society considered beyond reproach. In its zeal to protect children from their own parents, it often took them out of their families and forced them into institutional care. This appears to have been particularly true in the United States as compared to England, where child protection was more directed toward preserving and supporting family unity (Katz, 1986). By 1898, the New York SPCC had become a residential service provider and refused to allow state inspection of its facilities (Bremner, 1971a). In subsequent years, the Society came under heavy criticism for its appointments of untrained and inexperienced, but politically connected, people as child protection workers (Bremner, 1971b). Good intentions had not been sufficient to protect against the development of bureaucracy over time, the natural conflict between advocating for children and protecting the service provider, the lack of technical expertise and competence, and the powerful influence of money over human behavior. Nevertheless, progress was being made, even if it was slow and erratic. The American Humane Association (1951), a federation of children's rights societies, eventually formulated basic standards for protective services.

The development of progressive child protection resulted from the work of a number of groups with overlapping interests. Feminists were among the earliest and most productive advocates for children. For example, the Society for the Protection of Women and Children from Aggravated Assaults was formed in England in 1857. While its primary activities were directed at protecting wives from the violence of their husbands, it also publicized violence against children and advocated for reforms to protect them (Parton, 1985). Civil rights advocacy groups also have made a substantial contribution. For example, §1981 of the Civil Rights Act of 1866 (42 U.S.C., 1981) is aimed at reducing race-related inequities, suggesting that "all persons within the jurisdiction of the United States" shall have the same rights "enjoyed by white citizens." Advocates have used this section to argue the rights of all individuals to be free of discrimination based on age, ability, gender, and country of origin, and some courts have held "that the scope of the law is not limited to racial discrimination" (Burgdorf & Falcon, 1980, p. 436).

Labor unions were also among the first organized groups to advocate for children's rights. The inclusion of children in the work force not only led to their widespread exploitation and abuse, but it also reduced the economic value and power of adult workers. Protecting children from exploitation in the labor force was therefore essential to the union movement's agenda and became a social imperative that extended beyond the factory walls. Even after most children had left the work force, unions continued to advocate for quality child care and other child welfare issues.

Law enforcement, the courts, and criminologists also began to play an increasingly important role. Controlling domestic violence, including child abuse, has become more and more recognized as a priority for police. Special legislation, along with the growth of child protection systems and family courts, are further examples of crucial legal developments that also help to protect children.

The Second Wave

While the first wave of concern for child welfare never died out completely, a second wave of interest substantially added to the movement's slowing momentum after World War II. With the arrival of the second wave, health care professionals began to take a much more active role in the child protection movement. There are several possibilities for this occurrence. First, the extensive experience gained by treating trauma during the war may have enhanced the ability and concern of physicians who began to recognize similar traumatic injuries in children. Second, the end of the war caused the reintroduction of large numbers of fathers into homes where they had previously been absent, producing changes that forced child abuse to the attention of health care professionals. Finally, the increasing availability of antibiotics that followed the war substantially reduced the number of illnesses and deaths from disease, allowing physicians to begin to focus on other concerns.

In 1946, Caffey described some common patterns of injury seen in abused children. This work began to establish criteria for differentiating abuse from other forms of trauma. The involvement of medical and other health care professionals was further accelerated in the early 1960s when two socially conscious pediatricians, Helfer and Kempe, began publicizing the battered child syndrome (Antler, 1981). Scientifically, much of their work was a direct extension of Caffey's (1946) work a decade and a half earlier (although they added their own original contributions); however, Helfer and Kempe presented the information in a manner that urged action. They avoided esoteric medical jargon and replaced it with simpler language and transparent meanings. The battered child syndrome they described was now viewed by the public as a disease that was killing and disabling children. Thus, the medical community's interest in child abuse mobilized public concern, and medical science, with its extraordinary advances and its fresh victory over polio, seemed the logical choice to combat this threatening menace as well.

As this brief history of the child protection movement suggests, child abuse has only been considered a social problem since the 1870s. Since that time, however, it has become one of society's major concerns, and other forms of family violence (e.g., spousal and elder abuse) have also been given increasing attention. Since the 1960s, child abuse and other forms of violence have been the focus of much research. A brief review of some aspects of that research follows, with emphasis on findings particularly relevant to the abuse of people with disabilities.

PHYSICAL ABUSE

Physical abuse is probably the most obvious form of maltreatment. Children are beaten, shaken, thrown, burned, poisoned, smothered, and subjected to an almost infinite list of other tortures. Physical mal-treatment often takes the form of excessive punishment, blind rage, or systematic torture. Often it is justified as necessary or even beneficial to the child. For example, the Bible tells parents to "Withhold not correc-tion from the child: for if thou beatest him with the rod, he shall not die. Thou shalt beat him with the rod, and shalt deliver his soul from hell" (Proverbs 23:13–14).

The line between socially acceptable punishment and socially un-acceptable abuse has never been clearly marked, but evidence of per-manent physical damage and long-standing psychological harm leave little doubt that the line is often crossed. The effects of chronic or se-vere abuse are frequently devastating, and, in many cases, severe abuse can be causally linked to various forms of disabilities.

Types of Physical Abuse

Homicide   Although recent attention has been given to the mur-ders of children in random and gang violence, children are much more likely to be killed by their caregivers, and the number of these deaths appears to be growing rapidly (Adelson, 1991). An unknown number of children die throughout the world every year as a result of child abuse (Greenland, 1987); at least 1,000 children die from abuse an-nually in the United States, and experts estimate the true figure to be 2,000–5,000 child fatalities each year (Murphy et al., 1991).

For example, a sample of 96 children under 6 years of age who died in New York City in the first half of 1980 was reanalyzed by ex-perts. Death certificates originally indicated that about 50% were acci-dental, 24% were homicides, and 24% required further investigation. Expert analysis suggested that 47% were child abuse and neglect (CAN) deaths, and an additional 25% were possible CAN deaths, leaving only 28% as clearly resulting from other causes. Almost half (49%) of the families of the confirmed CAN death cases and 17% of families in the possible cases had previously been reported to authorities for child abuse, but none of the families of the children who died from other causes had been previously reported. Almost a quarter (24%) of the children whose deaths were confirmed as CAN deaths were under ac-tive supervision of child protective services at the time they died (Greenland, 1987). These findings suggest that child deaths due to vio-lence are likely to be two to three times as frequent as the statistics com-monly reported.

Shaking and Smothering   Two forms of abuse that often go un-detected are shaking and smothering. Shaking of young children can cause severe internal injuries, such as bruising of the brain or tearing of the major blood vessels entering the brain, or death, while leaving few, if any, external signs of injury ("Child Abuse," 1984). However, improved diagnosis is helping to identify more of these cases (Sobsey, 1989b). It is now clear that some of the infants once believed to have died of sudden infant death syndrome (SIDS) or "cot death" are actually victims of smothering (Newlands & Emery, 1991). Unfortunately, distinguishing between the two is very difficult in a postmortem examination, and it is often only when several such deaths occur in a family or when other suspicious circumstances surround the death that the possibility is even considered (Cooper, 1978). In one family, for example, as many as nine infants died of "SIDS" before charges were preferred (Egginton, 1989). Although one child was adopted (making a genetic connection hypothesis unlikely) and several children were outside the age range normally associated with SIDS, no conclusive evidence of abuse was detected. Several of these children experienced nonfatal "near-SIDS" attacks before finally being killed, while their mother received sympathy and recognition for saving these children through her heroic actions.

DiMaio and Bernstein (1974) relate another case, in which seven children in the care of the same woman died over a period of 23 years. Death certificates listed such diverse causes of death as enlarged thymus gland, bronchopneumonia, diptheria, and SIDS, but cyanosis (a dark bluish coloration of the skin) caused by lack of oxygen was noted in each case. Some of the children were the natural offspring of the caregiver, but others included an adopted child, a niece, a nephew, and a child the woman was babysitting. None of these children experienced any episodes of cyanosis or airway obstruction in the presence of any other caregivers. Only when the court ruled that evidence related to the general pattern of these deaths could be admitted in court (typically such evidence is prohibited since the deaths of other children are considered irrelevant to current charges) was this woman finally convicted of murder. Perhaps most relevant to consideration of the relationship of abuse to disability is that investigation revealed that this woman had been involved in many other smothering episodes that did not kill the victims, but did leave the children with severe disabilities. Ironically, the offender was often viewed as a hero who saved children with mouth-to-mouth resuscitation or viewed as a bereaved victim who required empathy and support.

These two cases with their striking similarities are not unique. While no estimates of prevalence are available, emerging information suggests such occurrences are much more common than was formerly believed, and that the vast majority of cases go undetected or unconfirmed. One study (Newlands & Emery, 1991) found that one in 30 of the children on the Child Protection Register had a sibling whose death was certified as being caused by SIDS, and suggests that about 10% of deaths of children diagnosed as SIDS are actually due to infanticide. In a second study (Armstrong & Wood, 1991), nine SIDS deaths were reported among 375 infants (under 12 months of age) identified as being at risk for child abuse; subsequent autopsy findings in six of the nine cases suggested the deaths were not accidental, and in the other three significant doubt was raised by the history. Another report documents 14 cases of children whose airways were deliberately obstructed by caregivers. These cases were substantiated when, after multiple episodes of life-threatening air obstruction, surveillance cameras captured the crimes in progress (Samuels, McClaughlin, Jacobson, Poets, & Southall, 1992).

No clear criteria currently exist to differentiate between SIDS and quasi-SIDS abuse. Table 1 suggests some differences that can frequently help differentiate, but it is important to remember that none of these criteria are absolute. Only careful investigation and analysis of individual cases can provide definitive conclusions.

The emergence of these findings suggests one mechanism by which child abuse may cause disability, yet it also raises many additional questions that remain unanswered. Does the large number of deaths attributed to a few perpetrators reflect an obsessive need to repeat these offenses, or do these cases represent the emerging tip of a much larger iceberg, reflecting that those who kill or disable less than

Table 1. Features commonly associated with SIDS and quasi-SIDS cases

SIDS	Quasi-SIDS
Occurs regardless of which caregiver is present	Always occurs in the presence of the same caregiver
Caregiver typically compliant with prevention measures (e.g., monitor)	Caregiver often noncompliant with prevention measures
Less likely to have history of abuse in family	More likely to have history of abuse in family
Can occur in more than one child in family, but rarely does	Often involves more than one child
Rarely occurs past first year of life	Occurs more frequently in older children
Usual range of medical histories in family	More unexplained illnesses and injuries
Physical examination typically unremarkable	Small blood vessels in mouth or nose are sometimes broken; there may be other evidence of shaking
Normal caregiver behavior	Caregiver may demonstrate manipulative or attention-seeking behavior
Caregiver very upset	Caregiver may be unusually calm
More frequent in male infants	Infant may be either gender

six children are almost certain to go undetected? Why would a parent want to smother his or her own child? Both the abusive mothers described above adopted children as well as having more of their own children after apparent murders of previous children. Why would a parent who has already smothered one or more children want to have more children?

One of the most interesting and most difficult questions that is raised by the pattern of these cases is "why would a caregiver who smothers a helpless child stop and resuscitate the child or seek help for the child, yet repeat the smothering at the next opportunity?" Four hypotheses that might answer this question require further investigation. First, there is a rage hypothesis, suggesting that the offenders become enraged by their inability to control crying or other behavior. When the children become unconscious, their crying stops and the offenders' rage may subside. Second, there is an ambivalence hypothesis, suggesting that these offenders do feel some genuine love for the children whom they attack. When the children appear lifeless, their anger is overcome by their grief and they now want desperately to save the children. Third, there is an incompetence hypothesis, suggesting that these offenders are trying to kill the children who survive, but are unable to, possibly because they are interrupted or because they believe that the children are dead when the victims become unconscious. Finally, there is a pragmatic hypothesis, suggesting that these offenders commit these acts because of the social consequences. They may seek the disruption of routine living, the chance to play the role of a hero by "saving" the children, the compassion shown by others when these crises occur, the attention of the health care team, or other social outcomes created by these emergencies. The deaths of the child are unnecessary to achieve any of these goals and may even interfere with some of them. Furthermore, the children who die cannot be exploited again to achieve such goals, but the children who survive can be used again and again. Perhaps some other explanation for the many near-SIDS smotherings will emerge, but it is likely that one or some combination of these hypotheses provides the explanation.

Ungrounded suspicion of families of children who die or become disabled as a result of natural causes will not solve these problems, and great care must be taken not to encourage a generalized stigma against families who have experienced SIDS. Hopefully, future techniques will clearly differentiate SIDS from CAN deaths and help to vindicate those who might be unfairly suspected, while deterring those who hide their crimes behind this tragedy. Parents of children who die from real SIDS or who become disabled through legitimate near-SIDS episodes generally support the need for better discrimination between abusive parents and genuine SIDS parents. For example, when a law was proposed in Pennsylvania that would require autopsies and investigations following the unexpected deaths of all children under 3, SIDS parent support groups backed the bill because they felt it would facilitate SIDS research and help discriminate between SIDS and abuse ("Lawmaker Wants," 1993).

Münchausen Syndrome by Proxy Münchausen syndrome is a pattern of fabrication of clinically significant and convincing symptoms by a patient in order to gain medical attention (Stedman, 1990). Münchausen syndrome by proxy (MSBP) is a similar pattern of behavior where caregivers (typically mothers) fabricate or cause symptoms in individuals for whom they provide care (typically their children) in order to gain medical attention (Rosenberg, 1988). However, MSBP has been known to occur with adult victims, as well as children (Sigal, Altmark, & Carmel, 1986), who are dependent or become dependent on the care provider as a result of abuse. Some of the falsified or induced symptoms that have been associated with MSBP include bleeding, seizures, central nervous system depression, diarrhea, vomiting, fever, and as previously mentioned, SIDS and near-SIDS episodes (Rosenberg, 1987). Since MSBP was first defined by Meadow (1977), many cases and some distinct variants have been identified. Three variants of MSBP have been described.

Type 1 The caregiver may really believe that the child requires medical attention and be unaware that the information he or she is giving the health care team is false. For example, a parent may report that the child is hyperactive and really believe it although there is no objective evidence to support the belief.

Type 2 The caregiver deliberately falsifies information given to the health care team. For example, a parent may report a seizure that never occurred or report an elevated temperature when it was actually normal. This may be done to get attention from the health care team or to manipulate the treatment that the physician prescribes. For example, a parent who wants antibiotics prescribed for the child might claim that the child has an elevated temperature to influence the physician's decision regarding the prescription of medication.

Type 3 This is often the most dangerous type of MSBP, in which the parent actually causes the symptoms that require health care intervention. The false SIDS cases described previously in this chapter are probably extreme examples of this type of MSBP. Other cases may involve drugging or poisoning children, deliberate exposure to dangerous diseases, or a variety of other harmful activities.

These types are not entirely distinct. Two or even three types can exist in the same caregiver and one type may evolve into another. For example, a mother who really believes that her child is ill (Type 1) and needs treatment may falsify an elevated temperature (Type 2) to encourage the physician to prescribe medication. Other caregivers may begin to actually harm the individuals whom they care for after their attempts at falsifying symptoms fail. While the definition of MSBP stresses the pragmatic effect of getting attention from the health care team, other researchers have pointed to possible social functions within the family. For example, a woman who fears losing her husband may attempt to falsify or create an illness in a child to divert attention from the spousal conflict or to increase her husband's inhibition related to leaving (Griffith, 1988).

It is important to recognize that features associated with caregivers who exemplify MSBP may vary, yet, although no single set of features can be used to diagnose all cases, some features are fairly common. MSBP caregivers often appear to be extremely concerned and will actively seek medical care for the individual(s) in their care, but paradoxically they often fail to follow medical advice or only follow the parts they like. For example, parents who seek help for a child they describe as hyperactive may be unwilling to follow changes in diet (recommended for children with specific allergies) or exercise prescribed for their child, but some may give prescribed tranquilizers (if incapacitating their child is part of their personal agenda). Often the described episodes only occur in the presence of a single caregiver. For example, the child reported to have a near-SIDS incident may be fine throughout weeks of hospital observation, but have a second incident as soon as he or she arrives home. Many of these perpetrators have had prior training or experience in the health care professions. In spite of a great deal of concern voiced by MSBP caregivers, they are often surprisingly calm in the face of medical emergencies. Precise diagnoses of the medical condition are often impossible or confounded by some atypical findings. Often more than one child in the family is affected, but typically siblings are affected at different times rather than concurrently. Other forms of child abuse are more likely to occur in the homes of children of MSBP caregivers, although in many cases this is the only identified form of abuse in the family. Most frequently young children or individuals with limited communication skills are affected because they lack the defense of being able to report the caregiver's behavior. MSBP caregivers sometimes have a tendency to go from one doctor or hospital to another, especially after any incident that might cast suspicion on their role in the illness.

MSBP has some important potential implications related to people with disabilities. First, individuals with disabilities are more likely to have limited communicative ability and may be more dependent on caregivers. If so, they may be more likely to become MSBP victims than other individuals, especially in later childhood and adulthood when this syndrome is rare for people who do not have limited communicative ability. Meadow (1982) suggests that MSBP becomes rare in children beyond 6 years old because developing communication skills after this age will allow children to disclose the deception. Clearly, individuals with limited communicative ability remain at risk beyond this age.

Second, Type 3 MSBP is a form of child abuse that causes an indeterminable, yet significant number of disabilities and thereby increases the association between abuse and disability. Other forms of MSBP can also lead to disability because the victims are often subjected to highly dangerous diagnostic and therapeutic measures in an effort to diagnose or cure their apparently life-threatening, but fictitious, illnesses (Meadow, 1982). Furthermore, MSBP can produce significant psychological disturbances in children, including feeding disorders, withdrawal, hyperactivity, and hysteria that may be severe enough to produce long-term disability or to aggravate the effects of other disabling factors (McGuire & Feldman, 1989). While 83% of children diagnosed with MSBP fully recover, 8% have been reported to have long-term disability or illness, and 9% have been reported to die (Rosenberg, 1987).

Third, in some cases the symptoms described by MSBP parents can create the appearance and expectation that these children have disabilities (Stevenson & Alexander, 1990). Thus, some of these children become classified as having disabilities, even when this classification is erroneous.

Finally, sometimes MSBP can take the form of false disclosures of physical, emotional, or sexual abuse, and this form has been frequently reported as involving individuals with disabilities. This phenomenon is further explored in Chapter 3 because it appears to have the greatest implications for sexual abuse.

Violence-Induced Disabilities

In addition to MSBP, shaking, and smothering, there are other forms of overt or covert violence that can lead to *violence-induced disability syndrome* (VIDS). These include gross head injuries, other internal injuries, choking, drowning, and a variety of other violent attacks (Greenland, 1987).

Traumatic Brain Injury Traumatic brain injury (TBI) is a major cause of disabilities. These head injuries can be caused by accidents or violence, but emerging information suggests that violence may be the more frequent cause. While it is known that about 12% of all traumatic brain injuries result from assaults (Silver, Yudofsky, & Hales, 1987), this estimate is likely to be low, as young children and individuals sustaining severe injuries are often physically unable to give the real cause, and some victims give false information out of fear or loyalty, in order to protect their attackers.

Falls, commonly blamed for the violent injuries of young children, have rarely been found to cause serious head injuries. A study of 246 children under 5 years of age who were injured in falls out of bed or off physician's examining tables showed that none received serious injuries (Helfer, Slovis, & Black, 1977). Another study of 84 infants (under 1 year old) with head injuries found that 30 (36%) were the result of abuse, and 54 (64%) were probably actual accidental results of motor vehicle accidents or falls (Billmire & Myers, 1985). However, most of the accidental injuries were superficial and involved no intracranial damage and were thus not associated with potential disability. Of those involving intracranial injury with the potential to cause disability, most (64%) were the result of abuse; of those categorized as serious and highly likely to cause disability or death, 95% were the result of abuse. The full impact of these figures can only be appreciated when one considers that 5,000,000 children sustain head injuries each year in the United States alone. 200,000 of these children require hospitalization and 5,000–10,000 are left with severe disabilities, such as cerebral palsy, mental retardation, and behavior disorders (Silver et al., 1987).

Psychogenic Disabilities The direct physical effects of violence in causing disabilities are the most obvious, but physical effects are not the only way that abuse causes disability. The powerful psychological outcomes of all forms of abuse can also cause disabilities or contribute to those already existing. Often emotional and physical neglect accompany abuse, and when the neglect is severe, the disabling effects may be as significant as the violence. Psychogenic disabilities resulting from abuse include impaired cognitive functioning, learning, and communicative abilities. Abuse can also produce behavioral changes that simulate a variety of other disabilities (e.g., developmental disabilities, autism, and movement disorders).

The Toll of Violence-Induced Disabilities The total number and percentage of disabilities caused by violence remains unknown and for the foreseeable future will remain unknown for several reasons. First, because perpetrators of abuse have a powerful incentive to hide abuse and the harm it does, they will normally use every means possible to obscure the true etiology of VIDS. Second, due to the fact that etiology studies are almost always retrospective, it remains difficult to separate causes from associations (Garbarino, 1987). For example, most people with disabilities will encounter some form of violence or abuse during their lifetimes (e.g., Stimpson & Best, 1991), but this does not necessarily mean that all of their disabilities are caused by abuse. Third, violence can cause disabilities by a number of different mechanisms; therefore, studies that look at a single mechanism (e.g., traumatic brain injury) may obscure several other contributing causal factors. Many disabilities are not caused by single factors alone, but may result from a multitude of interacting factors; therefore, attempting to assign single causes artificially may distort the real picture. Finally, McLaren and Bryson (1987) determined that no direct cause is identified for more than half of developmental disabilities classified as mild and for about 30% of disabilities classified as severe. The large number of unknown etiologies reported in such studies leaves great latitude for speculation, but little basis for testing these hypotheses.

Nevertheless, VIDS is certainly a significant cause of developmental disabilities, if not possibly the single most critical causal factor, and is likely to be among the most prevalent single causes of other forms of disability as well. Only a few studies of the etiology of disabilities report on abuse as a cause, and the rates reported vary substantially. One of the first studies to report on the effects of abuse found that 11% of the 300 children followed in the study died and 28% suffered some permanent disability as a result of the abuse (Kempe, Silverman, Steele, Droegemueller, & Silver, 1962). Another study of abused infants found only 10% to be free of residual damage resulting from the abuse (Elmer & Gregg, 1967); 10 years later a follow-up of these children found that 24% had neurological problems and 47% had significant learning difficulties (Elmer, 1977). Rose and Hardman (1981) reviewed available evidence and concluded that between 20%–50% of abused children will suffer mild to severe brain damage. By using United States national incidence figures of 3.4 physically abused children per thousand children per year (approximately 5.9% of all children under the age of 18) (Burgdorf, 1980), it can be estimated that between 1%–2.5% of all children would be expected to suffer brain damage as a result of physical abuse sometime before reaching adulthood. This also suggests that physical violence toward children is a major cause of disabilities. Furthermore, this estimate does not factor in the physical damage effects of severe neglect or the psychological harm done by all forms of abuse. For example, neglect causes 39% as many child fatalities and 83% as many severe and moderately serious injuries as does physical abuse. Damage done to infants born to mothers abused during pregnancy further increases the toll of violence. Adding the disabling effects of these other forms of abuse to the estimated damage done to physically abused children suggests that 3%–6% of all children will have some degree of permanent disability as a result of abuse, and that abuse may be a causal factor in as much as half of all disabilities in children.

Abuse also appears to be a significant factor in the etiology of cerebral palsy. Diamond and Jaudes's (1983) study of children with cerebral palsy found that 9% of these disabilities probably resulted from abuse and that 21% of the children studied experienced postnatal traumatic brain injuries that may also have resulted from abuse. Other studies report that about 20% of cerebral palsy is caused by traumatic head injury (Mullins, 1986). When all VIDS mechanisms are considered together, it is likely that violence is a significant causal factor in 10%–25% of all developmental disabilities.

Much remains to be learned about the actual numbers of disabilities caused by child abuse and other forms of violence, and it is important to recognize that the estimates presented here remain speculative. While there is no doubt that violence and disability are closely related, more research is needed to determine the process that links them.

Signs of Abuse

Regardless of whether or not abuse causes disability, the signs of abuse are generally the same. Occasionally, evidence of physical abuse will be obvious. Coercive or threatening interactions can sometimes be observed between abusers and their victims. When overt abuse is observed, it often signals a situation that is critical because the abuser may no longer be able to control violence, even when sources of external inhibition are present. However, it is typically far more difficult to determine abuse with certainty. Table 2 lists some common signs of physi-

Table 2. Some common signs of abuse

Physical signs	Behavioral signs	Circumstantial signs
Abrasions	Aggression	Aggressive behavior in caregivers
Bites	Atypical attachment	Alcohol or drug use
Bruises	Disclosure	Devaluing attitudes
Burns and scalds	Fearfulness	Isolation of social unit
Coma	Learning disabilities	Other forms of abuse
Dental injuries	Noncompliance	Other violence in setting
Dislocations	Regression	Previous history of abuse
Ear injuries	Sleep disturbances	
Eye injuries	Withdrawal	
Fractures		
Lacerations		
Ligature marks		
Welts		

cal abuse. Common signs may be physical, behavioral, or circumstantial. Rarely does a single sign provide conclusive proof; rather, it is typically a combination of signs and other factors that must be considered and analyzed before any definitive conclusion can be drawn.

Physical Signs Physical signs often provide compelling evidence of abuse, but the wide variety of normal childhood injuries and predisposing medical conditions can make interpretation difficult. Careful examination by a physician can help to clarify the significance of injuries; however, in some cases, even a qualified physician will need expert consultation.

Abrasions Frequent, repetitive, unexplained, or inadequately explained scrapes, particularly in atypical locations (i.e., other than on the palms of hands or the tops of knees), may be signs of abuse. It is important to remember that minor abrasions (and many of the other injuries described below) will commonly occur due to accidental causes.

Bites Bites inflicted by adults can typically be easily distinguished from those inflicted by animals or other children by their size and shape. Occasionally, bites are explained as self-inflicted, but the location and position of the bite will prove to be inconsistent with this explanation.

Bruises Frequent, unexplained, or inadequately explained bruises can be found in many cases of abuse. Bruises that are patterned (e.g., hand print, belt buckle) in specific locations (e.g., infants sometimes show oval fingerprints on chest or back from shaking episodes; bruises to both sides of the body are rare from accidental causes) or temporally dispersed (i.e., bruises change color over time, a series of bruises of different colors is inconsistent with a single "accident" explanation) are often intimations of abuse (Langlois & Gresham, 1991). Bruises typically appear pink or red at first, turn blue in about 6–12 hours, turn dark purple in 12–24 hours, take on a green tint in 4–6 days, and finally turn pale green to yellow in 5–10 days (Mead & Westgate, 1992). While the range and overlap of these changes makes exact dating difficult, it provides a good indicator of the approximate age of bruises. Bruising of the face or blackened eyes are particularly worrisome because head injuries can occur from this kind of violence, and abusive caregivers who are concerned about long-term outcomes usually avoid hitting the child's head. Bruises are among the most common injuries noted in abused children and adults, but it is important to remember that occasional bruising is also common in people who are not abused, and some people with disabilities may be prone to bruising for other reasons. Mongolian spots are grayish or bluish marks on the upper buttocks or lower back that are found on some infants and young children with or without disabilities (Mead & Westgate, 1992). These may be easily mistaken for bruises, but are not normally tender to the touch and do not change color with time the way that bruises do. They usually fade gradually and disappear within the first couple years of life.

Burns and Scalds Repeated, unexplained, or inadequately explained burns or scalds (e.g., caregiver suggests that burn occurred when child leaned against radiator, but burn pattern suggests hot liquid) may indicate abuse. Patterned burns (e.g., round cigarette burns) or burns in specific locations (e.g., several burns on different parts of the body or on particularly sensitive locations) may also indicate abuse. Scalds caused by pouring hot liquid are usually more severe on the thighs of the legs than on the calves, and accidental scalds usually have a characteristic upper limit consistent with the explanation. Sometimes skin appears to be burned, but is actually infected (Mead & Westgate, 1992). This skin usually appears red, is tender to the touch, and may be slightly swollen. If the cause is indeed infection, the borders may expand to or withdraw from their original limits, and the pattern will follow the lymph system or other internal markers rather than the fall of gravity pattern resulting from burns caused by spilling liquids or the distinct object shapes of burns caused by solid objectives. Often it is hard to be certain, and if any uncertainty exists a physician should be consulted.

Coma Cases of coma of undetermined origin without external injuries sometimes occur as a result of shaking or other forms of abuse. Comas that are not associated with known accidental causes or clearly identified disease processes should be evaluated carefully.

Dental Injuries Lost or broken teeth—particularly if unrelated to dental disease, normal loss of children's first teeth, or accidental causes—as well as repeated, unexplained, or inadequately explained dental injuries (e.g., caregiver indicates child's "baby tooth" fell out, but bruising of cheek and gums suggest traumatic injury) are sometimes indications of abuse.

Dislocations and Joint Injuries Repeated dislocations of joints in the absence of known disease processes may indicate abuse, often in the form of shaking, twisting, or pulling. Frequent or multiple dislocations (e.g., in both arms or an arm and a leg) in the absence of a clear explanation are often signs of abuse.

Ear Injuries Sudden or unexplained hearing loss, cauliflower ears (i.e., thickened external ear structures), bruising to the outer ears, or blood in the ear canal can all occur as a result of abuse (Mead & Westgate, 1992). Blood in the ear canal can also be a sign of skull fracture and therefore requires immediate attention to determine its cause.

Eye Injuries Detached retinas and intraocular hemorrhage are among the eye injuries that can be signs of physical abuse (Riffenburgh

& Sathyavagiswaran, 1991), particularly when they are unexplained or inadequately explained. Careful diagnostic work is required to rule out disease processes that may cause these conditions and to assess if other signs of trauma are present. Eye injuries can be caused by direct impact to the eyes, but abnormal findings in the eyes (e.g., bleeding from the optic nerve) also may indicate damage to the brain (Mead & Westgate, 1992).

Fractures Repeated or multiple fractures in the absence of known disease processes or clear explanations often signal abuse. The discovery of old, untreated fractures often indicates chronic abuse. One study reported that 77% of diagnosed child abuse fractures were found as acute injuries, while the remaining 23% proved to be older fractures (Loder & Bookout, 1991). In the same study, 32% of the fractures involved the skull. Spiral fractures of the limbs often result from twisting. Osteogenesis imperfecta and some other physical conditions may result in frequent fractures in some children and may be difficult to differentiate from abuse. Laboratory tests can be very useful in cases where doubt exists (Gahagan & Rimsza, 1991).

Lacerations Patterned, repeated, unexplained, or inadequately explained lacerations may signal abuse. Self-inflicted cuts are not uncommon among abused children, and children who cut or otherwise mutilate themselves reveal histories of frequent abuse (van der Kolk, Perry, & Herman, 1991). Often lacerations that occur as a result of abuse are associated with bruises or other injuries (Cooper, 1978).

Ligature Marks Chafing and bruising is sometimes seen on the wrists, ankles, throat, or penis as a result of being tied up or choked, and may be accompanied by swelling. Nevertheless, even when choking is severe or fatal, bruising may be faint or entirely absent (Cooper, 1978).

Welts Welts unrelated to disease or clearly explained injury may be a result of whipping. Often these follow clearly defined stroke patterns, especially if the child was immobile during whipping.

Behavioral Signs In many cases, physical signs of abuse are not present or not yet discovered, and behavioral signs are the first indicators of abuse. Typically it is a combination of physical and behavioral abnormalities that can be detected in abused individuals.

Atypical Attachment Insecure or atypical attachment has commonly been seen in abused children. These children often appear insecure with strangers and compulsively seek the presence and attention of their primary caregivers, yet may express little affection toward this caregiver. For example, a preschooler might demonstrate insecure attachment by clinging to his mother and crying excessively both when she leaves him and when she returns.

Aggression Aggressive behavior is widespread among victims of abuse. In some cases, it may mimic the aggression committed against the child (e.g., a child who is whipped may whip smaller children), but also may generalize to other forms of aggression. Aggression may also be exhibited through excessively violent drawings, stories, or play.

Disclosure Direct disclosures provide powerful evidence of abuse, even when some details (possibly including the name of the abuser) are incorrect. All disclosures of abuse should be given attention and referred to the appropriate individuals (e.g., police, child welfare workers, and adult protection workers) for full evaluation.

Fearfulness Abused children often appear fearful of others. Fear can be specific to the abuser, but may generalize to other people as well. In some cases, fear may be age or gender specific, and this sometimes helps to identify the source of the fear. For example, some children turn away and raise their arms as if to deflect a blow whenever an adult who is nearby makes a sudden move.

Learning Disabilities Many abused children have difficulty learning. The reasons for this are complex. In many cases, much of the child's energies are being directed toward survival and coping with stress, leaving little energy left for learning or other typical childhood activities. Sinason (1992) describes children and adults whose apparent learning disability sometimes resulted entirely and sometimes partially from their psychological response to abuse and whose learning abilities improved after psychotherapy.

Noncompliance Children who are abused often become noncompliant. Noncompliance may be specific to particular people or situations, but also may be generalized. In some cases the noncompliance is specifically directed toward avoidance of the abuser or abusive situations. In others it appears to be a more general response to frustration, and perhaps reflects an effort to gain some small degree of individual control.

Regression Many abused children exhibit behavior more typical of children younger than themselves. This may reflect an inability to move through normal stages of development in the face of intense anxiety or it could reflect a mechanism of escape. Regression can be limited to affective and interpersonal behavior, but sometimes extends to developmental skills. For example, a child who has previously been toilet trained may begin to wet or soil after experiencing abuse.

Sleep Disturbances Sleep disturbances such as nightmares or difficulty in getting to sleep are characteristic of abused children. Unfortunately, these problems sometimes elicit further abuse.

Withdrawal Children who are abused will often withdraw from interaction with others and spend much of their time alone. Sometimes withdrawal is associated with other aspects of depression. Occasionally withdrawal and aggression will alternate in the same child. Aggression may occur as a way of discouraging interaction with others. For example, an abused child may keep to herself and avoid other children, but if unable to avoid interaction may become aggressive in order to end it.

Circumstantial Signs   Circumstances that are frequently associated with child abuse must be considered cautiously. In conjunction with physical or behavioral evidence of abuse, they can be useful for evaluation of the total picture and can help to identify risk factors. However, it is important to recognize that circumstantial signs alone are rarely strong enough to diagnose abuse without additional evidence, and false assumptions can have many negative effects, such as alienating families and caregivers, who are not actually abusive.

Aggressive Behavior in Caregivers   Caregivers who display difficulty controlling impulsivity, particularly impulsive aggression, are more likely to commit child abuse. Authoritarian attitudes have often been cited in association with several types of abuse. For example, caregivers who emphasize the need for compliance by the individuals in their care or who employ punishment as a primary teaching method are more likely to commit abuse.

Alcohol or Drug Use   Caregivers who frequently use alcohol or other disinhibiting drugs are likely to be abusive. One study found that 43% of parents who committed severe child abuse offenses had documented substance abuse problems, including alcohol (31%), cocaine (16%), and heroin (12%); an additional 7% had alleged but undocumented substance abuse (Murphy et al., 1991). One report indicates that 22 states reported chemical dependency as the dominant factor in determining child protective custody; Washington, D.C., reported that 90% of parents named in child protective custody petitions were active substance abusers (Dinsmore, 1992). By 1989, the number of drug-related custody petitions in the United States had increased to 30 times its 1984 level (Dinsmore, 1992).

Devaluing Attitudes in Caregivers   Negative attitudes toward children are associated with increased risk for abuse. Devaluing attitudes may act to disinhibit abusive behavior, and offenders' attitudes toward victims usually become more negative after abuse occurs, possibly as a means of rationalization. Anthropological data suggest that the values placed on children in general, and on specific categories of children (e.g., boys versus girls) can influence the likelihood of abuse (Korbin, 1987). Many societies permit the killing of children with disabilities, and rarely is such killing a source of disapproval by others (Daly & Wilson, 1988). Often this killing is rationalized by belief systems that dehumanize such children (e.g., viewing the children as demons or "vegetative organisms"). These belief systems facilitate a wide variety of abuses against the people who have been dehumanized.

Isolation of Social Unit　The isolation of a family or other living alternative from the mainstream of society is associated with increased risk for abuse. Abusive caregivers often seek isolation in order to conceal their actions. Isolation decreases contact with sources of external inhibition and magnifies the effects of existing power inequities.

Other Forms of Abuse　Children who are neglected, sexually abused, and/or psychologically abused are also more likely than other children to be physically abused. The presence or history of any category of abuse is associated with increased risk for all other categories. In many cases the same abuser engages in more than one type of abuse, but in some cases different caregivers may commit varying forms of abuse.

Other Violence in Setting　A history of other violence in the setting is associated with increased risk for child abuse (e.g., spousal abuse or abuse of another child in the family). One study of the children of battered women reports that two-thirds of these children were also victimized (Wildin, Williamson, & Wilson, 1991). Abusive caregivers rarely abuse only a single victim if more than one potential victim is available.

Previous History of Abuse　Children who have already experienced at least one episode of abuse are more likely to be abused again in the future, not only by the same caregiver, but also by other caregivers. Ironically, it is far too common that children removed from abusive homes will also be abused in the "protective" setting (Chase, 1976). A number of mechanisms work to increase the risk of future abuse for those who have already been abused. Natural defenses can be weakened as a result of abuse, causing the child to become compliant and submissive. However, in many cases the connection between past and future abuse has nothing to do with the behavior of the abused person. For example, if a child is abused by his or her parents and continues to live with them, the abusive parent(s) is (are) likely to abuse again. Ironically, if the abusive parent leaves the home, the child is then in a single parent home or also living with a stepparent—both conditions associated with risk for abuse. If the child is removed from the home, he or she is likely to be placed in foster or institutional care, also typically associated with elevated risk (Tower, 1989).

PSYCHOLOGICAL ABUSE AND NEGLECT

Psychological abuse is the most complex form of abuse to objectively define or detect. It is also difficult to isolate from other forms of abuse because sexual abuse, neglect, and even physical abuse all produce psychological harm, which can be the most devastating of all consequences. Even though psychological abuse frequently accompanies these other forms of abuse, it also occurs independently. Individuals who have power and influence over others' lives use that power and influence to exploit or harm, rather than to support. This kind of abuse can be especially treacherous during a child's developmental years. For example, children should be taught to have reasonably optimistic expectations of themselves and of other people, but sometimes they are taught to feel worthless and to expect the worst from others. No clear criterion exists to determine exactly when such treatment constitutes abuse. Psychological abuse can be committed by parents, teachers, health care providers, and a variety of other people who exercise authority. Although this book concentrates on forms of abuse that more clearly constitute offenses, it is important to remember that psychological abuse, even when it does not clearly constitute a criminal offense, is nevertheless an important issue. No formal research exists that directly analyzes the effects of psychological abuse on people with disabilities, but anecdotal reports suggest that this is a major concern. Considerable research is available regarding attitudes toward people with disabilities (e.g., Lyons, 1991; Murray & Chambers, 1991), and the negative and ambivalent attitudes found in such studies provide a strong rationale for assuming that psychological abuse is a particular concern for people with disabilities.

Neglect is perhaps the most insidious form of abuse; in extreme form it may be one of the most damaging. Physical neglect occurs when nutritional, medical, or other physical needs are deliberately ignored or withheld. Emotional or developmental neglect occurs when an individual is deprived of the basic human interactions required for the development of normal behavior. The failure to provide appropriate or required medical care is a form of medical neglect, and educational neglect refers to the failure to provide appropriate educational services. Often these forms of neglect occur simultaneously, although sometimes there may be only one type of neglect taking place. Neglect often occurs along with physical abuse, but either may occur without the other.

For people with disabilities, abuse by omission rather than commission may be the most frequent form of abuse. In the 19th century, for example, people with disabilities were often kept in unheated sheds and pens, often without benefit of clothing. Dix reports on one example: "[his] feet had been frozen, and had perished: upon the shapeless stumps, he could by some motion of his shoulders, raise his body partially up the side of the pen" (quoted in Deutsch, 1949, pp. 167–168). Ironically, reports of such conditions helped provide a rationale for the development of institutional care. Such institutions were intended to provide asylum from the harsh realities of the life in the community for people with disabilities. However, almost from their inception, reports of extreme abuse and neglect in institutions gave a new and sardonic meaning to the word "asylum."

ABUSE OF PEOPLE WITH DISABILITIES

The relationship of child abuse to disability has sparked discussion and debate since the late 1960s (Westcott, 1991). Cohen and Warren (1990) interviewed staff from about 20 agencies that served children with disabilities or children who were abused and reported that "over and over again we heard statements from professionals about the connection between disability and abuse, but these statements were based on personal experience rather than formal data" (p. 256). Such statements raise many important questions. Is this belief based on reality or myth? Has research been conducted to test the perceived connection between disability and abuse? If so, does research support this association?

Exploring the Relationship between Disability and Abuse

Disability acts to increase vulnerability to abuse. Sometimes the effects are fairly direct (e.g., limited ability to fend off or escape from an attack), but often they act indirectly, more as a function of cultural responses to disability than as a function of disability itself. The relationship between cultural belief systems and abuse of people with disabilities is discussed in greater detail in Chapter 6.

While many small scale studies (often methodologically weak) have reported that children with disabilities are more frequently abused than other children, inconsistencies in the estimates of the extent of increased risk, along with a few studies that fail to demonstrate a relationship, leave some uncertainty about the nature and the magnitude of the relationship (Sobsey & Varnhagen, 1989; Westcott, 1991). However, when these studies are considered as a group they provide powerful evidence of a link between the two (Sobsey, 1988). Sobsey and Varnhagen (1989) suggest that the risk of only a single incident of abuse for people with disabilities appears to be at least one and a half times as great as the risk for other people of similar age or gender. Because people with disabilities are often repeatedly or chronically abused, the increased risk becomes even greater when multiple victimizations are considered. When definitions of abuse are limited to more severe forms of abuse and multiple victimizations of the same individuals are factored in, the relative risk of abuse for people with disabilities is probably at least twice as high and may be five or more times higher than the risk for the general population. Differences in definitions of abuse, reporting rates, contextual variables, and sampling strategies probably mean that no single figure will ever reliably express differences in risk between people with and without disabilities. There-fore, it has been suggested that the time has come for research to go beyond merely trying to measure the strength of association between disability and abuse, by concentrating future research on determining why the relationship exists (Sobsey, 1988). Westcott (1991) points out that regardless of the precise level of risk, we know that significant numbers of individuals with disabilities are abused and that society's failure to respond to their needs for prevention and intervention must be addressed. Better knowledge of the nature of the relationship be-tween abuse and disability could be helpful in designing the appropri-ate prevention and intervention programs.

Studies Elmer and Gregg (1967) were among the first to show a relationship between physical abuse and mental retardation. They were also among the first to point out that abuse might result in disability, and disability might also increase vulnerability to abuse. Furthermore, while neurological damage can occur as a result of physical abuse, abuse can cause deficits in development in other ways. For example, Harlow's (1959) work with monkeys clearly demonstrated that social isolation could produce significant and enduring deficits in develop-ment without physical abuse. Harlow and colleagues removed infant monkeys from their mothers for varying periods of time and placed them with surrogates. These surrogates were not monkeys, but rather made of either wire or soft cloth with some facial features and nursing bottles. Some of these surrogates moved and others were stationary. The monkeys who were provided with soft and moving surrogates avoided many of the effects of isolation. Those deprived of maternal contact became withdrawn, rocked, mutilated themselves, and demon-strated other atypical behavior.

Table 3 lists some of the many studies that have examined the rela-tionship between abuse and disability. Each study mentioned follows one of two basic patterns. Either a sample of abused individuals is ana-lyzed to determine the percentage of people with disabilities, or a sam-ple of people with disabilities is analyzed to determine the frequency of known or suspected abuse. In most cases, the percentages that result are higher than might be expected if only a random relationship existed.

Unfortunately, most of the studies did not use matched control groups of individuals not abused or without disabilities, so that it is un-certain exactly how the findings should be interpreted. For example, Benedict, White, Wulff, and Hall (1990) compared the 10.6% of the 500 children with multiple disabilities that they studied who had "sub-stantiated maltreatment reports filed with the appropriate social ser-vices agency" (p. 209) with "national incidence study figures . . . includ-ing nonreported situations in their figures" (p. 214) and concluded that "these study data do not appear to confirm any increased reporting risk for this population" (p. 214). This conclusion, while unrelated to the primary purpose of the study, is potentially important. The sample studied were diagnosed at birth; therefore, their disabilities were not caused by abuse. However, comparing a figure for substantiated cases with a figure that includes unproven and even unreported cases raises some doubts about the conclusion. Using confirmed case incidence figures from the state of origin for the years covered by this study, Sobsey and Doe (1991) suggest that the 10.6% found by Benedict and colleagues to have known histories of abuse is 4.43 times as high as the figure for the population without disabilities.

Sandgrund, Gaines, and Green (1974) used a control group of nonabused children matched with groups of physically abused and neglected children. Their finding that abused children were 8.3 times as likely and that neglected children were 6.7 times as likely as nonabused controls to exhibit mental retardation suggests that the effect of physical trauma provides only a partial explanation for the association between abuse and disability.

Andre (1985) studied four groups including: 1) 308 maltreated children with disabilities, 2) 301 nonabused children with disabilities, 3) 295 maltreated children without disabilities, and 4) 319 nonabused children without disabilities who were drawn from a nationally representative stratified random sample of children receiving public social services. Findings revealed a higher prevalence of children with disabilities among maltreated children (23%) than among other children served by public social service agencies (16%).

Two studies included in the table (Doucette, 1986; Stimpson & Best, 1991) are based on interviews with women with disabilities rather than children, but are included here because they presented retrospective disclosures of childhood experiences. The Doucette (1986) study is of particular interest because it utilized a control group of women without disabilities responding to the same questions and found that physical abuse was 1.97 times as frequent among the women with disabilities.

Further Speculation Although these studies indicate a relationship between abuse and various disabilities, the relationship may be even stronger than it appears due to the fact that critical information about health and disability is often missing from abuse records (West, Richardson, Leconte, Crimi, & Stuart, 1992) and may be missing from the health care and educational records of people with disabilities as well. Failure to coordinate child protection, health, rehabilitation, and educational services adequately has presented a major obstacle to both recognition of and response to the causal linkages between abuse and disability. The combined evidence from these studies leaves little doubt,

Table 3. Chronology of studies of the relationship between abuse and disability

Year	Authors	Country	Subjects	Data	Results
1967	Elmer and Gregg	USA	50 abused children	Follow-up examinations and records	50% of the abused children had mental retardation; it is not known if this was the result of abuse.
1968	Birrell and Birrell	Australia	42 abused children under 3 years old	Records reviewed	25% had congenital disabilities and 24% experienced developmental delay as a result of abuse.
1968	Johnson and Morse	USA	101 abused children under 15 years old	Records reviewed	Almost 70% had a physical disability or mental retardation.
1970	Gil	USA	12,610 abused children 6 months to 15 years	Survey	22% showed some mental retardation (8%) or physical (14%) disability.
1970	Morse, Sahler, and Friedman	USA	25 abused children 2–7 years old	Family interviews	71% were considered to exhibit atypical behavior and below average intellect prior to abuse.
1974	Martin, Beezley, Conway, and Kempe	USA	37 abused children without known head trauma	Psychological testing	43% exhibited neurological dysfunction.
1974	Sandgrund, Gaines, and Green	USA	60 abused children, 30 neglected children, 30 nonabused children	Psychological interviews and testing	25% of abused sample, 20% of neglected sample, and 3% of nonabused sample exhibited mental retardation.
1977	Buchanan and Oliver	UK	140 children with mental retardation under 16 years old	Records reviewed	22% were physically abused, 10% were at risk, and 3% (possibly as many as 11%) had disabilities that resulted from abuse.

Year	Authors	Country	Sample	Method	Findings
1981	Green, Voeller, Gaines, and Kubie	USA	60 physically abused children, 30 neglected children, 30 nonabused children	Neurological exams (blind ratings)	More than 50% of the abused children were diagnosed as having moderate to severe disabilities, as compared to 37% of the neglected and 14% of the nonabused group.
1982	Frisch and Rhoads	USA	430 children referred for learning problems	Records reviewed	6.7% had been independently referred to social services agencies for possible abuse, 3.5 times the rate of the general population.
1982	Lightcap, Kurland, and Burgess	USA	24 families of abused children	Survey	22% of the children in these families were judged to have disabilities, but 43% of the abused children were judged to be without disabilities.
1982	Lynch and Roberts	UK	39 abused children and their siblings	Psychological testing	59% of the abused children and 33% of their siblings showed developmental delays on follow-up assessments. Language skills were the most severely affected. 25% of the abused children had moderate or severe neurological deficits, as compared to 7% of their siblings.
1983	Diamond and Jaudes	USA	86 children with cerebral palsy	Records reviewed	19% were abused; 22% were at risk.
1984	Oates and Peacock	Australia	38 physically abused children, 38 nonabused children	Follow-up intelligence tests after about 5 years	Abused children had IQ scores significantly lower than the control group. Severity of initial abuse did not account for differences.

(continued)

Table 3. (continued)

Year	Authors	Country	Subjects	Data	Results
1984	Souther	USA	125 children with disabilities in protective services in West Virginia	Survey	69% of the children had one or more disabilities.
		USA	263 child protection workers in West Virginia	Survey	35% of children served had disabilities caused by abuse or neglect, and 37% of the children served had disabilities that may have been a contributing factor to abuse or neglect.
1985	Andre	USA	609 children with disabilities, 614 without disabilities, stratified random sample	Correlation of social services records	23% of the children with disabilities served by social services were abused, as compared to 16% of the control group.
1985	Hawkins and Duncan	USA	126 abused and/or neglected children	Substantiated and unsubstantiated cases compared	9% were found to have mental retardation; 10% were found to have emotional disturbances.
1986	Doucette	Canada	30 women with disabilities, 32 women without disabilities	Interview disclosures	67% of the women with disabilities had been physically abused, as compared to 34% of the women without disabilities.
1987	Hochstadt, Jaudes, Zimo, and Schacter	USA	149 children placed in foster care after abuse or abandonment	Physical exams and reviews of history	24.2% had developmental delays, 23.1% had behavioral problems, and 50% had multiple physical disabilities. Only 13% had physical examinations that showed no disabilities.

40

1987	Hughes and DiBrezzo	USA	Children with and without history of abuse living in a women's shelter	Interviews with mothers	23% of the abused and 11% of the nonabused children had learning disabilities.
1987	Jacobson and Richardson	USA	100 psychiatric inpatients with multiple disabilities	Interviews	81% had experienced major physical or sexual assaults.
1989	Ammerman, Van Haslett, Hersen, McGonigle, and Lubetsky	USA	150 children with multiple disabilities	Records reviewed	39% exhibited evidence of abuse, including 19% with definite abuse histories and 9% with probable and 11% with possible histories of abuse.
1989	Erikson, Egeland, and Pianta	USA	Children of 267 abusive mothers in Minnesota	Prospective follow-up	44% of the physically abused children, 65% of the neglected children, 45% of the sexually abused children, and 37% of the psychologically neglected children were referred to special education in kindergarten as compared to 21% of control group.
1989	Lujan, DeBruyn, May, and Bird	USA	53 abused or neglected Native American children	Records reviewed	30% had disabilities.
1990	Benedict, White, Wulff, and Hall	USA	500 children with multiple disabilities	Records reviewed	10.6% had known histories of abuse.
1991	Stimpson and Best	Canada	85 women with disabilities	Questionnaire	73% indicated that they had experienced violent assault.
1992	West, Richardson, LeConte, Crimi, and Stuart	USA	150 abused children	Records reviewed	34% had confirmed, 11% likely, and 23% suspected developmental disabilities.

however, that some causality exists, and also suggests that not all of the association can be explained by the effects of physical trauma alone because disability is frequently found when abuse does not involve physical violence. Even studies that test the relationship where physical abuse does not occur prior to disability find that the association still exists.

Some cases of child abuse could be expected among children with disabilities as a result of random overlap between children with disabilities and those without disabilities who are abused. Common risk factors increase this association. For example, families with a history of violence or excessive alcohol use have an increased risk of having children with disabilities, and also an increased risk for child abuse. One study reports that 17% of parents of abused children had "long-term drug and alcohol abuse problems" and that "of those parents whose [abused] children were 1 year old or younger, 41% reported some drug and/or alcohol abuse" (West et al., 1992, p. 224). In 11% of the abuse cases reviewed in this study, mothers had used alcohol or other drugs during pregnancy.

Some professionals believe that drug or alcohol abuse during pregnancy is a form of child abuse because many children of such pregnancies are born with serious developmental problems. An estimated 100,000–400,000 infants are born each year who are affected by drug abuse during gestation and many of these have permanent disabilities. Only about 100 of these mothers are prosecuted for child abuse and the legal basis for such prosecutions remains questionable (Dinsmore, 1992). Furthermore, some lawmakers have been reluctant to develop new legislation to clarify this issue because such legislation protecting the unborn child would inevitably become entangled in the contentious abortion issue. If dangerous levels of prenatal drug and alcohol exposure were categorized as child abuse, the number of disabilities thought to be caused by abuse would rise substantially.

Generally, those who consider serious drug and alcohol ingestion during pregnancy to be abuse, also consider it to be a form of neglect. The mother is viewed as more concerned with her own needs than the needs of the developing fetus. However, in some cases, it appears that the use of drugs or alcohol is a deliberate attack on the fetus. While the number of cases of drug ingestion during pregnancy that represent deliberate attempts to harm the fetus remains unknown, some case studies present reason for concern. Condon (1986), for example, describes a 25-year-old woman who was a light drinker before her pregnancy who began drinking heavily in her second trimester. She indicated open resentment for the intrusion that the baby had made on her career, marriage, and other aspects of her life, and stated that she often wanted to "hit the baby," especially when it moved. When asked if her drinking might be her way of punishing the fetus, she replied, "I've thought of that many times. I think it might . . . I feel so guilty about it" (p. 511).

Other factors besides drug and alcohol abuse or preexisting violence in the family that link child abuse with disability include:

1. Disabilities caused by the physical effects (e.g., traumatic brain injury) of child abuse
2. Disabilities caused by the social–emotional effects (e.g., posttraumatic stress disorder) of child abuse
3. Child abuse that is associated with the increased vulnerability of children with disabilities (e.g., an impaired ability to escape abuse, dependence on the service system)

The relative influence of these factors remains unknown and is likely to vary substantially depending on exactly how abuse and disability are defined and measured.

Battery of Mothers During Pregnancy   One example of preexisting violence in the family includes the battering of pregnant mothers, which causes an unknown number of disabilities in their children. No precise figures are available, but various studies report that 4% (Hillard, 1985), 8% (McFarlane, 1989), or 23% (Gelles, 1975) of pregnant women in their samples were battered during their pregnancies. In fact, several studies suggest that physical violence increases in frequency and intensity during pregnancy. Richwald and McClusky (1985) suggest that this may result from: 1) transitional stress, 2) sexual frustration, 3) response to altered affect and behavior resulting from pregnancy, 4) a conscious or unconscious desire to hurt the fetus, or 5) decreased capacity of the mother to defend herself. The direction of aggression toward the fetus is of particular concern because such attacks are often focused on the abdomen and may account for the fact that battery appears to be more dangerous to the fetus than other forms of trauma (Goodwin & Breen, 1990).

Low birth weight babies are born two to four times as frequently to mothers battered during their pregnancies (Bullock & McFarlane, 1989). A separate and independent study confirms that about four times as many low birth weight infants are born to battered women, and also found that the average infant born to a battered mother weighed 229 grams less than the average infant born to a nonbattered mother (Schei, Samuelson, & Bakketeig, 1991). Some of this difference was related to other potentially confounding factors, but when the effect of all control factors was removed, a difference of 175 grams still remained. Another study found that although battery during pregnancy was associated with small group differences when potentially confounding variables were controlled, battered mothers did have babies born with lower birth weights and smaller head circumferences (Amaro, Fried, Cabral, & Zuckerman, 1990).

While it is important to remember that not all low birth weight infants have disabilities and that some infants injured through battery prior to birth may be of normal or above normal birth weight, this initial data raises serious concerns that large numbers of infants may be born with disabilities because of battering during their mothers' pregnancies. Low birth weight has generally been a weak predictor of long-term disability in children because it represents a symptom of many different conditions and etiologies (Susser, 1988) making low birth weight infants a heterogeneous group. For example, an infant girl born to parents who are short is much more likely to weigh less than 2,500 grams than an infant boy born to taller parents, but the girl is no more likely (actually slightly less likely) to have a disability. However, low birth weight is also associated with many genetic syndromes that are almost certain to be associated with a disability. Thus, the specific cause of the low birth weight is the critical factor in determining risk for disability. Since low birth weight associated with battery during pregnancy is likely to result from trauma, it is also likely to be predictive of disability. In fact, the risk due to trauma may be greater than the increased frequency of low birth weight suggests because trauma might produce disabilities in other cases (e.g., trauma later in pregnancy) without resulting in low birth weight. Also, some or all of the low birth weights associated with battery during pregnancy could result from nontraumatic causes (e.g., psychosomatic effects) that might prove to produce fewer disabilities. Goodwin and Breen (1990) studied pregnancy outcomes for mothers who experienced noncatastrophic trauma during pregnancy and found that mothers who were battered were more than twice as likely to have complications to their pregnancies than those who experienced trauma as the result of falls or those who experienced trauma in automobile accidents. Until the effects have been more thoroughly investigated, the safest assumption would be to assume that battery of women during pregnancy increases the risk of infants born with disabilities by about the four times currently suggested by birth weight data.

Further study to clarify these relationships should be a major priority of researchers concerned with violence and disability. The historical lack of research and clinical attention given to the effects of abuse during pregnancy has occasionally been pointed out, but little has been done to rectify this problem. In 1981, the staff of the Division of Genetics at Kansas City's Mercy Hospital wrote: "We consider it a delusion to think that the fetus is exempt from an environment in which child abuse and spouse abuse is commonplace. Are there others with similar concerns who can help elaborate the battered fetus prototype?" (Morey, Begleiter, & Harris, 1981 p. 1296).

While others have added their voices to this concern, no large scale or well-controlled study has followed. Clearly this work needs to be done, but the task is a complex one. Because spousal abuse within families correlates to increased risk of child abuse within these same families, the children whose mothers were abused during pregnancy would also experience greater risk for abuse as infants, children, and young adults. Care must be taken to separate the effects of prenatal and postnatal trauma. Furthermore, substance abuse is more frequent in families where violence takes place, and the potential effects of alcohol and other drugs on the fetus would require careful experimental control.

Underreporting Another problem that is difficult to address in currently available research is the relative influence of underreporting. Because studies can only measure reported or observable child abuse, we assume that covert cases exist and that the findings based on overt cases also represent the unknown relationships found in covert cases. We also assume that if a given percentage of children with disabilities are known to have been abused, a similar proportion of children with disabilities are most likely victimized in covert cases of abuse. This assumption is based on another underlying assumption that the proportion of reported to unreported cases is the same for children both with and without disabilities. If abuse were more likely to be reported in the cases of children with disabilities than those of children without disabilities, the link between disability and abuse might only reflect better reporting for this group. Conversely, if abuse were less likely to be reported in the cases of children with disabilities than those of children without disabilities, the actual differences in rates of abuse would be even greater than they appear. For example, if abuse occurred with equal frequency for children with and without disabilities, but only 10% of cases in one group was reported and 30% of cases in the other group was reported, the abuse would appear to be three times as frequent in the group with the higher report rate.

The important questions that arise from this will have to be answered by future research. Current research indicates that many case characteristics influence the likelihood of reporting, including some attributable to the child being abused (Zellman, 1991), but does not specifically indicate how disability may influence reporting. The answers will probably be quite complex because any differences in reporting could depend on the nature and severity of the disability, the environment in which the abuse occurs, the type of abuse, and any number of other factors. Preliminary indications do suggest, however, that unreported abuse may be a particular problem for children with disabilities, especially those living in institutions and other isolated environments.

For example, one study (Schilling, Kirkham, & Schinke, 1986) found that although most (82%) child protection workers considered children with developmental disabilities to be more likely to be abused, 84% could not recall serving even one child with a developmental disability, and only 4% had served more than one. Other studies suggest that people with disabilities often have difficulty obtaining services for protection and intervention (e.g., Sobsey & Doe, 1991). Children with disabilities may be underrepresented by samples drawn from such agencies that typically exclude them. The widespread failure to report abuse in institutional settings (see Chapter 4 for a fuller discussion) also contributes to an underrepresentation of people with disabilities in child abuse register studies. Initial findings of a study conducted by England's National Society for the Prevention of Cruelty to Children (NSPCC) suggested that more of the cases of abuse involving children with disabilities went unreported (Cohen & Warren, 1990).

Physical Assaults on Adults with Disabilities

Little research is available that addresses physical assaults committed against adults with disabilities. However, these offenses appear to be fairly common. One study of women who have been psychiatrically institutionalized (Firsten, 1990) reports that 59.8% had experienced severe physical assaults as adults, slightly more than the percentage that had been physically abused as children (56.6%). Another study of women with a variety of disabilities reported that 33.4% had also been victims of physical assaults (Stimpson & Best, 1991).

Adults with developmental disabilities are also frequently assaulted. In one such case, a 24-year-old man with mental retardation was tortured and beaten to death in an unprovoked attack by an adult and three teenagers with whom he had tried to make friends. Over a protracted period they took turns beating him, shaved his head, forced him to lick the toilet bowl, and tortured him in several other ways. He died several days later from blunt trauma to his kidneys sustained in the beatings. The court heard testimony indicating that the victim made no attempts to defend himself, but rather only redoubled his efforts to gain the approval of his assailants. Convicted of killing this man, the adult perpetrator was sentenced to only 6 years, two of the teenagers were sentenced to probation and community service, and the remaining teenager received only a suspended sentence (Engman & Crockatt, 1992). The judge who sentenced the two teenagers to community service and probation in this case is reported to have "said the assaults were not serious" (Engman, 1992, p. A1).

THE VIOLENCE AND DISABILITY CYCLE

As suggested earlier in this chapter, violence is a cause of an unknown but substantial number of disabilities, and people with disabilities experience a greater risk for abuse. As a result, some individuals become trapped in a vicious cycle of violence and disability; they experience permanent disability as a result of violence and become more vulnerable to violence because of their disability. They may enter the cycle at any point, but once caught in the cycle escape becomes more difficult.

Figure 1 illustrates some of the mechanisms that contribute to the violence and disability cycle. Some of these mechanisms receive further attention in subsequent chapters. Nevertheless, they are included here to illustrate the diversity of causal influences that maintain the violence and disability cycle. Of course, not all of these mechanisms apply in every case; usually there is a combination of several factors at work.

For example, a mother abused by her partner during pregnancy is more likely to have a child with a disability as a result of injuries sustained by the developing fetus (Morey et al., 1981). Because abused individuals are more prone to use alcohol and other drugs, and women with substance abuse problems during pregnancy have an increased chance of having infants with disabilities, the fetus is at higher risk as a result of this secondary effect of violence (West et al., 1992). Furthermore, if the abusive father stays in the family, he is inclined to also be an abusive parent, and if he abuses his child, the risk of disability is fur-

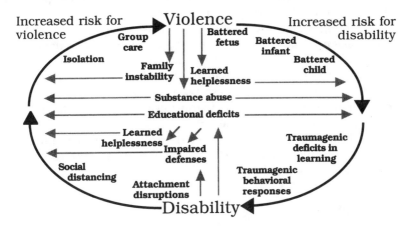

Figure 1. Mechanisms that contribute to the abuse and disability cycle.

ther increased. Sadly, the abusive father provides a violent role model, thus the child is also prone to experience violence from other family members (Bandura, Ross, & Ross, 1963). In addition, abuse of the mother along with substance abuse increases instability and thus increases the possibility of family break-up, but even if the abusive father leaves the home, the child is likely to be exposed to a wide variety of alternative caregivers, and this situation is also associated with increased risk for abuse and the danger of further injury-produced disability. Even when violence does not produce injury through physical assault, emotional trauma could interfere with the child's development and learning and can produce psychological and behavioral disturbances that contribute to disability.

If any of these mechanisms result in disability or even if the child has a disability resulting from an unrelated cause, the child is inclined to have impaired self-protective skills. Depending on the nature of the disability, the child may be unable to seek help, escape, or ward off abuse from others. As a result of society's responses to disabilities (Sobsey & Mansell, 1990), parents may experience difficulty establishing emotional bonds with their child (Youngblade & Belsky, 1989). Such attachment disruptions may increase the risk for abuse within the family and also increase the chance that the child will be placed outside the natural family where the risk of abuse is also high (Blatt & Brown, 1986). Dehumanizing attitudes about disability act to reduce inhibitions against violence and facilitate abuse (Sobsey & Mansell, 1990; Waxman, 1991). The child with a disability is more likely to be placed in a special education program and these programs also typically have an increased tendency toward violence because they often encourage dependency, compliance, and learned helplessness while failing to teach self-protection and assertiveness (Sobsey & Mansell, 1992).

While the violence and disability cycle is powerful, it is important to note that the relationship between abuse and disability is not universal and it is not inevitable. Not all people who are abused have disabilities, and not all people with disabilities are abused. In fact, many individuals and families avoid or escape this cycle. These families need acknowledgment and support. Inappropriately blaming families for their children's disabilities or assuming all families that include members with disabilities are dysfunctional would not only be unfair, but could also produce unnecessary external pressures, which can in turn lead to an increased risk for violence.

CONCLUSION

The child protection movement has evolved since the middle of the 19th century and has gained momentum in the latter half of the twentieth century. Since the 1960s, a strong relationship between abuse and disability has been noted and further research is required before that relationship can be fully understood. While much remains to be learned, several facts have clearly emerged. First, abuse is a major cause of disability. Second, even when individuals have disabilities that are not caused by abuse, the risk of abuse appears substantially greater than the risk for individuals without disabilities. Third, some circumstantial factors such as chronic alcohol abuse in families can substantially increase the risk for both abuse and disability, adding to the association between the two.

These conclusions provide useful preliminary information for the development of a model to explain the abuse of people with disabilities and for the planning of prevention programs. Before presenting such a model, however, it is important to consider information about sexual and institutional abuse and the resulting implications for people with disabilities, as well as to explore how some types of rehabilitative intervention can also be forms of abuse.

3

Sexual Abuse
and Sexual Assault

It is not surprising that outrage and concern were expressed in the community when five New Jersey high school boys were charged with a sexual attack. On March 1, 1989, 11 high school athletes gathered around a 17-year-old girl with mental retardation in a basement and took turns engaging in a variety of sexual behavior such as fellatio, penetrating her with a small baseball bat, and penetrating her with a broomstick while the others looked on and cheered. One boy was quoted later as saying that it was like "a group of guys watching a friend feed a tank of piranhas" (quoted in Schanberg, 1992, p. 17). What was surprising, however, was that most of the outrage seemed to be directed toward the young woman, and most of the concern was for the young men involved.

Schoolmates voiced dismay that the lives and future careers of these young men could be damaged by an unfortunate incident like this. One fellow male student who was not involved is quoted in the Associated Press as saying, "these kids are really not bad kids at all," and a female student, apparently having a little more empathy with the victim suggested, "you've got to have sympathy for both sides" ("5 accused," 1989, p. 1415). If there were others who felt that these young males had acted inappropriately, they apparently chose to keep their opinions quiet, especially after schoolmates who failed to stand behind the accused students reported threats—including at least one death threat, property vandalism, and physical attacks by friends of the accused ("5 accused," 1989). A female student attempted to discredit the young woman who had been victimized by pretending to be her friend and winning her confidence in order to covertly record her responses to leading questions about her sexual behavior (Schanberg, 1992).

Schanberg (1992) quotes the defense attorney at the subsequent trial, who described the young woman involved as a "Lolita" who "craved euphoria because her brain functioned that way" and described the young men involved as mere "pranksters" acting out "basic human boyish needs" (p. 17). Some observers felt that the prosecution presented an even more troubling image of the young woman as helpless and incompetent, unable to make her own decisions or to give her consent under any circumstances. Nevertheless, after a long and complex trial, four of the young men involved were convicted on major charges of sexual assault ("Four found guilty," 1993).

A similar report alleges that when the football coach at a Houston middle school found seven boys sexually assaulting a 13-year-old special education student in September 1992, he stopped the attack, but never reported the incident ("Houston students expelled," 1992). Only after the student who was assaulted disclosed the incident to another teacher the following day was any action taken.

Research now leaves little doubt that both children and adults with disabilities are likely to be victims of sexual abuse, assault, and exploitation, and that society often responds in a manner designed to protect offenders and blame victims (e.g., Carmody, 1991; Stimpson & Best, 1991). Such events are not unique to our time. For example, more than 100 years ago Dorothea Dix reported the case of a young woman with mental retardation who was chained and kept naked in a barn, "the helpless prey of profligate men and idle boys who were permitted to visit the place at will" (Deutsch, 1949, p. 167).

This chapter discusses sexual abuse of children with disabilities and sexual assault of adults with disabilities. Sexual offenses are among the most frequent crimes against people with disabilities. For example, one study of alleged crimes against people with disabilities found that more than 90% involved sexual offenses (Carmody, 1991). Before addressing unique aspects of sex crimes against people with disabilities, however, it is important to consider what is known about these crimes as they affect all members of society.

SEXUAL ABUSE OF CHILDREN

Sexual abuse of children is now known to be a fairly common event, but no one is certain exactly how common. Self-report studies (i.e., studies based on adults' personal recollections of childhood abuse) from the United States and Canada suggest that between 3% and 31% of males and between 6% and 62% of females are sexually abused as children (Peters, Wyatt, & Finkelhor, 1986). The extent of variability in these results may be due to real differences in the samples (e.g., Americans or Canadians, volunteers or college students), procedural differences (e.g., telephone survey, mail-in survey, or face-to-face interview), and differences in definitions of child sexual abuse (e.g., unwanted sexual acts before age 18 or sexual assaults prior to age 16, inclusion or exclusion of verbal or other noncontact offenses). Even the most conservative estimates based on inclusion of only severe offenses, however, suggest that millions of North Americans have been sexually abused. It is estimated that as many as 100,000–500,000 children become victims of sexual abuse in the United States alone each year (Waterman & Lusk, 1986).

Although child sexual abuse has been given more attention since the 1970s, it is certainly not a new phenomenon. Tardieu, a major contributor to the development of forensic medicine, reported on over 9,000 criminal cases involving rapes of children in France from 1858 to 1869 (Summit, 1988). Nevertheless, many continued to believe that children's disclosures of sexual abuse were either fantasies or malicious lies. Summit (1988) compares the unwillingness of society to accept the overwhelming evidence of child abuse to its unwillingness to accept the idea that the sun is the center of the universe, pointing out that "it took 18 centuries to give up the sacred notion that the world is the center of the universe . . . despite irrefutable accumulation of evidence to the contrary" (p. 51). Masson (1984) quotes Dr. Claude Bourdin, in 1882, in a powerful example of the attempts to discredit children's disclosures: "It is up to the educators and particularly the medical doctors to destroy the myth of the infallible sincerity of children" (p. 48).

In 1896, more evidence was presented suggesting that child sexual abuse was a significant problem. Freud presented a paper, "The Aetiology of Hysteria," indicating that childhood sexual abuse was often a cause of psychotic symptoms in women (Masson, 1984). Freud believed that he had made an important discovery that would be welcomed by his colleagues, but he soon discovered that he had made a grave error. The reaction to his presentation was immediate and "within two weeks he was feeling the pain of inevitable isolation" (Summit, 1988, p. 48). After being ostracized by his professional colleagues as well as the families of his patients for presenting his theory of childhood sexual abuse, he retracted it and replaced it with one that suggested that these disclosures were sexual fantasies produced by sick minds. Freud's recantation and the replacement of his earlier seduction theory with his later Oedipus complex vindicated those who were threatened by the realities of sexual abuse, saved Freud's career, and probably shaped the discipline of psychiatry for at least the next century (Summit, 1988).

It is not surprising that the general recognition by contemporary society of the existence of sexual abuse of children occurred only after its recognition of physical abuse. Physical abuse leaves more visible scars that are difficult to refute as fantasy, and our society remains more accepting of discussions of violence than of sexuality, as is illustrated by the open portrayals of violence in mass media, while sex generally remains a topic for innuendo or at least greater discretion. For example, young children watching television are likely to see frequent bombings, stabbings, and shootings, but will be shielded from watching sexual behavior because it is considered to have a dangerous influence. Some might argue that it is unfortunate that our society seems much more comfortable with the destruction of life than with its creation.

Still, with the growing concern about physical abuse and neglect that followed the publication of *The Battered Child Syndrome* (Kempe et al., 1962), it was inevitable that concern about the sexual victimization of children would follow. In 1969, DeFrancis published a survey of New York City child sexual abuse victims and their families (Dziech & Schudson, 1991) indicating that the vast majority of offenders went unpunished. Subsequent mass media attention, along with scientific studies, worked to fuel public concern.

Current Knowledge

Knowledge of sexual abuse of children remains very limited. Definitions of child sexual abuse still vary. It is now known that it occurs frequently and causes significant damage to children. There are still only a few clues that indicate why it occurs, and based on these clues, programs have been developed to try to prevent it. However, there is very little information to validate the effectiveness of these prevention programs. Programs to support victims of sexual abuse have also been developed, but, here as well, little data are available (Wheeler & Berliner, 1988).

Defining Child Sexual Abuse Definitions of child sexual abuse vary in several important ways (Peters et al., 1986). First, the age of the child may differ. Various definitions limit the age of the abused child to 15, 16, or 17. Others set the limit at puberty regardless of when it occurs. Second, the kind of behavior included may differ. Some definitions include verbal propositions and exhibitionism, others include only physical contact abuse. Third, specific conditions may be imposed. For example, a minimum age discrepancy of 5 years between the offender and the person abused is required by some definitions. This discrepancy is designed to differentiate between normal sexual exploration and abuse. Many definitions combine two or more of these elements. For example, a definition may include all contact and non-contact sexual behavior if the child is under 13 and the offender is at least 5 years older, but if the child is 13–16, will only include sexual behavior when the offender is at least 10 years older or when coercion or harm is evident. Another approach to definition has been taken by the National Center on Child Abuse and Neglect. It defines abuse as "any childhood sexual experience that interferes with or has the potential to interfere with a child's healthy development" (Tower, 1989, p. 105). This definition has strong conceptual advantages, but is difficult to apply with precision as a criterion for the inclusion or exclusion of specific cases.

As defined by this book, child sexual abuse means any sexual interaction between an adult and a child 12 years old or younger, or any sexual interaction involving an individual who is 13–17 years old when there is clear indication of harm, coercion, or the exploitation of a relationship of authority. This definition is a narrow one, restricting the number of cases included and eliminating many cases that might be disputed (e.g., mutually consenting adolescent sexual experimentation). When references are made to the work of other researchers and authors, it will be helpful to note that their definitions may differ. Sexual abuse can be categorized in several ways. For example, it may be intrafamilial or extrafamilial; homosexual or heterosexual; single incident, repeated, or chronic; planned or spontaneous; may or may not involve overt sadism or violence; and may or may not include various forms of sexual behavior (Tower, 1989).

Identifying Risks All children are at risk for sexual abuse. Children of every race, culture, and social class have been victims. Although both girls and boys are at risk, girls are more likely to be sexually abused than boys. Reinart (1987), for example, reports that one sixth of sexually abused children are boys. Differences between statistics from service agencies and self-report rates indicate that more cases of sexual abuse of boys go unreported, suggesting the apparent five to one ratio of female to male victims may overemphasize the difference in risk. However, even with improved reporting of male victms, it is unlikely that the difference in risk will be completely eliminated (Finkelhor & Baron, 1986). The relationship between gender and risk also appears to correlate with age. Preschool boys and girls appear to be equally at risk (Waterman & Lusk, 1986) and pedophiles who abuse young children often exhibit no clear gender preference. As boys and girls approach adolescence, however, abusers tend to exhibit gender preferences, and girls are more frequently selected for victimization.

There are a variety of other factors that appear to be consistently associated with increased risk (Finkelhor & Baron, 1986). Social isolation of children and families is associated with greater risk for child sexual abuse. Children in homes with single parents, especially those without their natural fathers present, as well as children living with stepfathers, are more likely to be sexually abused. Most studies suggest a greater probability that children in these kinds of families will be abused by all categories of offenders, not just by their stepfathers. Poor parent–child relationships are also associated with sexual abuse. Anthropological studies have shown that children who are valued by their families and cultures are less at risk for abuse than those who are not valued (Korbin, 1987). They also suggest that families who are strongly embedded in their communities and culture have a lesser tendency toward abusing their children (Korbin, 1987).

Studies of the relationship between socioeconomic status and child sexual abuse show inconsistent results (Finkelhor & Baron, 1986; Waterman & Lusk, 1986). Some studies indicate increased risk associated with lower socioeconomic status, whereas many others fail to demonstrate a clear relationship. Because many of the studies record the socioeconomic status of adult survivors of childhood sexual abuse, any measured association may be related to effects of the abuse rather than to causes. In addition, the complex interactions among socioeconomic status and a plethora of potentially related factors may suggest spurious relationships. For example, the absence of one natural parent from the home is associated with increased risk, and single parent families typically have lower incomes.

No simple and consistent correlation between racial or ethnic origin and sexual abuse has been established, although complex interrelationships may exist. For example, several studies have compared incidence among black and white Americans and have failed to demonstrate differences (Finkelhor & Baron, 1986). Other studies suggest that minority group families that are poorly integrated into the mainstream of society experience greater risk; however, data from these studies point to social isolation as the risk factor rather than ethnic or racial differences (Korbin, 1987).

The great majority of sexual abusers of children (both girls and boys) are males, although there are some female offenders. Some researchers believe that sexual offenses by women are more likely to go unreported, and as a result gender differences are exaggerated. Nevertheless, there is little reason to believe that measurement errors account for any significant misrepresentation as to the preponderance of male offenders.

Detecting Sexual Abuse   One of the unfortunate realities of sexual abuse is that it often goes undetected. Children may not disclose abuse for a variety of reasons. They may be struggling with confusing emotions regarding their abuse and may be inhibited by rational or irrational fears. Sometimes preliminary attempts to talk about the abuse are blocked by responses of disbelief or anger. For example, one child indicated that she had started to tell, but her father had responded, "If he ever touches you, I'll kill him." Later she indicated that she was afraid to discuss the abuse because she feared that her father would kill the neighbor who abused her and be sent to jail. Even physical examinations rarely provide conclusive evidence that sexual abuse has or has not occurred. Nevertheless, a number of indicators can help to detect sexual abuse and these signs are listed in Table 1.

Although none of these signs can provide conclusive evidence of abuse, some signs are more significant than others. However, all speculation should be evaluated in consideration of the child's age and other information. For example, sexually transmitted diseases (STDs) are rarely transmitted by other means; however some STDs transmitted congenitally may be found in very young children, and adolescents can contract STDs through sexual activity that does not necessarily constitute abuse. Similarly, caregivers who drink alcohol, use other drugs, or have their own unresolved histories of abuse do not necessarily abuse others. All signs of abuse must also be considered with regard to the particular situation and individuals involved. For example, people who have been sexually assaulted may exhibit unusual fear and resistance toward medical examination, and those who have been forced to have oral sex will sometimes react more extremely to dental examinations than to examinations of other parts of their bodies.

Table 1. Common signs of sexual abuse

Physical signs	Behavioral signs	Circumstantial signs
Bruises in genital areas	Atypical attachment	Alcohol or drug abuse by
Genital discomfort	Avoids specific adult	caregivers
Sexually transmitted	Avoids specific setting	Devaluing attitudes
disease	Depression	Excessive or inappropriate
Signs of physical abuse	Disclosure	eroticism
Torn or missing clothing	Eating disorders	Isolation of social unit
Unexplained genital	Learning difficulties	Other forms of abuse
abnormalities	Noncompliance	Pornography usage
Unexplained pregnancy	Poor self-esteem	Previous history of abuse
	Regression	Seeks isolated contact
	Resists physical	with children
	examination	Strong preference for
	Self-destructive behavior	children
	Sexualized behavior	Surrogate caregivers
	Sleep disturbances	(particularly males)
	Substance abuse	Unresolved history of
	Withdrawal	abuse

Recognizing the Harm

Some disagreement remains regarding the harm caused by sexual abuse. Alfred Kinsey, one of the foremost experts on American sexuality, proposed that it was only our cultural sexual inhibitions that made sexual relationships harmful between adults and children, and Karl Menninger, one of America's most highly esteemed psychiatrists, suggested that adult–child sexuality is rarely harmful and may actually stimulate the development of the child (Dziech & Schudson, 1991). Nevertheless, despite the fact that some organizations, such as Better Life Boy Love, the Childhood Sensuality Circle, and the North American Man–Boy Love Association continue to advocate for the legitimization of adult sexual relations with children, the vast majority of evidence points to very substantial damage done to sexually abused children (e.g., Tower, 1989).

Physical Harm STDs, pregnancies, physical injuries, and even deaths occur as a result of child sexual abuse. Most STDs can be treated successfully with antibiotics, but some, such as HIV infection and Hepatitis B, can be fatal. Furthermore, even STDs that can be easily treated are often left untreated, sometimes with serious consequences, because both the abuse and the STD have been concealed. Obviously, boys who are sexually abused do not face the risk of unwanted pregnancy, and female offenders do not produce pregnancy in children. The risk for girls becoming pregnant varies with age, and the nature and frequency of the abuse. Sexual offenders often take measures to prevent conception because pregnancy could lead to disclosure of the abuse. As a result of these and other possible factors, pregnancies are uncommon. Because sexual abuse that does not lead to pregnancy is more easily hidden, statistics may overestimate the probability of pregnancy. For example, a study from India of rape among children reports pregnancy in 18% of the cases (Metha, Lokeshwar, Bhatt, Athavale, & Kulkarni, 1979). Such a high rate is not surprising, however, because the authors suggest strong social pressure to conceal abuse, indicating that "marriage is beyond question and to keep social prestige of the family the only path left for this doomed girl is suicide" (pp. 671).

Associated physical violence may be used by the offender to force sexual compliance, to prevent disclosure, or to achieve sexual satisfaction. Bruising, lacerations and other physical damage can occur as a result of the abuse. Sexual abuse is often associated with other forms of physical and emotional abuse that compound the potential harm. For example, in a study of convicted child sexual molesters, 58% admitted that they had used more force with children they abused than the amount necessary to achieve sexual compliance (Marshall & Barrett,

1990). Half the victims of sexual abuse in this study required medical treatment for injuries.

Some manifestations of sexual abuse appear to be physical, but are typically considered to be psychosomatic in origin. These include stomachaches, headaches, sleep disorders, seizures, difficulty with bladder and bowel control, and a variety of other physical complaints (Lusk & Waterman, 1986). The mechanism of such complaints is not always clear, however, and physical causes should not be ruled out. For example, undiagnosed STDs can cause abdominal pain and frequent findings of abnormal electroencephalographic measures among some victims suggests that not all seizures are psychosomatic (Davies, 1979).

Psychological and Behavioral Harm Fortunately, many victims of child sexual abuse escape physical harm, although almost all suffer long-lasting behavioral, emotional, and social consequences. Sexual abuse that is chronic, violent or sadistic, or committed by a parent or individual in a close relationship to the child, and begins at an early age, is likely to cause more severe damage than sexual abuse that is less frequent, nonviolent, or committed by an adult who does not have a close relationship with the child, and begins at a later age (Tower, 1989).

Children who have been sexually abused may exhibit a wide variety of symptoms. Some of the more common ones include loss of self-esteem, guilt and self-blame, rational and irrational fear, depression, repressed or open anger, generalized loss of trust, role confusion, pseudomaturity (often accompanied by precocious sexuality) with failure to meet prerequisite developmental milestones, problems with self-control, and feelings of personal and social devaluation (Porter, Blick, & Sgroi, 1982). Post-traumatic stress disorder and multiple personality disorder are severe psychological problems that also can result from child sexual abuse. In addition, there have been strong suggestions that childhood sexual abuse substantially increases the risk of sexual dysfunction, revictimization, psychiatric illness, sexual abuse of others, drug and alcohol abuse, teenage prostitution, and a number of other difficulties later in life (McGregor & Dutton, 1991).

Some of the symptoms of child sexual abuse actually interfere with recognition of the problem both in general and in specific cases. Together these symptoms have been referred to as the child sexual abuse accommodation syndrome (Summit, 1988). These include:

1. Secrecy
2. Helplessness
3. Entrapment
4. Delayed and unconvincing disclosures
5. Retraction of disclosures

Prevention

While a great deal of attention has been given to preventing child sexual abuse, there is surprisingly little consensus among professionals and little scientific data available as to exactly how it can be prevented. Better information on the effectiveness of prevention programs may take a long time to generate because most available information regarding the prevalence of child sexual abuse comes from adult recall studies, and therefore, may require as much as 2 decades before the effects of interventions applied with children today can be measured in adults (Bagley, 1991).

The majority of prevention or risk-reduction programs focus on teaching children how to protect themselves. Contents typically include recognizing appropriate and inappropriate touching, saying "no," telling others, and avoiding high-risk situations. While children's learning can be measured in pre- and post-test measures, many researchers and clinicians suggest that cognitive assimilation of this material appears to be a weak predictor of how these children will act in critical life situations (Daro, 1991; Gentles & Cassidy, 1988). Furthermore, the assumption that applying the learned material will, in fact, enable children to prevent their own abuse seems unrealistic. This is especially true in situations where older, more powerful offenders, often in positions of authority, seek to manipulate and exploit children over whom they exert considerable control.

Some researchers and clinicians have attempted to use simulations to test children's responses to potential abusers. These studies have been useful in demonstrating the inadequacies of post-test evaluations. They have also pointed toward the requirement of self-esteem as a co-factor with knowledge for children to be able to apply what they have learned in abuse prevention programs (Gentles & Cassidy, 1988). However, using simulation as a means of validating prevention training creates some ethical problems. It has been suggested that such simulations may actually desensitize children to abusive situations and thus increase their vulnerability (Gentles & Cassidy, 1988). Also, abusers may actually conceal the abuse as a "test" (Bagley, 1991), further complicating the picture for children and those who wish to protect them. For example, a teacher might attempt to involve a child in a sexual interaction. If the child refuses and discloses the proposition to other adults, this teacher could simply tell them that the approach was an evaluation exercise. Thus, until data become available from longitudinal evaluations, sexual abuse prevention education programs will continue to be based on theoretical rather than empirical principles.

Other approaches to prevention focus on convicting and sentencing offenders as a deterrent to abuse, rehabilitating offenders to reduce the risk of future offenses, public education to help protective adults recognize high-risk situations, initiatives against substance abuse (often a factor in child sexual abuse), and attempts to support intact families (disrupted families appear to increase the risk for abuse). It is likely that effective prevention programs in the future will combine many of these components.

Intervention

In the United States alone, there are more than 2,200 child sexual abuse support programs (Keller, Cicchinelli, & Gardner, 1989). Most use traditional counseling and psychotherapeutic approaches. These inlude:

1. Individual psychotherapy
2. Group therapy
3. Family therapy
4. Mother–daughter dyad therapy
5. Crisis intervention
6. Behavioral therapy
7. Art therapy
8. Educational intervention
9. Eclectic programs combining elements from two or more approaches (Porter et al., 1982; Thomlison, 1991)

Environmental or protective interventions must also be considered because it is difficult to accomplish progress if support is provided, yet children remain in environments where threats continue. Therefore, ensuring safety from repeated victimization may be an essential prerequisite to effective intervention. Support goals should be individualized, but often include building self-esteem, eliminating guilt and self-blame, coping with anger, developing healthy relationships, restoring trust, communicating about feelings and experiences, normalizing development, and channeling reactions into constructive behavior (Furniss, 1991; Tower, 1989). Although the results of intervention are promising, well-designed evaluation studies are rare; much more work is required before definitive statements regarding the most effective practices become available.

Ritual Abuse and Conspiracy

Although little information is currently available regarding ritual abuse, increasing reports have made it an emerging concern. Experts have not yet formulated a common definition, but ritual abuse often involves psychological, sexual, and physical abuse of children and sometimes adults (Lloyd, 1992). It is typically characterized by multiple offenders who belong to the same organization or cult, ritualized (typically religious or supernatural) behavior, and an atypical set of beliefs or attitudes (Ryder, 1992). In many cases, elaborate measures are undertaken to maintain secrecy and ensure that victims cannot or will not identify their abusers (Lloyd, 1992). Often when victims disclose abuse, their stories include elements of the supernatural (e.g., people flying or walking through walls), making all aspects of their stories more difficult to believe. While the genesis of such supernatural memories is unknown, post-traumatic stress disorder, mind-altering drugs, and deliberate deceptions by perpetrators are considered likely contributors. Victims may be abducted by strangers, but are frequently recruited and indoctrinated by cult members. While the number of reports of ritual abuse is increasing, many disclosures remain unverified, making it difficult to even estimate the actual number of cases (Lloyd, 1992). Even the range of events associated with ritual abuse remains uncertain because cases that are publicized are often those with the most sensational disclosures, rather than those with the most thorough documentation.

Until more is known about ritual abuse, its implications for people with disabilities will remain uncertain. Nevertheless, indications that some cults seek socially isolated and devalued individuals with low self-esteem and limited communication skills as "ideal victims," suggests that people with disabilities are likely to be among the victims of ritual abuse (Ryder, 1992). Cultural attitudes that associate disability with evil or view people with disabilities as holy innocents may also make them more attractive to some cults. In a rare personal account of ritual abuse from a woman who is deaf, the author suggests that her deafness was probably largely irrelevant with regard to her chronic physical, emotional, and sexual abuse, but also recommends that "the disabled consumer's movement has a very important role to begin addressing and acknowledging ritual abuse in its work on violence against people with disabilities" (Amethya, 1992, p. 20).

Conspiracy is not unique to Satanic cults. Sexual abuse conspiracies have also been uncovered within communities, schools, churches, childcare centers, orphanages, and a variety of other settings (e.g., Gil, 1981). The degree of conspiracy varies from carefully planned abuse to negotiated cover-ups after the abuse has taken place. This type of sexual abuse or assault is particularly harmful because it is often chronic, involves multiple offenders, is committed by people in positions of trust, and leaves its victims feeling powerless and totally isolated. People with disabilities are particularly likely to become victims of sexual abuse conspiracies when they live in group-care settings where such abuse frequently takes place.

False and Unconfirmed Disclosures

Not all disclosures of abuse are validated or confirmed. Whereas unconfirmed reports of physical abuse also occur, confirmation is particularly difficult in cases of sexual abuse because physical evidence to corroborate allegations is often unavailable or equivocal (Adams, 1992). Nevertheless, most unconfirmed allegations are not proven false; they simply lack sufficient proof to be certain that they are true.

Considerable evidence suggests that false disclosures of sexual abuse are rare. Green and Schetky (1988) cite two studies that report about 6% of allegations are false and a third study suggesting that 8% of disclosures are false. Although this percentage is small, sometimes false allegations can and do occur, and alleged offenders must and should be considered innocent unless proven guilty.

False allegations have been associated with custody disputes, Münchausen syndrome by proxy, retaliation, displacement, and contagion (Green & Schetky, 1988). Allegations of sexual abuse are more common during divorce, marital separation, and custody or visitation disputes, and many of these allegations remain unconfirmed (Green & Schetky, 1988). However, not all allegations arising during custody disputes are false, and the increased number of allegations during marriage breakdown may occur for a variety of other reasons. For example, underlying family dysfunction that causes the break up of the family also increases the chances for abuse at that time, a child may be more willing to disclose abuse to her mother after the father leaves the home, separate residences may allow for better opportunities to commit abuse, and finally, angry fathers may abuse their children as a way of retaliating against their wives. Nevertheless, the large numbers of disclosures in custody disputes that remain unconfirmed suggest that significant numbers of these allegations may be false.

Münchausen syndrome by proxy, described in Chapter 2, is a less common phenomenon associated with false allegations of sexual abuse. Some caregivers, most often mothers, may become convinced that their children are being sexually abused and seek help for them despite the absence of evidence. Occasionally, they may even convince their child to disclose fictitious abuse. In some cases, the caregiver's own, sometimes repressed, experience of being victimized begins to surface when her child (typically her daughter) reaches a particular age or when the caregiver encounters a particular situation that triggers recall of the abuse (Furniss, 1991).

In a few instances, children, generally older children and adolescents, have been found to falsify charges of sexual abuse to retaliate against a caregiver (Green & Schetky, 1988). In other, uncommon cases, children who have been sexually abused accuse innocent people, often as a result of fear or of manipulation by the real offender. For example, an offender may tell a child to blame someone else or he will murder the child's parents, and the child may comply as a result of overwhelming fear.

Some people have suggested that *contagion* can also lead to false allegations. They suggest that impressionable children may be led into fantasies of abuse by parents or professionals who ask leading questions in an attempt to obtain a disclosure (Green & Schetky, 1988). A few nationally publicized cases of apparently widespread sexual abuse conspiracies involving many adults have failed to be confirmed in the courts, leaving some to wonder whether children may have been "brainwashed" into telling stories of abuse or if better methods of investigating and prosecuting such cases would have yielded different results. For example, the McMartin Preschool case in California involved allegations of sexual abuse by many children against many adults and led to one of the most protracted and costly trials in American history, but resulted finally in zero convictions (Summit, 1993). While many believe that the stories told by these children were false and resulted from leading questions and poor interview techniques, others believe that better investigative techniques could have provided physical evidence that would have corroborated the children's stories (Summit, 1993).

Although it is important to note that false allegations do occasionally occur, it is also important to recognize that research suggests that the great majority (90%–95%) of allegations are truthful (Green & Schetky, 1988). No allegation should be dismissed without careful investigation. Nevertheless, society must continue to develop better methods of ensuring that genuine allegations are validated and false allegations are identified and eliminated. This is not only essential for the protection of any innocent individuals who are wrongly accused, but to eliminate the defense of doubt and "righteous indignation" from those who are guilty.

SEXUAL ASSAULT AND SEXUAL EXPLOITATION OF ADULTS

Unfortunately, sexual assault of adults is a grim reality for many women and significant numbers of men. Women are much more likely to be victimized, whereas men commit the vast majority of sexual offenses; however, men can also be victims of sexual assault. It is typically an extremely, perhaps uniquely, traumatic emotional experience for victims and is often accompanied by other forms of violence. For example, Marshall and Barrett (1990) report that 71% of incarcerated rapists admit using more force than "necessary."

Blaming the Victim

People who are sexually assaulted are often blamed by some segments of society, and sometimes even blame themselves, for "allowing themselves to be victimized." Individuals who are attacked by people whom they know and trust are accused of having encouraged the attack or having been too trusting. People who are sexually assaulted by strangers are sometimes accused of having failed to take adequate precautions or of failing to fight off the attacker. The apparent expression of such attitudes by a number of judges not only provides some of the most outrageous examples, but also contributes to the social and political polarization of society on sexual assault as a gender issue.

Marshall and Barrett (1990) provide a long list of examples of such judges' opinions. In 1983, one judge acquitted the defendant of rape finding the complainant's testimony of nonconsent hard to believe for two reasons: 1) she had answered her door at 5:30 in the morning, and 2) although she had told the perpetrator that he could not come in, she had failed to lock the door when she closed it behind him. Another judge that year halved the 8-year sentence of a twice-convicted rapist who punched his victim in the face and kicked her crutches away from her. The judge "remark[ed] that the victim should have expected to be raped" (p. 111) if she accompanied the man home at 3 A.M. to drink beer and smoke marijuana. Another judge who gave a light sentence to a man who had sexually assaulted three young girls and his foster daughter repeatedly explained his leniency by saying that the man only used force when one of his victims tried to resist. A report by a Toronto action group based on similar views expressed by judges in over 1,000 sentencing reports provides strong evidence "that judges often blame the victims for provoking sexual assaults, downplay the severity of the crimes, and accept such factors as the offender's family background and employment records as reasons for leniency " (Marshall & Barrett, 1990, p. 108). Such attitudes expressed by judges (typically male) can only be viewed as providing support for the assertion presented by Brownmiller (1975) and echoed by many others that rape is not a sexual act, but an act of power used collectively by men against all women to maintain male social dominance.

Sexual Exploitation and Abuse of Trust

One of the most common forms of sexual offenses against adults involves the corruption of relationships of trust. While professional sexual misconduct can involve victims with or without disabilities, it is a special concern for people with disabilities because they typically have a great deal of contact with professional caregivers. Psychologists, psychiatrists, physicians, clergymen, teachers, and a number of other professionals often violate the prescribed boundaries of their relationships with their patients, clients, and students when they commit sexual exploitation (Rutter, 1989). Various studies report that from 7%–15% of physicians admitted having sexual contact with patients, and about 8% of female patients reported being sexually harassed by their physicians (McPhedran, 1992). Sometimes these infractions involve gross sexual assault; more frequently they involve "consent" or at least acquiescence, but that "consent" is distorted by the coercion or inappropriate influence of authority or even incapacitating drugs. For example, some male psychoanalysts treating women with sexual dysfunction tell these patients that having sex with them is part of their therapy, although such practice violates professional ethical standards and is clearly a criminal offense in some jurisdictions. In such cases, women may consent either because they trust their therapist to act in their best interest or because they are afraid they will lose the "therapeutic relationship" on which they have become dependent.

Some professionals who indulge in such misconduct are fully aware that it is a form of predatory exploitation (Newberger & Newberger, 1986). Others may deceive their victims as well as themselves that the relationship is therapeutic, rationalize that they are the ones who are being seduced, or simply consider the sexual attraction to be irresistible in spite of their better judgment. Such rationalizations are harder to support, but are nevertheless frequently present among physicians who sexually assault patients during physical examinations (Beck & Long, 1986) or dentists and anesthesiologists who sexually assault anesthetized patients (Mertz, 1986).

Clearly, sexual attraction is a motivating factor, but power and control are also critical motivators (Rutter, 1989). Another important factor may be the health professional's desire for rebellion or sabotage against the Hippocratic oath or the mandate of their agency of employment. Rutter (1989) points out that these abusers are aroused and reinforced by the very fact that such acts are forbidden. Mars (1982) presents a related anthropological paradigm suggesting: 1) that crime in the workplace often serves as a form of rebellion against authorities, and 2) that crimes in the workplace often require the same skills as those employed on the job. He provides the example of stevedores who load trucks, boats, and trains full of goods for other people. These same stevedores may become involved in pilferage and will utilize their job skills to load some of the goods into their own cars and trucks. Of course, an economic motive is clear, but Mars suggests that the need to rebel against the control of institutional authority is at least equally important. If we apply this model to people in human services whose duties generally involve caring for others, we should expect their rebellion to take the form of exploiting others for their own gratification. Furthermore, we would expect them to use the same job skills to accomplish this exploitation. Counselors might be expected to psychologically manipulate those they seduce; physicians might be expected to rely more on physical manipulation; and dentists and anesthetists might be expected to use the drugs that have made patients numb to treatment to make them docile for exploitation.

Discussions of this type of sexual exploitation have typically assumed that the abusive professional is an adult male and that his victim is an adult female without disabilities. Certainly most cases do involve male professionals, although a small minority of female professionals have been involved in similar offenses (Pope, Keith-Spiegel, & Tabachnick, 1986). Other abusive scenarios include homosexual as well as heterosexual offenses, the victimization of children (Bajt & Pope, 1989), and the sexual exploitation of people with disabilities by professional caregivers (Sobsey & Doe, 1991). Because people with disabilities are more routinely in contact with and dependent upon service providers than others, they are more likely to be victimized by those who commit sexual misconduct.

SEXUAL VIOLENCE IN THE LIVES OF PEOPLE WITH DISABILITIES

Children and adults with disabilities are particularly at risk for becoming victims of sexual abuse or assault (Senn, 1988; Sobsey, 1988). For example, one study of 87 girls and women with mental retardation between 11 and 23 years old who were referred for birth control found that 25% had a known history of sexual assault (Chamberlain, Ruah, Passer, McGrath, & Burkett, 1984). Other authors (Cruz, Price-Williams, & Andron, 1988) report frequently finding known or previously hidden histories of sexual abuse among women with developmental disabilities referred for intervention with behavior problems. Westcott (1993) reports a similar relationship between adjustment problems and history of sexual abuse in both women and men with disabilities, and Ryan (1992) found that severe behavior problems in both men and women with developmental disabilities were often associated with traumatic sexual abuse involving multiple perpetrators and typically beginning in childhood.

Children with Disabilities

Senn (1988) summarizes a number of studies suggesting that 39%–68% of girls with developmental disabilities and 16%–30% of boys with developmental disabilities will be sexually abused before the age of 18. Such findings are not surprising because many of the factors associated with increased risk for child abuse are also associated with disability. For example, one study lists eight risk factors that can be measured at less than one year of age, and seven of these (i.e., child in care outside the home, congenital defects, low Apgar scores, low birth weight, "difficult to handle," failure to thrive, frequent hospital admissions) are also closely associated with disability (Sigurdson, Marginet, & Onysko, 1991). Ironically, society appears to offer less protection to children with disabilities than to other children because it does not view children with disabilities as likely targets for sexual abuse (Senn, 1988).

Adults with Disabilities

Adults with disabilities are frequently among the victims of sexual violence. The Center for Women's Policy Studies (1984) estimated that more than 100,000 people are raped each year in the United States, including about 85,000 that are reported to the police and an unknown number of unreported rapes. If the government estimates of 3–10 unreported rapes for each reported rape are correct, the actual number could be in excess of 250,000 and may be as many as 850,000 per year (Koss, 1988). When these numbers are considered along with the percentage of people known to have developmental disabilities and the excess risk demonstrated among this population, it is likely that 15,000–90,000 people with developmental disabilities are raped each year in the United States alone. Hard (1986) found that out of a sample of 95 people with developmental disabilities, 83% of the women and 32% of the men had been sexually assaulted. Elvik, Berkowitz, Nicholas, Lipman, and Inkelis (1990) reported on a cohort of 35 women with mental retardation living in a single residence, where there was strong evidence of sexual assault in about half the women. No positive or negative judgment could be made regarding the other half; their status was simply unknown.

This phenomenon is not restricted only to the United States. In Australia, out of 855 cases of sexual assault reported to the New South Wales Department of Health in the first 6 months of 1989, 6.4% (55) involved victims with mental retardation (Carmody, 1991). Although this figure is more than twice as high as the 3% of Australians estimated to have mental retardation, it is considered likely to be an underestimate due to severe underreporting in this category (Carmody,

1991). Police action was anticipated in only one third of these cases. In a study of 144 crimes alleged to have been committed against people with developmental disabilities, 130 (90%) were sexual offenses (Carmody, 1991). Data from other studies indicate that as many as 86% of the women with developmental disabilities in some samples had been sexually assaulted (Hard, 1986).

Stimpson and Best (1991) suggest that more than 70% of women with a wide variety of disabilities have been victims of violent sexual encounters at some time in their lives. Sobsey and Varnhagen (1991) have suggested that when broad definitions of sexual abuse are employed and single occurrence incidence is used as a measure, the risks of being sexually abused or sexually assaulted are probably at least one and a half times greater for people with disabilities than for people without disabilities of similar age and gender. The extent of this elevation of risk, however, is probably even greater when more restrictive definitions of abuse are used and multiple offenses against the same individuals are considered. For example, under broad definitions of sexual abuse (e.g., any unwanted sexual behavior) the rate in the general population may approach 50%. Thus, the rate in any subpopulation cannot exceed two times (i.e., 100%) this level. As more restrictive definitions are used (e.g., requiring physical contact), the rate in the general population decreases allowing rates in subpopulations to exceed two times the risk. As single incidence measures do not differentiate between individuals who have been victimized once or many times, they may also tend to minimize the perception of increased risk. Using measures more sensitive to repeated victimizations and restricted to more severe offenses, the risk for people with disabilities may be five or more times greater than the risk for people without disabilities.

Patterns of Sexual Violence Against People with Disabilities

Estimates of the frequency of sexual violence in the lives of people with disabilities provide strong reasoning for the development of prevention programs; however, information about the incidence of such problems provides few details to help determine how these programs should be constituted. In order to better understand how to prevent these offenses, much more specific information is needed about how they occur. This information is beginning to emerge. Table 2 summarizes studies of sexually abused people with disabilities. Although these studies differ in their methods and results, common findings among the five help to establish reliable data, and differences among the studies may help to identify certain issues or areas that require further research. Whereas the first four studies are predominantly quantitative in their approaches, the fifth (Westcott, 1993) is predominantly qualita-

Table 2. Patterns of sexual abuse of people with disabilities

Authors	Number	Ages	Gender	Disabilities	Abuse	Sample
Sobsey and Doe (1991)	166	1–57	82% F[a] 18% M[c]	114 (69%) DD[b] 52 Other	All sexual (contact only)	Self-selected Report forms (Canada, U.S.)
Sobsey[d] (current)	215	1–57	79% F 21% M	159 (74%) DD 56 Other	All sexual (contact only)	Self-selected Report forms (Canada, U.S., New Zealand)
Sullivan, Brookhouser, Scanlan, Knutson, and Schulte (1991)	482	0–21	43% F 57% M	74 (15%) DD 408 (85%) Other	72% Sexual 28% Other	Treatment referrals Record reviews (U.S.)
Turk and Brown (1992)	84	18–61	73% F 27% M	84 (100%) DD	All sexual (contact and noncontact)	Survey of service providers (UK)
Westcott (1993)	34[e]	26–44	65% F 35% M	9 (53%) DD 8 (47%) Other	53% Sexual 47% Other	Interviews with volunteers (UK)

[a]F = females.

[b]DD = developmental disabilities.

[c]M = males.

[d]The data have not previously been reported and are based in part on the same sample as Sobsey and Doe (1991).

[e]This study also included a control group consisting of 17 adults who did not have disabilities but had been abused.

tive. It is included here for two reasons. First, its qualitative approach provides a rich subjective narrative description of findings that is unavailable from the quantitative studies and makes an important contribution to understanding the experiences of the abused individuals. Second, it includes a control group of people without disabilities who experienced abuse and thus allows some distinction between issues for all victims of abuse and those that are specific to people with disabilities.

The first two studies listed actually represent parts of the same study undertaken by the author of this book and colleagues at the University of Alberta Abuse & Disability Project. Thus, all of the cases in the first (Sobsey & Doe, 1991) table entry are also represented in the current study. The inclusion of current data has been added to this discussion for two reasons. First, the additional data increase the size of the total sample by about 30% and also include cases from a third country to broaden the scope of the study. Second, while the previously published data (Sobsey & Doe, 1991) provide figures for comparison with other studies, the inclusion of current data allows for comparison figures not reported in the earlier publication. Therefore, in presenting information regarding the patterns of sexual abuse experienced by people with disabilities, current data from the University of Alberta Abuse & Disability Project are presented, but data from the earlier studies are used to supplement this information and to determine areas of agreement and disagreement.

Offenses

Severity People with disabilities who are sexually abused typically experience severe and chronic forms of abuse. Sullivan, Brookhauser, Scanlan, Knutson, and Schulte (1991) record sexual abuse and combined sexual and physical abuse as the most frequently occurring categories of abuse reported in their sample of children with disabilities. They point out that this differs from the population of individuals without disabilities, in which physical and emotional abuse are reported more often than sexual abuse. Westcott (1993) reports fairly consistent findings among her 17 interviewees with disabilities. Sexual abuse was the most prevalent form of abuse, while emotional and physical abuse were slightly less common. Ryan (1992) also reports that sexual abuse was the most frequent form of trauma among her sample of people with developmental disabilities and post-traumatic stress disorder, but physical abuse and life-threatening neglect were also typical findings. Although Ammerman et al. (1989) found that both physical abuse and neglect were more common in their sample of children with multiple disabilities who were admitted to a psychiatric hospital, they also found histories of frequent sexual abuse to be present among these children.

Turk and Brown (1992) found that noncontact forms of sexual abuse of adults (e.g., exposure to pornography, indecent exposure, sexual harassment) occurred in 23% of the cases. Sullivan et al. (1991) reported noncontact sexual abuse in only 6.7% of cases involving physical and sexual abuse and 7.3% of cases involving sexual abuse only. These lower figures for noncontact sexual abuse may be due to the fact that the sample was limited to children referred for intervention services, possibly eliminating some of the less serious cases. Other samples of sexually abused people with developmental disabilities and emotional-behavioral disorders also point to extreme forms of abuse. Ryan (1992) found that severe sexual abuse involving multiple perpetrators and beginning early in childhood was a frequent finding, and Ammerman et al. (1989) found that 40% of children with multiple disabilities in their sample were sexually abused by numerous perpetrators.

Turk and Brown (1992) found that contact sexual abuse occurred in 87% of cases (10% involved both contact and noncontact forms). Vaginal or anal penetration occurred or was attempted in 67% of cases. This is reasonably consistent with Sobsey and Doe (1991) who reported penetration in 53% of reports involving both child and adult victims. Sullivan and colleagues (1991) found that penetration had occurred in 50% of the cases of children with disabilities who were referred for sexual (but not physical) abuse and that penetration had occurred in 44% of the cases of children referred for combined sexual and physical abuse.

Sobsey and Doe's current data indicates penetration in 56% of all cases and in 62% of cases involving victims with developmental disabilities. Age was also a factor, with penetration occurring in 61% of offenses against those 18 and over, 58% of those between 13 and 17, and 48% of those under 13. Comparing the youngest group to the child data reported by Sullivan and colleagues and the oldest group to the adult data reported by Turk and Brown approximates agreement with both studies. When this sample is further restricted to only adults with developmental disabilities, making the sample more similar to that of Turk and Brown, the percentage experiencing penetration rises to 63%, providing even stronger agreement with their finding of 67%.

Koss (1988), in her study of sexual aggression against women, found that of the university students in the study who had undergone sexual coercion, attempted rape, or rape, 51% had actually suffered the most serious category of sexual assault. Koss' definition of this most serious category was broader than that used in any of the studies of people with disabilities, adding "oral intercourse" to penetration (p. 8).

Using this expanded definition, however, increases Sobsey and Doe's percentage among adults with developmental disabilities only slightly to 65% because in most cases of oral–genital contact with the offender, penetration also occurred. Nevertheless, these figures suggest that the sexual offenses committed against people with disabilities are frequently devastating in nature and that more of these offenses fall into the most serious category of assault than do those committed against the population without disabilities.

Chronicity The chronic nature of the sexual abuse committed against people with disabilities is perhaps even more alarming. Sullivan and colleagues (1991) found that "only 17.4% of sexually abused youngsters were victimized on a single occasion. The remaining 82.6% endured multiple episodes over various time periods" (p. 191). Similarly, Sobsey and Doe (1991) found that "79.6% were victimized more than once" (p. 247) and "the largest group (49.6%) disclosed abuse on 'many' (greater than 10) occasions" (p. 247). Westcott (1993) points out that for many the abuse began in childhood and continued into adulthood. Sometimes the perpetrators remained the same, and sometimes different perpetrators committed abuse at different times. In Westcott's study, even after two stepfathers were convicted of sexual abuse of other children in the family, "professionals did not investigate the possibility that abuse has been perpetrated upon siblings with disabilities and these children were not interviewed" (p. 15). No one seemed to know or care about the plight of these children; they remained vulnerable and abused.

As shown in Figure 1, current data from the Sobsey and Doe project continues to show a similar pattern of chronic sexual abuse for both children and adults. In fact, younger children in the sample were more likely to be chronically abused and less likely to be abused on only a single occasion than adults (χ-square, $df = 6, p = .0041$). Whereas individuals with developmental disabilities do not appear different from those with other disabilities with respect to chronic sexual abuse, those diagnosed as having significant mental retardation ($N = 52$) appear particularly likely to experience chronic abuse, with only 10% experiencing single episodes and at least 56% experiencing 10 or more episodes.

Offenders

Gender It is an inescapable reality that men commit many more crimes against other people than do women. Homicide, physical assault, sexual assault, and most forms of child abuse are committed predominantly by men (Monahan, 1990). Neglect is the only form of child abuse more frequently attributed to women. This is likely due to the

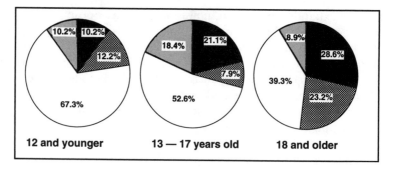

Figure 1. The number of episodes of sexual abuse or sexual assault experienced by children and adults with disabilities (■, once; ▨, 2–9 times; □, many [10 or more times]; ▨, repeated [number uncertain]).

fact that mothers are generally perceived as having most of the responsibility for the care of children, so when a child is neglected, the mother is typically held responsible.

Women appear to be less likely to abuse and more likely to report abuse (e.g., Marchetti & McCartney, 1990). Although some have suggested that bias in reporting may underestimate the actual percentage of offenses committed by women, it seems extremely unlikely that more accurate reporting will ever demonstrate gender equality in the commission of violent or sexual offenses. In fact, the risk associated with female care providers is probably overestimated in some respects because the relative amount of time spent in caregiving by males and females has rarely been considered.

For example, one study reported on 24 fatal cases of child abuse indicating 16 male and 8 female perpetrators (Krugman, 1985). A simple analysis would suggest that the risk is approximately half as high with female caregivers as with male caregivers. This estimate would be reasonable if we assumed equal exposure to children by male and female caregivers. However, the fact that many women have far more contact with children than do men suggests that the risk associated with male caregivers may be much higher than just twice the risk associated with female caregivers. Coverman and Sheley's (1986) study found that women spend about 3.5 times as much time caring for children than do men. Another study found that mothers spent about 2.1 times as much time caring for children than did fathers (Sanik, 1990). These findings would suggest that the risk associated with fatal abuse by men could be as much as four to seven times greater than the risk associated with fatal abuse by women. Margolin (1992) reported a similar conclusion. Comparing male and female caregivers, he found that females were the abusers more frequently than males; however, controlling for relative caregiving time, male caregivers actually abused more than 6.5 times as frequently as female caregivers. Males who were not blood relatives of the children they cared for were even greater risks. Some studies have shown that mothers of children with disabilities typically perform a larger proportion of overall child care than do mothers of children without disabilities (e.g., Bristol, Gallagher, & Schloper, 1988). This would suggest that the risk associated with male caregivers, at least within natural families, may be further underestimated considering the amount of actual contact time.

Most studies agree that sexual abuse offenders against people with disabilities are predominantly male. Turk and Brown (1992) reported 98% male perpetrators, Sobsey and Doe (1991) reported 91% males, and Sullivan et al. (1991) reported 88.5% males. Most, but not all, of the perpetrators described by Westcott (1993) were also males.

Relationships There is clearly less agreement among researchers regarding the relationship of these sex offenders to their victims with disabilities. Some of this disagreement may result from differences in the methods of classifying relationships, but other differences in samples or methods also appear to contribute. Figure 2a illustrates categories of relationship between abusers and their victims based on data from the University of Alberta Abuse & Disability Project's analysis of 215 cases. The four most prevalent categories of offenders include disability service providers (e.g., paid staff or volunteers who contact the abused person while providing services related to their victim's disabilities), acquaintances and neighbors (e.g., family friends), natural family members, and peers with disabilities (typically other recipients of special services).

As indicated in Figure 2b, almost half of the offenders contacted their victims through special services provided because of disability. Slightly more than half were victimized by people who contacted them through generic relationships (e.g., acquaintances, neighbors, dates, employers). This suggests the possibility that much of the excess risk of abuse experienced by people with disabilities may result from their exposure to the service system. For example, if we assumed that the risk from families and other generic social contacts was the same for people with disabilities as for those without disabilities, the additional risk resulting from exposure to special services could almost double their risk of abuse. Furthermore, 67% of offenders who abused people diagnosed as having severe or profound mental retardation contacted their victims through specialized services. This may help to explain the mixed findings regarding how differences in intellectual ability can predict abuse (e.g., Ammerman et al., 1989; Benedict et al., 1990; Zirpoli et al., 1987). Increasing differences in intellectual ability may be

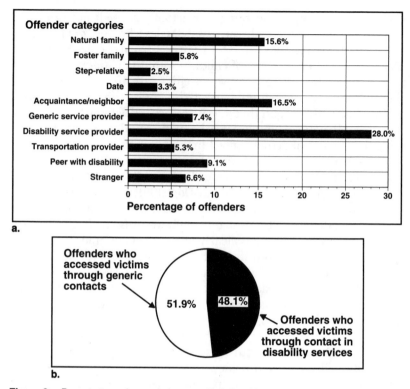

a.

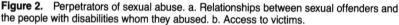

b.

Figure 2. Perpetrators of sexual abuse. a. Relationships between sexual offenders and the people with disabilities whom they abused. b. Access to victims.

correlated with increasing risk to the extent that this factor determines the frequency and nature of involvement with special services, but has little effect within levels of service involvement.

There is some disagreement among the various studies regarding the estimated percentage of disability service providers who have committed sexual offenses against people with disabilities. Table 3 presents data from our current analysis of 215 cases along with related figures from Sullivan and colleagues (1991), Turk and Brown (1992), and Westcott (1993). Data from the University of Alberta Abuse & Disability Project suggests that disability service providers constitute the largest category of offenders (28%). Similarly, Westcott (1993) reports that 33.3% of offenders in her study were providers of disability-related services, but Turk and Brown (1992) found only 14.3% of offenders in this category. Sullivan and colleagues do not use an equivalent category, and the wide possible range (at least 15% of male offenders and at least 14% of female offenders) suggested by the categories used in Sullivan's study could approximate either of the other studies. Restricting

Table 3. Perpetrators of sexual abuse

Perpetrators	Sobsey (Current)	Sullivan et al. (Males)	Sullivan et al. (Females)	Turk and Brown	Westcott
Natural family members	15.6%	N/A	N/A	N/A	[24.9%]
Parents	N/A	14.2%	21.0%	N/A	8.3%
Siblings	N/A	5.4%	14.5%	N/A	8.3%
Relatives	N/A	6.1%	6.5%	N/A	8.3%
Foster family members	5.8%	N/A	N/A	N/A	0.0%
Step-family members	2.5%	5.0%	0.0%	N/A	16.6%
Family members	[23.9%]	[25.7%]	[42.0%]	17.8%	[41.7%]
Acquaintances and neighbors	16.5%	N/A	N/A	[≤16.7%]	24.9%
Dates	3.3%	N/A	N/A	N/A	0.0%
Older child	N/A	18.4%	14.5%	N/A	0.0%
Generic service providers	7.4%	[≤14.8%]	[≤8.0%]	[≤16.7%]	0.0%
Other person without disabilities	N/A	N/A	N/A	16.7%	0.0%
Teachers	N/A	0.4%	4.8%	N/A	0.0%
Disability service providers	28.0%	[15.3%–30.1%]	[24.2%–32.2%]	14.3%	33.3%
Houseparents	N/A	15.3%	24.2%	N/A	0.0%
Transport providers	5.3%	N/A	N/A	N/A	0.0%
Peers with disabilities	9.1%	[18.6%–37.0%]	[≤11.3%–25.8%]	41.7%	0.0%
Peers	[9.1%–20%]	18.6%	11.3%	[41.7%–57%]	0.0%
Strangers	6.6%	2.1%	0.0%	5.0%	0.0%
Others	0.0%	14.4%	3.2%	4.5%	0.0%

N/A = comparison figures are not available.

Figures in brackets are estimates based on extrapolations of other listed categories to allow rough comparison across studies.

Sobsey and Doe's current sample to only adults with developmental disabilities reduces this category from 28% to 22.2%, but this figure remains significantly higher than the figure reported by Turk and Brown.

There is even stronger disagreement regarding abuse of people with disabilities by their peers with disabilities. Current data from the University of Alberta Abuse & Disability Project indicate 9.1% of all offenders fall into this category. Westcott (1993) reported no instances in this category, but Turk and Brown (1992) report that 41.7% of identified offenders in this category. Again, restricting the University of Alberta sample to cases involving adults with developmental disabilities reduces the discrepancy because 18.9% of offenders against the adult group fell into this category; however, the difference remains worth noting. Because Sullivan and colleagues did not indicate whether peers had disabilities and both their "peer" and "older child" groups could include individuals in this category, their findings might be consistent with the lower estimate or could approach the higher estimate of Turk and Brown.

Other categories remain fairly consistent across studies. However, the unresolved discrepancies discussed above suggest that more research is needed to resolve these differences. Some of the discrepancy may be explained by the variation of sampling methods. Turk and Brown restricted their sample to proven, highly probable, and highly suspected cases; they eliminated an additional 35 cases with less available evidence. As they pointed out, this may have increased the percentage of offenders with disabilities because offenders with disabilities were likely to be detected. The University of Alberta study collected anonymous reports on forms distributed through advocacy groups, treatment programs, and other agencies, whereas the Turk and Brown study collected reports from service providers. Also, the University of Alberta sample was restricted to contact abuse and eliminated noncontact forms. If milder forms of abuse were more likely to have been committed by other people with disabilities, and more severe forms of abuse were associated with disability service providers, this sampling difference could have produced much of the difference reported between this study and the Turk and Brown study. Each sampling method may have contributed its own bias. Abuse by peers with disabilities may have been underreported in the University of Alberta, or abuse by caregivers may have been underreported in the Turk and Brown study, or likely both.

In spite of the disagreement in precise percentages, these studies agree that significant numbers of offenders are sometimes: disability service providers; other people with disabilities; natural, step-family, and foster family members; peers without disabilities; other acquaintances (e.g., dates, neighbors); and in rare instances, strangers. Whether caregivers constitute 14% or 28% of the offenders, the number in either case is significant enough to cause concern. Furthermore, assuming that most of the offenders with disabilities described by Turk and Brown contacted their victims through clustered services, we can extrapolate that up to 56% of the offenders in their sample contacted their victims through specialized services, a figure similar to that from the University of Alberta sample (48.1%). Thus, offenders appear to represent a diverse group and more research is needed to clarify the emerging picture.

   Outcomes for Offenders   All of the studies discussed above agree that convictions of offenders were rare in spite of the chronic and severe nature of abuse. Figure 3 illustrates outcomes for the offenders in the University of Alberta Abuse & Disability Project sample. Although convictions occurred in more than a third of the cases where charges were laid, a large number of cases went unreported and thus made convictions impossible. Ironically, many who failed to report abuse indicated that they lacked faith in the justice system to secure convictions. This appeared to become a self-fulfilling prophecy, as crimes that go unreported cannot be punished.

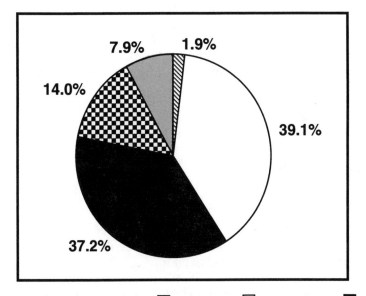

Figure 3.   Outcomes for offenders (, unidentified; , never reported; , reported/not charged; , acquitted; , convicted). Less than 8% of offenders were convicted. Most were never reported or never charged by authorities.

Turk and Brown (1992) report similar findings. For 48.2% of offenders in their sample, there were no consequences for their offenses; 18.5% were either prosecuted or underwent disciplinary hearings, and of these, only 4.7% were convicted and an additional 3.6% were actually disciplined. In 3.7% of cases the offender resigned and no further action was taken, and in an additional 8.6% of cases, only a caution was given. Some (13.6%) of the offenders with disabilities were moved to another unit or facility. The remaining 7.4% of cases resulted in a variety of other consequences.

Westcott (1993) reports that none of the perpetrators were prosecuted for their offenses against people with disabilities, although two of the offenders were convicted for offenses against children without disabilities. Westcott points out, however, that this was not unique to offenders against people with disabilities because no prosecutions occurred for the offenders against the individuals in her sample of individuals without disabilities.

Environments

All of the studies discussed agree that residences were the most common setting for abuse, but differences in categories make precise comparison impossible. Turk and Brown (1992) found that 58% of the offenses took place in the homes of either the victim (48%) or the perpetrator (10%), 14% took place in day/leisure facilities, 12% in public places, and 16% in vehicles or various unspecified locations. Sullivan and colleagues found that 34.7% of offenses occurred in the child's home, 9.4% in the offender's home, 0.5% in foster homes, an additional 8.5% in both school and homes, 39% in schools (including residential schools), and 8% in other environments.

Data from the University of Alberta Abuse & Disability Project suggest a similar picture. Private homes were the most frequent setting for abuse (49.8%), but institutions (15.8%), vehicles (9.3%), public places (7.4%), group homes (6.5%), other disability service environments (6.5%), and hospitals (2.3%) also were settings for abuse with some frequency. The remaining 2.3% occurred in a variety of generic environments.

Abused Individuals

Gender Both males and females with disabilities were among the victims of sexual abuse. Females constituted 78.9% and males constituted 21.1% of the University of Alberta sample. A similar figure of 73% from the Turk and Brown (1992) sample were females and 27% were males. Westcott (1993) reported that 70% of the sexually abused people with disabilities in her sample were women and 30% were men.

Considering the general consistency of these findings, it is surprising that Sullivan and colleagues (1991) found that 53.8% of those who reported abuse in their sample were males, and only 46.2% were females. This difference is probably due to several factors. First, the three studies reporting higher percentages of females included adults, whereas the Sullivan study indicating more males included only children. Restricting the University of Alberta sample to those 12 years old and younger increases the percentage of boys to 35.4%. Second, Sullivan's use of a treatment referral sample involving many children who experienced multiple forms of abuse may have increased male representation in the sample. More than a third of the boys in the sample who were sexually abused were also physically abused and this may have increased their likelihood of referral for intervention. Third, the inclusion of a large number of children abused in residential institutions may have contributed to the frequency of abuse because boys in institutions are more likely to be sexually abused than those in other settings. Turk and Brown (1992) also comment on the relatively large majority of men in their adult sample. Although these factors explain the discrepancy among the studies regarding the percentage of male victims, they do not contradict the conclusion that males with disabilities constitute a larger percentage of victims of sexual abuse than might be expected from studies of populations without disabilities (Sullivan et al., 1991).

Several hypotheses could explain the larger than expected number of men and boys among people with disabilities who have been sexually abused. First, it has been argued that because sexual abuse and assault of males have been underreported and underestimated in the general population, studies of people with disabilities simply might be more accurate. Second, because people with disabilities are sometimes treated as children, they may be viewed more like children by offenders, and as a result patterns of abuse might approximate those associated with younger children (i.e., less differential risk related to gender). Third, the increased risk for males may be a further reflection of the service system that many people with disabilities encounter. Sullivan and colleagues provide evidence to support this hypothesis, finding that 30% of the abuse of boys in mainstreamed settings was sexual abuse; that figure rose to 58.8% for boys living in residential settings. Data from the University of Alberta sample is also consistent with this hypothesis as 36.1% of victims sexually abused in institutional settings (regardless of age) were males, and of children 14 and younger sexually abused in institutional settings, 76.9% were males.

Why does sexual abuse appear to be a more frequent problem for boys living in institutions than for girls? The simple answer appears to be institutional structures. Because all of the studies agree that the great majority of offenders (about 9 out of 10) are males, we must consider whom males have the greatest opportunity to abuse. The traditional sexual segregation of institutions clusters male staff together with male residents and female staff together with female residents (partly as a means of minimizing heterosexual interaction). Thus, because most offenders are male, gender-clustered service systems permit greater access to potential male victims.

In addition, many institutions allow residents to go home for an unescorted weekend with a staff member of the same gender, but do not allow a similar outing with a staff member of the opposite gender. Such practices limit opportunities for heterosexual abuse more than they limit opportunities for homosexual abuse. In fact, many male pedophiles indicate that they choose to abuse boys rather than girls precisely because approaching or spending time with boys is usually tolerated and sometimes encouraged, while similar behavior with girls is often viewed with great suspicion (Marshall & Barrett, 1990).

While the strict sexual segregation of the past is gradually eroding, males continue to have greater access to other males, with little or no supervision in contemporary institutions. Male offenders with no gender preference will therefore abuse more males. Male offenders who prefer male victims will also have more opportunities than male offenders who prefer female victims and may even be drawn into the system because of this easy access. Male offenders who prefer female victims will have fewer opportunities to exercise this preference and will likely be less drawn to the system. Of course, female offenders also have more opportunities to abuse other females, but the lower rate of female offenders results in a smaller number of female victims.

Disabilities   Because all of the five studies of patterns of abuse discussed used different nonrandom sampling procedures, it is not surprising that the relative distributions of disabilities in the sample varies. Figure 4a illustrates the disabilities described in the University of Alberta sample. Mental retardation was the most common cause of disability in this group, comprising 74% of the victims of sexual abuse. Hearing impairment was reported among 14.9% of this sample. Reports indicated that 37% of the sample had multiple disabilities. This contrasts sharply with the sample of children with communicative impairments reported by Sullivan and colleagues, with 53.4% of this sample having hearing impairments and only 39% having mental retardation. While these differences appear to result from sampling procedures and highlight the need for a study using a large random sample, both studies suggest that a number of different disabilities are associated with risk for abuse.

Turk and Brown's (1992) study included only individuals with mental retardation, but the authors included information on levels of disability. The report determined percentages by IQ scores indicating that 40.2% of their sample had IQs between 51 and 80, another 40% had IQs between 36 and 50, and 19.6% had IQs below 36. Since many more people have mild disabilities than severe disabilities, this suggests that those with severe disabilities were overrepresented among the abuse victims. The University of Alberta data indicate a similar over-representation of people with severe disabilities. As shown in the outer ring of the pie chart in Figure 4b, people diagnosed with severe and profound mental retardation represented almost half of the victims of sexual abuse in this sample, whereas they would have been expected to represent less than one-fifth (as indicated by the inner circle) based on the proportions of these categories in the general population. In spite of these findings, however, it may be premature to assume that greater severity causes increased risk because sampling procedures in both studies may have resulted in overinclusion of people with severe disabilities. The only clear conclusion that can be safely made at this time is that people with all levels of severity are among the victims of abuse and need our protection. People with severe disabilities may also require different approaches to some aspects of prevention and intervention. Those with severe disabilities in the University of Alberta study were more often victims of chronic abuse, more likely to be abused in institutions, younger, tended to be males, had a greater possibility of being abused by special service providers, were more likely to be injured and to contract sexually transmitted diseases, were inclined to develop behavior problems as a result of their abuse, tended to have difficulty gaining access to intervention, and, when they did gain access, were less likely to receive support that accommodated their needs.

Harmful Consequences Physical violence was often associated with sexual abuse. Sullivan and colleagues report that 35.9% of sexually abused boys with disabilities and 27.8% of sexually abused girls with disabilities were also physically abused. Of the cases in the University of Alberta sample, 43.7% indicated no injury, 19.1% indicated mild injuries (e.g., bruises, abrasions), 8.6% indicated severe injuries (e.g., fractures), 7.4% were reported to have contracted STDs, 1.9% reported pregnancies resulting from the abuse (3.1% of females 14 and over), and 0.9% of the cases resulted in death. Data were not available for the remaining 8.4%. Thus, physical injury or illness was a common outcome, although far from a universal experience.

Negative social, emotional, and behavioral consequences were far more common. In the University of Alberta sample, only 2.8% indicated no signs of observable emotional trauma. Most (65.1%) were ob-

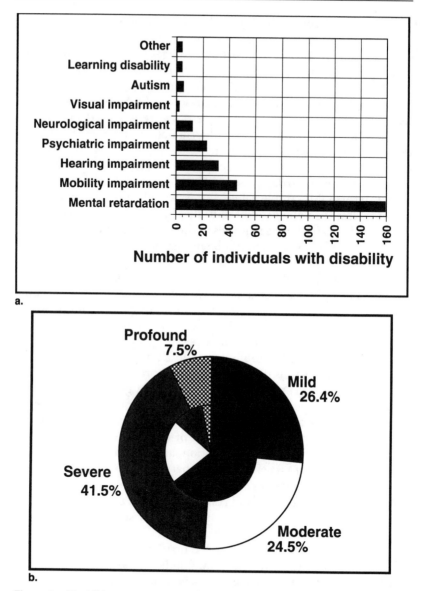

Figure 4. Disabilities among people who were sexually abused or sexually assaulted. a. Number of individuals and the type of disability represented. $N = 215$. b. Percentage of abused individuals with mental retardation by severity. Center circle indicates expected distribution.

served to show emotional distress (e.g., anger, crying), others simply withdrew (29.8%). Many exhibited noncompliance, aggression, or sexually inappropriate behavior (29.3%) as a result of their abuse. The latter was often the first noted symptom of the abuse, and those exhibiting this behavior were placed on intrusive behavior management programs or incapacitating drugs to control their behavior. Another 10.7% were moved out of their homes or programs to prevent further abuse, sometimes creating additional trauma for the abused individual. Turk and Brown (1992) reported emotional trauma in 55% of the victims. This lower percentage may be due to the inclusion of noncontact offenses in their sample as well as the exclusion of children because trauma has often been linked to more severe offenses and younger victims. Westcott's (1993) qualitative approach presents the trauma experienced by victims of abuse in their own words, providing the most powerful testimony as to the effects. Her inclusion of victims with and without disabilities in the study also allows some degree of comparison. While the effects on both groups of victims was basically the same, she points out that "interviewees with learning difficulties appeared to still be feeling much more fear and vulnerability" (p. 24).

Services As indicated in Figure 5a, many of the abused individuals (45.8%) in the University of Alberta sample had difficulty obtaining intervention services. Figure 5b breaks down how the needs of those requiring intervention services were met. Of the 173 subjects who received services, 5.2% found that generic services provided to other abuse victims met their individual needs, and 19.4% felt that the program was adequately adapted to meet these needs. For 22.8%, attempts to accommodate their individual needs were inadequate, and for the remaining 52.6% accommodation was needed but not provided. Thus more than 60% of abused individuals found services unsatisfactory. Turk and Brown (1992) report similar, if slightly more optimistic, figures. Counseling was provided to 71% of the victims in their sample; however, they point out that the counseling was minimal and typically delivered by those already providing other kinds of services rather than by trained counselors. Most of the interviewees in Westcott's (1993) study were already in counseling, and the comments of her interviewees eloquently demonstrate the value that counseling had for them. She quotes one of her interviewees with a developmental disability as follows: "Women's group—can talk to—made feel happier, couldn't tell anybody else before group" (p. 27).

Summary of Studies on Patterns of Sexual Abuse

Although some areas of discrepancy remain to be clarified in future studies, certain patterns are clearly emerging. Both children and adults with disabilities experience risk for sexual abuse. The abuse that these individuals experience is often chronic and severe. While they may be abused by many of the same perpetrators as other victims of sexual abuse (e.g., family members, neighbors, babysitters), they appear to experience additional risk from offenders with disabilities and caregivers

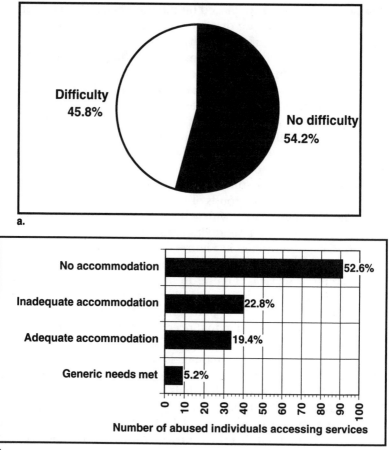

a.

b.

Figure 5. Support services. a. Percentage of sexual abuse victims with mental retardation experiencing difficulty in obtaining intervention services. b. How effectively the needs of abused individuals were being accommodated by intervention services.

with whom they come in contact through disability services. When people with disabilities are abused, they suffer traumatic effects similar to other victims of abuse. In some cases they suffer additional harm from interventions applied to eliminate their behavioral symptoms of trauma or from involuntary moves away from their homes or programs. In spite of these traumatic effects, support services often exclude them, and even when they gain access to treatment, it often fails to accommodate their special needs.

CONCLUSION

This chapter included information on sexual abuse of children and sexual assaults against adults. Although sexual abuse and sexual assault have long histories, concern over the frequency of these events and the harmful effects on those who are victimized is relatively recent. Interest in child sexual abuse began to grow in the 1970s and has continued into the 1980s and 1990s. We now know that it is a fairly common, but usually well-concealed experience, often producing long-term trauma and adjustment problems that continue into adulthood. While considerable effort has been put into prevention and intervention programs, little information is available to evaluate their success.

Sexual abuse of children and sexual assault of adults with disabilities has long been the subject of anecdotal record; however, systematic study of the problem only began to receive attention in the last half of the 1980s. Nevertheless, it has become clear that children and adults with disabilities experience more risk for sexual abuse than people without disabilities of similar age and gender. Although girls and women with disabilities are more often sexually abused than boys or men with disabilities, males, especially those living in institutions, may experience a greater degree of risk associated with their disabilities. Recent studies reporting the patterns of sexual abuse for people with disabilities have helped to identify some of the patterns of risk and may serve as a basis for the development of future prevention programs. While disability is associated with risk for abuse, it is important to avoid the assumption that disability is a direct cause of vulnerability. Several studies suggest a more complex relationship, one that is characterized by interactions between disability, society, culture, and violence. Westcott (1993) stresses this point:

> Disabled and non disabled children alike are victim to power dynamics operating in society, and particularly to the inequities found in abusive relationships. However, children with disabilities are extra vulnerable as a result of being seen as "different" and treated in ways not experienced by their non disabled peers. (p. 43)

Thus, she argues that increased vulnerability may be associated more with society's response to disability than to disability itself. Logically, our first step in controlling this vulnerability may be to set right the harm of previous intervention with people with disabilities, rather than to apply additional intervention to counterbalance the effects of what has already been done.

4

Institutional Abuse

This chapter describes institutional abuse, a subject that has had a long and controversial history. In spite of the relative infrequency of confirmed reports of institutional abuse (Marchetti & McCartney, 1990; Sundram, 1984), there is no doubt that chronic abuse has occurred and continues to occur in a variety of institutional settings (Rindfleisch & Rabb, 1984; Sullivan, Vernon, & Scanlan, 1987). While the problem of institutional abuse has been recognized for at least 2 centuries (e.g., Howard, 1929), the fundamental causes of abuse and the actions required to control or eliminate it remain topics of much dispute.

For example, Goffman (1963) and Wolfensberger (1975) emphasize the stigmatizing and dehumanizing nature of institutions as factors involved in disinhibiting coercion and violence by staff. Blatt and Brown (1986) suggest that a variety of environmental influences contribute to institutional risk. Rusch, Hall, and Griffin (1986) feel that "abuse-provoking characteristics of institutionalized mentally retarded individuals" contribute to the problem (p. 618). Hirschbach (1982) suggests the unrealistic expectations of staff, and Gil (1981) identifies the lack of legal safeguards as contributing factors to the institutional abuse problem. This lack of consensus regarding the causes of institutional abuse is not surprising considering its "limited attention in the research literature" (Marchetti & McCartney, 1990, p. 367). In view of this disagreement, this chapter begins by defining institutional abuse and describing some of its typical characteristics, without drawing conclusions about its fundamental causes or suggesting methods of prevention.

The term *institutional abuse* refers to neglectful (e.g., Blatt & Brown, 1986; LeGrand, 1984; Payne & Patton, 1984), psychological (e.g., Marchetti & McCartney, 1990; Weicker, 1987), physical (e.g., Marchetti & McCartney, 1990), or sexual abuse (e.g., Crossmaker,

1991) that takes place in the managed institutional care of human beings. Institutional care is not necessarily restricted to large custodial institutions; it includes an array of living arrangements and related programs paid for with government or other public funds that would normally be provided through less formal family and community resources. Thus, institutional abuse can take place in group homes, foster care, hospitals, residential schools, prisons, and a variety of other environments. Any individual, whether with or without disabilities, who lives in institutional care can become a victim of institutional abuse. For example, Smith (1992), relating her own experience in foster care and how it compares to life in institutions recalls, "Oh my God, you never know. A lot of foster homes I was in you'd be lucky if you even got fed. It's either that or they'd sort of rape you on the side and nothing's being done about that" (p. 12). Furthermore, institutional abuse need not take place within the physical boundaries of the institution. In some cases, institutional abuse occurs outside the institution walls in public places, staff homes, vehicles, or a number of other settings. Nevertheless, abuse in these settings should be considered institutional abuse if the nature of the interaction between the offender and victim is determined, at least in part, by the institution or its service system.

CHARACTERISTICS OF INSTITUTIONAL ABUSE

Although institutional abuse is similar to abuse in other environments, it is distinguished by four factors that make it unique. In varying degrees, these four factors can be identified in most and probably all cases of institutional abuse. These factors are addressed below.

First, institutional abuse is characterized by the extreme power inequities that exist between staff and residents. In extreme cases, staff control when residents wake up, sleep, eat, go to the bathroom, wash, communicate, exercise, rest, and virtually every other aspect of their lives. This control is achieved through the use of various tools, such as compliance training, drugs, locks, keys, restraints, aversive therapy, ward routines, and, when deemed necessary, physical force. These conditions in themselves are viewed as abusive by some people—but not by everyone. Regardless of whether such power inequities constitute abuse, they inevitably lead to other abuses. Crossmaker (1991) points out that the power and control dynamics of institutionalization are practically identical to those that characterize sexual assault and abuse.

Glasser (1978) points out that the extreme disempowerment of institutional residents is rationalized by the paradoxical notion of "good intentions." Because institutions are viewed as agencies that help rather than punish people, they are permitted to intrude deeply into the residents' lives. As an example of how this disempowerment begins early on, Glasser points out that records from just 2 of 12 New York State training schools showed 130 children were kept in solitary confinement for a total of 542 days within a 3-month period. The total powerlessness experienced by institutional inmates was profoundly illustrated by Rosenhan's (1973) experiment, in which volunteers without mental disorders were placed in mental institutions as patients without the knowledge of institutional staff. The profound sense of powerlessness, depersonalization, and humiliation experienced by these volunteers was beyond their anticipation, and had strong negative effects on their emotions, thought processes, and behavior.

Second, institutional abuse is collective in nature. There is typically more than one offender and more than one victim. In some cases, the great majority of caregivers are perpetrators of abuse and all of the residents are victims. For example, in one group home, 250 charges of abuse were laid against 14 staff (VanDusen, 1987). In another example, the placement of an undercover police officer in a large residential institution led to abuse charges against 41 staff members ("Workers at mental health center," 1986).

An abusive subculture often exists among staff in institutions and sometimes predominates. Within such an abusive subculture, abuse is not viewed as either deviant or socially unacceptable. It is viewed as normal, and becomes expected of one socially, with peer pressure to encourage abuse. In this looking-glass world, individuals who report on or otherwise attempt to thwart abuse become the targets of social outrage and administrative retaliation, whereas the people who commit abuse are implicitly or explicitly encouraged. The subculture often intercepts any reports of abuse; thus, even when reported incidents clearly fit the criteria for mandatory reporting to outside agencies, studies suggest that 80%–85% never reach the proper authorities (Powers, Mooney, & Nunno, 1990). Under such conditions, abuse may be the rule rather than the exception, and residents might not differentiate between abuse and other aspects of their care. Wambold (1990) describes an example of his 54 years of institutionalization in Ohio:

> They used clubs and broom handles and kicked you in the ribs and with mop handles. They hit you over the head with them. Is that good treatment? That's the treatment I got. A lot more got the same. . . . You had to scrub on your knees and the morning police walked back and forth with the damn mop handle in his hand. (p. 54)

The third typical characteristic of institutional abuse is the cover-up. People working within the institution where abuse takes place know more about the abuse than they share with the general public (Gil &

Baxter, 1979; Marchetti & McCartney, 1990; Sundram, 1984). Staff with knowledge of abuse do not usually report it to their supervisors. Supervisors and administrators who are aware of abuse sometimes attempt to control the problem internally, but when they do, they avoid taking any action that could lead to public recognition. Even when authorities beyond the confines of an institution become aware of abuse, they often respond by referring the problem back to "institutional authorities." For example, an inquiry into decades of abuse at Mt. Cashel orphanage in Newfoundland heard testimony indicating that police, social services, and other responsible agencies had received reports of abuse on at least 25 different occasions, but failed to take action, believing that the problem should be handled internally (Underwood, 1989).

The reasons behind institutional cover-ups are complex, and conflicts of interest occur at many levels. The same individuals who are responsible for supervising and administering services to prevent abuse are also typically responsible for investigating and responding to abuse complaints. Any confirmation of abuse also confirms their own failure to prevent it, and can therefore lead to their own demotions or perhaps to the actual closing of the service that they oversee. Attempts to ensure investigation by "disinterested parties" provide some solution to these conflicts, but further improvement is needed. For example, some county-run programs have entered into reciprocal cooperative arrangements with programs from other counties, investigating each other's programs instead of their own (Rosenthal, Motz, Edmonson, & Groze, 1991). There can be little doubt that reciprocal investigations are an improvement over self-investigations, but questions remain as to whether the providers of similar services, likely to be subjected to investigation by the very people they currently investigate, should really be considered "disinterested parties." Low confirmation rates of reported institutional abuse could result from fear on the part of interested parties working in these settings. However, in at least some cases, it merely reflects a lack of determined effort or the necessary prerequisite skills to carry out a proper and thorough investigation.

In addition to such deliberate cover-ups of blatant abuse, a more subtle form of cover-up occurs in the rationalization of intrusive and abusive intervention. As mentioned earlier, the fact that institutions are viewed as agencies of protection and healing allows them to intrude on the freedom and dignity of the people they purport to help. Lewis (1970) captured this paradox suggesting that:

> Of all tyrannies, a tyranny sincerely exercised for the good of its victims may be the most oppressive. . . . Those who torment us for our own good will do so without end for they do so with the approval of their own conscience. (p. 292)

Finally, institutional abuse is characterized by clearly defined patterns of environmental influence. Institutions can differ in size and location, and some are better than others. Nevertheless, in spite of the social isolation that characterizes most institutions, most are remarkably similar. For example, staff of institutions in three different countries many thousands of miles apart report broom and mop handles kept in closets, in order to be readily available to staff for use in controlling residents. Such institutions seem as much alike as fast-food franchises run by the same home office, yet there is no unifying management and no procedure manual telling staff where to place or how to use the mop handles. How then do such similar events develop? They appear to develop in response to basic environmental conditions. In other words, if a situation is created in which staff members are given very few resources, but a great deal of power over a large number of residents in an isolated environment, it is likely that one might find a mop handle behind the door before much time has gone by. This suggests that institutional abuse cannot be easily remedied only by dealing with individual occurrences. Unless the environmental conditions are changed, institutional abuse will continue to pervade.

IS INSTITUTIONALIZATION INHERENTLY ABUSIVE?

Two conflicting views exist regarding institutional abuse. One view sees institutions as essentially constructive havens for people with disabilities where care and habilitative services can be provided, and where abuse may occur to a greater or lesser degree, but is mostly preventable or correctable. This view typically leads to a position that institutions need only to construct better policies and procedures.

The second view considers institutionalization to be an inherent intrusion on human liberty and dignity, with no potential for habilitation and an inevitably negative influence on individual development. This view has been clearly stated by Andrejs Ozolin who suggests that "even if institutions were put in the best working order, they would be intrinsically abusive at their best and their best would be difficult to sustain" (cited in Schwartz, 1990, p. 7). This view typically leads to a position that closing institutions is the best and perhaps only meaningful deterrent against abuse.

Many readers of this book may have already developed strong views of their own regarding institutions. Others will need to develop their own positions. Nevertheless, five facts seem clear:

1. Institutions in various forms have been part of our society for many years.

2. Institutions have a long history of severe abuse.
3. Institutions have a long history of attempts to prevent, control, and eliminate abuse.
4. Efforts to prevent and eliminate abuse have never been entirely successful and have rarely provided more than superficial progress.
5. Hundreds of thousands of people with disabilities continue to live in institutions with little hope of rapid return to their communities.

A BRIEF HISTORY OF INSTITUTIONAL ABUSE

Institutional abuse is not a new phenomenon. The trend toward serving people with developmental disabilities in separate institutions did not become established until the 19th century and still progressed slowly in many places. Thus, the "almshouses," "lunatic asylums," and "workhouses" described by early reformers probably included many people with developmental disabilities. In at least some cases, people with developmental disabilities constituted the majority of residents in early "lunatic hospitals" (Judge, 1987). A variety of cages, retrains, chains, and camisoles were utilized in these settings. "Treatment" included pouring cold water over people's heads, placing them in isolation cubicles, hanging them by their feet, starving them, and whirling them around in specially made chairs (Judge, 1987). *A Mad People's History of Madness* (Peterson, 1982) provides 3 centuries of personal narratives of the mistreatment of people with mental illness.

John Howard's (1929) account of his visits to institutions of all varieties, first published in 1777, was among the first to document the extent of cruelty and neglect. During the 1800s, Dorothea Dix was one of the most eloquent advocates for service reform (Deutsch, 1949). She visited many people with developmental disabilities and mental disorders who were maintained under brutal conditions in public poorhouses and jails as well as in private facilities, and she described the horrible conditions that they endured. Many were kept chained or caged in unheated pens or cells that were infrequently cleaned of accumulated urine and excrement. Those who were provided straw for bedding or clothing were more fortunate than others who were provided with no such luxuries. Those capable of performing work were sold at auction and subjected to the whims of the highest bidders. To remedy these conditions, Dix proposed that states build more institutions and reform the standards of care in those already existing.

In response to these calls for more and better institutions to protect people from abuse, many new institutions were opened in the last half of the 19th century. Safeguards were incorporated in these institutions to ensure that abuse would not occur (Schwartz, 1990). For example, superintendents were housed on the grounds, usually as close as possible to areas of greatest concern; boards of visitors were created and mandated regular inspections; policies and procedures were developed; new laws were enacted; and employee training was undertaken. Schwartz wrote about the opening of New York's Willard Asylum, pointing out that "barely were the celebrations over than Willard found that it was not itself immune to the persistent problems of abuse and neglect" (p. 7). In a more general discussion of these attempts at humane institutionalization, Schwartz concludes that "instead of 'refuge,' the word 'asylum' would come in time to be an ultimate symbol of abandonment and despair" (p. 7).

Elizabeth Packard's (1973) eloquent personal account of institutional life in the mid-1800s was first published in 1873. She refers in her account to the way in which institutions rob people of their most basic personal right to self-defense and suggests that this fundamental abuse is the source of a multitude of others. Her account reveals that little positive change had taken place.

Shortly thereafter, Nellie Bly, a newspaper writer well known for her exploits, conspired to have herself committed to the New York City Lunatic Asylum in order to "reveal asylum horrors." Her descriptions of horrid living conditions, brutal staff, and treatment that resembled torture were published in Joseph Pulitzer's widely read New York World (Deutsch, 1949). Bly's revelations generated widespread public interest in the problems of institutional life.

The New York State Board of Charities recommended closure of the Ladies' Deborah Nursery and Child's Protectory in 1896 (Bremner, 1971a). They cited falsified records of healthy children, yet examination showed disease and neglect, frequent complaints of abuse, and little expenditure of funds on the children, although large sums were paid for salaries, rentals, and furniture. The managers of the trust had coincidentally supplied many of these items at inflated prices. While these same managers admitted that many of the abuse complaints were founded, they stated that these problems were beyond their control.

Early 20th Century

Institutionalization spread rapidly during the early part of the 20th century. This growth may have been the inevitable outcome of urbanization and industrialization, but it was supported and facilitated by a new view of intelligence fused with a subconscious expression of moral chauvinism. The association between intelligence and morality was presented as scientific fact, and this new view portrayed those with mental retardation as a menace that must be controlled and eliminated for the safety of the brighter and morally superior members of society.

Goddard (1919) warned society that "if there is little intelligence the emotions will be uncontrolled and whether they be strong or weak will result in actions that are unregulated, uncontrolled, and, as experience proves, usually undesirable" (p. 272). Terman (1916), another prominent educational psychologist of that era whose work continues to influence the field today, suggested that ridding society of these "defectives" would result in "the elimination of an enormous amount of crime, pauperism, and industrial inefficiency" (p. 7). Terman proudly presented his own experiences of shattering the positive expectations of parents so that the guardianship of their children could be assumed by the state as a good example for others to follow (Gould, 1981). Statements such as these had a direct, positive impact on the support of institutionalization, sterilization, and euthanasia. This kind of thinking also implanted in society the subtle, but implicit, message that intelligence is a single and immutable measure of morality as well as cognitive functioning.

Mid- to Late-20th Century

During World War II, the staff at many institutions were seriously depleted by conscription and about 3,000 conscientious objectors were assigned to work in American institutions under the Civilian Public Service Program. Many of these individuals were horrified by the conditions they encountered and were articulate enough to advocate for change. This process was repeated to some degree during the Korean conflict and the Vietnam war. Although this advocacy contributed to reform or at least to public recognition of the problem, institutional life for thousands was not fundamentally changed.

Blatt and Kaplan (1966) provided a powerful photographic record of some of the horrifying conditions of institutional life faced by people with mental retardation in five American institutions. As they pointed out, much of what they saw was the inevitable product of a system vastly underfunded and overextended. However, some of the incidents they describe constitute deliberate abuse; others, perhaps more alarmingly, illustrate a total lack of human compassion or even recognition of the humanity of the residents. For example, they describe a physician who seemed anxious to demonstrate to his visitors the guttural voice of a child with a rare syndrome: "He pinched her again and again—harder, and still harder. Finally in desperation, he insured her response with a pinch that turned into a gouge and caused the child to scream in obvious pain" (p. 34). The physician inflicting this pain on the child seemed totally unaware that his behavior might be seen as abusive or unacceptable. For him, it was merely a casual demonstration of a scientific curiosity.

A few years later, Cole (1972) visited children's institutions in four states reporting similar results in each. Children were being raped and sodomized by caregivers. Babies and young children were kept in cages. Fists, belts, and a variety of other weapons were used in chronic beatings. Education, rehabilitation, and even the bare necessities of life were either nonexistent or barely provided.

Willowbrook Institution

That same year, Rivera's (1972) television exposé of New York's Willowbrook institution provided more horrifying examples of unsanitary conditions, solitary confinement, abuse, and a complete lack of any educational or rehabilitative programs for the majority of the more than 5,000 (at one point Willowbrook housed more than 6,200) people clustered in an institution with a maximum capacity of less than 3,000. Cattle prods were routinely used to control the behavior of residents. Instances of overt physical abuse were common, and overwhelming neglect was apparent (Glasser, 1978). For example, when investigators cleaned the debris from the infection of the eye of one resident, they found a thumbtack sticking in the eye that had apparently gone unnoticed for a considerable period of time. The appalling conditions of Willowbrook were televised and recognized as a national disgrace, but public outrage generated by this national television exposé was inadequate to ensure meaningful change.

Willowbrook, like many other institutions, had a long established board of visitors to oversee living conditions. Obviously the board had failed miserably. Appointments to the board of visitors were made on a political basis, and no training was provided for the appointees. Thus, appointees depended on the institutional staff and administrators whom they were supposed to police. Visits were extremely rare and almost always prearranged (Rothman, 1984).

A legislative investigation followed and then a lawsuit (Chase, 1976). In 1975, after 3 years of fighting the suit and facing imminent court action, New York State signed a consent agreement pledging to reduce the population to no more than 250 beds by 1981. By April of 1982, the failure of the state to comply with this and other standards of the consent decree related to living conditions, sanitation, clothing, and programs led to court intervention and the appointment of a special master task force to ensure compliance (Herr, 1984). Willowbrook became a symbol of the worst realities of institutional care.

Other Investigations

Unfortunately, Willowbrook was not unique. Around the same time, similar conditions came to public attention in at least seven other states, and these can only be viewed as the small tip of a very large iceberg (O'Brien, O'Brien, & Schwartz, 1990). Table 1 lists some of the institutions cited in exposés of abuse in the late 1960s and early 1970s. In fact, efforts to eliminate the problems that were exposed at one institution often meant redirecting funds earmarked for other institutions with equally serious, but less public, problems.

In 1974, a Senate investigation heard testimony from United States military personnel regarding the treatment of children in private psychiatric institutions in Florida and Michigan. These children had been handcuffed, placed in solitary confinement for long periods, subjected to "shock collars," injected with urine, and beaten with bullwhips (Chase, 1976). In a separate investigation, testimony presented at the *Halderman v. Pennhurst State School and Hospital* trial (1977) provided more accounts of overcrowding, dehumanization, medical neglect, beatings, sexual assault, and unsanitary conditions (Payne & Patton, 1984). The average resident received about 75 minutes per week of potentially beneficial programming. These, and many other investigations like them, have forced institutional abuse into the public consciousness. Unfortunately, they have not succeeded in stopping this disgrace.

Similar neglect was recorded in descriptions of the lives of the 6,000 children with multiple disabilities living in institutions in England and Wales. Oswin (1979) found that these children received an average of 5 minutes direct care and attention during a 10-hour shift. Most of these children received no education or rehabilitative therapy, and "as a result of that neglect there were some horrifying incidences of deformities" (Oswin, 1979, p. 90). Nevertheless, Oswin considered the deprivation of normal childhood experiences and emotional stimulation as horrifying as the physical neglect.

Table 1. Influential exposés of abuse in U.S. institutions in the late 1960s and early 1970s

State	Institution
Alabama	Partlow
Maryland	Solomon State Hospital
Massachusetts	Belchertown
Nebraska	Beatrice State Hospital
New York	Willowbrook
North Dakota	Sandhaven
Pennsylvania	Pennhurst
Tennessee	Cloverbottom

Ironically, in spite of the pleas for reform, the exposés, and the litigation of the recent and distant past, Gil and Baxter (1979) found that institutional administrators reported that they were completely unaware of the problem. Those they approached were

> consistently surprised at the need for a program which focussed on abuse and neglect of children in out-of-home care. Some were overtly hostile at the Project's receipt of funding . . . but none felt that abusive behavior towards children in their facility by their staff was a potential or existing problem. (p. 694)

Blatt (1980) whose trip through what he described as "hell on earth" 15 years earlier (Blatt & Kaplan, 1966) had been among the most influential of institutional exposés, returned to review progress a decade and a half later. He acknowledged that improvements had been made through reduction in overcrowding, more staffing, and better funding. However, his review revealed that institutions continued to control people with disabilities by abusively intruding into every aspect of their lives. He found that, though indeed they had become much more expensive to run, they had failed to solve the fundamental problems of dehumanization, neglect, and abuse. Blatt concluded that only the closure of institutions and their replacement by appropriate community-based services could solve these problems.

In September of 1986, the United States House Select Committee on Children, Youth, and Families conducted a hearing on children in out-of-home care. Witnesses from various states testified that circumstances were deplorable and sometimes fatal in institutions, group homes, and foster care (Nunno & Motz, 1988). In 1987, the 50-state survey published by the National Center on Child Abuse and Neglect indicated a sharp *increase* in the deaths of children due to abuse and neglect (Nunno & Motz, 1988). Ironically, some of these deaths occurred at the hands of foster parents and other paid caregivers after these children had been removed from their natural homes in order to "protect them" (Nunno & Motz, 1988).

Such problems of abusive managed care are not confined by international boundaries. In what Cunningham (1991, p. 1) described as Britain's "worst child–sex scandal," boys at a residential school were subjected to a shocking regime of brutality and abuse by social workers. In this case, allegations of torture, rape, and physical violence by several staff members against 14 children were supported by other staff, spanned 13 years, and included victims as young as 8 years old. In New Zealand, one set of foster parents were charged with beating children; forcing them to eat their own vomit; "putting spring clothes pegs on their testicles, penis, ears, nose and other 'bits of skin'," and other cruelties ("Former foster parents," 1991). Although the couple resigned as foster parents in 1987 after complaints had been made to the Department of Social Welfare, they reapplied to become foster parents again in 1989, and no action was taken to oppose their reappointment. Yet another tragic example of institutional abuse occurred in Romania, where in the wake of the Ceausescu regime, an estimated 40,000 Romanian children were found abandoned in warehouse-like institutions ("Project Concern," 1991). Although many of these children were placed in institutions for social reasons, most of the children showed clear signs of devastating social, medical, and physical neglect resulting in developmental disabilities, and many showed signs of active abuse.

Similar cases were reported in Australia. The Community Visitors Board (1991) of Victoria referred to institutional abuse in their annual report. They suggested that "the more we applaud the closure of Caloola on the grounds of its inability to meet the needs of its residents, the more the similar problems at other Centers [will] press us to reach the same conclusion in the future" (p. 2). The common problems among the institutions they reported on included child abuse, battery, sexual assault, illegal restraint and seclusion, violation of legal rights, degradation, denial of medical treatment, unsafe and unsanitary conditions, unusually high death rates, chemical restraint, missing or diverted resident funds, wrongful imprisonment, overcrowding, failure to attempt to prevent residents from assaulting each other, lack of programs, and neglect. They acknowledged that the problems addressed in their report probably represented only a small fraction of the actual magnitude of the problem of abuse. Despite a total of 96 community visitors to inspect 23 institutions, frustration was voiced over the difficulties in dealing with the extent and severity of the problem. These difficulties were often "aggravated by management disinterest and worse," a strong philosophy of nonreporting, and anonymous reports that were often unsubstantiated (p. 43).

An intensive investigation at one of these institutions culminated in 51 charges of rape, indecent assault, and false imprisonment against one staff member and additional indecent assault charges against another. The Community Visitors Board was "saddened that they were unable to penetrate the web of subterfuge which allowed such terrible things to happen at Pleasant Creek" (p. 43). The special inquiry that resulted in these charges required 3 months of full-time investigation by highly trained investigators. Nevertheless, Pleasant Creek was not targeted for closure because this institution was thought to provide a better standard of care than others.

Also in the Community Visitor's Board (1991) report was the example of a man who had been in an Australian prison, but was transferred to one of the institutions because of his mental retardation. He pleaded to be returned to prison for a better quality of life; however, his request was denied until he set fire to one of the institution buildings and threatened to do it again. His desire to return to prison is hardly surprising because, as the report points out, "society provides better living conditions for offenders than it does for people with intellectual disabilities" (Community Visitors Board, 1991, p. 124).

The recent situations described in Victoria are not all negative. In fact, the report points out that in the 5 years prior to the report, considerable improvements had been made. Furthermore, as the report also suggests, the large number of abuses that were uncovered represents a fresh and laudable effort to come to grips with the problem.

In a demonstration of this type of renewed effort, government officials in Canada announced that they would not renew the license of two group homes for autistic adults run by the same service provider. The announcement was made only one day after allegations of abuse were presented on an investigative television news report (Aikenhead, 1993). Allegations included neglect and physical abuse. The news report featured an interview with a former employee who described losing his temper and breaking the collarbone of one resident. A second employee had been convicted of an assault reported by an external inspection team (kicking a resident in the face), but was allowed to continue his employment after the conviction. According to government documents, "between 1985 and 1990 the facility was staffed by workers with criminal records and alochol problems" (Aikenhead, 1993, p. A7). The documents revealed that conditions at this particular home were known by officials for at least 4 years, yet action was taken only after the television exposé brought the situation to the public's attention. A third group home run by the same agency continued operation because homes in Alberta with less than five residents did not require a license.

After considering the abuses found and efforts to control them, the Community Visitors Board (1991) in Victoria, Australia, concluded:

> that while the Department's policy of prosecuting the worst offenders is praiseworthy, these abuses cannot be remedied simply by police measures. The abuses stem in large measure from the nature of the institutions in which they occur. The pervasive culture of large institutions isolated from the community creates the atmosphere where such things seem commonplace. (p. 7)

Even prosecuting the worse cases is a staggering demand. For example, the Public Advocates Office, which was set up to protect the rights of people with mental retardation in Victoria, receives between 150–180 calls each day, with a range of complaints including murder, rape, incest, beatings, financial exploitation, and other infractions. With seven full-time and two part-time staff, the office takes on about

20 new cases per week, forcing difficult decisions for its overworked staff (Dixon, 1988).

Sadly, such stories of institutional abuse are not restricted by time or geography. The stories of abuse of institutionalized individuals with disabilities in England and Wales (Oswin, 1979), Australia (Community Visitors Board, 1991; Davies, 1980), Canada (Sobsey & Varnhagen 1991; VanDusen, 1987), Romania ("Project Concern," 1991), and the United States (Weicker, 1987) are among the many examples that add to an extensive record. The few examples cited here represent only a small sample of known cases of institutional abuse. In addition, the isolation of victims, unwillingness to report by staff, and the coverups of administrators all ensure that the known cases represent only a miniscule fraction of the true extent of abuse.

Chase (1976) pointed out that "there are far more children mistreated in institutions than suffer neglect or injury at home" (p. 151). As suggested by Québec officials when they dropped 250 charges of sexual abuse against 14 staff members of a group home, there is no wide-scale public interest in abuse that occurs out of the mainstream of society (VanDusen, 1987). Chase (1976) referred to society's double standard of institutions over human beings that allows us to "take children from parents who beat them and put them in institutions where guards will strike them instead" (p. 152).

Again, the examples of institutional abuse presented here do not by any means constitute a comprehensive history. Institutional abuse is not a new discovery. It has been discovered and rediscovered over at least the past 2 centuries. Nevertheless, it continues in spite of all efforts to understand and to control it. There are, however, several identifiable factors associated with institutional abuse, and these are addressed in the next section.

FACTORS THAT CONTRIBUTE TO INSTITUTIONAL ABUSE

Unrealistic Expectations

The gap between the reality of institutional life and the public's expectations is very wide. People continue to believe that institutions provide safe havens, protecting people from society while offering sophisticated educational and rehabilitative services in a supportive environment. Sadly, this view represents naive wishful thinking, and the gap between this and reality is too wide to be crossed. Politicians cannot face the public with the truth. Bureaucrats cannot face the politicians with the truth. Administrators cannot face the bureaucrats, supervisors cannot face administrators, and direct care staff cannot face supervisors with the truth. This fundamental dishonesty at every level makes real change impossible.

From high on top of this pyramid, abuse may be viewed as individual infractions to be punished—the only way it can be acceptably acknowledged. In this frame of reference, it cannot be addressed as inherent to a system that needs radical change because to do so would require honesty about the current state of affairs. For example, few if any staff, regardless of how well-intentioned or caring they may be, can work indefinitely with large numbers of aggressive and assaultive residents and never use force to defend themselves or to protect residents or other staff. Yet this fact is generally ignored, and those who use very little force may be viewed as being just as guilty as the most sadistic offender. As a result, the person who uses minimal force cannot honestly report this or ask for help in finding ways to reduce the need for it. Such individuals may also be stopped from reporting the more severe abuses of coworkers. Because they too have violated the formal guidelines, they are also vulnerable to discipline.

Other people are equally unable to cope with these problems because they feel they cannot be honest. In a number of cases reported to the University of Alberta Abuse & Disability Project, offenders were not charged because facility administrators felt that to do so would create bad publicity for their agency. One parent indicated that he was certain that his child had been abused, but that he would not disclose it because he was advocating to keep the center where his son was abused open and did not want to jeopardize that. Those advocating for the closure of institutions might feel differently. However, if and when quality community services can become available for all remains unclear; until that time, the suffering continues. Alarmingly, this same "hide the abuse to protect the agency" mentality has already begun to emerge in some of the community-based programs.

Isolation

People who live in institutions are isolated from the mainstream of society. They rarely interact or communicate with people outside the institution. In some cases, as was suggested in Chapter 1, the institution is even inviolate from intrusion by police. Yet, experts in child abuse and family violence tell us that isolation is one of the few consistent predictors of abuse.

Lord's (1991) study of the disempowerment versus the empowerment of people with disabilities suggests that isolation is a major contributor to powerlessness in the lives of people with disabilities. Although individuals with disabilities in the study who lived in the community also experienced some forms of isolation and powerlessness, institutions provided by far the most extreme situations. The unique depth of disempowerment found in the residents of institutions often elicited rebellion from the residents, leading to further repression by the staff. In many residents, the ultimate outcome was learned helplessness and subsequent psychological and physical deterioration.

Ironically, the same almost impenetrable isolation of institutions that breeds abuse hides the abuse that it breeds. Opportunities for direct observation or reliable accounting of abuse are difficult to obtain. As a result, little information is available to assist with efforts toward prevention or correction. Public apathy is facilitated by the lack of connection between disempowered people within institutions and potential help from outside. The general public knows little about institutional realities and displays little interest in obtaining this knowledge. Ridington (1989) refers to her lack of access to women living in institutions for her research on the self-image of women with disabilities as "blunt testimony to the isolation of many women with disabilities" (p. 3).

Administrative Structures

Marx (1981) describes the processes of *nonenforcement, covert facilitation,* and *escalation*. Through nonenforcement, institutional administrators permit abuse and implicitly condone it. Covert facilitation refers to how administrators take actions that deliberately encourage abuse, and escalation refers to how they put pressure on certain situations, pressure that often provokes an even more deleterious result.

Some administrators exhibit nonenforcement by making strong and sincere statements against abuse, while at the same time, they are unwilling to confront it. Therefore, they take great care not to be aware of its existence. Avoiding the discovery of abuse during an extended administrative career in most institutions is analogous to spending 20 years in the desert without discovering sand. Considerable effort is required. If they are forced to recognize abuse, they respond inadequately. For example, although they might be willing to take administrative action that has little effect and at the same time claim that their hands are tied by the union, they will be unwilling to lay criminal charges merited by the offense. It is sad that many instances of abuse that are police matters in the community are trivialized as institutional administrative infractions to be handled by employee relations or other similar departments. The result of such nonenforcement strategies is the encouragement of abuse, as there would seem to be little serious consequence for partaking in it. Covert facilitation by administrators who deliberately encourage abuse may also occur. For example, super-

visors will punish those who report abuse (e.g., by unfavorably changing their shifts or assignments) in order to reduce the number of complaints that they receive. As a result, they have demonstrated that they
are on the side of the abusers rather than the reporters.

In the process of escalation, administrators will respond excessively to even the most trivial complaint. For example, an employee may
have to defend him or herself against an attack by a resident, and there
may be some uncertainty as to whether the force used was truly the
minimal amount required. Such situations certainly do occur and do
require attention, but overreacting can be as dangerous as ignoring
them. Threatening the employee with discipline or criminal charges in
this type of situation may erode the line between serious and minor or
questionable offenses and increase the chance that more force will be
used next time as the consequences would be the same.

Administrative structures within institutions often make reform
difficult or impossible. Direct care staff are typically at the bottom of a
large and complex bureaucracy and have little real power or influence.
Administrators who are at the top of this bureaucracy are so far removed from the realities of the lives of the residents and direct care
staff that they lack the basic information required to establish appropriate policies and procedures. Both the administrators and their staff
might recognize that something is terribly wrong, but neither has the
necessary information, power, or inclination to correct the obvious
problems. In their powerlessness and frustration, they often blame
each other. For example, the quote below from an attendant at a state
institution for people with developmental disabilities illustrates the
contempt of living unit staff for their institution's professionals and
administrators.

> Let me tell you that those psychiatrists are all crazy. . . . They just don't
> know what they are doing. They tell us to sit down with 'em and talk to
> them when they start going at it [fighting]. Christ, if I tried that I'd get my
> fuckin' brains kicked out. (Bogdan, Taylor, deGrandpre, & Haynes, 1974,
> p. 144)

Attendants angry at their powerful superiors in the institutional
chain of command are frustrated by their own lack of power and
may displace their anger toward more vulnerable targets. This often
means the residents of the institution. Administrators and supervisors
may intentionally or unintentionally encourage this redirection of anger because it allows them to avoid being directly confronted with it. By
creating strong policies against abuse, but providing no real enforcement of them, they encourage their staff to redirect anger from a
stronger adversary to a more vulnerable one. As a result, unenforced
or unenforceable policies can be worse than no policy at all.

Dehumanization and Detachment

Institutions depersonalize the individuals who inhabit them and inhibit any bonds of human attachment between caregivers and the individuals who receive services from them. Rutter (1989) cites research suggesting that young children reared in institutional settings typically encounter 50–80 caregivers before reaching school age, making the development of any healthy attachment virtually impossible. A comparison of infant–caregiver interactions at Greek institutions with those taking place in Greek family homes showed that paid caregivers failed to provide nurturant behavior, whereas natural caregivers provided more eye contact, touching, rocking, and vocalization combined with eye contact. The authors point out that the institutional caregivers "were quite persistent and frequently disregarded the infant's cues, suggesting a certain insensitivity in caregiving" (Roe, Feldman, & Drivas, 1988, p. 365).

Labeling people according to categories of disability along with negative attitudes toward disability are a powerful depersonalizing influence, but the rigid hierarchy of the institution provides even greater depersonalization (Rosenhan, 1973). For example, when Rosenhan (1973) introduced eight healthy pseudopatients into mental hospitals as part of an experiment, they were given more than 2,100 doses of psychoactive medications although none displayed symptoms. Furthermore, their fellow patients were much better at discriminating the pseudopatients from the genuine patients than were the trained institutional staff. This may not be surprising because extensive record keeping and staff meetings took up most staff time, and patients averaged only a few minutes of contact with staff per day.

Clustering

Although this chapter focuses primarily on abuse of institutional residents by their caregivers, it should be noted that many residents of institutions are abused by other residents. For example, about 10% of people with disabilities analyzed by the University of Alberta Abuse & Disability Project were victims of sexual assault or abuse by others with disabilities. The mixing of vulnerable individuals with others who are known to be aggressive offenders is common in institutional settings. Institutions have created this problem, but usually they fail to acknowledge their own responsibility and typically take little or no action to control it. Clustering in an environment where abuse takes place also teaches abuse to the residents who are victimized or who simply observe it (Bandura et al., 1963). Thus, abuse often feeds on itself as a result of a kind of chain reaction where each incident of abuse puts all the residents at greater risk.

Abusive Subcultures

Society generally considers violence to be an aberration that is unacceptable to the majority, however, within many institutions violence is the norm. For example, when researchers Nibert, Cooper, and Crossmaker (1989) asked 58 residents (i.e., 30 women, 28 men) of a midwestern psychiatric center about their experiences, 71% indicated that they had been threatened or abused while in institutional care. More than half (53%) had been physically assaulted, and 38% had been sexually assaulted. Although in many cases other patients had committed these infractions, staff themselves were more often the offenders. Under circumstances like these, abuse cannot be considered the exceptional acts of just a few deviant individuals. In fact, as McGrath (1991) points out, the abusive subculture of the institutional environment is so pervasive that it "often remains so, even after the 'problem' members leave" (p. 61).

Unfortunately, institutions and the people who inhabit them rarely seem conscious of the abusive subculture and are typically powerless to confront it (Ross & Grenier, 1990). Even professionals and researchers who attempt to understand institutional abuse have often supported the stereotypical notion that institutional residents provoke the abuse that is perpetrated against them. Powers et al. (1990) reviewed the literature and pointed out that many authorities suggest that "sadism does not produce neglect in institutional residential settings, rather the maltreatment results from the frustration and inability of providers to handle their deep anger at youth who remain elusive and defiant" or "frustrated attempts to treat children who are not treatable" (p.88).

Frustration of various kinds plays a role in institutional abuse, as it may play a role in other forms of abuse such as child abuse, spousal abuse, lynchings, and many other forms of violence. Yet trying to explain away the incessant physical, psychological, and sexual violence found in many institutions as mere acts of frustration by well intentioned staff is totally inconsistent with existing research and common sense. The widespread sexual abuse of children and adults in institutional settings (Crossmaker, 1991; Sobsey & Doe, 1991; Sullivan et al., 1991), for example, is particularly difficult to reconcile with this notion.

A Personal Comment

In Chapter 1, I described some of my own experiences with abuse in an institutional setting. No single explanation was adequate to explain the variety of abusive behavior that took place; rather, it seemed to be the result of many interwoven causes. Frustration was certainly a contributing factor in some cases. Staff were held responsible for controlling residents (e.g., keeping them in their beds at night, lining them up to go to the dining room) who were often difficult to control. Of course, the degree of control demanded of the residents themselves was in itself excessive and abusive, and, if necessary at all, was only needed because of crowded conditions. At any rate, frustrated staff sometimes lashed out at residents.

Although sometimes the residents were the source of the frustration, more often frustration was exacerbated by the demands of the job, coworkers, or supervisors. However, coworkers and supervisors were a lot less vulnerable than were the residents. So, even when the source of the frustration was not the fault of the residents, the residents were the ones who were hurt.

Fear was also sometimes a contributing factor. At times, some of the residents of the institution did, indeed, attack employees. Those who felt confident to defend themselves against such attacks typically did so with minimal force. Those who felt less confident and feared for their own safety often overreacted and seriously injured their attackers.

Sadism was apparent in some, but certainly not all of the staff. Some of these individuals chose to work in the institution primarily because access to vulnerable victims was one of the benefits of the job. Such individuals generally pushed the limits of what was acceptable even to other abusive staff. Often, they would spend time and energy devising new tortures. For example, one attendant discovered that a great deal of pain could be induced by squeezing residents' hands in a mop-ringer.

Abuse of residents won a certain amount of acceptance and respect from other abusive staff. This was particularly apparent in some younger staff members who were abusive when they worked with other abusers, but did not abuse residents when working with nonabusive staff. Of course, learning from other staff was another interrelated factor. People witnessed abuse on a regular basis, and for most new staff, the more abuse they witnessed, the more they learned to be abusive.

Sexual abuse was less acceptable than physical abuse. Rumors and occasional accusations of sexual abuse were common, and certain staff members were considered by others to be sexual abusers of residents. These individuals, however, were generally not fully accepted by the group, and when allegations of sexual abuse arose against staff members, others would typically deny the possibility or disassociate themselves from the accused.

Often people became more abusive simply because it was easier. Despite the fact that less abusive means could frequently be taken, severe punishment provoked the quickest responses from residents, with the least energy requirement by staff. This and many of the previously named factors overlapped with the fundamental issue of control, and control was the central issue of every aspect of institutional life.

ATTEMPTS TO CONTROL INSTITUTIONAL VIOLENCE

Public recognition of institutional abuse remains minimal, and despite the developing initiatives being taken against child abuse and family violence since the 1960s, progress against institutional abuse has not moved forward. The established agencies and mechanisms for addressing family violence have neither a clear mandate nor the necessary tools for addressing violence in the institutions. By the same token, child abuse agencies and prevention legislation are aimed specifically at children and do not address the issues of vulnerable adults. Thus, as many of the individuals residing in institutions are adults, and all are separated from their families, institutional residents escape attention from the child and family protection movements, in particular, and from the rest of society in general.

Legal attempts have often been made to stretch child abuse and other generic statutes to cover institutional abuse, but these attempts have never been successful (Powers et al., 1990). In 1984, an amendment was made to the United States Child Abuse Prevention and Treatment Act requiring states to adopt statutes or procedures to ensure that complaints of institutional child abuse are reported to and investigated by independent agencies. Unfortunately, the great majority of states have been slow to comply, and old and ineffective statutes continue to be in place (Powers et al., 1990).

The repatriation of as many institutional residents as possible to good community placements certainly is an ideal approach toward the reduction of problems associated with institutional abuse. However, failure to address the protection of people who remain in institutions in the hope that they will soon be released or in the belief that institutions are not worth the effort required to address their problems abandons thousands of people who urgently need society's help and protection. When communities adequately respond to the needs of people with disabilities with well organized community living alternatives, institutions will naturally cease to exist. Unfortunately, progress toward that goal continues to be slow, and many leave traditional institutions for nursing homes, large group residences, and other alternatives that offer few, if any, demonstrated advantages over traditional institutions

(Sobsey, 1983). Therefore, it is essential that efforts are made to provide all possible safeguards against institutional abuse and to ensure the best possible life for people who continue to live in these settings.

CONCLUSION

Two important questions arise from any discussion of the long-term history of institutional abuse. First, can institutions be reformed? Second, can institutions be eliminated?

Institutions can and do change, and much of the progress that has taken place in the 1970s, 1980s, and 1990s has been significant. Many institutions are smaller, better staffed, and better supervised. Nevertheless, Taylor and Bogdan (1992) suggest that the totalitarian nature of institutional life has not changed, and much of the apparent transformation has only been accomplished through increasingly sophisticated image management.

5

For Their Own Good . . . Caregiving or Abuse?

Are psychological, sexual, and physical abuse merely isolated aberrations that defy society's prevalent desire to safeguard people with disabilities? Or, are these criminal forms of abuse mere extensions of society's prevalent desire to rid itself of people with disabilities? These are questions that must be answered before abuse can be fully understood or meaningful efforts toward prevention can be undertaken. The history of societal attitudes and actions toward people with developmental (and other) disabilities provides a useful context in which to begin.

Several excellent histories of the care of people with developmental disabilities have already been published (e.g., Kanner, 1967; Scheerenberger, 1983). However, this chapter is not intended to provide the same kind of comprehensive or balanced point of view. It simply recounts some of the more outrageous responses to people with disabilities that have been regarded by society as examples of caregiving practices.

In reading any of the aforementioned histories, however, it is important to recognize a qualitative difference between the history of people with developmental disabilities and most other histories. The names and faces of people with developmental disabilities are noticeably absent; their opinions and concerns are missing. They are not the subjects of these histories; they are the objects of the programs and services whose histories are recounted. Scheerenberger's (1983) history, for example, includes pictures of Hippocrates, J. Langdon Down, Dorothea Dix, Lewis Terman, Alfred Strauss, and about 20 other people who have studied or worked with people with developmental disabilities. There are only a few pictures of people with disabilities, however, and these individuals remain anonymous or are provided with false names (e.g., "Village idiot," "Cretin child," "Deborah Kallikak").

This concern about the objectification of people with developmental disabilities should not be viewed as a criticism of the authors of these histories who have done an excellent job of describing the sciences and services that surround disability. Nevertheless, the history of these people remains largely unwritten, and therefore, they remain voiceless, faceless, and nameless in the thoughts of society.

Most of the chapters in this section discuss overt physical and sexual abuse or criminal neglect of people with disabilities, but any discussion of abuse of people with disabilities would be incomplete without consideration of caregiving practices that border on the criminal. People with disabilities have been incarcerated in institutions and segregated from the rest of society. They have been sterilized and denied the right to sexual expression and reproduction against their will. They have been passively "allowed to die" or purposefully killed by individuals who have judged the lives of people with disabilities to have no potential quality or value. They have been compelled to provide labor with little or no compensation. They have been punished and subjected to other forms of unpleasant and sometimes dangerous treatment, often with no evidence of potential benefit. They have been stereotyped as being subhuman "vegetables" incapable of human emotions and unworthy of human compassion. All of these things have been done by caregivers.

Not everyone considers these actions against people with disabilities to be abusive. Some of them have been permitted, even condoned, by law. For example, the sterilization programs in the United States and Nazi Germany were both permitted by law (Wolfensberger, 1975), and the euthanasia of infants with severe disabilities has been approved at various times by courts in the United States and other countries. The individuals who carried out these actions were not considered to be criminals, and some may even have viewed their actions as noble. The Americans with Disabilities Act (1990) provides formal recognition "that people with disabilities have been subjected to a history of purposeful unequal treatment" (42 USC 12101 [a][7]); yet, it too falls short of labeling this treatment as abuse. Should such actions of "unequal treatment" be viewed in fundamentally the same light as criminal abuse, or are these two different things? Would these actions be deemed appropriate or criminal if carried out against individuals who have not been labeled as disabled? Is there any rationale for a double standard? Perhaps the double standard that allows these actions to be carried out against people with disabilities while prohibiting them against other members of society, as well as the attitudes that permit such a double standard, are the underlying problems that facilitate abuse and link all of its separate manifestations.

How does one differentiate between caregiving and abuse? When reading the history below, it will be useful to apply the definitions of abuse presented in previous chapters. These acts of commission or neglect have resulted in physical injuries, deaths, emotional harm, psychological distress, and damaged human development. We can differentiate caregiving from abuse only by analyzing another criterion—intent. The individuals responsible for these actions tend to assure others that they have no intentions to harm; in fact, they claim to be performing deeds of great humanitarianism. Lewis Carroll (1978) presented this absurdity in Alice's dilemma in the looking-glass wonderland where she is forced to decide whether she likes the Walrus better because he cries sympathetically for the poor oysters even as he devours them.

Waxman (1991) cautions us not to be misled by sympathetic rhetoric, but to judge on the basis of actions rather than words. She suggests that the attitudes that link all of the separate forms of abuse of people with disabilities are manifestations of deeply entrenched hatred. She proposes that it is our failure as a society to recognize this hatred of people with disabilities that is a measure of how deep-seated and widespread that hatred has become. Thus, we accept as rational actions that would quickly be denounced as criminal, discriminatory, and abusive if directed toward any other group. Söder (1990) suggests that society's attitude is best described as ambivalence arising from conflicting values of benevolent sympathy, avoidance, and devaluation. The interplay of these motivations often allows situational contexts to play a particularly powerful role in determining responses. Experimental studies of interactions between people with and without disabilities support this model of ambivalence (e.g., Doob & Ecker, 1970).

Söder's notion of ambivalence does not actually conflict with Waxman's concept of hatred, but it does make it slightly more complicated and far more insidious. It suggests that under certain circumstances people can act to avoid, dominate, or eliminate people with disabilities while justifying their actions as somehow being beneficial for the victims. It explains how society can ruin the lives of individuals with disabilities, and, at the same time, weep for these ruined lives. Waxman's (1991) perspective suggests that "the tears of the Walrus" are hypocritical and are used to hide the Walrus's true malicious intent. Söder's (1990) view evokes an even more frightening perspective. The Walrus has come to genuinely believe he is a great friend to the oysters, but he is unaware that he has made them his victims.

EARLY EFFORTS TO
ELIMINATE PEOPLE WITH DISABILITIES

Efforts to eliminate people with disabilities have a long history in many different cultures (e.g., Edgerton, 1970). Often these efforts took the form of abandonment of infants who had apparent impairments (Orelove & Sobsey, 1991). Some societies not only killed children with deformities, they also killed their mothers (Meyers & Blacher, 1987).

Enough is known of ancient Greek philosophy and customs to provide a reasonably clear record. Scheerenberger (1983) quotes Plato's suggestion that "the offspring of the inferior, or of the better when they chance to be deformed, will be put away" (p. 12) and Aristotle's plea for "a law that no deformed child shall live" (p. 12) as examples of that philosophy. The Spartans threw unwanted infants with disabilities from a cliff at Mt. Teygetus to die (Scheerenberger, 1983). Spartans considered these infants unlikely to make significant contributions to their society, which emphasized physical beauty, strength, intelligence, and aggression, and so they simply disposed of them. The site of these killings is still marked by a public historical sign declaring that these children were killed "for the good of the development of the human race" (illustrated in Judge, 1987, p. 4).

Athenians, typically viewed as more humanistic than the Spartans, also practiced infanticide. They placed unwanted infants in jars and put them by temples where they could be removed by anyone who might choose to adopt them. Infants who were female or seemed to have disabilities were particularly likely to be destroyed in this manner; however, parents did have the option to abandon any infant less than 10 days old (Scheerenberger, 1983). This practice was so common during some generations that it would significantly deplete the population. Infanticide was also common practice during much of the Roman era. Some of these abandoned children were rescued, only to be mutilated by their rescuers in order to make them more effective beggars (Scheerenberger, 1983). Even now, in some parts of the world, mutilations for this purpose still occur. With the growth of Christianity, people with disabilities were sometimes executed as devils. Martin Luther, for example, recommended drowning because "idiots are men in whom devils have established themselves" (quoted in Judge, 1987, p. 4).

Genocide

The term *genocide* is relatively new. It was first applied during the 1930s to the intended extermination of Jews by the Nazis (*Webster's New World Dictionary*, 1988). Since that time it has been used to refer to attempts to eliminate other groups of people either through mass

murder or through less direct alternatives such as limitations on reproduction. The appropriateness of application of this concept to people
with disabilities is a complex issue. Efforts to eradicate disability without actually eliminating the individuals who have disabilities would not
typically be categorized under the definition of genocide. However,
some might view this as cultural genocide (e.g., elimination of all deafness would likely eliminate the culture associated with it).

The concept of genocide might be more easily applied to endeav-
ors to eradicate disability through the actual elimination of human
beings with disabilities. Although the most obvious example of this
would be murder, a similar result could be attempted through sterilization, selective reproduction, or abortion. Wolfensberger (1981) refers
to the particular effort to eliminate people with disabilities as *eugenocide*.

Euthanasia

Another term that can be applied to attempts to eliminate people with
disabilities is *euthanasia*. Its first and oldest definition implies a "gentle
and easy death" typically at the choosing of a dying individual (*Oxford
English Dictionary*, 1971, p. 904). Its second meaning, "the intentional
putting to death of a person with an incurable or painful disease"
(Stedman, 1990, p. 544) is distinctly different and clearly more current.
For example, starving a hungry infant to death who has no part in the
decision would not meet the criteria of the first definition, but under
the second definition, such an act has been legitimated as euthanasia
(Schaffer & Sobsey, 1991). Starvation has never been recommended because of its benefits for the individual who is killed; it is a method
selected for the benefit of the caregivers who implement it. Such a
method might better be termed as *altruistic murder*, the term used by
Resnick (1980) to describe the most frequent motive of mothers who
commit infanticide to "relieve the infant of real or imagined suffering"
(p. 145).

Nazi Euthanasia Program   History provides support for applying the concepts of genocide and euthanasia to plans to eliminate people with disabilities, as these attempts have often been accompanied by
parallel efforts to dispose of racial, ethnic, and religious minorities
deemed unfit. Wolfensberger (1981) points out that the Nazi euthanasia
program initially targeted people with severe mental or physical disabilities, referring to them as "useless eaters." Gradually this target
group was expanded to include people with less severe disabilities, people who were atypical but not disabled, those suspected of carrying unacceptable genetic and racial traits, and those devalued solely because
of their cultural attributes. Under the Nazi extermination program,
more than 100,000 mental hospital patients and 5,000 other children

with developmental disabilities were exterminated between 1939 and 1941 (Scharfetter, 1984), along with millions of Jews, Gypsies, Blacks, Slavs, prostitutes, homosexuals, people with physical disabilities, juvenile delinquents, vagrants, and other human targets (Sengstock, Magerhans-Hurley, & Sprotte, 1990). At first, people with developmental disabilities were systematically starved to death, but the program became more efficient with the introduction of gas chambers, and later, lethal injections (Scheerenberger, 1983).

Hitler considered the elimination of the unfit to be of the utmost importance. "Doing this," he wrote, "will one day be seen as a more important accomplishment than the greatest military victories of our time" (Hitler, 1934, p. 447). Physical extermination was only one component of a complex Nazi campaign that utilized methods of sterilization and sexually segregated institutionalization aimed at total elimination of people with disabilities. More than 300,000 special education students and residents of institutions with mental retardation were sterilized under this program (Sengstock et al., 1990).

Although there was some resistance, the majority of special educators in Germany at the time supported and cooperated with the effort to exterminate people with disabilities. The introduction of eugenic policy was also facilitated by the previous policy of segregated special education. German special educators in the pre-Nazi era believed that removing people with disabilities from the mainstream of education would allow remedial education to prepare them for living with the rest of society (Sengstock et al., 1990). These isolated students were easily targeted by the Nazi regime. Already removed from the mainstream of society, it was only necessary to ensure that they would not return to it.

Similarly, many health care professionals enthusiastically supported the Nazi euthanasia program. Dr. George Renno was the medical superintendent at Hartheim, an Austrian Castle converted to a hospital serving children with mental retardation where more than 14,000 were murdered in the early years of the war. He and his medical staff were thought to be so efficient in their work that they were promoted to positions in the extermination camps of central and eastern Europe (Hume, 1991a). Renno's career path was not unique; of the 450 men who ran the Nazi extermination centers, 92 (one-fifth) were promoted from the euthanasia program. These men were considered to be among the most important leaders at the camps because they "brought with them the knowledge and experience in setting up and operating gassing institutions for mass murder" (Arad, 1987, p. 17). Sereny (1974) points to the career paths of such central figures in the holocaust as a demonstration of the preparatory role played by the euthanasia program for the Nazi's "Final Solution."

In 1941, prominent physicians, psychiatrists, and nurses, along with other members of the multidisciplinary team, were served free drinks at a celebration in honor of the extermination of the 10,000th patient at Hadamar Psychiatric Hospital (Hume, 1991b). The role of health care professionals in administering the extermination program was essential to the validation of these murders as a necessary medical intervention. However, not all German physicians cooperated with the euthanasia program. Martin Hohl, director of the Wendelhöfen mental institution at Bayreuth, for example, used a number of stalling tactics to prevent the implementation of euthanasia. When these were exhausted, he directly confronted his Nazi superiors with the fact that he would not murder innocent people (Kater, 1989). Still, no other profession cooperated with the Nazi regime as often or as enthusiastically as did the medical profession (Kater, 1989); although, certainly some of those who did cooperate were cowed by considerable pressures.

In addition to the influence of the direct authority of the government, there were several other factors at work. First, medical resources were in short supply; the war had put huge demands on a system also strained by the loss of a very significant number of well-qualified Jewish physicians. Thus, eliminating people with chronic needs served a triage function, allowing the diversion of resources toward the war effort. Second, in Germany the tradition of Freudian psychology had become enmeshed with the idea that most disabilities are the result of environmental rather than genetic cause. This became extremely unpopular because espousing such a view not only ran contrary to the central racist–hereditary theory, but was also seen as reflecting the ideology of the so-called "Jewish conspiracy," as Freud was considered a spokesperson for this conspiracy. Furthermore, early indoctrination of new physicians in the ideology of genetic purification began in their early schooling. In medical school, this indoctrination was intensified, and students learned that their primary duty was to upgrade the German race through health care for the fit and eradication of the unfit (Kater, 1989). Elimination of people with disabilities and the extermination of racial, ethnic, and political minorities were not separate objectives that developed from disparate motives. They were one unified plan based upon a single racist philosophy.

After World War II, only a few physicians were found guilty of war crimes, and the degree of involvement of many others remains controversial to this day. Hans Sewering, for example, was a member of the Nazi Party and the Shutzstaffel (SS) by the time he graduated from medical school. Although few records exist, there is one from 1943 that clearly shows that Sewering sent 14-year-old Babette Fröwis from the Schönbrunn hospital to Eglfing-Haar, a euthanasia center where she was killed (Kater, 1989). Since that time, Hans Sewering established himself as a leader in his profession. In 1992, Dr. Sewering was elected to the presidency of the World Medical Association, which, in reaction to the Nazi medical atrocities, was founded in 1947 to uphold medical ethics and human rights. Before taking office, Sewering was forced to resign in 1993 when it was confirmed that he had indeed sent Fröwis to her death. It was also determined that in 1943, when Sewering was the attending physician at Schonbrunn, 203 people with disabilities were sent to their deaths (Leaning, 1993). The day after this information was released, Sewering resigned and "blamed 'world Jewry' " for his downfall (Leaning, 1993, p. 121).

American Euthanasia Ideology   In 1941, the same year that the medical staff at Hadamar Hospital were toasting their success, an American physician, Foster Kennedy, was invited to present an address before the American Psychiatric Association. In this speech, Kennedy suggested that the Nazi agenda should be partially adopted by North America (Kennedy, 1942). Although he advocated that people with schizophrenia and manic depressive psychosis should be allowed to live, he proposed death for "hopelessly unfit" children with mental retardation and developmental disabilities at the age of 5 years. He rationalized this by stating that "it is a merciful and kindly thing to relieve that defective—often tortured and convulsed, grotesque and absurd, useless and foolish, and entirely undesirable—of the agony of living" (p. 14). Kennedy believed that the Nazi agenda of purification through extermination is a natural step in evolution and that "the social organism [should] grow up and forward to relieve the utterly unfit, sterilize the less unfit, and educate the still less unfit," so that "thereafter civilization will pass on and on in beauty" (p. 16). The speech was well received and was published the following year in the July issue of *The American Journal of Psychiatry*.

An editorial in the same issue of the so-called "Official Organ of The American Psychiatric Association," suggests that parental attachment might be an obstacle to exterminating their children. It declares that this attachment results from "an accusing sense of obligation on the part of the parents toward the defective creature they have caused to be born" ("Euthanasia," 1942, p. 142) and suggests that "anything that can be said or done to relieve a parent's mind of the unhappy obsession of obligation or guilt, and bring him to a more dispassionate view of a hopeless situation would seem to be good mental hygiene" (p. 143). Parental caring and efforts to keep their children with severe disabilities alive were judged to be "precisely the psychiatric problem that this overlengthy discussion has been trying to get at" (p. 143). Only 5 months after the publication of these two articles, the bombing of

Pearl Harbor plunged the United States into a war that made Nazi ideology and policies far less popular. Whether such policies would actually have been adopted had the United States stayed out of World War II will never be known.

Eugenics

Eugenics Policy in Nazi Germany Eugenics is defined as the "science that deals with the improvement (as by control of human mating) of the hereditary qualities of a race or breed" (*Webster's Ninth New Collegiate Dictionary*, 1989, p. 425). The earlier application of eugenic methods in the United States, where tens of thousands of eugenic sterilizations and massive institutionalization had taken place, was cited as part of the rationale for the employment of similar methods in Nazi Germany (Sengstock et al., 1990). The Nazi regime utilized sterilization and restrictive sexuality and reproduction laws for people with disabilities, as part of their eugenics program. The application of similar laws to the Jewish population provides a further parallel between the ethnic holocaust and the euthanasia–eugenics program. For example, in 1942, a Reich secret document called for the sterilization of 2–3 million Jews as a means of eliminating their reproduction while keeping them alive as a labor resource (Arad, Gutman, & Margaliot, 1981). During the Third Reich, special education students who tested below the educable level were exterminated, while those who passed at the educable level were sterilized and used as part of the labor force in support of the war effort (Sengstock et al., 1990).

Ironically, the United States Military Government made it unlawful to sterilize people with mental disabilities in Germany in 1947, declaring it to be a crime against humanity (Sengstock et al., 1990); however, involuntary sterilizations continued in the United States long after that date (e.g., Dickens, 1982). Although the practice remains illegal, more than 1,000 involuntary sterilizations of people with mental retardation have taken place during the 1970s and 1980s in Germany, and legislation has again been introduced to legalize this practice (Finger, 1990).

Eugenics Movement in the United States American eugenicists, like the Nazis who followed their examples, believed that they could "conserve mental virility and the moral integrity of the race" (Schlapp, 1915, 321). Wolfensberger (1975) points out that the term, *Final Solution*, in reference to the proposed eugenic elimination of people with mental retardation, was actually in use in the United States as early as 1918, and the idea that the "disability question" might be resolved with the same methods used to solve the "Indian problem" was suggested as early as 1885. The link between people with disabilities and various devalued racial or ethnic groups appears many other times in the literature of American eugenics.

The eugenics movement in the United States had three major components. First, beginning in the late 1800s restrictive marriage and reproduction laws were passed that prohibited marriage or sexual intercourse involving anyone with mental retardation, epilepsy, and other disorders if the female participant was of reproductive age. Many of these laws remain in effect today. Second, compulsory sterilization soon followed as the failure of marriage and reproduction laws became apparent. Finally, institutionalization with strict sexual segregation was implemented when sterilization programs failed (Scheerenberger, 1983; Wolfensberger, 1975). All of these components were aimed toward the common goal of eliminating mental disabilities by controlling human reproduction. Each failed for a multitude of reasons, including two essential flaws in the theoretical basis for eugenics.

Flaws in Eugenics Theory   First, while supporters often suggested that Darwin's theory of evolution provided a basis for their actions, their practices actually conflicted with Darwin's model. Darwin's theory maintains that natural environmental forces control evolution; if traits are developed and maintained in a genetic population, they have value. Proponents of eugenics suggest the contrary—that traits that are arbitrarily defined or chosen (e.g., IQ scores) are valued and that there is some advantage to manipulating the environment in order to achieve enrichment in these traits. The Darwinian view trusts in nature to exercise selection over genetically determined traits. The eugenic view attempts to defy nature and usurp its role as selector in favor of a privileged class who exercises control over the rest of humanity.

Second, proponents of eugenics overestimated the role of genetics as they underestimated the role of environment in determining disability. For example, Goddard (1919) declared that "there is not the slightest evidence that malnutrition or any other environmental condition can produce feeble-mindedness" (p. 283-284). It is now known that child abuse and neglect, parental alcohol usage, communicable disease, accidental injury, and a host of other environmental factors are significant causal and contributing factors for developmental disabilities. It is also known that many inheritable categories of developmental disability are not typically transmitted genetically. For example, most cases of tuberous sclerosis occur as new mutations, and children with Down syndrome born to parents with Down syndrome account for only a tiny fraction of 1% of all children born with Down syndrome (Hayes & Hayes, 1982).

The "science" that provided the rationale for the eugenics movement was not based on objective research, but rather on a philosophy of personal superiority and a series of fraudulent findings that appeared to provide a basis for the applicaton of biased policies (Gould, 1981). Just as people with disabilities and other devalued attributes were exterminated as witches for supposed religious reasons during the 17th century, an era dominated by religion (Scheerenberger, 1983), they have been eliminated for alleged scientific reasons in the 20th century, an era dominated by science. Gould (1981) gives an example of how racial and ethnic discrimination have often been linked with prejudice against people with disabilities. He describes the pseudoscientific evidence that was introduced showing that various racial, ethnic, and national groups were considered intellectually unfit to immigrate to North America, thereby justifying restrictive immigration policies.

It is interesting to note that efforts to eliminate people with disabilities were more widely accepted than attempts to eliminate particular racial, ethnic, or religious groups. Thus, the "scientific determination" of intellectual incompetence of immigrants of various nationalities through IQ testing programs at Ellis Island and other portals was used as a rationale for restricting access to the United States. Eugenics, under the pretense of science, was a social tool wielded with deadly results.

Although the underlying motivation of eugenics policy (i.e., to protect society from the burden and menace created by people with disabilities) was never in doubt and often clearly articulated, American proponents of elimination appealed to a more philanthropic sensibility. Johnson (1903) suggested that society should "improve [its] methods of support of the weak ones so that [it] may add . . . the needed element of control" (p. 252), that element being the combination of institutionalization and sexual segregation. In similar fashion, Nazi proponents of extermination propagandized that their "mercy killing" and sterilization programs were for the "benefit" of their victims (Sengstock et al., 1990).

The eugenics movements in the United States and Germany were similar in many respects to those in various other countries (e.g., Barker, 1983; Hayes & Hayes, 1982; Tully, 1986). For example, the United States was not the only allied nation to utilize some of the practices for which Nazi Germany was condemned. Discussing his treatment in a Soviet psychiatric hospital and its relationship to Nazi attempts to eliminate people with disabilities, Soviet dissenters Zhores and Roy Medvedv (1971) pointed out that "at the Nuremberg Trials this practice was declared to be a crime against humanity," yet, he remarked, Soviet practices "move in the same general direction" (p. 202). In England, the Mental Deficiency Act of 1913 established a Board of Control for the management of people with developmental disabilities (Radford &

Tipper, 1988). Involuntary, sexually segregated incarceration and sterilization were England's primary tools for management (Tully, 1986). New Zealand also developed a Eugenics Board based on the recommendations of the Committee of Inquiry into Mental Defectives and Sex Offenders (1925). An earlier report by New Zealand's Committee of the Board of Health to Study Venereal Diseases (1922) had already proposed that "mentally defective or morally imbecile girls" were a major cause for the rise in cases of venereal diseases (p. 13).

Perhaps the most ironic aspect of the eugenics debate was that its central, underlying assumption was clearly known to be false by most credible scientists, even at the height of the movement. Most of the traits that the eugenicists wanted to eliminate were carried by recessive genes. Elimination of such traits by killing or sterilizing homozygotes (those who carry two recessive genes and actually display the trait) would take hundreds of generations. For example, if an autosomal syndrome occurs in 1 out of 10,000 births and we eliminate that individual from the gene pool we have destroyed two "defective genes." However, as 1 person in 100 would be a heterozygote (carry only one of the defective genes) another 99 people out of that 10,000 would be expected to carry that gene. Hence, the frequency of the defective gene in the next generation would not be substantially changed. Researchers estimate that such eugenic practices would take as long as 2,500 years to reduce the frequency of a genetic trait from one in 100 to one in 200 if they were perfectly efficient and no new mutations appeared (Suzuki, Griffiths, & Lewontin, 1981). Unquestionably, the simple facts make even the latter impossible for several reasons: 1) such perfect killing efficiency would be difficult to achieve or maintain for 2,500 years, 2) most developmental disabilities are unrelated to genetic causes, and 3) new mutations appear to account for many developmental disabilities that are genetically related. Only by identifying and killing carriers of recessive deleterious genes could such a eugenic goal be accomplished. Unfortunately, researchers believe that every human being on our planet carries at least several deleterious genes (Suzuki et al., 1981). To rid the gene pool of all of these traits, *everyone* would have to be killed or sterilized.

PRESENT-DAY EFFORTS TO ELIMINATE PEOPLE WITH DISABILITIES

The history of past atrocities committed against people with disabilities may seem remote. Certainly attitudes have become more benevolent and enlightened, but how much has really changed? As the Americans with Disabilities Act went into effect in January 1992, many physicians were complaining that it might interfere with their policies and procedures of withholding life-sustaining care ("Denial of health," 1991). Ironically, the article covering the latter debate was published immediately after Hume's (1991a) article covering the Nazi extermination efforts half a century earlier.

As the 21st century rapidly approaches, the fallacies of the reasoning behind the eugenics movement are widely recognized, and the Nazi holocaust is behind us, hopefully never to be repeated. The issues surrounding the elimination of people with disabilities through incarceration, death, and sterilization, however, still remain. Though the rhetoric and rationales have changed, the means are more subtle. The actual numbers may have been reduced, but efforts to eliminate people with disabilities continue. The human beings who were sterilized as threats to racial purity, burned as witches, or sent to the gas chambers in the past are now being "allowed to die for their own good" or sterilized for "hygienic reasons" in this era.

Active and Passive Euthanasia

Duff and Campbell's (1973) classic review of 299 consecutive neonatal deaths at Yale-New Haven hospital revealed tha. in spite of hospital treatment, 86% of these infants had died. The remaining 14% identified as being disabled died because treatment was withheld or discontinued. Gross, Cox, Taytrek, Polloway, and Barnes (1983) reported on 24 babies with spina bifida who were given only supportive care and another 36 babies with spina bifida who were given vigorous care. Within 6 months of birth, all 24 babies in the first group were dead, whereas all of the babies in the second group survived. Other cases of passive and active euthanasia involving infants and children with severe disabilities in the United States (Orelove & Sobsey, 1991) Canada (Gregory, 1983), Australia (Judge, 1987) and England (Hayes & Hayes, 1982) have been the subject of various court actions. *Active euthanasia*, in which an individual carries out an act that results in death (e.g., injecting a legal dose of morphine), is more likely than passive euthanasia to result in criminal charges because responsibility can be linked to a specific individual. However, even in a case of active euthanasia, sympathies often lie with the offenders and punishment is often mild or nonexistent. Judge (1987) lists 13 examples from Australia dating from 1964 in which parents killed their children with disabilities. The means of death included drug overdose, poisoning, strangulation, drowning, bullet wounds, burns, and skull fractures. Only two of these 13 cases resulted in jail terms, and only one other parent was committed to a mental hospital.

Passive euthanasia, the failure to provide the necessities required to sustain life (e.g., withholding medical care or food), results less frequently in criminal charges as it is harder to place the responsibility for the death with any specific individual(s). However, the legal and ethical differences between passive and active killing become especially relevant in the case of children with disabilities. For example, a parent who starves his or her child to death is no less responsible for murder than a parent who shoots his or her child. Judge (1987) provides the example of infants with disabilities who were placed on rocks in the middle of streams. When the infants turned over or moved, they fell in the water and drowned. Because the person placing the child on the rock did not actually drown the baby, he or she was considered to have less personal responsibility. Obviously, such a distinction between active and passive euthanasia is strictly a technical one. There is no less deliberate and irreparable harm being done to a child who is being starved to death or allowed to die of infection, than the harm done to a child dying of strangulation or other more "active" methods. It is ironic that those defending methods of passive euthanasia would suggest both that the child does not suffer during such an ordeal and that the child is better off dead because he or she will be prevented from further suffering.

Quality of Life Argument

The stance that the child is "better off dead" is referred to as the *quality of life* argument. This philosophy maintains that the individual with severe disabilities has so small a possibility of experiencing pleasure in life and so great a potential for suffering that he or she would be better off dead. Thus, killing such a person becomes a sort of assisted suicide. The problem with this concept is that the decision to die is not made by the individual, nor is it voluntary in any sense. Schaffer responds to the quality of life argument by suggesting that this rationale "just provides a good reason instead of the real one, and the real one" is "to get rid of this baby" (Schaffer & Sobsey, 1991, p. 605). Hauerwas (1986) points out that there is no objective reason to believe that people with developmental disabilities enjoy their lives less than any of the rest of us, except that they are often badly treated by others. He proposes that "if justice comes to mean the elimination of the victim of injustice rather than the cause of the injustice, we stand the risk of creating a less troubled but deeply unjust world" (p. 65).

Burden on Society

Advocates of euthanasia suggest that there is no choice but to allow children with severe disabilities to die because of the tremendous burden that increasing numbers of these children place on society. This argument implies that increasing numbers of children with disabilities are now living because advances in medicine have allowed children to live who probably would have died in the past. This myth is not supported by research that suggests that improvements in medicine are actually reducing the overall number of certain disabilities among children (Sobsey, 1989a). To be certain, some children with disabilities now survive who would not have survived 50 years ago, but these numbers are much smaller than the number of children whose disabilities are prevented (Robertson & Etches, 1988). Immunizations against polio, pertussis, rubella, mumps, and a variety of other diseases, along with better neonatal care, genetic counseling, and other such factors have all been responsible for substantial cuts in the number of children with disabilities that more than offset any increases created by saving children with severe impairments.

Nevertheless, although euthanasia of people with severe disabilities clearly violates civil rights, child abuse, and homicide laws, widespread termination of life through the withholding of food, fluid, or other lifesaving care continues ("Medical discrimination," 1989). Decisions to terminate these lives are often "grounded in misinformation, inaccurate stereotypes, and negative attitudes about people with disabilities" (p. 149). While parents are typically the nominal decision makers, their decisions are often manipulated by professionals, and "in practice the doctors are often the prime movers in denying treatment" (p. 149).

Passive Euthanasia in the Health Care System

Although they may share similar motivations, health care workers who clandestinely murder their patients are viewed differently from those who openly advocate for passive euthanasia (Blissland, 1984). Often these murders remain hidden because of the probability that death will be ascribed to some underlying medical condition. Even when suspicious deaths are discovered, identification of the actual perpetrator remains extremely difficult because of the large number of health care workers who have the opportunity to commit these crimes. Rashes of such murders appear to have taken place in New Jersey in 1966, Michigan in 1975, Maryland in 1978, Illinois in 1979, Ontario in 1981, California in 1984, Georgia in 1985, again in Maryland in 1985, and at many other places at various times (Newton, 1990a, 1990b). The deaths in such cases have been caused by tampering with equipment; injections of insulin, potassium, curare, or a multitude of other drugs; or by smothering. Many, but not all, of the victims were either very old or very young.

Frequently suspicious deaths are discovered only after a pattern has been established involving dozens of similar deaths. Some of these offenders openly advocate for euthanasia, yet many of the patients that they kill seem to have had a fairly strong potential for recovery. Often these killers appear to be driven by an insatiable need for power over others and, quite possibly, by displaced anger toward a more powerful individual (Newton, 1990a, 1990b). Most were not involved in murders outside of their professional careers; their violence appears limited to the unique opportunities they possessed for exercising the power of life and death over extremely vulnerable individuals. "Medical murderers" probably represent the most prolific group of serial killers in contemporary society, but their crimes receive much less attention than other kinds of crimes because they usually remain undiscovered or unsolved. Even when solved, these murders might be considered less shocking because the victims are portrayed as close to death anyway, and the murderers are often portrayed as compassionately wishing to end the victim's suffering.

Those cases that are solved, however, reveal far more complex and insidious motivations. Dorothy Matajke, a nurse's aide in Little Rock, killed her patients with drugs and insecticide after forging checks and emptying her patients' bank accounts (Newton, 1990b). Richard Angelo, a registered nurse on Long Island who injected patients with lethal doses of drugs, apparently did so in order for him to appear to arrive just in time to save them and gain recognition for his heroism. Unfortunately, estimates suggest that more than 10, and possibly as many as 38, people died in spite of his "heroic" efforts (Newton, 1990a). Carl Menarik killed patients at a New York nursing home to create space for admission of younger, easier to care for patients (Newton, 1990b). Fritz Rudolf, a German registered nurse, feared and resented a surgeon whom he worked for and displaced his anger to poisoning the surgeon's patients (Newton, 1990b). Although he was convicted of only 22 murders, Arnfinn Nesset was believed to have killed as many as 62 patients at the nursing home he managed in Norway. He first claimed these murders were mercy killings, but later confessed that it was the simple pleasure of killing that motivated him. In court he pleaded insanity, saying that the godlike power of life and death he held over his patients had driven him mad (Newton, 1990b). These medical murders are another example of contemporary society's attempts to rid itself of its more vulnerable members. And although society's attitudes toward people with disabilities may have improved over the years, darker motivations are still cloaked under the blanket of protection and compassion.

INCARCERATION, SEGREGATION, AND ISOLATION

People with disabilities often live and learn in settings segregated from their contemporaries. The majority of contemporary society knows little of the reality of the lives hidden in these isolated settings, and most do not want to know. After World War II, tribunals attempted to determine how much typical German citizens knew about Nazi atrocities. Many said they knew nothing. Some said that they believed the lies they had been told. Others said that they had only vague suspicions, but were powerless to change things anyway. If someday we are asked what we know about the thousands of people with disabilities who continue to suffer in institutions or what we did to try to stop their suffering, how will we answer?

Institutionalization

The practice of institutionalization is often justified as necessary to protect and educate people with disabilities. This rationale argues that through the congregation of people with mental retardation in institutions, it will be possible to provide them with the highly specialized medical and educational services that they require in a setting protected from the dangers of life in the community (Tully, 1986). Unfortunately, the reality of institutional life contradicts this view. Many communicable diseases that are rare in community settings are common in institutions (Benenson, 1990). Physical and sexual abuse are at least twice as common in institutions as in community settings (Blatt & Brown, 1986; Rindfleisch & Rabb, 1984). Accidental death rates for people diagnosed with severe mental disabilities have been found to be about three times as high for those living in institutions as those living in community settings (Dupont & Mortensen, 1990).

Periodic exposés of institutional atrocities and abuse such as those discussed in Chapter 4 have publicized the hard realities of institutional life. As Chase (1976) succinctly pointed out, institutions are "society's wastebaskets, public garbage bins [that] are only carrying out the wishes of the public" (p. 154). The social control function of institutions was never completely hidden; it was presented alongside the care and rehabilitation functions (Wolfensberger, 1975). *Management* and *control* are common terminology used in the philosophy, guidelines, and procedures that shape institutional life.

The unparalleled power of institutions to exert control over human beings is illustrated by the choice of the Soviet Union's use of institutions to "rehabilitate" their most challenging dissidents and the United States' choice of institutions for their experimentation with mind control techniques (Thomas, 1988). Soviet authorities chose psychiatric institutions to control dissidents because they allowed them "to deprive a man of his freedom for an unlimited amount of time, keep him in strict isolation, and use psycho-pharmacological means of 're-educating' him" (Fireside, 1979, p. 92). Dissenters who had learned to defend themselves in the legal system, found that institutional life rendered them "absolutely powerless" (Fireside, 1979, p. 93).

If the rationale of institutional care and rehabilitation was ever viable, the reality of abuse and neglect suggests that only the social control function—the ridding of society of its unwanted members—was maintained. The pretense of care and rehabilitation served primarily only to ease the conscience of a society that was occasionally discomforted by fleeting glimpses into the harsh realities of institutional life.

Lovett (1985) provides an example of this social control function describing his own experience working in an institution for people with disabilities. He describes how professionals met to make decisions regarding how to best control behavior of the inmates; yet, the very people whose fates were being decided "never came to the meetings at which they were discussed" (p. 1). Control was achieved through the application of coercion to maintain domination. As an example, he describes an incident in which a woman refused to take a shower when commanded to do so. As a consequence for her decision, she was overpowered, stripped, and forced to shower by two staff members, not because skipping one night's shower would harm her or anyone else, but because being allowed to disobey an order threatened the institution's absolute control over its inmates.

Did those who overpowered this woman and forced her into the shower believe it was abuse to deprive her of even this small degree of free will? Did they believe that teaching her this lesson in compliance was somehow in her best interest? Whatever the answers to these questions, many thousands of human beings with disabilities, as in the example of this woman, have been incarcerated in institutions against their will and deprived of their liberty, privacy, and every last vestige of personal control over their own lives. Again, the line between caregiving and abuse blurs until the difference becomes indistinguishable.

Segregated Education

Like euthanasia, sterilization, and institutional incarceration, segregated education serves a primary function of eliminating people with disabilities from participation in society. Like all of these other practices, it has often been rationalized as being for the benefit of the excluded individuals. Educational segregation has often been justified in terms of its educational advantages. Special education settings have been portrayed as essential to maximizing learning so that children with disabilities can become more independent adults. Thus, institutions can be viewed as protecting people from the dangers of community living, and segregated education settings can be viewed as allowing people with disabilities to obtain specialized services. However, does empirical evidence support these claimed advantages?

Dunn (1968), in a classic review of the existing literature, found that students with mild mental retardation "made as much or more progress in regular grades as they do in special classes" (p. 8). After decades of further research, the overwhelming majority of findings agree with Dunn's assessment. The academic performance of students with disabilities is at least as good, and quite often measurably better, in inclusive education.

Carlberg and Kavale (1980) reported on the results of a major meta-analysis based on 50 studies that met their research criteria out of an initial pool of 860 studies and reports. They found significant differences between inclusive and segregated placements for students with mild mental retardation. Those placed in segregated classrooms showed lower academic achievement than those placed in inclusive classrooms. Students with scores on intelligence tests of between 75 and 90 lost 13 percentile ranks on average as a result of being denied inclusion, while those with scores on intelligence tests between 50 and 75 lost 6 percentile ranks. The authors concluded that "the results . . . demonstrated that special class placement is an inferior alternative to regular class placement in benefitting children removed from the educational mainstream" (p. 304). Although not everyone agrees that IQ scores or achievement test percentiles are the best determinants of academic performance, similar results have been obtained using a variety of different measures. For example, Brinker and Thorpe (1984) found that students in integrated settings achieved a larger percentage of the objectives identified on their individualized education programs (IEPs).

Wang, Anderson, and Bram (1985) replicated the results of the earlier meta-analysis with another large-scale investigation involving 50 studies and approximately 3,400 students. The results showed a significant advantage in educational performance for students placed in inclusive education settings. In addition, these results indicated that students spending 100% of their time in a general classroom significantly outperformed their peers who were included only on a part-time basis.

If educational segregation does not actually serve the needs of the students who are segregated, whose needs are being served? McKnight (1977) suggested that the growing service-driven economy requires service consumers, and that in order to maintain these service consumers, the economy seeks to cast certain individuals into roles of increasing dependency. Support for this theory exists in the calls by educational fraternal groups and professional organizations to expand their programs in order to absorb the teacher surplus that emerged in the 1970s. Reiger (1972) specifically proposed the further development of special education classrooms, adult education programs, and early education in order to absorb the excess in teachers.

Yet, for many students with disabilities, separate education was viewed as a step toward inclusion because the previous alternative had been total exclusion from the education system. As isolation was accomplished either through total exclusion from the schools or by segregated programs within the schools themselves, the growth in the service sector cannot be viewed as the driving force behind segregation; it merely influenced the degree of segregation involved.

Finally, it is important to realize that segregation is not an inherent requirement for special education. Individualized curriculum content, instructional methods, and teaching materials can certainly be extremely valuable for some students; however, it is unnecessary to provide these alternatives in segregated settings. In fact, segregation often undermines the value of these interventions because it defeats the central purpose of contemporary education—that of socializing children to fully participate in future society.

Slavery and Exploitation of Labor

Many individuals locked away in institutions are capable of producing economically valuable work. The English workhouse institutions established in the 17th century set a precedent of exploiting individuals for labor that remains in place to this day (Judge, 1987). Until the 1960s, as pointed out by Lusthaus (1991), in United States institutions, "the more able-bodied and developmentally capable residents were used to perform labor with no pay" (p. 34). As few records were kept of this practice, it is difficult to estimate its full extent or to describe its impact on people's lives.

The labor of institutionalized children was contracted out to private enterprise in New York State until the 1880s. These children were pushed to their limits by supervisors who received gifts from the contractors to ensure that shops would be run in their interests. Testimony given in 1882 by W. P. Letchworth to support abolition of this practice (Bremner, 1971a) indicates the ferocity with which it was enforced:

> One institution in the State, in order to meet the expectation of contractors, was forced in a single year to inflict on the boys employed, upon the direct complaint of contractors, their superintendent, overseer and employers, corporal punishments *two thousand two hundred and sixty three times*. This was administered with a strap or rattan on the hand, or on the posterior bare or covered, as the gravity of the case demanded. During the same period the punishments in school, in order as it was said, to "wake up" their already overtaxed attention, was so considerable as to swell the aggregate punishments for the year to the magnitude of *ten thousand*. (pp. 470–471)

Personal Accounts Observation at one American institution over a 10-year period[1] and accounts reported by other individuals involved provide an idea of more recent practices. In an institution serving more than 5,000 residents, about 400 were identified as "houseboys" or "housegirls." These were typically individuals with the least physical impairment and a more advanced use of language. Some of the houseboys and housegirls walked to work in units separate from their own living quarters. Many others lived and worked in the same area. Thus some men and women were forced to live with children because their labor was required in those units.

The duties demanded of these workers were diverse. They swept, mopped, and waxed floors; folded laundry; moved furniture; and made beds. They fed, dressed, showered, cleaned, supervised, and disciplined other residents. Paid employees were sometimes ridiculed by their peers or scolded by their supervisors for doing low status jobs that should have been reserved for the houseboys or housegirls. Many worked 16 hours a day, seven days per week, with only occasional breaks for coffee, meals, church, medical care, and similar intrusions. After their 16-hour workday ended, they would often be awakened several times during the night to change beds that less-able residents had wet or soiled as they slept. For many, this schedule commenced when they were in their teens and continued until their mid- to late-60s when they were no longer capable of working.

These residents received no pay for their work, but were allowed to stay up later, were granted other privileges from time to time, and were given tobacco, extra coffee, and bread. Most houseboys had "parole cards." These cards permitted them to leave the locked wards where they lived to travel around the grounds of the institution without the accompaniment of a paid employee. These unpaid workers clearly had a higher status than other residents, and many emulated the paid employees who supervised them. For example, although they were not issued keys, many attached "shoelace keychains" to their belts and would walk around the wards twirling them in circles imitating the paid attendants whom they had seen twirling keys on heavy steel or nylon keychains.

The actual skill levels of the houseboys and housegirls varied. Some were limited to only a small numbers of jobs that they could do well. Some performed their specific duties adequately, but lacked generic language or social skills. Others were easily as competent as their paid counterparts. In fact, significant numbers were elevated to paid employee status for a brief time during their extended careers. During World War II, shortages of staff (particularly male staff) in institutions

---

[1]This account is based on the author's own observations between 1968 and 1978.

became critical. Chronically understaffed before the war, institutions could not hire enough staff for their sexually segregated male units. The more capable houseboys were issued keys and promoted from inmate to staff status; moved to staff quarters; took charge of wards; and, for the first time, received paychecks. Most made the adjustment easily and performed well during the war years. When the war ended and the troops returned, the majority of these individuals were promptly demoted to the status of inmate once again. Their keys were taken away, and they returned to their long unpaid careers as houseboys.

In fact, wars and labor shortages have repeatedly redefined who has mental retardation, what kind of care they require, and what contributions they can make to society. Gould (1993) quotes from the 1946 Annual Report of the Mansfield Training School, a large institution for people with mental retardation:

> Although the returning of men and women from the service will mean fewer jobs for our boys and girls, the war years were of help to the mental defective. The public learned that with a little understanding and patience on their part, mentally deficient persons could do productive work, were dependable, and less inclined to drift from job to job. (p. 3)

Many people also left institutions during World War I and II to fight in the United States armed forces. Of 13 men from Southbury (Connecticut) Training School who enlisted to fight in World War II, four were promoted to higher ranks and seven were wounded in action (Gould, 1993). Advocates for enlisting formerly institutionalized people with mental retardation in the armed forces argued that the regimentation of institutional life well prepared them for the military and that they made excellent soldiers because they obeyed orders without question or hesitation (Gould, 1993). Nevertheless, as Gould points out, when the wars ended and manpower shortages eased, people with mental retardation were no longer required for military or civilian jobs. They were consistently fired, and many returned to institutional care.

Barron (1981) describes his experiences in an institution in 1930s England. Although he was only 13 years old, Barron was required to scrub toilets 6 hours a day, 5 days per week. In return, he was paid a small sum each week to buy sweets. However, he preferred this job to his later assignment working in the sewing room, or performing such punishment tasks as scrubbing the concrete with a brick for a scrub brush. Other residents worked 55–60 hours per week in the laundry. The pay for this work started at a half-penny per week, but a more proficient and responsible worker could earn up to four pence per week. However, Barron recalls that "patients could never guarantee on receiving their 'spends'" (p. 19) because the pay was often withheld for a fortnight, and sometimes as long as 2 months, as punishment for such infractions as talking without permission, failing to say "thank you," or even reaching out to accept the pay with one's left rather than the required right hand.

Mavis May (1989) provides a similar personal account (expanded upon in the first foreword to this book) of her experiences in institutions in New Zealand. She relates, "I never went to school. They wanted me to work because I was so good at it" (p. 28). While working in an institutional laundry, May asked to be excused from work because she felt sick, but was forced to continue until she fell unconscious onto an electric stove, sustaining severe burns that required a long period of hospitalization.

Cotter (1967) described how his work program paid inmates of a Vietnamese institution one *piastre* (less than one U.S. penny per day), no doubt worth less than the half-penny to four pence per week described by Barron (1981). Cotter defended himself against criticism that the wage was too low by pointing out that because prices were kept low at the institution store, a day's wages were enough to buy a glass of chocolate-flavored powdered milk.

Economic Viability   The forced and unpaid labor of these individuals was a key factor in the economic viability of many institutions. Cost estimates were traditionally calculated on a per capita basis by simply dividing the total institutional budget by the number of residents. By including in this calculation the vast unpaid workforce as institutional residents, the total costs were distorted in two ways. First, the number of residents actually requiring care was lower than reported because close to 10% of the residents were actually a part of the workforce. Second, the expenses were kept artificially low through the utilization of forced labor. As many unpaid laborers worked twice the normal work week and received little time off, a paid workforce of about twice the size of the unpaid workforce would be required to replace them.

Many of the early attempts to move more capable residents out of institutions were met by strong resistance from administration and staff who feared the loss of free labor, a valuable economic asset. By the mid-1970s, growing legal pressure was forcing institutions to prohibit the use of forced labor. Reductions in the institutionalization of children with less severe disabilities was eroding the free labor pool through natural attrition, and many more capable residents were making the transition to community group residences and other alternatives. Together these changes made it difficult for institutions to continue their widespread use of forced labor; however, practice of forcing labor from people with disabilities has not entirely eroded. In 1988, for example, the U.S. Supreme Court heard a case involving farm workers with mental retardation who had worked 17 hours a day,

7 days a week, for little or no pay. The Court ruled that the case could not be prosecuted under the 13th Amendment to the U.S. Constitution that prohibits slavery (*United States v. Kozminski*, 1988) despite the fact that these workers had been threatened with institutionalization if they refused to work or attempted to escape from the squalid, unheated trailer where they were kept (Luckasson, 1992).

Links to Other Forms of Abuse

Not surprisingly, many examples of forced labor are also connected with physical and sexual abuse. For example, the University of Alberta Abuse & Disability Project data include a number of cases of sexual assaults within the context of forced labor. This is consistent with the establishment of the master–slave relationship that extends far beyond the narrow contractual limits of employer and employee. As Patterson (1982) suggested in his comprehensive cross-cultural analysis of slavery, "I know of no slave-holding society in which a master, when so inclined, could not exact sexual services from his female slaves" (p. 173).

In some cases, sexual services became the ultimate focus of master–slave relationships between therapists and institutional inmates. Breggin (1991), for example, describes how one of America's leading psychotherapists surrendered his license in order to avoid charges involving a number of women whom he "physically and sexually assaulted, virtually turned into mental patient slave[s]" and whom he "tormented . . . in isolated cottages in which he imprisoned them under guard" (p. 339).

The use of institutionalized people as subjects in experiments is another form of abusive exploitation. For example, smallpox vaccine was tested on large numbers of institutionalized children by first vaccinating them and then injecting them with smallpox virus. The logic was simple. If the children got sick or died, the experimenters would know that the vaccine needed further work. Fortunately, this particular vaccine was a success; however, a number of other tests conducted in the same way failed (Lederer, 1992).

AVERSIVE INTERVENTION AND CHEMICAL RESTRAINT

People with developmental disabilities have often been targets of intervention intended to increase compliance or eliminate undesirable behavior. Many issues arise related to the application of such intervention. Are people with developmental disabilities much more likely to exhibit severe behavior problems? Is the intended control justifiable or does it intrude unreasonably on the lives of the individuals who are targeted for intervention? Would the same interventions be used with individuals without disabilities who exhibit similar behavior? Are the intrusive interventions used effective, and, if so, are they significantly more effective than less intrusive alternatives? Are these interventions harmful or associated with significant risks, and, if so, do the potential benefits outweigh these risks? While debate over these and related questions continues and more complete discussions of some of these issues can be found elsewhere (e.g., Helmstetter & Durand, 1991; Repp & Singh, 1990), consideration of these issues is included here to help identify underlying attitudes and assumptions regarding caregiving practices.

Menaces to Society

The view of people with developmental disabilities as menaces to society is a common one. Wolfensberger (1975) considers this myth to be rooted in humanity's fear of the unknown and distrust of anything unfamiliar. As an individual, the person with a disability has often been viewed as destructive and aggressive, with a propensity toward antisocial behavior. As a group, people with disabilities have often been viewed as a threat. Anthropologists have linked the fear of children who are different with the concern for maintaining the parental bloodline, and they point out that infanticide is often acceptable when children are born from adulterous pairings, nontribal fathers, or even previous husbands, as well as when children are considered diseased, disabled, or deformed (Daly & Wilson, 1988). The concepts of changelings or abominations have been incorporated into many religions; these concepts regard any child who is deviant in any way as a demon or menace. English author John Wyndham (1955) provides a masterful exploration of the fundamental fear of deviance in his novel, *The Chrysalids*. The novel depicts the conflict of a child struggling to reconcile the deeply ingrained notion that all deviance is blasphemy with the frightful and deadly secret of his baby sister's extra toes: "A blasphemy was, as had been impressed on me often enough, a frightful thing. Yet there was nothing frightful about Sophie. She was simply an ordinary little girl" (p. 14).

Inappropriate and noncompliant behavior are assumed to be "common in the repertoires of persons with developmental disabilities" (Luiselli, 1990, p. 79). Certainly, among some people with disabilities, extreme cases of aggressive, disruptive, and self-injurious behavior do exist. However, these individuals represent only a small minority of people with disabilities. Many people with developmental disabilities exhibit less antisocial behavior than their peers without disabilities.

Psychoactive Drugs

In spite of the fact that serious problem behavior is uncommon among people with mental retardation, the use of medication and other intrusive behavior management programs to control it is common. The use of psychoactive medications as chemical restraint in understaffed programs grew quickly after their introduction (Beyer, 1988). Although the use of such drugs could be and sometimes has been implemented for limited periods to allow for the implementation of less aversive programs, drugs have often been used as inexpensive alternatives to programming, incapacitating people in order to make human warehousing easier for the service providers. Although controlled studies provide little support for their effectiveness (Sobsey & Cox, 1991), about 20% of school-age children classified as having severe and profound mental retardation receive tranquilizers (Gadow & Poling, 1988). About half of all adults with mental retardation living in institutions and about one-third of all adults with disabilities making transitions to community living also receive tranquilizers (Harder, Kalachnik, Jensen, & Feltz, 1987).

In addition to tranquilizers, sedatives, stimulants, anticonvulsants, and other psychoactive drugs are sometimes prescribed (Sobsey & Cox, 1991). When these other psychoactive drugs are included in the overall estimate, it is likely that the majority of people with mental retardation are receiving psychoactive medication. For example, Harder et al. (1987) found that 59% of their successful community placement follow-up sample and 81% of those requiring readmission received at least one of these drugs. Such figures only represent the percentage receiving these drugs at a given time; therefore, the estimated percentage of those who will receive them at some point in their lives is probably very low. Aman and Singh (1988) state that "it is quite clear that psychoactive drugs represent a prevalent mode, perhaps the single most common mode of treatment with developmentally disabled children and adults" (p. 6).

In addition to their incapacitating effects, psychoactive drugs have a multitude of serious side effects—some of which are lethal. Side effects can include:

Cataracts
Liver damage
Confusion
Lowered seizure threshold
Difficulty swallowing
Drowsiness
Blood abnormalities (Sobsey & Cox, 1991)

The rate of death from airway obstruction has been found to be almost 100 times higher among institutionalized men with mental retardation than in the general population (Dupont & Mortensen, 1990). Carter and Jancar (1984) found that the rate of deaths by asphyxia increased by 2,400% in the 25 years following 1955 (the advent of the widespread use of tranquilizers) as compared to the previous 25 years. While not every death by asphyxiation could be attributed to tranquilizers, a large group was found "who choked to death as a result of impaired swallowing reflex due to . . . various combinations of major tranquilizers" (p. 693). Ironically, behavior problems are an additional side effect that can emerge as a result of drug treatment, and more drugs are sometimes prescribed to manage these problems, creating an inescapable cycle (Sovner & Hurley, 1982).

Although there is a specific physiological rationale for the use of tranquilizers (which suppress dopamine) with schizophrenics (who produce excess dopamine), this rationale does not extend to people with mental retardation (who do not produce excess dopamine). These drugs are used to suppress behavior, "however, they do so regardless of whether it is appropriate or inappropriate" (Evenden, 1988, pp. 232–233). Werry (1988) concludes that the administration of psychoactive drugs to people with mental retardation is widespread, the doses tend to be exceptionally high, medical supervision of this treatment is poor, drugs most commonly used are those with the greatest incapacitating effects, research on the effects has been scarce and often flawed, and these drugs are typically used as chemical restraint. Such use of drugs has been labeled as a form of abuse (e.g., Barowsky, 1976) and has consistently been found to violate the law (Beyer, 1988), yet chemical restraint continues to be practiced and accepted as standard intervention.

Other Aversive Intervention Methods

In addition to chemical restraint, many children and adults with mental retardation are subjected to aversive behavior management procedures to achieve similar ends, with similarly equivocal results. The use of noxious tastes and smells, sensory deprivation, restraint, electric shock, and a variety of other unpleasant stimuli makes it difficult to separate behavior management from abuse. Furthermore, the application of aversive intervention by professionals serves as a model for untrained staff and other clients to devise their own methods to control behavior. Perceived control of behavior through "punishment" has been shown to exceed the actual level of control (Sobsey, 1990a), and this misperception often leads to the application of aversive procedures to an ever-growing list of minor behaviors, without consideration of less intrusive alternatives (Evans, 1990). Electric shock used to stimulate attention in picture-naming or to reduce rocking is an example of the unnecessary use of severe restraint (Guess, 1990).

Ironically, although aversive programs have been rationalized as a means of controlling violent and self-destructive behavior, they have also been utilized to induce rage. They are used to force compliance on people who are not passive and to provoke noncompliance from those who appear too passive. Cameronchild (1980) describes how she was institutionalized as a result of abuse by her family, then deliberately abused in a similar manner in the institution, as part of a program that was intended to provoke her rage.

Torture   Torture as a form of treatment has a long history. Benjamin Rush, considered the father of American psychiatry, practiced medicine in Pennsylvania during the late 1700s and early 1800s. He was well known as a reformer, humanitarian, and great thinker. Nevertheless, he believed that "terror acts powerfully on the body and through the medium of the mind, and should be employed in the cure of madness" (cited in Deutsch, 1949, p. 80). He also believed that people with mental disorders and developmental disabilities must be "broken" like the taming of wild animals. He invented the *tranquilizing chair* that provided total restraint of head, trunk, and limbs for extended periods (including a visual screening device), and the *gyrator*, a device that strapped the patient to a rapidly rotating board to force blood to his or her head.

Rush's devices were considered to be far more humane than the procedures that were commonly used by others, such as a pump that directed an agonizingly powerful stream of water against the spine or the *bath of surprise* that employed a concealed trap door to plunge the patient into a pool of cold water. Some advocated chaining the patient in the bottom of an empty well and gradually filling it with water, or placing the patient in a box with holes which was lowered into water until the bubbles stopped coming out; they were then removed and revived for further treatment (Deutsch, 1949). In considering such methods, it is important to recognize that they were designed and carried out by people who believed in the scientific merit of these procedures and the humanitarian right to effective intervention for their patients. The thin line between abuse and aversive intervention dissolves completely in these cases.

Bien Hoa Mental Hospital in Vietnam   Modern examples of torture continue to emerge. Cotter (1967), for example, who was "tremendously impressed" (p. 23) by Lovaas' work with children with autism, describes a behavior management program that he instituted with hundreds of individuals living in the Bien Hoa Mental Hospital in Vietnam. Lovaas's work included punishments such as superficial electric shock to establish control over the self-injurious or disruptive behavior of students with autism. Cotter applied electro-convulsive shock therapy (ECT) and withheld food from his patients until they were willing to work. The ECT was unmodified; no medication was given to minimize the risk of bone-crushing injuries that often result from the severe convulsions that occur during shock treatments. According to the author's account, the program was highly successful. In this case, success meant that he was able to get most of his subjects to plant crops in battle zones, while heavily drugged with phenothiazines and other tranquilizers for one piastre (less than 1 cent U.S.) per day. Levy (1968) criticized Cotter's program suggesting that Cotter's one visit to Dr. Lovaas's laboratory and his conversation with ward personnel at Patton State Hospital was inadequate training, that the methods employed by Cotter were coercive and cruel, and that the pay was far too low. Cotter (1968) responded by accusing Levy of being motivated by "negative feelings on the subject of [U.S.] national policy in VietNam" (p. 1137). In defense of his methods, Cotter cites the endorsement of another leading behaviorist: "In correspondence with Dr. Skinner concerning my paper, he commented that he would in no way endorse Dr. Levy's criticisms and felt him quite unduly alarmed" (p. 1137). However, only Cotter's word for Skinner's response is available, and if Skinner did endorse the work at Bien Hoa, he may have done so without the knowledge of certain information that was not included in the published study.

While he acknowledges Lovaas' influence on his work and claims Skinner's endorsement, Cotter omits the mention of another apparent influence, the CIA. Thomas (1988) reports that Cotter and two other physicians arrived at Bien Hoa under the auspices of the U.S. Central Intelligence Agency. Viet Cong prisoners of war were kept along with patients with chronic mental disorders at Bien Hoa to allow for more severe torture and experimentation than could be conducted in the prison camps. Thomas (1988) reports on the experiments at Bien Hoa to try to confirm the depatterning experiments that Cameron conducted earlier in a Montréal institution for the CIA:

> Using a Page-Russell electroshock machine they had brought with them, the agency doctors gave the man six separate electric shocks. Twelve hours later he received a further series of multiple shocks. Within a week Dr. Cotter began to see 'evident improvement in the behaviour of his patients'. (p. 392)

Thomas goes on to report that this patient died after receiving 7 more days of treatment involving 60 more shocks. After 3 weeks, all the prisoners of war receiving this treatment had died, and "the agency men packed away their machine and flew home" (Thomas, 1988, p. 392). In an associated group of experiments at Bien Hoa, electrodes were implanted in the war prisoners' brains and then activated to try to get the prisoners to kill each other. When the experiments failed, the prisoners were taken out and shot (Thomas, 1988).

Cameron's Depatterning Experiments Cameron's depatterning experiments, which were the forerunners of the work at Bien Hoa, were conducted for the CIA in Montreal's Allan Memorial Institute over a period that spanned much of the 1950s and 1960s (Thomas, 1988). These experiments utilized extensive ECT, sensory deprivation, drug-induced sleep, LSD and curare injections, and a variety of other techniques in an attempt to break down a person's psychological constitution to allow for deprogramming. Ironically, a lengthy obituary of Cameron (Braceland, 1967), a former President of the American Psychiatric Association, appears in the same volume as Cotter's study. The first of several unethical treatment lawsuits against Cameron's estate and the Allan Memorial Institute was launched several months before the printing of Cameron's obituary by one of his former colleagues, Dr. M.M. Morrow. Dr. Morrow launched the suit after suffering through 17 days of Cameron's experimental treatment. Despite the lawsuit, the obituary makes no mention of Cameron's CIA brainwashing studies, his work with the greatest negative impact on society and, no doubt, the work for which he will be best remembered. Related court actions based on Cameron's alleged gross disregard for the patients he exploited while trying to develop better brainwashing techniques continued into the 1990s. Nevertheless, his obituary only describes, "the softness, lovingness, warmth, and kindliness of this understanding man" (p. 861).

In Cameron's (1956) own description of his *psychic driving* technique (endlessly playing back a tapeloop of the patient's own words), the lovingness and warmth are less apparent. He fails to mention the source of funding—the CIA's Project M-K-Ultra—and describes one patient's treatment, a "minimum of 25 hours of psychic driving—with part of her thinking partially disorganized under LSD-25" (p. 506) as highly therapeutic. He also describes how other patients received treatments of "10 or 20 hours each day for 10 to 15 days" (pp. 503–504) while kept in sensory deprivation and injected with stimulant, depressant, and hallucinogenic drugs. Cameron compares the effects of this treatment on his patients to "the fire blizzard of World War II—when the hotter the conflagration grew under the rain of incendiary bombs, the more air poured in, and hence the more intense the conflagration" (p. 508).

Although he does not specifically mention the brainwashing application for which psychic driving was developed, he does suggest that its effects are analogous to "the breakdown of the individual under continuous interrogation" (p. 508). How many of Cameron's colleagues were aware of the true nature and intent of his work remains uncertain. One colleague comments in Cameron's obituary on how Cameron was viewed, saying, "professional men, psychiatrists, do not choose their leaders by whim. They knew him" (Braceland, 1967, p. 861).

Intrusive behavior management procedures and the use of incapacitating drugs have also been utilized to suppress noncompliant behavior that served as the only defenses of some individuals with disabilities against sexual abuse (Sobsey, 1990b). Even when such behavior does not result from abuse, it does serve some function for the individual, and suppression of the behavior will not solve the underlying problem. Although aversive procedures cannot be used against the will of adults without disabilities or against convicted criminals in most civilized countries, there are few controls concerning if or how it is applied with children or adults with mental retardation. Lutzker (1990) points out that "the data are not evident or sufficient in quantity to justify the use of aversive procedures with severely impaired individuals" (p. 500) and "there are not sufficient safeguards to suggest that mediators of aversive procedures would apply them in a conscientious, ethical manner" (p. 500). Nevertheless, these procedures continue to be used.

CONCLUSION

In summary, people with developmental disabilities have been blamed for a variety of social problems; denied lifesaving medical treatment and other necessities of life that would be given to their peers without disabilities; incarcerated against their will in overcrowded, unsafe, and unsanitary institutions; and forced into compliance with a variety of drugs and intrusive behavior procedures. Who does these things to them?

Surprisingly, the perpetrators of these acts do not identify themselves as enemies, nor does society label them as abusers. These are the acts of certain "caregivers" and "service providers" who typically identify themselves as friends to and advocates for people with disabilities. Like the walrus in *Through the Looking Glass* (Carroll, 1978), they appear to be painfully compassionate with their victims, yet still continue to victimize them. Society rewards them for their duplicity, honoring their compassionate intent while ignoring their destructive behavior. Like Alice, we focus on the apparent intent, and fail to comprehend the obvious outcomes of their actions (Heath, 1974).

Society has placed the care and protection of people with disabilities in the hands of such guardians and views them as being beyond reproach. In all probability, many perpetrators believe in what they are doing. Few mechanisms have been developed for protection against these well-intentioned guardians. After all, they are the experts who devote their lives to serving people with disabilities. They are the ones who profess their sympathy so eloquently and so publicly. Because they are beyond reproach, caregivers are given almost absolute power, and such power can only lead to abuse. To quote Acton: "Power corrupts and absolute power corrupts absolutely" (Acton, 1887, as cited in Bartlett, 1980, p. 615).

Because caregivers are seen as helping people with disabilities, they are allowed to do things that would not otherwise be permitted. For example, people who are convicted as criminals cannot be incarcerated indefinitely; are allowed to make an appeal and speak in their own defense; cannot have food, fluids, or required medical care withheld; and cannot be placed on aversive behavior management programs or given psychoactive medications against their will because these things violate their rights. People with disabilities do not receive the same protection, however, because they are thought to be "helped, not punished" by these interventions.

This chapter has not discussed acts typically treated as criminal offenses or perpetrators typically identified as criminals. This chapter is about so-called "friends of the disabled," often the people who win awards for years of outstanding service. Maréchal Villars, taking leave of Louis XIV, is quoted as saying, "Defend me from my friends; I can defend myself from my enemies" (Bartlett, 1980, p. 422). Villars, it appears, was not the only one who needed protection from such friends. C.S. Lewis (1970), provides a similar warning against such "humanitarians":

> They are not punishing, not inflicting, only healing. But do not let us be deceived by a name. To be taken without consent from my home and friends; to lose my liberty; to undergo all those assaults on my personality which modern psychotherapy knows how to deliver . . . who cares whether this is called punishment or not? (p. 290)

This chapter began by asking if overt and criminal abuse is a social aberration or a mere extension of prevailing social attitudes and actions toward people with disabilities. It presented examples of intervention that defy the establishment of meaningful boundaries between care and abuse. The conclusion is inescapable: overt abuse of people with disabilities is closely linked to the actions and attitudes that characterize society's overall response to abuse. Perhaps the most dangerous and difficult to control abuses are those that masquerade as intervention, and the most difficult offenders to suppress are those who pose as friends.

This discussion of abuse by some professionals and caregivers may seem self-righteous and may assume that the author is somehow exempt from this criticism. Although it may be easier to conceive of the world in such simplistic terms, simplistic conceptions of good and evil are inadequate. We are *all* products of our environment, and we are *all* influenced by the attitudes and beliefs in which we remain immersed.

To understand and to ultimately combat abuse, a model is required that includes the social attitudes and cultural beliefs that facilitate all forms of abuse of people with disabilities, and prevention strategies are needed to protect them from abuse in any form. Such a broad-based model is presented in Chapter 6.

6

An Integrated
Ecological Model
of Abuse

One essential goal of this book is to provide practical guidelines for abuse prevention. In order to work effectively, these guidelines must be based on a detailed model that is consistent with the nature and extent of abuse. The purpose of this chapter is to present that model.

Abuse of people with disabilities has occurred at many different times in a variety of places. The preceding chapters of this book have presented grim images, implying that various forms of abusive treatment have been the rule rather than the exception. The overwhelming prevalence of this type of abuse makes it impossible to limit its explanation by analyzing it in terms of a few aberrant offenders. By the same token, explanations that blame abused individuals for provoking or facilitating their own abuse are equally inadequate, and this kind of "blame-the-victim" mentality, along with society's willingness to accept it, can only be viewed as yet another form of devaluation and abuse of people with disabilities and other vulnerable people who are victimized. In addition, attempts to explain abuse of people with disabilities solely in terms of victim characteristics are contradicted by empirical research (Pillemer, 1985; Pillemer & Finkelhor, 1989; Sobsey, 1990c). Nevertheless, the characteristics of victims and offenders cannot be totally rejected when developing a model of abuse. The fact that people with disabilities are more likely to be abused than others implies that some real or perceived characteristic associated with disability acts either directly or indirectly to increase risk.

Chandler and Lubeck (1989) believe that child-focused views of jeopardy for child abuse are misleading and propose that a family-focused view is more appropriate. The observation that abuse and disability often coexist, they suggest, has been mistakenly interpreted as a demonstration of a direct link between the two. Although their suggestions are specific to children living with their families, they may easily be extended to other children or adults with disabilities and the particular social contexts that they inhabit. For example, some people with disabilities may be at risk because they live in institutions or with socially isolated families. The risk for abuse in these cases results from the social context, not from the disability. A narrow focus on disability can hide the real implicit dangers while encouraging unjustified preoccupation with the role of victim characteristics.

The fact that some offenders victimize a large number of people with disabilities and commit particularly brutal crimes suggests that offender characteristics cannot be entirely ignored. Gary Heidnik, the self-ordained minister who abducted, raped, tortured, and murdered a number of women in Philadelphia, provides a horrific example. Heidnik's ministry was exclusively directed toward people with disabilities who were also his most frequent victims. Englade (1988) quotes from a psychiatric report on Gary Heidnik that was presented to the court:

"He appears to be easily threatened by women who [m] he would consider to be equal to him either intellectually or emotionally" (p. 54).

"He impresses me as one who sees himself as superior to others, although apparently he must involve himself with those [he sees as] distinctly inferior to himself to reinforce this" (pp. 54–55).

"[He is] perhaps a greater danger to others in the community, especially those he perceives as being weak and dependent" (p. 55).

At the time these reports were written, Heidnik had already been apprehended for abducting and sexually assaulting a woman with severe disabilities. However, reports of that crime were filed years before he committed a series of abductions, tortures, sexual assaults, and murders involving many more victims with disabilities for which he was sentenced to death and 320 years in prison. The existence of such prototypical offenders makes it difficult to ignore offender traits, and the research demonstrates that personality profiles of caregivers have measurable, but limited, power in predicting caregiver abuse (Pillemer & Finkelhor, 1989).

The fact that some settings appear to be associated with increased risk while others appear to be safer (e.g., Rindfleisch & Rabb, 1984) suggests that context influences the interactions between potential offenders and potential victims. Therefore, environment must be considered along with offender and victim characteristics (Garbarino & Stocking, 1980). The integrated ecological model of abuse presented in this chapter provides a framework for understanding abuse as an interaction between individuals within a specific social unit that is part of a broader cultural context. However, before presenting this model, the section below considers the various models that have been developed by other researchers.

VARIOUS MODELS OF ABUSE

The Dependency–Stress Model

The traditional model used to explain higher risk for abuse of people with disabilities focused on family stress and dependency as illustrated in Figure 1. In this model, the disability of the individual is thought to increase his or her dependency on family caregivers beyond their limited resources for coping with these demands. The family caregivers are perceived as responding to this stressful situation with abuse, which at least temporarily reduces their stress. The model has been applied to the abuse of children with disabilities by family members (Friedrich & Boriskin, 1978, Herrenkohl & Herrenkohl, 1981; Mullins, 1986) and to the abuse of dependent elders by their children and other family members (e.g., Steinmetz, 1983).

The characteristics of the abused individual, particularly those associated with disability, are portrayed as being abuse provoking. The model suggests that reducing the dependency of people with disabili-

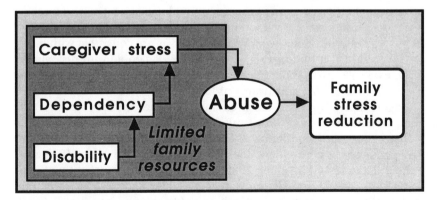

Figure 1. The dependency–stress model of abuse. This model assumes that abuse occurs as an outlet for increased family stress associated with the abused individual's disability and the family's limited resources.

ties on their families and increasing family coping resources will reduce the overall risk. For example, teaching children with disabilities to be more compliant with adult caregivers should reduce their risk for being abused because parental stress is thought to be increased by child noncompliance. Also according to this model, removing people with disabilities from their family homes and placing them in residential institutions should reduce risk because caregivers in institutional settings work with clients only a defined number of hours and are not restricted by limited resources.

The dependency–stress model is subject to several important criticisms. First, it can be viewed as blaming the victims for the actions of the people who offend against them. Victim-blaming theories are not restricted to abuse of people with disabilities. They reflect the rationale provided by abusers to justify their abuse. For example, one study (Dietrich, Berkowitz, Kadushin, & McGloin, 1990) reports that 62.5% of caregivers who abused children believed that their abusive actions were justified, and of these, 50.7% assigned the blame to the child. Many (41.1%) felt no remorse for their actions. In another example of victim blaming, it is possible that perhaps there may always be individuals who feel that women invite sexual assault by assuming certain dress and behavior or that minority groups provoke lynchings by demanding equal treatment. In fact, some people might apply the dependency–stress theory to spousal abuse, suggesting that the abuser is only responding to a particularly stressful spouse. Such explanations, however, have been widely refuted on both ethical and empirical grounds. Placing the blame on the victim is no more acceptable to explain abuse of people with disabilities than it is for any other social problem. The fact that the dependency–stress theory has been relatively unchallenged as an explanation for abuse of people with disabilities does not make it any less objectionable as a victim-blaming theory.

Second, the dependency–stress theory is not consistent with many of the empirical findings regarding abuse of people with disabilities. For example, stress should decrease when the number of caregivers increases because the constraints of limited family resources should no longer apply. However, research supports the contrary finding that placement in settings with multiple caregivers increases risk rather than reduces it (Rindfleisch & Rabb, 1984; Sullivan et al., 1987). The dependency level of elders does not predict risk for abuse (Pillemer, 1985; Pillemer & Finkelhor, 1989). The most dependent group of people with mental retardation have been shown to be less frequently abused than some of those identified as less dependent (Zirpoli, Snell, & Loyd, 1987). In fact, of people living in institutions, those with higher IQ scores and more adaptive behavior appear to be at somewhat greater risk for abuse than those with lower IQ scores and less adaptive behavior (Marchetti & McCartney, 1990). Minor deviations in development have been found to increase risk for abuse more than larger deviations that produce greater dependency (Starr, Dietrich, Fischhoff, Ceresnie, & Zweier, 1984). These and many other findings clearly contradict this model.

Third, research connecting disability, dependency, stress, and abuse does not provide a clear demonstration of these relationships. For example, Herrenkohl and Herrenkohl (1981) did find a positive association between parental stress and abuse; however, it is important to note that it was parental *perception* of stress that was measured. Green, Gaines, and Sandgrund (1974) point out that abusive parents often view their nondisabled children as deviant or defective and will justify their abuse with this imagined or exaggerated deviance. The perception of stress by abusive parents provides scant evidence for adopting this theory. Flynt and Wood (1989) found that the stress levels of mothers of children with mental retardation were a product of the mothers' characteristics, not of the children's characteristics. Similarly, Krauss (1993) found the stress levels of parents of children with disabilities to be below clinical levels (i.e., levels typically associated with any mental or physical symptoms) and found little correlation between the characteristics of children (including the severity of their disabilities) and the stress reported by their parents.

Undoubtedly, many parents of children with disabilities do experience stress related to their child's disability or behavior or to difficulties in obtaining services for their child (Stagg & Catron, 1986). However, parental stress is not unique to these parents, and the role of the child with disabilities in contributing to stress may be overemphasized. Schilling, Kirkham, and Schinke (1985) found that family stress levels were typically associated with financial worries unrelated to disability in families both with or without children with disabilities. Measures of parental stress often include a child scale as well as a parent scale, and items on the child scale bias the results to reflect stress if a child has a disability. For example, if a parent perceives the child as being different from other children or slower to learn, the parent is assumed to be more stressed, even if the parent is merely reporting objective reality. Thus, Cameron, Dobson, and Day (1991) found that "parents of children with delayed development experience high stress levels on the Parenting Stress Index (PSI) Child Domain" (p. 16) and go on to state that "stressors were related to particular attributes of the child" (p. 16). However, these parents exhibited no significant differences on any measure related solely to parental experience of stress; all quantitative differences were the result of presumptions made assuming that children with disabilities cause intensive stress for their parents.

Glidden (1993) points out that families of children with disabilities have been persistently misrepresented as dysfunctional "despite substantial methodological problems with research on which the belief is based" (p. 482). She points out that, as in the study by Cameron et al. (1991), these tests often use child characteristics as measures of parental stress or family dysfunction. Yet because many of these characteristics merely describe the child's disability they become both the independent and dependent variable, hopelessly confounding the results.

Although stress may indeed be a factor that contributes to abuse in at least some cases, methods of dealing with stress may prove to be better indicators of potential abuse, and more work is needed to explore this possibility. Research has shown that abusive parents have an increased physiological response to stress (both child and non–child-related) and this increased response can trigger abusive reactions (Casanova, Domanic, McCanne, & Milner, 1992). Dependency-related stress in the families of children with disabilities, however, must be considered to be an unsupported and largely disproven model for understanding the abuse of people with disabilities. As such, it has little potential value for guiding prevention efforts.

The Counter-Control Model

Figure 2 illustrates the counter-control model of abuse. In this model, individuals react to each other by reinforcing behavior that is pleasant and punishing behavior that is aversive. When each individual equally controls the consequences for the other's behavior, a healthy equilibrium is established between the two. To establish this equilibrium at an equitable level, each of the interacting parties must have equal command. Thus, when one exerts control, the other responds with an equal amount of counter-control.

However, when one of the individuals controls the vast majority of the consequences, the interaction becomes abusive. Once substantial inequities exist, the dominant individual can take away any control that still remains with the abused individual. The greater the inequity, the more severe the abuse is likely to become. For example, parents are typically bigger and stronger than their young children and have much better developed skills and resources for exercising control. As a result the potential for abuse of children exists. Sexual exploitation is also common in power inequities. For example, slaves were subjected to their masters' sexual whims as well as to physical assaults and exploitation of labor (Patterson, 1982)

Figure 2. The counter-control model of abuse. Interaction becomes abusive when power inequities affect the participants' abilities to have an equal amount of control over the consequences for the other's behavior.

Fortunately, exercise of consequences is not limited to individuals, and modern democratic societies, as well as other kinds of cultures, have developed many counter-control mechanisms to help minimize power inequities. Slavery is prohibited, and parents who use superior physical strength to dominate their children can provoke social consequences administered by the police and the legal system. Thus, at its best, law in a democratic society can be viewed as a complex set of counter-controls. In spite of the imperfections of such a system, in at least some cases, there can be little doubt that the potential for social consequences will restore the balance of power between interacting individuals. If abuse is to be prevented or eliminated, victims and potential victims must be empowered to exert equal counter-control against their abusers. If they cannot do this themselves, external mechanisms must be put in place.

This model recognizes the interactive nature of abuse and is consistent with both research and common knowledge. It suggests that it is the victim's lack of control over consequences, and not some inherent trait, that contributes to the problem. The counter-control model strongly conflicts with the dependency–stress model previously discussed. Whereas the dependency–stress model suggests that abuse is likely to occur as a result of noncompliance on the part of the abused individual, the counter-control model suggests that it is too much compliance that increases risk. This contradiction illustrates the importance of determining the most appropriate model before formulating prevention strategies, as these two models alone lead to conflicting prevention methods (i.e., teaching compliance vs. teaching assertiveness). According to Zantal-Weiner (1987), although many abusers justify their behavior by citing the defiance of their victims, more objective research fails to support this notion and suggests that too much compliance intensifies the problem.

The counter-control model does suggest some useful abuse prevention strategies. People with disabilities are vulnerable to abuse both as a direct result of their impairments, and as a result of disempowering actions on the part of caregivers and society as a whole. For example, impaired physical abilities reduce the potential for self-defense and may interfere with ability to contact others who might assist. Of equal importance, social decisions that disempower people with disabilities (e.g., teaching compliance) and give excess control to caregivers (e.g., the right of institutions to incarcerate people against their will) contribute as much or more to existing power imbalances. As such, this model is an improvement over the one previously discussed. The ecological models that follow include the basic elements of the counter-control model, but differ in their emphasis on the *context* in which abusive interactions occur. These models are viewed not simply as additional sources of counter-control, but as essential factors that can either facilitate or inhibit abuse.

The Social Learning Theory Model

A different perspective on abuse is provided by the social learning theory model illustrated in Figure 3. This model emphasizes the influence of modeled behavior on individuals. An individual who witnesses abusive interactions being rewarded is more likely to abuse others (Lorber, Felton, & Reid, 1984). Conversely, an individual who sees abusive interactions being punished is less likely to abuse. Similarly, witnessing nonabusive social behavior either being rewarded or punished can also influence the likelihood of abuse.

Figure 3a illustrates inhibited abuse and Figure 3b illustrates imitated abuse. For example, a child who sees an adult coerce another child with physical force is more likely to use force when interacting with other children. Bandura et al. (1963) conducted a classic experiment, in which they showed one group of children 5 minutes of filmed sequences of aggressive play behavior that was rewarded, while a second group viewed similar aggressive play behavior that was severely punished. A third group was shown vigorous but nonaggressive play behavior, and a control group was not exposed to any model. Following viewing, the children who saw the rewarded aggressive model exhibited the most aggression in their own play, children who saw the nonaggressive play and those shown no model exhibited less aggression, and those who saw the punished aggressive model demonstrated the least aggression in their own play. Exposure to aggressive models who are either punished or rewarded is seen as discouraging or encouraging aggression by the observer through a process of vicarious punishment or vicarious reinforcement. Three different, but related, processes have been identified that link the behavior of the model to that of the observer. First, *modeling* and *imitation* facilitate the learning

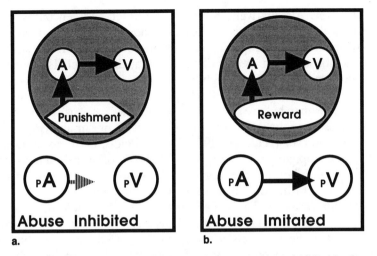

Figure 3. The social learning theory model of abuse. a. Abuse inhibited in observer. b. Abuse imitated by observer. (A = abuser, V = victim, pA = potential abuser, pV = potential victim.)

of new behavior through observation. The observer actually learns how to do something simply observing another's actions. Second, *inhibition* or *disinhibition* result from the observer vicariously experiencing either punishment or reinforcement of the behavior by directly witnessing or having knowledge of its consequences. Third, elicitation is the observer's performance of related responses after observation. These related responses are not direct imitations of the observed behavior and may not have previously been in the observer's repertoire; nevertheless, these responses are in the same general behavior class. For example, verbal aggressiveness in observers may increase after viewing physical violence.

Heisler (1974) showed that verbal threats of severe punishment without an actual model was ineffective in reducing inappropriate behavior and may have even increased it. However, the combination of severe threats with a punished model proved to be an effective deterrent. This finding has strong implications for training staff who may be presented with verbal or written information that conflicts with what they actually see happening on the job.

Although the basic social learning theory model is a simple one, its application is often complex. For example, an observer sees a film in which an aggressive individual abuses several victims. In the end, the hero (a previous victim) reluctantly confronts the abuser in combat and prevails. Force is ultimately overcome by force. Because the abuser is severely punished, this model could inhibit aggression on the part of the observer. Alternatively, however, the observer is encouraged to identify with the protagonist in the story whose aggression is portrayed as a justifiable and appropriate punishment for the abuser. Are aggression and abuse encouraged or discouraged by this model? Is it possible that the same observation might encourage violence in one observer and discourage it in another? Such questions are not easily answered. There is reason to believe that the perceived power, status, and physical characteristics of the aggressive model affect his or her ability to influence the observer (Feldman, 1977). Nevertheless, extreme caution is required in applying models using hostile forms of punishment to control aggression because the aggressive behavior could be encouraged and imitated, rather than discouraged and inhibited.

Manifestations of Social Learning Two particularly unfortunate manifestations of social learning appear in the *victim–offender* and the *multiple-victimization cycles*. In the victim–offender cycle, children who were abused become abusers of children as adults. In the multiple-victimization cycle, people who are abused assimilate the role of the victim and are more likely to find themselves repeating that role in the future. Evidence of these cycles appears in various studies of both adult offenders and victims who report high rates of abuse during their childhoods (e.g., McGregor & Dutton, 1991).

Of course, social learning does not provide the sole link between childhood victimization and adult violence. Robert Harris, who was executed in the California gas chamber in April 1992 for the murder of two 16-year-old boys, provides an example of the complex nature of such relationships. Harris and his parents were all alcoholics, and Harris showed some signs of *fetal alcohol syndrome* (fetal malformations that can have long-term effects resulting from *in utero* exposure to the mother's alcohol abuse). Before he was even born, he probably suffered damage from the beatings that his father gave his mother, including kicks to her stomach aimed at trying to end her pregnancy. He suffered convulsions and brain damage after his father knocked him unconscious at the age of two. This was not the first or last severe beating Harris experienced as a child, and he appeared to suffer from post-traumatic stress disorder as a result (Perske, 1991). Physical trauma, fetal alcohol syndrome, and posttraumatic stress disorder may all have contributed to Harris's violence, in addition to the effects of social learning. It is unlikely that anyone will ever be able to determine with any certainty how much any one of these contributed, but emerging information suggests that a combination of such factors is more dangerous than any one factor alone. Robert Harris's case is not unique. A study of 14 juveniles on death row in the United States reported that only two had IQs above 90, 12 had been severely physically abused, nine had major neurological impairments, seven had histories of psychological disorders that predated their offenses, and five had been sodomized by relatives (Lewis et al., 1988).

In the multiple-victimization cycle, people who have been victimized once are victimized again and again in seemingly unrelated situations. Although the underlying mechanisms of the multiple-victimization cycle are unclear, several factors may contribute. The initial victimization can lead to learned helplessness and damaged self-esteem that makes an individual more vulnerable to future abuse. Social mechanisms external to the victimized individual can also play a role. An individual who is victimized may become isolated, devalued, or blamed for the abuse, which can result in social conditions that lead to further victimization. As an obvious example, a child abused within his or her natural home will sometimes be removed to alternative care. Unfortunately, "protective care" alternatives, such as group home, foster care, or institutional residences, are often abusive environments (Chase, 1976). In some cases of sexual abuse of children and adolescents, *traumatic sexualization* can confuse the negative aspects of abuse with positive aspects of sexual arousal and thus interfere with the development of normal sexuality (Finkelhor & Browne, 1985). This too can contribute to the multiple-victimization cycle.

Implications The social learning theory model has at least two significant implications for the abuse of people with disabilities. First, some service environments may provide aggressive models who not only go unpunished, but are sometimes even rewarded for their abusive behavior. For example, new employees in an institutional setting might be placed with experienced employees for a period of orientation. The experienced employees who serve as models may provide aggressive or even abusive models for the new employees to imitate. In another example, a professional may use a shock wand to control the behavior of a resident in an institution as part of an "ethically approved" behavior management program. Other staff viewing this behavior may then become disinhibited in their own applications of aggression to control the behavior of clients. Cotter's (1967) reference to Lovaas's work using electric shock with children with autism as a rationale for his own alleged use of repeated and unmodified electroconvulsive shock therapy provides a clear example of the inherent danger of such models (see Chapter 5, p. 138). Aggressive models may play a role in disinhibiting a variety of other related forms of abusive punishment. For example, Frechette and Rimsza (1992) report on the increasing number of children who experience electrical burns and other injuries as a result of abusive punishment inflicted by stun guns. Gary Heidnik's punishment procedure for noncompliance consisted of placing several women chained together in a waist-deep pit of water while he applied electric wires to their chains. Eventually he killed one of the women whom he punished in this manner (Englade, 1988). We can only wonder at the models that he may have observed, or perhaps, personally experienced in the development of this technique.

Second, a significant portion of the violence experienced by people with disabilities is perpetrated by other people with disabilities (Sobsey & Doe, 1991). Many of these abusive individuals have been previous victims of abuse themselves, and some of their victims will probably become future abusers. In clustered settings where many people with disabilities are kept under crowded conditions, the victim–offender cycle and modeled aggression can develop chain reactions that make violence among residents a chronic problem. If this cycle is to be broken, effective intervention and support for both offenders and victims is required (e.g., Griffiths, Quinsey, & Hingsburger, 1989; Vogel, 1982). Furthermore, large clustered settings must be eliminated or controlled to reduce the proliferation of these cycles.

The social learning theory model of abuse, like the counter-control model, is consistent with research findings and is useful for guiding prevention efforts. Nevertheless, a complete model requires further consideration of the context in which abuse occurs.

The Ecological Model

Bronfenbrenner (1977, 1979) describes an ecological model of child development that considers the relationship of individuals within interactive dyads (e.g., parent–child dyads). These interactions are influenced by the context of the family within the broader context of the community and culture. Bronfenbrenner's model has greatly influenced contemporary concepts of child development. Previous models tended to view the child as being either ontogenetically programmed, with little consideration of environmental influences, or as being totally controlled by environmental stimuli. The ecological model provides a framework for incorporating both child characteristics and environmental factors. This model has become well-established, and it has been applied to many different facets of family dynamics. Shortly after Bronfenbrenner introduced this model, Belsky (1980) applied it to child maltreatment, emphasizing the interactive nature of factors at different levels. Figure 4 illustrates this model.

The ecological model of family systems portrays child development as children's accommodation to the immediate environments with which they directly interact. These interactions are inseparable from the overall influence of the interplay of all other systems de-

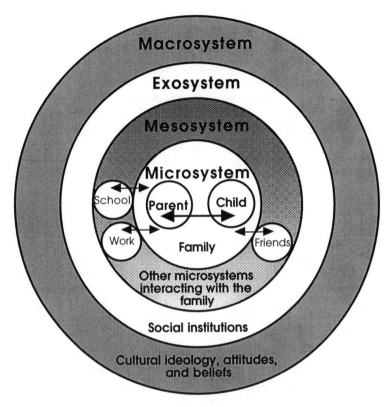

Figure 4. The ecological model of abuse. Family interactions are considered within the broader context of social influences, which can strongly affect the probability of abuse.

scribed within this model. Thus, parent–child relationships and inter-actions take place within the context of the family *microsystem* by which they are strongly influenced. For example, the relationship between a husband and wife may determine whether one or both parents will in-teract abusively with their child. The family is also strongly influenced by other microsystems in which family members participate. For exam-ple, a parent's workplace or social circle may influence that parent's attitudes, behaviors, and expectations within the family system. Taken together, all of the interacting social units that affect participating family members and consequently influence the family system are de-fined as the *mesosystem*. The *exosystem* is the surrounding set of environ-ments or social units that influence the family either directly or through other mesosystem components. Family members do not par-ticipate (or at most play only minimal roles) in these settings, but are nevertheless affected by them. For example, religious, educational, health care, social, and law enforcement agencies can influence family relationships and interactions. The *macrosystem*, the outermost layer of this model, is composed of cultural, ideological, and religious attitudes and beliefs that shape relationships and interactions within the inner exo-, meso-, and microsystems that are contained within the culture. For example, some cultures may expect little of children until they reach physical maturity, whereas other cultures may demand adult behavior at an early age; alternatively, some cultures might place more value on certain categories (e.g., first-born children, boys) than do others (Korbin, 1987). These cultural expectations are transmitted to parents and will influence interactions within the family.

Caudill and Frost (1975) demonstrated the influence of cultural attitudes on family interactions. In their study, they observed that as Japanese mothers were integrated into American culture, they began to behave toward their children more like American mothers. Just as outside environments can influence the family, the family can influence the outside environments, and all levels of the ecological model interact. Thus, cultural institutions, attitudes, and beliefs can also be affected, perhaps even altered, by the actions of individuals and families (Garbarino & Stocking, 1980).

Designed to explain the more general process of child development, and not necessarily to address abuse or the particular concerns of families with disabilities, this model can nevertheless be extremely useful for both of these applications. Seligman and Darling (1989) provide a good example of how this model could be applied to families of children with disabilities. They point out that families that include children with disabilities are not substantially different from other families. They share the same basic family systems and dynamics. Nevertheless, these systems and dynamics are affected on all levels of the ecological model by the presence of the disability. Direct interaction between the child and parents (microsystem) will be influenced by any increased needs of the child. Interactions with other families, friends, and acquaintances (mesosystem) will also be affected. Some families may withdraw from outside interactions; others may increase their social contacts. Interactions with schools, social services, and other community agencies (exosystem) are likely to change, particularly if the child is involved in or being considered for a special program. The influence of the cultural beliefs and attitudes toward the family (macrosystem) will also change; the family will be perceived differently because of cultural views of disability and related expectations.

The value of an ecological model for understanding abuse of children with disabilities can be understood by considering how the micro-, meso-, exo-, and macrosystems interact to increase or decrease the probability of abuse. Cultural attitudes place values on various characteristics of children. These values are likely to be internalized by parents who perceive their children differently because of these values. Various traits of children are associated with abuse, not because of an inherent relationship to abuse, but because of the culturally mediated devaluation of the child. For instance, some cultures have portrayed people with disabilities as menaces to society or even as devils (Judge, 1987; Wolfensberger, 1975). Such attitudes in the macrosystem can facilitate violence in the family. For example, parents who become frustrated with their child may exhibit aggressive responses, disinhibited by culturally influenced beliefs that it is the child's fault and that a less violent response would be futile. Other social units in the mesosystem (e.g., coworkers, neighbors) are more likely to accept or condone this response depending on whether they share the belief that the child is at fault. Even social agencies within the exosystem are less likely to protect the child because of this cultural devaluation, and they may even encourage the family to place the child in an institution, where the risk of abuse is likely to increase.

The ecological model allows us to understand abusive interactions and relationships within the context of the family, society, and culture. Individual characteristics and power inequities are viewed within the context of social systems that must be considered in order to fully understand abuse. This model mandates that prevention strategies respond to these interacting social systems, in addition to intervening at the individual level where the abuse directly occurs.

THE INTEGRATED ECOLOGICAL MODEL OF ABUSE

Figure 5 illustrates the integrated ecological model of abuse that is used throughout the rest of this book. This model is based on, remains strongly influenced by, and is consistent with Bronfenbrenner's ecological model, but differs in its focus by integrating elements from the counter-control and social learning theory models. Several modifications have been made. Because this model is being used for abuse prevention, greater emphasis is placed on the interactive relationship between a potential offender and a potential victim and the power inequities that may exist, develop, and grow in that relationship. As this model includes intrafamilial and extrafamilial abuse, the social unit that provides context for that relationship is referred to more generally as the environment, rather than as the family or microsystem. Interacting social units that would comprise a separate exo- and mesosystem in the previous model have been grouped together. When the basic social

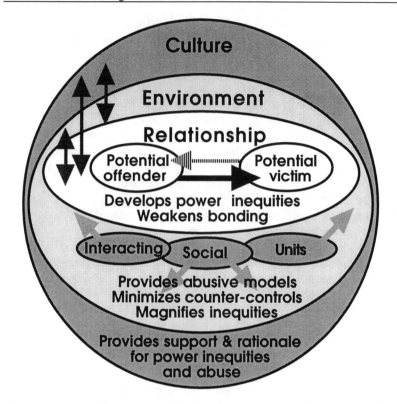

Figure 5. The integrated ecological model of abuse. Physical and psychological aspects of the interacting individuals are considered within the context of environmental and cultural factors.

unit is no longer assumed to be a family, and may change over time (e.g., when a child moves from a natural home to foster-care to group home), the distinction between those social units in which family members participate and those in which they do not becomes blurred. Cultural attitudes, beliefs, and ideology, specifically attitudes toward people with disabilities, remain important influences over all the remaining components of this model.

Integration and isolation are terms that describe the degree of interaction between the environment and other interacting social units. If a family or group home is well integrated into the community, it interacts frequently with neighbors, schools, and other social units who exert considerable influence. Although integration and interaction with other social units can occasionally contribute to increased risk due to exposure to abusive individuals or the abusive attitudes held in some subcultures, these situations are exceptional. A large body of research indicates that isolation from society increases risk and inclusion in society decreases it (Smith, 1984; see also Chapter 4, section on Isolation).

A related theory explores the power of the bond between a culture and a particular social unit. The more firmly an environment is embedded within a culture, the greater the power of the cultural beliefs and attitudes to influence behavior within that environment. For example, Ritchie and Ritchie (1981) found that child abuse was a rare occurrence within Polynesian families who were embedded in their native culture, but when these families moved away from Polynesian society, abuse was more frequent than within either the native or the adopted culture. They attributed this finding to the fact that these families were estranged from their native beliefs and attitudes that inhibited abuse, but were not sufficiently embedded in the new culture to be influenced by its abuse-inhibiting attitudes.

Attachment and bonding are related concepts that refer to the strength and durability of the relationship between individuals in a social unit. Attachment can be broadly defined as an ongoing and unique positive relationship between two individuals (Egeland & Vaughn, 1981). Bonding refers to the process through which attachments are developed. It has sometimes been associated with theories that require parent–child bonding to be formed during critical periods or events in order to ensure a healthy relationship (Egeland & Vaughn, 1981). Attachment often refers to children's attitudes and behaviors, whereas bonding is more commonly used to refer to the attitudes and behaviors of parents. However, the words are often used interchangeably, in that reciprocal bonding can be conceptualized as the process that creates mutual attachment.

Healthy attachment and bonding result in vicarious pleasure and pain; if one individual suffers, the attached individual suffers. Strong attachment between individuals encourages nurturing behavior and inhibits abuse (Smith, 1984). Child abuse leads to disruptions in the child's attachment to the abusive caregiver and subsequently to difficulties in the child's forming secure attachments with peers or with his or her own children when they are born (Youngblade & Pelsky, 1989). Thus, attachment theory, as well as social learning theory, can be used to explain the victim–offender cycle.

Attachment between parents and children with disabilities may be disrupted by a number of factors, and this disruption in attachment may increase risk for abuse (Blacher & Meyers, 1983). For example, many children with disabilities have intensive health care needs immediately after birth, and interventions to meet these needs an reduce the amount of contact between the infant and his or her parents, making attachment more difficult. Sadly, information given to parents by professionals at the time disability is diagnosed often implicitly or explicitly contains the message—"Don't get too attached to this child." In the most extreme case, parents may be advised to institutionalize their child.

Blacher and Bromley (1987) found that attachment is stronger between mothers and children with severe disabilities than between teachers and these children. Although this finding is not surprising, there are clear implications for children cared for by paid staff. When these children leave their homes and receive their care from paid caregivers, attachment is discouraged by rapid staff turnover and the rotating shifts, locations, and client responsibilities of the staff. Often paid caregivers are deliberately discouraged from becoming attached to clients by the ethic of professional detachment and the organizational needs of agencies that require staff and clients to be treated like interchangeable parts. The relatively weak bonds that formulate between staff and the people they serve cannot be expected to deter abuse to the same extent as the typically stronger bonds that occur within natural families.

Attachment disruptions may contribute both directly and indirectly to violence and other forms of abuse. Some social scientists suggest that "there is probably no more graphic example of the failure of adequate mother–infant bonding than physical abuse or neglect" (Egeland & Vaughn, 1981, p. 188). Others even propose that "failure to develop affectional bonds in human relationships is the primary cause of [all] human violence" (Prescott, 1990, p. 95). One study compared 56 fathers who committed incest with 54 nonabusive fathers and found that those who committed incest were not involved in the early nurturance of their children (Parker & Parker, 1986). Much remains to be learned about attachment and bonding, including their precise relationship to both disability and abuse, but what has been learned thus far suggests that these concepts may be vital in linking abuse and disability.

Applying the Model to Abuse of People with Disabilities

The integrated ecological model of abuse provides the structural framework for understanding the abuse of people with disabilities. Table 1 lists some of the factors associated with this model. Although the following section attempts to separate these factors and describe them in a linear sequence, it is important to remember their fundamentally dynamic and interactive nature.

Abused Individuals with Disabilities Some characteristics of abused individuals with disabilities can make them more vulnerable to physical and/or sexual abuse. Of course, not every individual with a

Table 1. Individual, environmental, and cultural aspects of the integrated ecological model of abuse

Potential victim	Potential offender	Environment	Culture
Impaired physical defenses	Need for control	Emphasizes control	Devalues victims
Impaired communicative functioning	Authoritarian	Attracts abusers	Objectifies victims
Lacks critical information	Low self-esteem	Isolated from society	Teaches compliance
Learned helplessness	Displaced aggression	Provides awarded models of aggression	Emphasizes vulnerabilities
Learned compliance	Exposed to abusive models	Covers up allegations	Disinhibits aggression
Undeveloped sense of personal space	Little attachment to victim	Many caregivers	Denies problems
Dependency	Devaluing attitudes	Transient caregivers	Discourages attachment
	Impulsive behavior	Dehumanizes potential victims	Discourages solutions
		Eliminates nonabusers	
		Clusters risks	
		Discourages attachment	

disability has all or even any of these attributes, which are not necessarily inherent traits of the individual or the disability. In fact, many of these characteristics result from the kind of treatment received by individuals with disabilities. Some of these attributes are as much or more the perceptions of others than real traits of the individuals to whom they are being attributed. Recent research and analysis suggest that caution must be exercised in ascribing too much weight to the characteristics of abuse victims as factors contributing to increased risk (Ammerman, 1991).

Limited Skills   Many people with disabilities have impairments that make it more difficult to protect themselves from abuse. Impairments in motor skills can make it harder to fight back against or impossible to escape from an aggressor, and can also interfere with communication skills necessary for seeking help. Cognitive and language impairments may also obstruct necessary communicative functions for seeking help and/or defending oneself verbally. Hearing and visual impairments may restrict the amount of information available to the individual, and as a result, they may lack information necessary for protecting themselves or seeking help. Several studies have demonstrated that overt aggression is suppressed when the potential target is believed to have the capacity for retaliation and released when there is no apparent capacity for retaliation (Feldman, 1977).

Learned Helplessness People with disabilities who exhibit inappro- priate behavior become vulnerable to abuse in several ways. For exam- ple, an individual may bite others or tip over furniture as a way of esca- ping from outside demands. The social control that this individual wants to exercise may be appropriate, but the means of attaining it are unacceptable. The inappropriate behavior may provide a rationale for abusive responses by caregivers, such as slapping this individual, and may also provide an alternative explanation for injuries that resulted from prior abuse. In addition, tranquilizers or even physical restraints may be used to control the behavior problem, incapacitating the indi- vidual's defenses and leaving him or her more vulnerable to abuse. Fi- nally, compliance training may be used as a means for controlling the inappropriate behavior (Luiselli, 1990). Learned compliance can also generalize to situations where compliance is not warranted and further decrease the individual's ability to fight against abuse.

Some of the attributes that make people with disabilities vulner- able to abuse are learned through individual experience and/or through specific programs. Learned helplessness and learned com- pliance are two closely related examples of these attributes, which have important implications for chronic abuse. Learned helplessness can be defined as the belief that one's actions have no influence on future out- comes or as a generalized lack of responding after previous attempts to exert control fail. Victims of abuse may respond initially by fighting back. If these efforts are successful at least some of the time, their resis- tance is reinforced. If, however, their attempts are futile, their resis- tance decreases and eventually ceases altogether.

Learned helplessness has two important applications to under- standing vulnerability of people with disabilities. First, learned help- lessness is seen in many victims of chronic abuse and increases their risk for future abuse (Kelley, 1986). Because many people with dis- abilities have already learned to tolerate chronic abuse with little or no resistance, they have become more vulnerable to the multiple- victimization cycle discussed in this chapter under manifestations of social learning. Second, learned helplessness is common in institutions and other environments that give people little decision-making power or control (Mercer, 1983); many people with disabilities live under these kinds of conditions.

Compliance training can aggravate learned helplessness. Com- pliance is considered by many to be a functional skill for people with disabilities primarily because it is useful for service providers who must manage them, not because it is useful for the individuals themselves. Sobsey and Varnhagen (1991) found that being too compliant was cited as a factor linking disability to sexual assault or sexual abuse in 24% of the cases they examined. Whereas people without disabilities in many Western societies tend to choose assertiveness training programs for themselves, people with disabilities continue to be forced into the opposite. The fact that they already have little or no decision-making power, as evidenced by the fact that they are placed in compliance training programs against their will, is ignored by service agencies demanding more control. Although it is true that many of these individuals exhibit some form of unacceptable behavior, that behavior often results from desperate attempts to exercise the last remaining bit of control that they have over their own lives. The elimination of unacceptable behavior without teaching any positive alternative obliterates these last attempts at self-empowerment, leaving them in a state of learned helplessness and extremely vulnerable to all forms of abuse (Sobsey & Mansell, 1990).

There are other educational outcomes that can increase vulnerability. For example, the emphasis on generalization across trainers in programs to teach people with disabilities suggests that their compliance should be generalized to whomever gives them instructions, including total strangers. While this kind of generalization serves the needs of service agencies who may need to place new staff in control of residential, vocational, learning, or leisure settings, it leaves those who have learned to generalize their compliance even more open to abuse. For example, children who have been taught to comply with every adult who gives them directions cannot be expected to defy a stranger who stops them on their way home from school and tells them to get into his car.

Physical prompting, when used appropriately, provides information and assistance to the learner. The teacher's and learner's movements should be coordinated. It does not involve the teacher's use of superior force to overcome the efforts of a resisting student. Excessive and inappropriate use of physical prompting can also contribute to vulnerability in at least two ways. First, physical prompting often involves physical coercion of a passive or resistant individual. If physical prompting is applied by forcefully overpowering the learner's attempts to resist until passive compliance is achieved, it subsequently teaches learned helplessness. Although this practice may not be perceived as abusive because of the practical intentions of the trainer and the socially valid educational goals of the program, this distinction is not likely to be clear to the learner. Second, as most children grow to adulthood, they develop a sense of personal space. In other words, they learn that other people should not touch or even get too close to them without their consent. This concept of personal space is important for the healthy development of a number of social skills, including skills that protect people from abuse. Failure to react to violations of personal space often signals potential offenders, particularly sexual offenders, that a victim is likely to comply with, rather than resist, abuse Therefore, failure to develop a sense of personal space leaves people exposed to greater danger that they will be chosen by an offender for victimization.

Dependency People with disabilities are likely to be more dependent on others, and the disability can contribute directly to this dependency. For example, some people with mental retardation may require a great deal of assistance and protection in many areas of their lives (e.g., Orelove & Sobsey, 1991). People with significant physical disabilities may require assistance to eat, dress, bathe, get from place to place, or any number of other daily living skills (e.g., Bigge, 1991). Successful education and rehabilitation programs should be aimed, at least in part, at reducing this dependency, but weaker programs may actually increase dependency. For example, people with disabilities may be taken out of the mainstream of community life and thus have no opportunity to learn independent community living skills. As a result, they often become more dependent on special services and programs.

Dependency creates the necessity for intensive interaction with caregivers, including some who may be abusive. As previously discussed, much of the abuse of people with disabilities is committed by their caregivers (Sobsey & Doe, 1991). Dependency on caregivers also creates or exaggerates already existing power inequities. When a caregiver becomes abusive, the person with a disability who is dependent on that caregiver may have little choice but to acquiesce. Many individuals with disabilities who have been victimized by abuse do not report it, for fear the report will cause disruptions in necessary services (Sobsey & Doe, 1991). For example, women with disabilities who are sexually abused often do not expose their abuse because reporting may lead to a breakdown in their community service alternatives, followed by institutionalization with its loss of freedom and risk of further abuse (Doucette, 1986). People with disabilities sometimes exhibit other traits, probably as a result of their life experiences, that make them vulnerable to abuse. These may include an inordinate desire to please authority figures, impaired judgment, and a lack of understanding of their rights (Perske, 1991).

Abusers of People with Disabilities Identifying offenders and potential offenders might provide one of the most effective methods for eliminating abuse; however, few details are known about those who abuse people with disabilities. Charges and convictions are rare, and systematic study of this group has not yet been carried out. Furthermore, the great variability in available information implies that the offender group is diverse and complex. Jones, Pickett, Oates, and Barbor (1987) describe 11 different patterns of various characteristics seen in abusive parents, and others could easily be added to the list. Yet, as few abusers fit precisely into any identifiable pattern and elements of several different patterns are present in many offenders (and to some degree in nonoffenders as well), it is difficult to define precise criteria. Nevertheless, some information is available that may be useful in forming a preliminary definition.

Offenders vary widely in age. For example, Sobsey and Doe (1991) reported an age range of 10–87 in their sample of perpetrators of sexual abuse and sexual assault against people with disabilities. Males appear more likely to abuse than females. Marchetti and McCartney (1909) reported that 62% of the confirmed cases of abuse (73% physical, 7% sexual, 20% other) in residential institutions for people with mental retardation were committed by male staff, although only 36% of the total staff were male. This suggests a rate of about three times higher for male offenders than for females. Sobsey and Doe (1991) found that in cases of sexual abuse and assault against people with disabilities, more than 90% of the perpetrators were male. However, McCartney and Marchetti (1990) report that 38% of their group of institutional abusers were females and Sobsey and Doe (1991) report almost 10% of their group of sexual abusers were female. Thus, the risk of abuse by female offenders is too large to be ignored. (For more information on the gender of offenders against people with disabilities, see Chapter 3, section on Gender.)

Abusers can be strangers (8%), casual acquaintances (15%), or generic service providers (10%), but they are more frequently natural family members (17%) or paid service providers (28%) (Sobsey & Doe, 1991; see also Chapter 3, Figure 2a). An additional 7% of sexual offenders against people with disabilities are other individuals with disabilities often brought in contact with the victims through segregated or clustered services. The remaining offenders are transportation providers (5%), foster-family members (4%), dates (4%), and step-family members (2%). More victims of sexual abuse or assault diagnosed with severe and profound mental retardation (49%) than victims labeled with milder categories of disability (22%) are abused by paid service providers (Sobsey, 1990a). (See Chapter 3, section on Offenders, for more on this breakdown.)

Need To Exercise Control   The frequency of abuse by caregivers raises troubling questions about how and why offenders enter caregiving professions. Preliminary information suggests that the process is not always random. For example, a number of cases have been recorded where known sex offenders or child abusers have selected careers providing "care" to people with disabilities (Sobsey & Mansell, 1990). In other cases, people who may not yet have committed offenses, but nevertheless display a pathological need for power and control, have selected caregiving professions. For example, in the spring of 1971. Gary Heidnik, responsible for the murder and torture of people with disabilities, said he was "visited by the Almighty. He told Heidnik to go back to Philadelphia and start a new church. Someone needed to care for the mentally and physically handicapped" (Englade, 1988, p. 41). During his earlier army career, Heidnik had applied for the military police and had become a medic and a licensed practical nurse, all career choices that gave him a degree of control over other human beings.

This need for control is not unique to offenders against people with disabilities. It has been noted in offenders against all categories of abuse victims. For example, Elbow (1977) categorized many wife batterers as "controllers," and Groth (1979) categorized many rapists as "power-oriented." The need to exercise power over those who appear to be especially vulnerable, as in the case of Gary Heidnik, also manifests itself in offenders against child victims. These kinds of offenders often lack self-esteem and fear confrontation with those they consider to be more able to defend themselves. Evidence suggests that frustration from difficulty in resolving conflicts with those whom these offenders perceive to be more powerful is redirected into aggression against those whom they perceive to be weaker (Feldman, 1977). Some offenders, especially those who are impulsive, may direct their displaced aggression at anyone, but others limit their violence to a specific category or class of victims (Monahan & Klassen, 1982). Stress from an external source, along with the availability of a vulnerable victim, may be the critical combination for such displaced-aggression offenders.

Exposure to Abusive Models Abusers have often been victims of abuse as children (Jones et al., 1987) or have been exposed to other abusive models, as discussed in the victim–offender cycle of abuse. Many seem to lack stable attachments and healthy relationships in their lives. Even if their other relationships appear normal, the relationship with the individual whom they abuse often lacks secure attachment and is characterized by rejection. Such parents and caregivers often attribute malevolent intent to their victims whom they view as provoking the abuse (Jones et al., 1987). These attitudes of rejection and blame are often mixed with devaluing attitudes toward the class of people they abuse (Megargee, 1982). Paradoxically, abusive parents and caregivers often set unrealistically high demands for their victims and are angered when these are not achieved (Jones et al., 1987).

Devaluing Attitudes   Megargee (1982) describes the role of values and attitudes in disinhibiting violence. Belief that violence is justified because "the victim provoked it" is common in a variety of criminal acts. He suggests that "inhibition can also be diminished by decreasing the empathy felt for the victim" (p. 155). Emphasizing the potential victim's differences rather than similarities is viewed as a typical method employed to achieve this lack of empathy. Megargee (1982) proposes that minimizing personal responsibility by exaggerating group responsibility and depersonalizing victims by conceptualizing group rather than individual identities also disinhibit violence. All of these have specific applications to abuse of people with disabilities.

Impulsive Behavior   Many abusers lack control over impulsive behavior, and this is sometimes associated with the use of alcohol or drugs or with brain damage. Studies suggest that alcohol is strongly associated with domestic violence. One study of offenders (Bradbury, 1983) reports 84% drank shortly before the violent episode, and almost 75% had been drinking within 30 minutes before the incident. The use of alcohol within family units has also been associated with high rates of incest, child abuse, and wife battering. One study of families with chronic alcohol problems identified an incest rate of 26% (O'Sullivan, 1989). Alcohol use has been identified as a causal factor in the offenses of 38% of abusing parents, 50% of rapists, 72% of robbers, and 86% of murders (Whitfield, 1990). Offenders who use alcohol and other disinhibiting drugs have been found to commit twice as many crimes against other people as those who use neither, and are significantly more likely to reoffend after being released from prison (Monahan, 1990). Several studies provide support for greater impulsiveness in offenders, although methodological concerns (e.g., greater impulsivity may increase the chances of getting caught rather than of offending) suggest the need for some caution in drawing a causal conclusion (Feldman, 1977).

Many studies have linked physical and sexual aggression to brain abnormalities. Abnormalities in the cerebral cortex in areas related to inhibition and impulse control have been most clearly identified, but limbic anomalies in areas that affect rage or sexual arousal have also been identified (Pontius, 1988). In a small minority of cases, the relationship appears to be direct. For example, Lehne (1986) reports a case of a man who developed an obsessive attraction to his daughter's breasts after sustaining a brain injury. Investigations that employ CAT scans of the brains or the regional cerebral blood flow of male sex offenders in psychiatric facilities suggest that these subjects have thinner and less dense skulls and lower blood flow values compared to controls (Hendricks, Fitzpatrick, Hartmann, Quaife, Stratbucker, & Graber, 1988).

Nevertheless, the frequency and extent of the role of brain abnormalities in most physical and sexual aggression remains controversial. Some have argued against the funding of further studies in this area because of the potential abuse of such findings to support racist doctrines linking violence to particular ethnic and racial groups or because of the possibility that focus on brain abnormalities might divert funding from important research regarding environmental factors (Pontius, 1988). Considering the distortions and misuse of other scientific work discussed previously in this book (e.g., intelligence testing, genetics), such concerns regarding the grave dangers of potential abuse of emerging information must be paid serious attention and great caution is necessary. People with developmental disabilities or emotional–behavioral disorders of any kind seem likely to be among those who would suffer from the misuse of such findings. Despite these concerns, suppression of knowledge has rarely, if ever, been a useful tool for protecting human rights, and efforts to halt this line of research when strong evidence is already emerging may only appear to give greater legitimacy to those who would use it for the worst purposes. Therefore, it is probably more appropriate to proceed cautiously and to advocate for the ethical use of this research rather than for its suppression.

In summary, there are a number of social, psychological, and demographic factors that are more common among offenders than in the general population. However, many offenders do not fit these patterns, and many individuals who exhibit some of these traits are not offenders. Environmental, cultural, and situational factors must be considered along with individual traits in considering the likelihood of an individual becoming either a potential offender or a potential victim. Even when these factors are taken into consideration, the prediction of future offenses is a quasi-scientific process, fraught with difficulties and full of potential for violating individual rights.

Interactions and Relationships   The previous information regarding people with disabilities who are abused and the people who abuse them tells a great deal about their interactions. People with disabilities who are victimized are often compliant and disempowered. The people who abuse them typically have a strong need to exercise control and are empowered to create dependency in their victims. The results of these dynamics are interactions marked by power inequities and relationships characterized by domination. Goffman (1961) described this type of relationship as inmate management through which those being managed are depersonalized and rigid, ritual-like practices are instituted by the managers. Although these procedures are generally for the convenience of institutional efficiency, they are often applied because they contribute to the underlying goals of depersonalization, social distancing, and control (King, Raynes, & Tizard, 1971). The power of institutions to "manage" people is well illustrated in descriptions of the employment of Soviet psychiatric facilities to (supposedly) care for Jewish refuseniks and political dissidents, while caregivers in American and Canadian mental hospitals conducted Central Intelligence Agency mind control research on their patients (Thomas, 1988). Institutions were chosen for these projects because they provide a greater degree of coercion and control than do prisons or any other contemporary setting.

The asymmetrical nature of caregiving relationships is not unique to institutional settings. Parents are often encouraged to implement behavior "management" programs, health care professionals "manage" children's conditions, and teachers learn classroom "management" strategies. In discussions of the laws of reinforcement and punishment, many people assume that it is the controllers who administer all the contingencies and the individual with a disability whose behavior must be modified. Counter-control, or the lack of it, has simply not been a subject for discussion (Sobsey, 1990a). Reciprocal interactions have received little attention in the professional literature despite the resulting secondary problem of *trainer dependency*. It can be argued that some degree of control is required to provide care and that complete equality between caregivers and those receiving services is unrealistic. Nevertheless, the inequities that characterize these relationships are so pronounced that undoubtedly very significant changes would have to take place before total equality could even begin to be achieved. Even if this degree of control were to be entirely justified, no amount of rationale can wipe out the fact that such huge power inequities inevitably invite abuse.

The extensive institutional use of drugs, physical restraints and intrusive behavior management techniques described in Chapter 5 leaves those who are managed defenseless against abuse. Relationships that emerge from such management and control functions are characterized by domination and dependency and not by secure attachment. Because attachment interferes with management functions and is incompatible with depersonalization, attachment is deliberately discouraged. Such actual or perceived social power inequities based on status, physical capabilities, age, or a number of other factors are "a crucial factor impinging upon the victim, affecting his or her behavior vis-a-vis a criminal adversary" (Claster & David, 1981, p. 185). If the inequity is so great that the victim does not resist the abuse, the perceived inequity is increased by the lack of consequences (or counter-controls) for the abuse, and future offenses become even more probable.

Environments   The role of different environments in facilitating or inhibiting abuse is a key issue for people with disabilities, but the importance of environment is not unique to offenses committed against this group of victims alone. Environments can bring together people who are likely to be offenders with people who are likely to be victims, and can create, enlarge, or minimize power inequities. Environments can provide models of prosocial or antisocial behavior. They can depersonalize and dehumanize potential victims and provide rationale to offenders. They can hide abuse and isolate victims from any source of relief. In these ways, and in many others, the physical and social characteristics of environments are key considerations in preventing crime.

Newman (1972) provides some guidance on *defensible space*, suggesting that small, stable communities are much safer than larger, transient environments. He suggests that many of the social mechanisms inherent in small communities that inhibited offenses are weakening with increased urbanization and mobility. Herbert (1982) discusses vulnerable environments that will attract criminals because they believe that relatively defenseless victims can be found in them, that crimes are unlikely to be reported, and that law enforcement efforts will be weak. Community-based crime prevention efforts attempt to build or restore the social structures that deter crime, while bringing social welfare, law enforcement, and criminal justice into the community (e.g., Trojanowicz, Trojanowicz, & Moss, 1975).

Westcott (1993) points out that "children who have disabilities are extra-vulnerable, since they are situated in locations not usually imposed on non-disabled children (p. 33). Environmental factors that facilitate or inhibit violence have particular relevance for people with disabilities because the general response to disability has often been to place the individual in a special environment, one that is particularly risky for abuse. Based on information already presented, less risk is associated with environments where there are small social units within a contained and stable population of caregivers. Depersonalized management should be minimized, and the environment should be well integrated into a community network. Demands for compliance should be minimized and counter-control should be clearly evident.

Environments that encourage abuse may develop a subculture of violence. Megargee (1982) describes this kind of environment as:

> a group committed to a violent lifestyle with supporting attitudes and values. This includes both normal people who learn that violence is ex-

pected of them in certain circumstances . . . and psychopaths who fail to develop adequate inhibitions against violent behavior because of disturbed developmental patterns. (p. 123)

This description fits some of the worst service environments for people with disabilities. The majority have learned that violence toward their victims is an unwritten job requirement. Mixed into the group are a minority of more seriously disturbed individuals who have found a home in a setting that provides them with an abundant supply of easy victims.

Violence within such a subculture not only achieves the acquisition of power and dominance for the aggressive individual, it also is required for acceptance of the offenders by their peers and for the maintenance of group solidarity. Once a subculture of violence has been established, the social system provides many rewarded models of aggression to teach new members to participate and uses coercion to eliminate individuals who fail to participate or who attempt to thwart some of the violence. It is not adequate for a member of such a subculture to remain passive and allow others to commit offenses. Members must actively participate in the violence or they will be perceived as a potential threat. They threaten the subculture not only because those who do not participate in the abuse can potentially report it, but also because they defy an essential belief of the subculture of violence that one must abuse to survive.

For such a subculture to survive within a broader culture that is less tolerant of violence, it must achieve some degree of isolation from the larger society. Physical isolation may be achieved through remote locations and locked doors. Social isolation can occur even in the absence of physical isolation when interaction between those in a service setting and members of the community is effectively discouraged. Organizational isolation separates members of the abusive subculture from potential agents of counter-control. For example, group home supervisors who spend much of their time out of the home at the main office doing paperwork provide little deterrence to abuse. Physical integration of residential services for people with disabilities within a community will not effectively deter abuse or the development of a violent subculture among staff unless interactions among staff, residents, and other members of the larger community take place freely and routinely both inside and outside the premises.

Culture and Value Systems Some of the attitudes that are commonly expressed toward people with disabilities include depersonalization, dehumanization, objectification, devaluation, blame, distancing, asexualization, disenfranchisement, imposed hopelessness, and emphasized vulnerabilities. Some of these attitudes are discussed in greater detail in Chapter 11, along with strategies for changing attitudes, but it is important here to consider how attitudes can contribute to the risk for abuse.

Williams (1976) reports studies suggesting that offenders received heavier sentences for committing crimes against more "respectable" victims than against those who were viewed as being less "respectable" and that sentences were less severe when crimes were committed against "unattractive" victims as opposed to "attractive" ones. She also points to research supporting the *just-world* theory that suggests that people view those who are easily victimized as deserving of their misfortune; therefore, the offender is seen as guilty of a less serious crime. Thus, attributes are ascribed to the victim and to the situation that support pre-existing concepts, values, attitudes, and beliefs that are transmitted by our culture. These influence the probability of the offense occurring, the choice of potential victims, the likelihood of intervention, and both the probability and the severity of consequences to the offender. Therefore, it is imperative to examine the concepts, values, attitudes, and beliefs relevant to disability to understand how they influence the probability of abuse (Denno & Cramer, 1976).

CONCLUSION

This chapter presented an integrated ecological model of abuse that helps to explain some of the myriad reasons why people with disabilities are likely to be victimized. Much of the vulnerability attributed to and experienced by people with disabilities appears to be a socially constructed phenomenon (Westcott, 1993). Thus, only a model grounded in social and cultural ecology can be expected to control that vulnerability. The integrated ecological model will serve as a basis for the prevention strategies in the chapters that follow.

II

PREVENTING ABUSE

7

Empowering Individuals To Resist Abuse

Section II of this book discusses methods of abuse prevention. Many different, yet interrelated, factors place people with disabilities at risk for abuse, and no single or simple approach to prevention would be sufficient. Violence and abuse are all too common in contemporary society and affect all of us; thus, it is not realistic to believe that total elimination of abuse can be achieved for people with disabilities. However, a substantial reduction in risk is a legitimate goal for comprehensive abuse prevention programs.

Because abuse occurs in the context of power inequities (see Chapter 6, section on Counter-Control), empowering vulnerable individuals is a logical approach to abuse prevention. Personal safety and child abuse prevention programs typically attempt to accomplish this empowerment through educational interventions, such as teaching individuals to avoid risky situations, know their rights, assert themselves, seek assistance, escape from an abuser, and/or defend themselves.

The word *empowerment* is a popular, but deceptive, term that implies relinquishing some of one's own power to someone more vulnerable than oneself. Although there has been a great deal of contemporary discussion of empowering people with disabilities and other individuals who experience power disadvantages, the discussion usually becomes vague when determining who is supposed to give up the power that these individuals are receiving (Sobsey, 1992). Often, service providers seem to want to empower people with disabilities to do all the things that the service providers think they should do, but not those things that might offend them. Such power is never truly given; rather, it is placed with the individual on a sort of conditional loan, payable on demand to those who exert real control over that individual's life. Some people argue that true empowerment can only be achieved when individuals empower themselves by taking power from others, with or without their consent. Thus, the use of the word *empowering* in the title of this chapter may be somewhat idealistic. Nevertheless, the concept of empowerment is essential to abuse prevention, and if the training strategies presented in this chapter cannot empower others, they can at least help others to empower themselves.

Training can and does help to prevent abuse, but it is important to recognize that many abused people with disabilities, as with other victims of abuse, face extreme power inequities that no amount of individual training can overcome. For example, it seems unlikely that learning personal safety skills could have helped the thousands of people with disabilities murdered at Hartheim Castle and Hadamar Hospital during the Nazi Third Reich (see Chapter 5). Furthermore, placing the exclusive responsibility for abuse prevention on those individuals who are likely to be victimized by requiring them to learn to resist abuse ignores the responsibility of the remainder of society for the problem. It also implies that the potential victims are themselves solely responsible for their own victimization. Therefore, training individuals to resist abuse must be accompanied by efforts to change the administrative, legal, social, and cultural conditions that foster abuse. This chapter focuses on training individuals to resist abuse, and subsequent chapters address the broader social and cultural contexts of abuse prevention.

The basic contents of abuse prevention education for people with disabilities are basically the same as they are for all members of society. There are several overlapping areas of curriculum. These include:

1. Personal safety skills training
2. Individual rights education
3. Assertiveness and self-esteem training
4. Communication skills training
5. Social skills training
6. Sex education
7. Self-defense training

Before discussing the things that *should* be taught, however, it may be useful to identify some things that *should not* be taught (Sobsey & Mansell, 1992). These are teaching practices that can produce *iatrogenic harm*, a term that refers to damage done by treatment. Although this term is borrowed from medicine, it is an important concept to consider in all human services because many efforts to improve other people's lives also have the potential to make them worse. Sometimes the most significant action we can take to make things better is to simply stop doing the things that make them worse. Concerns about iatrogenic harm in services for people with disabilities have been most clearly expressed in the philosophy of normalization, which assumes that treating people with disabilities in the same ways as others in society are treated is a more humane process that generally produces more desirable results (see Chapter 9, section on Normalizing Risks).

NORMALIZING EDUCATIONAL PRACTICES AND OUTCOMES

A hypothetical scenario:

A stranger entered the young woman's bedroom without knocking and approached her. This stranger was not the first to enter her room, there had been many others. She looked up blankly as the stranger approached and asked her to remove her shirt. Confused, she hesitated for a few seconds, but as the command was repeated she complied, slowly at first, then quickly and mechanically she did exactly as she was told. Realizing that she was under control, the stranger looked pleased. Just then, the door began to open and the young woman's caseworker entered the room yelling with enthusiasm, "She did it! She's completed every objective on her program plan, and she's demonstrated mastery by generalizing across three novel instructors." This was real cause for celebration.

The chilling similarities between modern special education and many actual scenarios of victimization sometimes go far beyond those suggested in the hypothetical situation described above. Students with disabilities must learn to *indiscriminately* do as they are told as part of their educational programs. If they fail to comply, they are given as much physical "assistance" as might be required to ensure that they do.

This criticism of special education is not a new observation. In 1972, Winnett and Winkler (1972) published their classic indictment of special education entitled "Current behavior modification in the classroom: Be still, be quiet, be docile." As the title implies, the authors found special education to be aimed at developing passive respondents who exerted no spontaneous control over themselves or others. Subsequent examinations continue to reveal problems with programs that encourage compliance to the demands of others, but fail to teach initiation, reinforcement, or other forms of social control (Orelove & Sobsey, 1991).

While a number of negative outcomes have been associated with these educational practices, little attention has been given to their effects on increasing vulnerability to abuse. Educational practices discussed below that increase vulnerability to abuse include the following:

1. Teaching too much compliance
2. Focusing on indiscriminate generalization across trainers

3. Overutilizing physical prompting
4. Teaching dysfunctional sexual behavior
5. Utilizing intrusive behavior management without identifying the function of the behavior being suppressed
6. Teaching age-inappropriate behavior

Compliance and Generalization Training

Compliance (following the directions given by another person) has been the dominant theme of special education. It is taught explicitly and implicitly through curricula that present a command as a stimulus condition for every objective (e.g., Luiselli, 1990). Of course, all students, not just those with disabilities, learn to follow instructions. However, students with disabilities, particularly those with mental retardation, have been subjected to more compliance training and aversive interventions to achieve compliance than any other group (Guess, Helmstetter, & Turnbull, 1987).

Compliance is generally recognized as a functional skill for people with disabilities (e.g., Luiselli, 1990), but some might argue that it serves an even greater purpose for their caregivers. For a skill to be functional to the individual who employs it, it must give its possessor at least some degree of power or control. Thus, compliance training is actually functional for the caregivers and agencies that manage and control the lives of people with disabilities, not for the individuals who receive it.

It might be argued that the emphasis on compliance in training people with developmental disabilities results as a reaction to an inherent tendency toward noncompliance among this group of children—but no such tendency has been demonstrated. Floyd and Phillippe (1993) found that observations of parent–child interactions indicated no significant differences in the rates of compliance between children with and without disabilities. Both groups of children in their study complied with about 80% of parental commands. Although the children with developmental disabilities did demonstrate higher rates of noncompliance than the children without disabilities, they also demonstrated higher rates of compliance. The reason that both of these rates were higher for this group is that the children with disabilities were given more than twice as many direct commands. This was not just a function of greater frequency of interaction in this group because the number of positive interactions between parents and their children with mental retardation was significantly lower than between parents and their children without disabilities.

While the authors of this study recognize that "high rates of parental commanding and directiveness are part of a process of coerciveness . . . that fails to attain control for the parent[s]" (p. 682) of children without disabilities, they suggest that:

> This is not the case in families of children with mental retardation. Instead, directiveness in these families is part of the teaching role filled by parents, and it is a role in which they excel, as evidenced by their highly "skillful" behavior management strategies, such as their more frequent use of clear commands and follow-up directives than the comparison parents. (Floyd & Phillippe, 1993, p. 682)

The positive view presented by these findings is not without merit, but any advantages gained by this style of caregiving must be weighed against its negative aspects. Any suggestion that children without disabilities need more acceptance and nurturing, whereas children with disabilities need more directive demands, should be carefully scrutinized from both ethical and educational perspectives. The fact that authoritarian parenting styles have been associated with both poor language development and greater risk for abuse (Mitchell, 1987) is among the reasons that this style of parenting should be of particular concern to readers of this book.

The generalization of compliance across instructors also primarily serves the needs of agencies. Children who grow up in their natural families should be taught to discriminate between the individuals whose instructions they must follow and those whom they need not obey. Institutional care with its rapidly changing paid caregivers, however, makes such discrimination impossible because a total stranger could be put in charge at any time. Thus, requiring generalization across trainers also serves a function for such agencies, and it is not surprising when mastery of objectives includes demonstration of compliance over three trainers, including at least one whom the student has never seen before. Through compliance training, people with disabilities are taught to obey whomever commands them and whatever command is given. This situation can obviously lead to their victimization.

Improving Practices   Training should be provided to help students understand when to comply and when to refuse the demands of others. They should be taught that no one has a right to hurt or abuse them. Noncompliance to unreasonable requests should be rewarded, not punished. Mixed messages should be avoided. For example, many parents teach their children that they have a right to refuse intimacy or touches that make them uncomfortable, but they are then forced to give relatives or friends of the family kisses in spite of the fact that these people are strangers to them or make them feel uncomfortable. Respecting children's right to be free of such touching, even when it is not objectively abusive, helps prepare them to resist abuse if and when it occurs.

Less emphasis must be placed on teaching compliance and more emphasis should be placed on discrimination of the appropriate and inappropriate conditions for following the instructions of others (Sobsey & Mansell, 1990). This might be accomplished in several ways:

1. Assess when and how much compliance is actually necessary.
2. Teach people appropriate ways to refuse to do things, and accept their refusal as legitimate whenever it is reasonable.
3. Teach students to distinguish when compliance is required and when they should assert their right to refuse.
4. Carefully examine curricula to determine if some of the objectives include unreasonable standards for compliance or for generalizing compliance indiscriminately.
5. Rationalize criteria that are associated with various objectives to levels of compliance that are reasonable for the content of the objective. It may be reasonable to expect near 100% compliance for some objectives with direct implications for health or safety (e.g., getting out of the road when cars are coming), but unreasonable to expect this level of compliance on other objectives (e.g., not talking to classmates during lessons), especially objectives where children without disabilities are not generally expected to meet the same standards.

Physical Prompting

Physical prompting and various forms of "hands-on" guidance are used extensively to teach students with disabilities who require higher levels of assistance to perform a variety of tasks. Because these students often lack the language skills required for verbal instruction and may also have difficulty imitating models, physical guidance is often seen as the best (or only) available alternative. Heavy emphasis on physical prompting, however, may be a poor solution for several reasons.

First, while physical prompting often produces rapid initial results, fading to independent functioning is often difficult and sometimes fails completely. Success under conditions of total guidance, however, often reflects more of the instructor's behavior than the student's. For example, in teaching color discrimination, a student may be told to "pick up the red sock" from an array of four socks of different colors. The student may not hear the direction and may not even look at the socks, yet the task is successfully completed through physical guidance. Under such prompted conditions, the student may appear to be demonstrating progress or even mastery, but in actuality, he or she has learned nothing.

Second, the power of modeling to teach students with severe disabilities has often been underestimated. In many cases, the same teachers who feel that learning appropriate behavior through modeling and imitation is beyond the limits of their students complain that these same students quickly learn inappropriate behavior from each other. This suggests that the problem is not related to a lack of the students' ability to imitate, but rather to a lack of meaningful reinforcement or some other failure in the method of instruction.

Third, physical prompting is not an age-appropriate method for teaching most skills to students (except perhaps very young children). Again, a professional double standard appears to operate. This double standard requires students with disabilities to learn to use behavior appropriate to their chronological age, but allows trainers to use intimate physical contact as a teaching method far beyond the age where it might be seen as acceptable with a student without disabilities.

Fourth, the extensive, age-inappropriate use of manual guidance and physical prompting makes it impossible for the student to develop a sense of his or her own personal space by constantly violating its limits. It leaves individuals exposed to it more vulnerable to both physical and sexual abuse because they have no sense of a right to control over their own bodies or of the space that surrounds them.

Improving Practices To ameliorate the deleterious effects of physical prompting, the following steps should be taken:

1. Minimize the use of physical prompting. When it is used, it should function to convey information through coordinated movement with a student, not to overpower a student who is resisting or to manipulate a student who remains totally passive. The distinction between coordinated and coercive physical prompts cannot always be visually observed; however, in most instances, the instructor carrying out the procedure can easily feel the difference.
2. Always ask students if it is acceptable before they are touched, and allow them to have the right to refuse (through their own words or actions) any time that they do not want to be touched.
3. Give careful consideration to the appropriateness of the prompting strategy to the task under instruction.

Physical prompting normally functions as a response prompt and is most useful in teaching new responses. Its use in teaching discrimination tasks is of questionable instructional value and other strategies should be given prior cosideration. For example, if an instructor is trying to teach someone to grasp an object who has not previously performed that task, response prompts may be very helpful. However, if that individual already knows how to grasp and the instructor is trying to bring the response under stimulus control (e.g., grasping the spoon when it is put on the table), response prompts are unlikely to help make that discrimination. Physical prompting is probably most effective when the student and teacher are working together and coordinating both of their movements. Under those circumstances, the student is trying to make the response and the teacher is providing some additional guidance or support. If, however, the student is resisting or remains totally passive, there is little chance that the response will actually be learned and understood.

Teaching Dysfunctional Sexual Behavior

It is unfortunate that many students, especially those with disabilities, go through school with little or no sex education; it is even more unfortunate that many others receive miseducation. Such miseducation is rarely intentional. Rather, miseducation is usually the result of misguided, well-intentioned attempts by poorly prepared teachers who feel uncomfortable about teaching sexuality. Sometimes miseducation occurs because of administrative decisions or inadequacies in the curriculum. Failure to correctly assess the student's perception of what is being learned further compounds the problem.

One typical example of this problem occurs when sex education is taught like a biology class. This "objective" approach to sexuality is inherent in many curricula, but also commonly develops because the teacher is uncomfortable with the topic. We have been well socialized in maintaining the privacy of our "private parts," and for most of us, the most private of our private parts is our emotions. Through practice and self-control the teacher may feel adequately prepared to objectively define such words as "penis" or "clitoris" to describe the mechanics of sexual intercourse, or to display photographs of various sexual interactions, but this teaching is often accomplished with incredible dispassion. Thus, the important social and emotional contexts of sexuality are often carefully withheld from sex education. Unfortunately, these are not only among the most enjoyable aspects of sexuality, they are also among the most essential ones.

Ironically, critics of contemporary society have often mourned the loss of love and romance in modern sexuality, yet sexuality is persistently taught in a manner devoid of its natural emotional content. This has potentially negative consequences for *every* student who undergoes emotionally neutral sex education; however, those with learning and developmental disabilities are the most vulnerable because they are the least likely to integrate this isolated learning content with their other life experiences. Thus, many people with disabilities are taught the objective anatomy and physiology of sexuality, but are never taught that sex can be a joyful or loving experience and that they have a right as human beings to expect it to be. If and when these students are later sexually exploited or assaulted, the experience is consistent with the objectified version of sexuality that they have been taught. If they later initiate sexually inappropriate behavior, this is the unfortunate outcome of learning sexuality outside of its social and emotional contexts.

This objectification of sexuality is probably the underlying cause of other more specific and extreme examples of dysfunctional sex education. Hingsburger (1990a) relates an example of a young man with a developmental disability who was taught that breasts, buttocks, penises, and vaginas were private parts. He was quite surprised to be arrested after putting his hand on the thigh of a young woman sitting next to him on the bus.

Other dysfunctional information in our sex education curricula may reflect dangerous attitudes. The author of this book recently reviewed a curriculum for people with developmental disabilities that included information such as *"when the man becomes excited,* his penis becomes hard, and *the woman's vagina becomes wet and slippery."* Whether this represented a mere error in grammatical construction or a more fundamental attitude problem is difficult to judge, but the harm to any student who might hear such a statement at face value is potentially fraught with immense consequences.

Improving Practices Misguided attempts at sex education can be worse than no sex education at all. Educational practices can be improved in several ways:

1. Ensure that the instructor feels comfortable and competent before providing instruction.
2. Be certain that sex education includes discussions of the emotional and social aspects of sexuality, not just instruction on the anatomy and mechanics of sexuality.
3. Review curricula carefully to eliminate incorrect or misleading information.
4. Always ask students what they have learned following the class. Be prepared to make revisions if they have not learned what was intended.
5. Individualize instruction based on students' current situations and past experiences. Individuals who are already sexually active often still need formal sex education. As these individuals already possess an experiential base for learning, education can sometimes proceed more quickly.

Intrusive Behavior Management

The suppression of the challenging behavior of individuals with disabilities through the use of drugs or aversive intervention has also contributed to their abuse. As discussed in Chapter 5, these procedures are viewed as abusive in themselves by some people with disabilities and their advocates; they can also leave the individuals who experience these treatments more vulnerable to other forms of abuse. All behavior serves some function for the individual, and challenging behavior often fills a critical function for the person who exhibits it (Sobsey, 1990a). Often these individuals either lack a more appropriate form of behavior to achieve the same function, or they do not use the more appropriate behavior because it is ignored (Donnellan, Mirenda, Mesaros, & Fassbender, 1984). For example, an individual may indicate that he or she wants to stay home from work by simply not going or by saying "no," and staff may respond by ignoring this preference and leading the person to the bus. However, when the same individual has a violent and self-destructive tantrum, he or she may be kept at home. Thus, the individual learns that the only way to exercise control is through catastrophic behavior. Suppressing such behavior through drugs or intrusive behavior management programs simply strips the individual of any remaining control and causes the individual to develop a state of learned helplessness.

Suppressing "inappropriate behavior" that allows an individual to avoid or escape from abuse results in two interrelated problems—one is immediate, the other cumulative. The immediate problem is that the individuals are deprived of the opportunity to protect themselves from the immediate harm. The cumulative problem is that these individuals learn that self-protection is futile, and they gradually abandon any natural or previously learned defenses in their repertoire.

The learned helplessness that develops as a result of this kind of treatment eventually eliminates any innate ability to escape from or resist abuse. Learning that it is futile to resist, these individuals become passive even in the face of violence or other forms of abuse. In extreme cases, they fail to show any signs of distress and may appear to be willing victims.

Improving Practices   Whenever possible avoid intrusive behavior management practices. Always make an attempt to understand what has caused the unacceptable or challenging behavior and the function that the unaccepted behavior has for the individual. Once the actual function of the behavior is understood, the following is recommended:

1. If the behavior is associated with pain or a health problem, attempt to cure the pain or problem before trying to suppress the behavior.
2. If the behavior is associated with a history of previous emotional trauma, consider evaluating the individual for post-traumatic stress disorder (Ryan, 1992).

3. If the behavior serves a legitimate social or communicative function for the individual, try to teach a more acceptable behavior that will serve the same purpose (Evans, 1990).

For example, if an individual screams, attacks others, or injures himself or herself in order to get attention or escape from the demands of a specific task, he or she might be taught to communicate those needs through speech, graphic symbols, or gestures. This training can only be effective if those in contact with the individual understand and respect the appropriate communication.

Although inappropriate behavior is not necessarily a result of abuse, it can sometimes be an indicator of abuse. Therefore, when this type of behavior occurs, and especially when it has a sudden onset, the possibility of abuse should be carefully evaluated. Sometimes behavioral outbursts take place in response to specific environmental stimuli that trigger disassociative reactions (Ryan, 1992). For example, whenever one 8-year-old boy saw cotton candy he would scream and run away in such great fear that he often fell or ran into things. This behavior developed in response to an incident in which his hand was held against the hot metal part of a cotton candy machine and burned as a punishment for not waiting his turn in line. When such dissociative triggers can be identified, they may provide clues to past trauma. In some cases, individuals can be gradually desensitized to the stimuli that elicit such responses, but suppression of the behavior through coercion will only aggravate the trauma itself.

Teaching Age-Inappropriate Social Behavior

Although considerable attention has been given to the need for teaching age-appropriate skills to people with developmental disabilities, the principle is often poorly applied to social skills. The following real-life example may help illustrate this point. Several consultants had been called in to develop sophisticated behavior management plans for an adolescent boy who persisted in grabbing women's breasts whenever they entered his special education classroom. None of the plans were successful. When he did the same thing to a woman in the supermarket one day, she punched him. His mother tried to prevent this by yelling, "Don't hit him; he's retarded," but the woman simply replied, "I don't care." From that moment, he never was seen to carry out this behavior again.

Readers should not misinterpret this example as a plea for corporal punishment, especially as some of the sophisticated programs that failed included strong aversive stimuli. It does, however, illustrate the power of normal expectations and logical consequences. This adolescent's inappropriate behavior developed because many of the caregivers who worked with him failed to have normal expectations and to exercise natural consequences for his behavior. The woman in the supermarket didn't care about his mental retardation and simply responded to his behavior as she would have if anyone else had acted as he did. She simply exercised normal social expectations and applied natural consequences. Those few moments in the community taught something that a half dozen structured programs in his segregated special education classroom had failed to teach him.

As children with disabilities grow into young adults, they must learn appropriate behavior for their age. Although the behavior in this example was blatantly inappropriate for any age, many people with disabilities are encouraged to act in more subtly inappropriate ways that might be appropriate for younger children. For example, they may display affection in ways that are inappropriate to their social relationships (e.g., it is typically acceptable for a young woman to give her brother a casual goodbye hug, but typically unacceptable for her to give the same kind of hug to her teacher). Often this kind of mildly inappropriate behavior will be tolerated in people with developmental disabilities by those who pass it off as harmless social immaturity. This kind of behavior, however, is not harmless because it increases the individual's risk of victimization by others who see the behavior as a sign of vulnerability or who interpret any show of affection as sexual seduction.

Improving Practices   Normalize social expectations for the ages, settings, and relationships of the individuals involved. Encourage appropriate demonstrations of affection, but observe carefully for those that may be inappropriate or likely to increase the risk of exploitation and shape them into more acceptable behavior. Two approaches may be used to accomplish these objectives.

In the first approach, inclusion and community-based instruction are used as powerful teaching tools. Attempting to teach people social behavior in artificial and segregated environments is like trying to teach them to swim on dry land. Full inclusion in a variety of age-appropriate social environments and activities with only the degree of intervention and support that is actually needed is enough to achieve the normalization of social behavior for many students. Ecological assessment, conducted with the student in the actual environment, can determine where support and intervention are needed. As the student becomes more independent, support can be withdrawn.

The second approach utilizes structured training to help normalize social behavior. Such structured instruction cannot take the place of inclusion or community-based instruction, but it can be a useful addition. Although they must be tailored to address the specific needs of individual students, there are some useful programs for teaching these concepts. The Circles program, for instance, uses a visual model of concentric circles to help teach the concept of varying degrees of social distance (Champagne & Walker-Hirsch, 1982). Students are taught to place people that they know in the appropriate circles and to recognize the kinds of social interactions that are acceptable in each. The program also includes videotapes featuring a young woman who describes her relationships with various people in her life, placing each person with whom she relates in a specific circle as the tape shows the appropriate interactions for that particular circle.

The Circles program can be used in conjunction with community-based instruction. A trainer who accompanies the student in various community activities can observe for appropriate and inappropriate interactions. A minimal prompt, such as, "Remember your circles," can be used if behavior becomes mildly inappropriate. More intrusive intervention should be avoided when in the community, unless the behavior is so inappropriate as to create some immediate danger. If necessary, later, in private, roleplaying can be used to act out some of the community interactions and to work on improving responses.

Page (1991) suggests four major areas of information that must be addressed in teaching self-regulation of social and sexual behavior to people with developmental disabilities:

1. The individual must understand his or her own abilities and limits.
2. The individual must learn the requirements of his or her current situations.
3. The individual must select and carry out appropriate responses to each situation.
4. The individual must monitor and evaluate his or her own responses.

Programs such as Circles concentrate on the first three issues. Community-based instruction where friends and other trusted significant others are recruited to provide additional feedback will help the individual with self-monitoring. For example, until self-regulation is fully achieved, double dating or other group activities that include friends who will provide input and assistance can be helpful. As the individual becomes more independent in self-monitoring his or her behavior, the external feedback can be gradually decreased.

BUILDING RISK-REDUCTION CURRICULA

The first section of this chapter discussed educational content to be avoided or improved upon if necessary. This section discusses educational options to be included in programs for students with developmental disabilities. Unfortunately, no conclusive research is available that can supply empirically validated content or methods that should be included in risk-reduction programs. It is hoped that future research will help to clarify current information and beliefs. The information presented here, however, is based on the following: 1) a review of the literature currently available regarding risk-management programs for people with disabilities, 2) current practices in risk-reduction programs for individuals without disabilities, 3) the integrated ecological model described in Chapter 6, and 4) our own survey of experts on abuse and disability (Sobsey, Mansell, & Wells, 1991). In this study, over 100 experts, including police and researchers, as well as people with disabilities, family members, and other caregivers indicated how they ranked the importance of various abuse prevention program components. Although this chapter does not attempt to present full curricula or instructional programs for each of these areas, some further sources of information are suggested to assist those interested in design and implementation of these programs.

Principles for Risk-Reduction Programs

Before presenting specific content areas, eight general principles that should be applied to each area of risk-management must be considered:

1. Individualizing content and instructional delivery
2. Providing activity-based instruction
3. Ensuring ecological validity
4. Coordinating team efforts
5. Facilitating active participation
6. Accepting and encouraging reasonable risks
7. Drawing on a variety of resources and techniques
8. Assessing progress and revising programs

Individualizing Content and Instruction   No single teaching program or approach will prove best for all students. This is true for students without disabilities, but it is particularly true for students with disabilities who exhibit a broad range of abilities and learning styles, and who are typically less adaptable to methods that are not directly suited to them. Because they are less likely to adapt to fit programs, programs must be adapted to fit them. This does not mean that unique curriculum content and instructional designs must be constructed for each student; predesigned programs can provide a good starting point. However, teachers and administrators must be prepared to modify them to meet the students' individual needs.

Providing Activity-Based Instruction   Teaching as much as possible within the context of natural activities has been suggested as an approach that improves generalization of skills and maximizes learning (Orelove & Sobsey, 1991). This does not mean that all skills can be taught completely within the realm of natural activities; some are difficult or even dangerous to teach entirely in this manner. Nevertheless, there are many opportunities where this teaching style would be appropriate. For example, some aspects of sex education, such as learning to label different body parts, can be combined with learning to bathe, shower, and dress. Areas of personal safety skills instruction, such as learning situations and places to avoid or where to go for help, are easily combined with community travel instruction.

Ensuring Ecological Validity   Individualization of risk-reduction programs must consider the environment as well as the student. For example, the skills needed to minimize risk of abuse are as substantially different for students who live with natural families, or in group homes or institutions, as they are for students who live in inner city or rural settings. Thus, learning how to react differently to strangers as opposed to immediate family members is valuable in family settings, but these distinctions are often meaningless in institutional settings that are staffed by constantly changing and often unfamiliar shift workers. Learning not to give strangers too much personal information on the telephone is useful at home, but may be irrelevant in institutional settings where only staff are permitted to answer the telephone. Knowing how to avoid or resist aggression by other residents is a necessary skill in most institutional settings, but is less frequently required in home settings. It is also important that the demands and expectations of caregivers in various environments are reasonably consistent. For example, in school a child may be taught that hitting is always wrong, but at home some kinds of hitting may be tolerated. To avoid situations like this, families should be involved in planning and implementation, so that some consistency in the expectations of the student can be reached.

Coordinating Team Efforts   Coordinated team efforts are important in every area of education for people with significant disabilities (e.g., Sobsey & Orelove, 1991). They are particularly important in risk-reduction education and are of increasing importance for individuals whose disabilities are of greater severity. Failure to coordinate team efforts often results in confused or conflicting messages about personal safety. For example, a student may be taught to be more assertive in a personal safety-skills class, but then also taught to be more compliant through a behavior management program provided by a different consultant.

Students with disabilities who require a great deal of assistance generally need more support in coordination of programs because they often have more programs and caregivers to deal with than children who require less assistance. These students are also typically less able to sort out or identify the areas of confusion. A coordinator should be assigned to each student who will take primary responsibility for ensuring that program components fit together. The coordinator may be a parent, teacher, other professional, or advocate. Students expected to develop independence as adults should be increasingly involved with coordinating their own programs as they approach adulthood.

Facilitating Active Participation Efforts to protect people with disabilities from abuse sometimes mistakenly isolate them from society. This has at least two major problems. First, because social isolation is associated with increased risk for abuse (Smith, 1984), trying to protect people with disabilities by isolating them is likely to increase risk. Second, by confining people with disabilities in institutions or other agencies where they will have little contact with the rest of society, these efforts often restrict the rights and opportunities of the individuals whom they are intended to protect. Therefore, protection through isolation can become a form of abuse in itself. Full and active participation in community social networks reduces risk for abuse (e.g., Meier, 1978; Smith, 1984) and should be implicit or explicit goals of educational risk-reduction programs.

Accepting and Encouraging Reasonable Risks Although one goal of educational programs should be risk reduction, no program can ensure perfect safety, and unwillingness to accept reasonable risks is often counter-productive. Risk-management must be a process of accepting reasonable and legitimate risks, while also attempting to control the overall level of risk. For example, a child with a disability who is included in a general classroom in an elementary school will probably encounter some teasing and perhaps even some physical aggression from classmates. In fact, virtually all children with and without disabilities encounter some teasing and physical aggression from their elementary school peers. Expecting special immunity for children with disabilities is probably unrealistic. Therefore, this risk should be considered normal; our goal should not be to eliminate it, but simply to teach children how to respond in an appropriate manner. Teaching them to tolerate the normal behavior of others and to recognize and respond to such mild forms of aggression may actually help prepare them to react self-protectively should they encounter more serious forms of mistreatment later in life.

Drawing on a Variety of Resources and Techniques Although community-based training and incidental learning methods are absolutely necessary for some of the social learning goals essential to risk reduction, an eclectic approach to risk reduction is an absolute requirement. Nevertheless, the infrequency of certain natural learning opportunities, along with some of the associated risks, makes it impossible to teach all of these skills in their natural contexts. Thus, simulation, vicarious learning through stories or audiovisual materials, and a variety of other formats for instructional delivery need to be included in the educational program. For many teaching objectives and for many students, generic personal safety materials designed without regard for disability are valuable educational resources, but for most students with disabilities additional instruction and support will be necessary, and some of the materials will require modification. For others, programs specifically designed for students with disabilities will be the best resources.

Many curricula have worthwhile components that are well suited to a wide range of students, but all curricula also appear to have some areas of weakness. Group instruction is ideal for many objectives related to personal safety because it allows for discussion, and participants often learn as much from each other as they do from the instructor. Groups involving people with a full spectrum of abilities often work well. Some students, however, need individualized instruction on specific objectives. Thus, no simple rules make one program or approach the best for every student, every content area, or every situation. Good programs have to be eclectic in order to take advantage of the best available tools for each objective and to individualize them for each student.

Assessing Progress and Revising Programs Clear-cut goals and objectives and the periodic assessment of progress are essential to all risk-reduction programs. Formative assessment, evaluation that occurs regularly as part of instruction and helps to guide the instructional process, is particularly crucial because the objectives are often complex, and the instructor may find that what the student is learning is actually something different than the intended educational goal. This situation typically requires a revision of the objective or instructional procedure to ensure that the proper goal is achieved.

Specific assessment strategies must be individualized to the student, situation, and objective. Many social skills can be assessed through direct observation in natural environments and situations. Knowledge of program content can be evaluated through gestural, iconic, or verbal communicative responses to questions; however, knowing the program content does not necessarily ensure that this knowledge will be applied to potentially abusive situations. Role-play situations can also be used as a method of program assessment. In using role playing to teach or assess personal safety skills, instructors must be cautious because creating threatening simulations could frighten some students; create greater confusion regarding the discrimination of abusive behavior, as some offenders may use similar role-playing interactions to mask their own abuse; and could even result in allegations against the trainer. For example, if a trainer threatens a child or asks a child to participate in sexual activity as part of a role-playing situation, the trainer's behavior could be reported to law enforcement or child protection agencies as abuse. This situation may result from well-intended efforts to assess the child's response or from an abusive trainer attempting to mask his or her offenses behind training.

Role playing of potentially abusive situations should be used only when:

1. The student clearly understands the difference between simulated and real-life interactions.
2. The student feels comfortable with role playing such situations.
3. The role playing is part of a well-documented and approved program.
4. The role playing is adequately supervised.
5. The student understands that he or she should not act out similar interactions with others.
6. The instructor is carefully selected and well-trained.

Social and subjective validation based on parents', teachers', and others' perceptions of the student's behavior are useful components for assessing maintenance and generalization of learned social skills to situations where the instructor is not present.

Content Areas for Risk-Reduction Programs

All of the program components listed in this section could be included under the heading of personal safety skills, but most have been grouped under other more specific headings. This is because most of the goals of risk-reduction programs are also important for reasons other than their potential role in abuse prevention. For example, enhancing communication skills is important to reducing the risk of abuse, yet communication skills are also necessary for a multitude of other reasons. They improve the quality of life, form the basis of social interaction, allow people to learn faster, contribute to better health care, and serve a variety of other valuable functions. They are also very useful in the other areas of risk-reduction curriculum described here. For example, communication skills allow people to assert their personal rights and are fundamental to healthy sexuality. In fact, all of the curricular areas described here overlap and interact in a variety of ways. They are divided into separate components largely for convenience, and those designated as personal safety skills are included under that heading because personal safety is typically the primary reason for including them in the curriculum.

Personal Safety Skills Training As used here, personal safety skills refer to those patterns of behavior that are intended to reduce an individual's risk for abuse, exploitation, and violence. Students are taught how to avoid situations of excessive risk or to respond to identified risks in a manner likely to restore safety. Many of the training materials that address personal safety focus on preventing sexual assault or sexual abuse and are particularly designed to control risks associated with strangers. These are certainly important aspects of personal safety, but they are not the only important aspects. One study of abuse of people with disabilities, for example, found that although 37% of the cases involved sexual abuse or sexual assault, about 29% involved physical violence and abuse, and the remaining 34% involved psychological abuse, neglect, theft of property, and a variety of other offenses (Brooks & Gowers, 1993). In addition, many studies of abuse and assault of people with and without disabilities have shown that only about 10% of these crimes is committed by strangers. (See Chapter 3, Figure 2a, this volume, for more on this topic.)

O'Day (1983) provides a good example of sexual abuse prevention curricula for students with hearing or visual impairments, physical disabilities, and developmental disabilities. Each curriculum contains lessons that cover vocabulary, types of touching, myths and facts about sexual abuse, acquaintance rape, what to do if victimized, reactions and feelings of victims, personal safety, and assertiveness. Some variations are made depending upon the group being addressed.

The Assault Prevention Training (APT) program (Crossmaker, 1986) teaches a variety of personal safety skills. Although this program is particularly suited to people with developmental disabilities living in institutions or other group care settings, it can also be easily used with those living in other settings. Participants learn how to get help, assert their rights, yell, and escape. Specific training deals with prevention of abuse by family members and other caregivers in positions of authority.

Toward a Better Tomorrow (Medicine Hat Regional Association for the Mentally Handicapped, 1993) is a personal safety skills curriculum that addresses physical, sexual, emotional, financial, and material abuse, but focuses on general training to recognize abuse, to say "no," to avoid or escape abuse, and to seek assistance. It also includes information for families and caregivers to help them recognize and respond effectively to abuse. Lesson plans include specific goals, training materials, and activities. While these curricula are not comprehensive, they do provide a good starting place for designing programs.

Individualization of personal safety skills training is required based on the student's age, gender, current abilities, level of independence, activities, identified risks, possible previous history of victimization, and a number of other factors. Families should usually be involved in the training of children (Comfort, 1985), but team involvement is desirable for students of all ages.

Individual Rights Education   The right to be free from abuse seems so fundamental that it is assumed that everyone knows that they have this right. This is not the case. People generally believe what their experience has taught them, and many people with disabilities must learn that they have rights before they can exercise those rights. The inability to recognize one's rights does not typically appear to result from a disability, but rather from a lack of the kinds of experiences that are necessary in order to learn about them. Many people with disabilities need to be specifically trained about their rights as individuals and such training can only be meaningful to those who are given the opportunities and encouragement to exercise them. Teaching people in the classroom to identify or list their rights while denying them opportunities to practice them may be worse than not teaching them at all because this will encourage them to view their rights as rhetoric, not reality.

Although basic human rights remain the same regardless of geographic and political boundaries, some specific rights and how they are protected may differ according to the laws of different jurisdictions. Therefore, people need education in general human rights as well as in their specific rights as a citizen of a particular nation, state, or province. Good materials from one jurisdiction may still be of use in developing programs in another; however, some care must be taken to ensure that modifications are made to conform to local laws. For example, one excellent Canadian resource for teaching adolescents and adults with developmental disabilities about their rights (Felske & Barnes, 1992) discusses the Universal Declaration of Human Rights, The Canadian Bill of Rights, The Canadian Charter of Rights and Freedoms, and The Individual's Rights Protection Act of Alberta. Some modification is necessary for students in other provinces and states, but much of the content of the training manual and audiotape (for nonreaders) would apply in most Canadian states and provinces, as well as in many other democratic countries.

The United States Constitution, The Canadian Charter of Rights and Freedoms, or other similar documents make excellent curricula when teachers are prepared to simplify the language and provide examples that indicate how students can apply what they have learned to their own lives. The United Nations Convention on the Rights of the

Child (1989) also provides powerful principles, although it is often difficult to understand how a child might compel others to recognize these rights. Nevertheless, where other more specific protections are not available, the provisions of this document provide a sound context for understanding the rights of children. For instance, Part 1, Article 2, requires every nation to take measures to protect all children against all forms of discrimination on the basis of disability and a variety of other attributes. Under Article 6, all nations must ensure every child's right to survival and identity. Under Article 23, children with disabilities have a right to care, education, and services provided "in a manner conducive to the child's achieving the fullest possible social integration and individual development" (p. 7). Under Articles 34, 35, and 36, sexual and other forms of exploitation are forbidden. Under Article 37, "[n]o child shall be subjected to torture or other cruel, inhuman or degrading treatment or punishment" (p. 11). Many of these provisions have implications for at least some children with disabilities.

There are some educational materials that deal with specific rights or categories of rights. One example, *The Right to Control What Happens to Your Body* (MacFadden, 1991), addresses sexual and reproductive rights in some interesting ways. For example, it includes a "Choice or Abuse" game that is similar to "Chutes and Ladders." All of the materials discussed above can be useful in designing programs to teach people with disabilities their rights and to encourage them to exercise these rights. Of course, responding positively in support of students' attempts to assert their rights is a necessary concurrent condition to any individual rights curriculum.

Assertiveness and Self-Esteem Training   While assertiveness and positive self-esteem are partially independent traits that have been associated with reducing risk for abuse, they are also closely interrelated. For the individual with low self-esteem, assertiveness is often difficult or impossible. When people who lack adequate self-esteem try to assert themselves, their attempts are often somewhat ineffective, either because they lack the necessary confidence to be truly assertive or because their uncertainty results in overly aggressive and negative attempts at self-assertion that could result in retaliation. Therefore, self-esteem and assertiveness are often best addressed at the same time. Positive and successful assertiveness helps to build self-esteem; healthy self-esteem serves as a foundation for attempts at assertiveness and improves their chances for success.

Self-esteem is related to abuse in a number of ways. Low self-esteem appears to be a typical characteristic of both victims of abuse and their offenders (Green et al., 1974). In fact, it may be one of the factors that is most characteristic of abusing families and helps to perpetuate violence and neglect by increasing the probability that victims of abuse will go on to abuse others. Fryer, Kraizer, and Miyoshi (1987) attempted to measure actual effects of abuse prevention training by creating covert simulations in which children were asked to leave the building with a stranger. They correlated results with other program evaluation data and found that higher self-esteem was one of the best predictors of less vulnerable responses to the simulation procedure.

Self-esteem cannot be taught solely through a series of instructional objectives. Although some specific activities can help students to understand their feelings about themselves and to build a positive self-concept, this is better developed through a multitude of interactions with others. When most of our interactions are characterized by acceptance and encouragement, we tend to build positive self-esteem and to gain confidence in our own abilities. When most of our interactions are characterized by rejection and emphasis on our failures, we tend to develop poor self-esteem and to doubt our ability to succeed. People with developmental disabilities often have difficulty developing positive self-concepts, but there is little evidence that this problem results from their disability. It is much more likely to result from the types of parenting and teaching that they encounter. Overly directive caregivers making unrealistic demands, expecting failures, and responding predominantly with negative feedback are likely to produce poor self-esteem in any child. Children with disabilities are particularly likely to experience these kinds of interactions (Floyd & Phillippe, 1993).

The following list of suggestions for parents and caregivers may be useful toward developing interactions that build children's self-esteem:

1. Begin early. It is much easier to develop self-esteem in young children than to repair damaged self-esteem in older children and adults.
2. Support and encourage the development of affectionate bonds between yourself and the child.
3. Whenever possible, encourage learning through reinforcement and minimize the use of punishment.
4. Accept each individual for who he or she is. Avoid focusing on the things that he or she cannot do.
5. Do everything possible to build your own self-esteem. We need to feel good about ourselves before we can help others to do the same.
6. Interact with the child. Avoid domination.
7. When correction is necessary, focus on building the desired behavior and not overly much on eliminating problems.
8. Arrange for the child to have opportunities for success.

9. If things go wrong, seek solutions, not someone to blame.
10. Do at least some things just because they are fun. Encourage your children to do the same.
11. Seek out the people who make you feel good about yourself and your family.
12. Celebrate the positive things in life. If they are rare, that is even more reason to celebrate them.

Hingsburger's (1990b) book on self-concept and people with disabilities provides an excellent discussion of self-esteem. It includes a number of practical suggestions for families and other caregivers, along with some powerful stories that illustrate his major points. Although the book itself is not intended to serve as a curriculum, it is extremely useful to those developing programs to help build self-esteem.

Assertiveness training is intended to increase an individual's expression of his or her personal choices and to encourage affirmation of his or her own decisions in spite of the influence of others. Self-esteem appears to be an important precondition for appropriate assertiveness. People with low self-esteem may have difficulty being assertive or become overly and inappropriately aggressive in their attempts to assert themselves.

Craft and Hitching (1989) discussed the critical need for assertiveness training for individuals with developmental disabilities as an integral part of efforts to reduce their risk for sexual abuse or exploitation. They make some general and specific suggestions for developing programs to address these issues. Crossmaker (1986) also provides useful curriculum materials for teaching assertiveness along with other assault prevention content. Her materials are particularly useful in training individuals to resist coercion by others who are in a position of authority.

People with developmental disabilities can be taught to be more assertive. Bregman (1984), for example, described a successful assertiveness training program that was used to train 128 participants from 4 rehabilitation centers for people with developmental disabilities. The participants became more assertive and also perceived themselves as having more control over their own lives. Methods of teaching assertiveness included focused instruction, modeling, behavior rehearsal, and feedback.

Learning to be assertive goes beyond simply learning how to stand up for one's rights. It is also about learning the appropriate and inappropriate times for asserting one's choices in a manner suitable to a particular situation. These are sophisticated skills and are often best taught through role playing and incidental teaching. Of course, providing instruction in assertiveness can not be expected to be effective unless the students' real life experiences allow for successful applications of these skills.

Communication Skills Training Communication skills are closely related to assertiveness and many of the other components of instruction addressed in this chapter. If students cannot communicate, they cannot assert their rights. If their communication is severely impaired, they will appear more vulnerable to offenders and are more likely to be selected as potential victims (Sobsey & Mansell, 1990). If they are in situations of actual or potential victimization, they will be less able to request assistance and therefore less able to escape. Behavior problems associated with communication deficits may provide a rationale for maltreatment. In addition, students with limited communication will be more difficult to teach other aspects of risk reduction, further compounding their risk.

Thus, communication skills are fundamental to virtually every aspect of risk management. Because communication training is a large and complex topic that has been well addressed in many other books and articles (e.g., Reichle, York, & Sigafoos, 1991; Warren & Reichle, 1992), this book does not cover the broader issues of communication training. However, some of the more specific issues pertinent to communication and abuse are addressed in Chapter 10, which discusses legal issues relevant to prosecution of complaints of abuse.

Three issues regarding training in communication skills as they relate to abuse prevention do require some mention. First, it is essential that communication be taught in a manner that encourages initiation, not just response, by the individual with a disability. Second, many behavior problems exhibited by people with disabilities can be best improved through communication training that teaches the individual exhibiting the inappropriate behavior a more effective way to express his or her needs, making more intrusive interventions unnecessary, and teaching valuable skills at the same time. Third, people with disabilities must be taught to consequate the behavior of others, and reinforcement is a particularly important form of consequence for them to learn to use.

Many authors have criticized the typical communication training programs for people with disabilities that encourage passive responses and discourage spontaneous initiations. For example, Cirrin and Rowland (1985) found that students with disabilities had low rates of initiation and high rates of dependence on others for interaction. This may explain why many individuals with disabilities do not report that they are in situations of potential or active abuse unless they are specifically asked. This can also be a problem when disclosure of abuse by an individual is necessary to prosecute the case. If the individual depends on direct questioning to communicate and gives little information spontaneously, the disclosure may be invalidated because the interviewer could be seen as leading the individual making the disclosure. Currently recommended teaching practices suggest a variety of stimulation methods to encourage children with disabilities to initiate communication, but a limited use of questions and other related response demands, as these tend to develop greater dependency (e.g., Yoder, Davies, & Bishop, 1992).

Understanding the Pragmatics of Communication   The recognition that behavior problems can often be symptoms of communication deficits received much attention in the 1980s and research on this subject continues to emerge. This line of research in linking the pragmatic functions of communication to challenging behavior has proven useful both for identifying nonintrusive methods for dealing with difficult behavior and for its value in helping to determine important areas of communication for teaching (e.g., Steege, Wacker, Berg, Cigrand, & Cooper, 1989). Where the employment of these and other related methods of nonaversive behavior management can make more intrusive methods unnecessary, they reduce the risk for abuse through inappropriate and excessive aversive intervention, while allowing the student to develop more effective ways to communicate. Dyer (1993) provides a good review of these methods that includes a number of additional resources for those who wish to learn more.

The pragmatics of communication are not only relevant to individuals with disabilities who have developed challenging behavior patterns, and communication skills should be taught before these problems develop. The increasing emphasis on teaching people with disabilities socially functional communication skills has moved the major emphasis of communication training away from mass trial instruction in the classroom to functional activities in a variety of natural environments. This development has been extremely helpful for producing communication of greater functional value. Thus, the emphasis in communication has shifted from semantics (meaning) and syntax (structure) to the pragmatics (social functions) of communication.

Reinforcement and Punishment   Pragmatic analyses of basic communication used by educators or communication and language therapists generally include such functions as getting others' attention, making requests for material needs or information, and labeling objects and events. Some of the lists used by researchers covering the pragmatic functions of communication are long and detailed, and there is no universally accepted list of categories. Certain important functions, however, seem to be ignored by most researchers and clinicians. These categories are reinforcement and punishment (Orelove & Sobsey, 1991). Reinforcement and punishment are responses to the behavior of others. Ironically, experts in communication have placed great emphasis on the use of reinforcement and punishment as functions used by parents, therapists, and teachers, but not as functions to be taught to or used by students with disabilities. Yet these communication functions could very well be the most important social functions that any human being can learn and are of even greater importance to those people who are more dependent upon others.

It is difficult to identify exactly why these language functions have been neglected; most likely it represents the continuing influence of *misapplied behavior analysis*, that is, the attempt to move operant conditioning from the laboratory to the real world without recognizing the inherent differences in rules. In the laboratory, the experimenter exercises imperial power over the subjects being studied. This power to control every aspect of the environment (also known as experimental control) meant that only the experimenter was allowed access to reinforcers and punishers. Rats, pigeons, and other experimental subjects were only to be the recipients of food pellets, electric shock, and other consequences; they were certainly not expected or allowed to administer these consequences to the experimenter. Unfortunately, this artificial distribution of power was mistakenly transferred from the laboratory into instructional and therapeutic programs for human beings.

There are many reasons why learning to consequate others' behavior is fundamental to abuse prevention. Obviously, if someone is being abusive, some form of punishing consequence is needed to make the person stop. This may be particularly important in the early development of abusive behavior when even subtle consequences may be adequate to stop the abuse and when easy acquiescence can lead to an escalation of the abusive behavior, making it harder to stop the behavior later on. Reinforcement may be even more important to preventing abuse. Making it pleasant for those who treat an individual well to continue this interaction helps to form protective bonds and to keep that individual in situations where abuse is less likely to occur. For example, if a parent receives reinforcement for providing good care to the child, he or she is more likely to continue as primary caregiver and less likely to seek caregiving alternatives that are often associated with greater risk. People learn to consequate behavior from the consequences others provide to them. This natural training should begin early. Caregivers should model the use of appropriate consequences for children, and also respond to the consequences that children give them. Clear and enthusiastic responses to smiles, frowns, and other subtle consequences help to encourage and strengthen children's consequating behavior. The ability to consequate others' behavior is an essential precondition for assertiveness, exercising personal rights, the development of more advanced social skills, and all forms of self-defense.

Social Skills Training   Teaching social skills is another large area that goes well beyond what can be covered in this chapter. Nevertheless, the importance of good social skills needs to be emphasized. Learning these skills improves the prospects for fully inclusive living and learning environments where the risk of abuse is lower. These skills can also help reduce the perceptions of others that the individual is "deviant" and thereby somehow deserving of abuse. Social skills also help to build friendships and other positive relationships that provide a degree of protection against abuse. In addition to reducing the student's risk of being victimized, learning appropriate social skills reduces the risk of the student victimizing others. Conversely, learning socially appropriate behavior is one of the primary methods of intervention for offenders (e.g., Griffiths, Hingsburger, & Christian, 1985), and successful treatment of offenders helps to prevent future abuse (see Chapter 12 for a fuller discussion) and may also help to reduce the risk of offenders being victimized by others.

Social skills develop best in natural and supportive environments through naturally occurring interactions; however, specific training can also be effective. Foxx and McMorrow (1985), for example, used games to teach social skills to adults with mental retardation. Not only did improvement take place, but testing 6–8 months later in natural environments indicated that these students had maintained their original levels of skill acquisition and, in some cases, even surpassed them.

Sex education and social skills training are often taught as parts of the same curricula or activities. Bellamy, Clark, Hamre-Nietupski, and Williams (1977) provided one of the first such programs for students with severe disabilities and many others have followed. Of course, some areas of sex education are more appropriately combined with other areas of risk-reduction curricula, and some areas of social skills training have little to do with sexuality. Nevertheless, combining areas of the curricula that do overlap provides an ideal format for addressing certain risk-reduction goals.

Developing friendships is a particular area of social skills that can be of great value in reducing the risk for abuse. People who lack the support of friends are vulnerable to abuse because they are often lonely and isolated. As a result of this isolation, they may enter into relationships of risk, exploitation, or clear abuse simply because it seems preferable to being alone. Few clear guidelines exist on effective ways of facilitating the development of friendships, but the topic is receiving increasing attention. Uditsky (1993) provides an interesting discussion on how friendships can be facilitated that emphasizes natural approaches. He suggests that creating the conditions under which friendships would naturally develop is generally more desirable than artificial interventions that can create volunteer–caregiver relationships that rarely become real friendships.

Sex Education   As indicated in Chapter 3, sexual abuse of children with mental retardation and developmental disabilities and sexual assault of adults with mental retardation are common events; these offenses are among the most common forms of abuse of people with disabilities. Sex education is essential for reducing the risk of sexual abuse (e.g., Monat-Haller, 1992; Sobsey & Mansell, 1990). It reduces risk in several ways. First, knowing and understanding about sex is essential to recognizing sexual abuse. Second, unless people understand the concept of sexual interactions, they cannot make informed choices about whether or not to participate in them. Third, those who are not taught about sexuality in a positive manner often learn about it through exploitation and abuse. Fourth, as people with developmental disabilities reach adulthood, they should be allowed and encouraged to participate in healthy sexual relationships. Those who participate will be less isolated and therefore less vulnerable to abuse.

Since the 1970s, many materials have been published that are useful in guiding program development (e.g., Craft & Craft, 1978; Gordon, 1979; Johnson, 1975; Kempton, 1975), but no standard curriculum or training materials should be expected to meet the needs of all students. Sex education programs must be individualized to fit the abilities, backgrounds, and situations that characterize the students. Trained sex educators and counselors can and should play a valuable role as part of service planning teams. Unfortunately, the value of expertise in this area is often overlooked, and it is sometimes assumed that anyone who has ever been sexually active (and sometimes those who have never been sexually active) is prepared to plan and deliver quality sex education programs. The American Association of Sex Educators, Counselors and Therapists (AASECT) certifies trained professionals, and certified educators and counselors are ideally suited for this work (Monat-Haller, 1992), although teachers, social workers, and counselors who have received training in this area would also be preferable. Many times, family members or program staff are drafted for the job and find themselves in the difficult position of either accepting a responsibility for which they feel ill-prepared or refusing, in which case this important task might go undone or be taken on by someone even less prepared or suited for the job than themselves. Those who are assigned the role of sex educator have a responsibility and a right to seek and demand assistance if they have any uncertainties about their abilities to carry out the job.

Anyone undertaking sex education or sexuality counseling with people with disabilities should take time to consider their own attitudes and biases relevant to sexuality, gender issues, people with disabilities, and other related topics. If there is discomfort discussing such topics, this must be resolved before it is transmitted to students. Two kinds of inhibition may interfere with providing effective sex education programs. The first kind (as mentioned earlier in this chapter) results from years of learning that sex is a private matter and not a subject for public discussion. This can usually be overcome through desensitizing oneself by discussing sexuality with others until the inhibition diminishes to a more comfortable level. In fact, it is probably better if this inhibition is not completely eradicated. The educator should be free enough to discuss sexuality comfortably, but should always convey that sexuality is a private matter to be discussed only with certain people and under certain conditions. The sex educator who conveys no trace of inhibition when discussing sexuality may be modeling behavior that is socially unacceptable. Students who imitate this lack of inhibition in front of unappreciative audiences might be considered offensive and be punished for this behavior. Group instruction should generally be conducted in private small-group settings (Hingsburger, 1990a). Usually gender-specific groups are desirable as these are more suited to the social conventions of privacy.

The second kind of inhibition experienced by some potential sex educators may be related to deeper discomfort with sexuality or some other aspect of the program. For example, a potential sex educator may have her or his own anger about previous sexual abuse or have negative attitudes toward people with disabilities. The exact area of discomfort may be difficult to identify or to change. Until such feelings are resolved, an individual who experiences them might not be a good candidate for this job. Some individuals might benefit from counseling to help them work through such feelings. Others may be able to resolve their feelings through group activities. Staff training has been shown to produce positive changes in attitudes (Sumarah, Maksym, & Goudge, 1988). Brown and Craft's *Working with the Unthinkable* (1992) provides some structured activities to help educators and counselors identify their own feelings about such topics.

Sex education for people with disabilities must be explicit. Verbal content needs to be in simple language suited to students' vocabularies and learning styles, and visual aids (e.g., pictures, videotapes, books, dolls) are also essential (Monat-Haller, 1992). Figure 1 illustrates an example of the use of explicit verbal content and visual aids from the

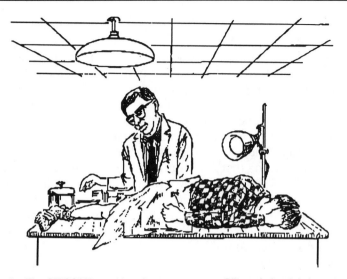

Figure 1. The SIECCAN sex education program uses Blissymbols, plain language, and simple illustrations such as the one shown here to make sex education more accessible to people with disabilities. (From Ludwig, S., & Hingsburger, D. [1993]. *Being sexual: An illustrated series on sexuality and relationships. Unit 15: Sexual abuse*, p. 31. East York, Ontario, Canada: Sex Information and Education Council of Canada; reprinted by permission.)

SIECCAN (Sex Information and Education Council of Canada) sex education program. This program combines the use of Blissymbols (semantically based icons), English writing, and line drawings to teach students with disabilities about all aspects of sexuality. While this combination would be most applicable to someone who reads English or Bliss, the program can also be used with nonreaders with the help of a reading instructor who signs or verbally interprets for the student.

Sex education classes should be pleasant and relaxed (Monat-Haller, 1992). Humor is sometimes helpful in reducing anxiety about the topic. However, too much joking or humor at inappropriate times can create problems. Laughing at someone or the ideas that he or she expresses is likely to hurt feelings and inhibit discussion. Finding humor in everything sexual may be the instructor's way of dealing with his or her own discomfort with the topic and could unintentionally increase anxiety and inappropriate responses to sexuality in the students (Hingsburger, 1990a).

As suggested previously, many aspects of sex education are well integrated with social skills training. *Just Between Us* (Edwards & Elkins, 1988) is a popular curriculum guide for teaching social/sexual content. It includes lessons on socialization; normalization; dignity; morality and ethics; menstruation; pelvic exams; parental concerns such as masturbation, homosexuality, pornography, exhibitionism, sublimation, and voyeurism; building self-esteem; sterilization; contraception; marriage and parenthood; and how to avoid sexual exploitation.

Sex education should be interactive. Students need information but they also need to express their own reactions and feelings toward the topic. Instructors should be good listeners and able to respond to what they hear (Hingsburger, 1990a). Through this interactive process, the instructor ascertains what the students are learning, and if there are any misunderstandings, the instructor can then determine what areas require retraining or modification of training. Incidental learning also has an important role in sex education. When students encounter sexual feelings or interactions in their own lives, these should be discussed with an intent to further their education.

Hundreds of books, articles, and materials related to sex education for people with disabilities have been published, and these contain a wealth of information that goes far beyond the scope of this chapter. Monat-Haller (1992), for example, provides an excellent review. Sex education allows people with disabilities to take control of their own bodies and their own lives. In doing so, it helps to reduce their risk of being abused.

Self-Defense Training Self-defense training may be suitable for many people with disabilities, provided that certain cautions are exercised in the planning and implementation of these kinds of programs. Individuals should be discouraged from false confidence in their abilities to defend themselves, especially so that they do not assume unnecessary risks because of this false confidence. The most important aspect of self-defense training is often developing the judgment to determine when it should be used and when it could actually increase risk. For example, attacking an adversary who cannot be defeated may only result in increased retaliation. Care should also be taken in teaching self-defense techniques to individuals who have a history of aggressive behavior to ensure that these techniques are not misapplied as aggression toward nonabusers.

Self-defense techniques also require individualization. Some methods require unimpaired physical abilities and complex reasoning to be effective. Teaching such techniques to those who are unlikely to master them is unlikely to produce useful results. Most people, however, can benefit from learning the most simple techniques of self-defense. Crossmaker (1986), for example, suggests that people learn to yell loudly to startle their adversary, then to run to escape. Wen-Do and other forms of self-defense can be taught to many people with physical or mental disabilities by qualified instructors (e.g., Rinear, 1985). Well-designed practical self-defense courses emphasize strategies for avoiding confrontation and minimizing risks as much or more than actual combat techniques. Small group instruction is often ideal and allows individualization to each student's needs and abilities. Self-defense training sometimes confers the additional benefits of increased self-confidence and self-esteem associated with the sense of accomplishment upon successful completion of the courses.

CONCLUSION

The ecological model of abuse presented in Chapter 6 portrayed abuse as a power imbalance between two people. Individuals with developmental disabilities typically have limited access to power, whereas their caregivers often have almost unlimited power. This chapter presented some areas of training that can either be improved upon or newly developed to help empower people with disabilities and thus reduce the imbalance of power that often leads to abuse. Education has the potential to play a key role in risk reduction, but it will only produce significant reductions in risk when other interventions are applied concurrently to help equalize the power balance between people with disabilities and those who interact with them.

8

Families and Other Caregivers
Support and Selection

Positive support and careful selection of caregivers are essential components of effective abuse prevention programs. Caregivers have the potential to be a source of great advocacy, support, and protection for children and for people with disabilities. Conversely, they also have the potential and the opportunity to abuse the people who are in their care.

Jason Carpenter is a child with disabilities caused by abuse. According to his grandmother, Jason's mother was addicted to cocaine and beaten by Jason's father. As a young child growing up in a crackhouse known as one of the "twin fortresses" in the midst of prostitution and drug addiction, Jason was neglected. All of these circumstances increased his risk for disability and for suffering further abuse (e.g., Helfer & Kempe, 1987). Social services intervened, taking him from his mother and placing him in foster care for his welfare and protection (Engman & Tanner, 1993).

This story should have had a happy ending, but within 42 days of being placed in foster care, 21-month-old Jason was rushed to the hospital unconscious and covered with bruises, pinholes, and cigarette burns. Jason's brain was severely damaged by the beatings he sustained in "protective" care, and his resulting profound disabilities are expected to last for the rest of his life. The foster parents who were chosen by social services to provide the safe and loving home that Jason had been denied were convicted of aggravated assault and withholding necessities of life after Jason's beating. The judge described the beating as sadistic and gave the foster parents stiff sentences.

Jason's grandmother, Carol Sheets, concisely summarized his removal from the crackhouse by child protection services and his subsequent placement in foster care as going "from the frying pan to the fire" (Engman & Tanner, 1993, p. A1). The social services department that placed Jason with the foster parents who beat him had investigated these foster parents five times previously concerning complaints of abuse of other children. This is a tragic case, but it is far from unique. All too often, attempts to help children who are at risk only result in further harm. If other children are to be spared this kind of experience, we have to find ways of getting them out of "the frying pan" without putting them into "the fire."

Jason's story illustrates how efforts to protect children can go horribly awry, and some might feel that it provides an argument for abandoning these efforts altogether. However, at the same time there can be little doubt that in many other cases, children have benefited from protective intervention (Reppucci & Aber, 1992), and these children would suffer if protective intervention was abandoned. Therefore, we must proceed with great caution. It is imperative that we recognize and build on the strengths and values of natural families. We must also recognize that, at least for the foreseeable future, some families cannot be made safe, and some children will be raised in alternative living environments.

There are other examples of abusive caregivers, who, like Jason Carpenter's foster parents, had a history of known or suspected abuse before being hired into caregiving positions. For example, Daniel Lee Siebert, also known as Daniel Spence, was so anxious to be hired at the Alabama Institute for the Deaf and Blind that he offered to teach there for free. Although he had a previous conviction for manslaughter, he was able to obtain work at the institute. As an art teacher there, he was unusually interested in and involved with some of his students. In 1986, he sexually assaulted and murdered two of them (Newton, 1990b).

Andre Rand was an attendant at Willowbrook State School in the 1960s. His original name was Frank Rashan, but he had his named legally changed to Andre Rand after his release from prison in 1972. Rand, however, became best known as the "Pied Piper of Staten Island" because of his ability to lure children (Newton, 1990b). Although his history of violence against children is believed to have begun much earlier, Rand was arrested in 1969 for the abduction and attempted rape of a 9-year-old girl, but he was allowed to plead guilty to sexual abuse and served only 16 months in prison for the crime. He was linked to the abduction of other children over the next decade, but these children were never found, and there was never enough evidence for a conviction. His next conviction, in 1983, was for the unlawful imprisonment of 11 children whom he abducted in a van and who were recovered unharmed. Abducting these children had not been difficult for him because he was employed as their school bus driver. Apparently, his previous history of child sexual offenses did not prevent him from obtaining this job. Because the children were recovered unharmed, Rand was sentenced to only 10 months in prison. He only served about 8 months and soon after became a suspect in the disappearance of other children.

Rand's behavior became more bizarre. Out of work and homeless, he went back to live in a makeshift lean-to on the grounds of Willowbrook, which by then was largely abandoned. He seemed to have been attracted there by his memories of better times. Considering this, it was perhaps not surprising that the next child he abducted was a 12-year-old girl with Down syndrome. Jennifer Schweiger was a happy child who lived with her parents and enjoyed dancing lessons and visiting neighborhood shops. She was last seen alive walking with Rand into the ruins of Willowbrook. Her dirt-encrusted body was found there in a shallow grave 35 days later (Neuffer, 1987).

Offenders like Rand often select jobs as care providers. It is frightening to realize that an individual like this would be hired as a school bus driver after already being covicted for the abduction and attempted rape of one child and while a current suspect in the disappearance of others. Clearly, any reasonable attempt at controlling the risk of abuse for people with disabilities must include a component that is aimed at known and potential offenders.

More than half of the abuse of people with disabilities is perpetrated by three groups of offenders: 1) family members, 2) paid caregivers, and 3) other people with disabilities, especially those clustered with their victims in service settings (Sobsey & Doe, 1991). In discussing these three groups as categories of abusers, it is important to recognize that the great majority of individuals in each group *do not* abuse others. Nevertheless, because some individuals in these three groups are responsible for a large percentage of offenses against people with disabilities, and each group represents an identifiable category, any intervention that reduces the possibility of offenses by any members of these groups has the potential to substantially reduce overall risk.

Intervention to reduce risk of abuse by other people with disabilities is addressed in subsequent chapters. Chapter 9, for example, discusses how reducing the number of people with disabilities living in clustered service settings and building safeguards into any remaining clustered settings can reduce risk. Chapter 12 discusses treatment programs for offenders with disabilities that can reduce the risk of future victimizations and treatment programs for victims of violence with disabilities that can reduce the risk that some of these victims will go on to offend against others.

Because people with disabilities who are abused are often victimized by their own family members and other caregivers, intervention aimed at reducing the risk of abusive behavior by these individuals is an essential component of prevention. This chapter discusses some of these prevention strategies.

HIGH-RISK FAMILIES

In general, natural families who are well embedded in their communities, with strong attachments among all members of the family, provide relatively safe environments for people with disabilities. Simply keeping children in their natural families and avoiding placement in service alternatives is an excellent abuse prevention strategy. Unfortunately, sometimes abuse can and does occur within the natural family itself.

Certain factors have been identified that are associated with higher risk for abuse within families. Recognizing these factors can help to identify these families, and intervention can help to reduce some of the associated risk. Prevention efforts are often specifically aimed at families considered to be high-risk. However, other prevention efforts are targeted more broadly toward all families of people with disabilities or toward all families in general, regardless of risk.

Care must be exercised in the assessment of and intervention with high-risk families. Although certain family attributes have been associated with a greater statistical probability for abuse, many families with these attributes are free of abuse. Also, family participation in prevention programs is generally voluntary and is more likely to be successful when participating family members have positive feelings about their involvement. Labeling a family as "abusive," "at-risk," or a "problem family" may cause the family to have negative feelings about becoming involved with a prevention program and could even increase the probability of abuse as a result of displaced resentment or negative expectations. It is essential that all families be treated with the greatest possible respect and that positive emphasis be placed on developing family relationships, skills, and resources, rather than a negative emphasis on suppressing abuse.

Similarly, it would be a serious error to stereotype all families that include a member with a disability as being high risk. Not all of these families could be said to suffer from isolation, excessive stress, or disruptions in attachment. Every family, and every family member, is unique. Successful family support programs must recognize and respond to individual needs and respect families as equal partners in the programs. This does not mean that families and professionals must always agree. Carney (1991) points out that disagreements and differences in perspective are natural and should be expected. She suggests that accepting differences and negotiating on the basis of common interests avoids stalemates that hurt those involved, while still allowing some benefits for everyone.

Determining Risk

The factors that need to be considered for determining risk for abuse within families that include a member with a disability are the same factors that are associated with risk in other families. However, many of these risk factors have special implications when applied to families of people with disabilities. Predicting risk for abuse is far from a perfect science, and abuse prevention programs are helpful for all families, not just those with higher risk. Why then is it necessary to consider the factors associated with increased risk? First, prevention programs typically have limited resources, and the identification of increased risk in some families may help to establish program priorities. Second, consideration of various risk factors may be useful in individualizing risk prevention programs on the basis of the risk factors identified. For example, one family may be identified as having increased risk because they are socially isolated, a second may be identified as having increased risk because they report difficulty coping with stress associated with managing challenging behavior, and a third may be identified as having increased risk because they show little attachment to their child with a disability. Some elements of various prevention programs may be common to all three, but the primary focus of each program should be directed at the particular area of identified risk for each family.

Isolated Families Family isolation has consistently been identified as a risk factor for violence and abuse within families (Meier, 1978). Smith (1984) points out that family isolation has been one of the most consistent findings associated with physical abuse of children. For example, when 152 women who had been identified as neglecting their children were compared with 154 nonneglecting mothers, the neglecting mothers were found to be more isolated and to live in less supportive environments (Polansky, Gaudin, Ammons, & Davis, 1985). Isolation has also been identified as a factor associated with incest (Mrazek, 1981), elder abuse (Moore & Thompson, 1987), and institutional abuse (Musick, 1984). The role of social isolation, like that of many of the other interrelated factors associated with child abuse, must be viewed with caution as it could be the result of family dysfunction or stem from some other factor (e.g., alcoholism, character disorder) that is the real cause. Nonetheless, current information suggests that isolation it-self may be an important factor.

Korbin (1987) analyzed child abuse from an anthropological point of view and found isolation to be a lack of embeddedness of the family within the community and culture. As a result, the preventive benefits of natural social interactions were unavailable to these families. She points out that families that have abandoned their original cultural heritage, but have not been fully assimilated into a new culture, are more likely to harbor abuse than families embedded in either the na-tive or the new culture (see Chapter 6, p. 161, for more on this subject).

Any family can become isolated from outside interaction, but fam-ilies that include a member with a disability are more likely to experi-ence this situation. Singer and Irvin (1991) point out that although the reasons for this isolation are poorly understood, four factors are likely to contribute. First, the demands of intensive caregiving may lead to fatigue. Second, difficulty obtaining child care may result in limited leisure time and restricted social interactions. Third, the stigma associ-ated with disability may result in social rejection or, conversely, the family may reject others who hold negative attitudes about their family member. Fourth, because family members with disabilities are often segregated from community activities, other family members lack nat-ural opportunities to become involved in social networks. For example, neighborhood mothers may get together to discuss the local school, but the mother of a child sent to a "special school across town" is unlikely to be included.

Family violence is only one of the negative outcomes associated with family isolation. When families become isolated, they are also at higher risk for a variety of mental and physical health problems (Weiss, 1973). These effects may include changes in personality and attitudes, substance abuse, increased perception of stress, and anger or resent-ment toward other family members. Such problems often contribute to additional risk for abuse and further isolation. Therefore, identifying family isolation can be a key element in assessing risk for abuse. A number of instruments are available for assessing the social networks and resources of families and determining their degree of embedded-ness in or isolation from the community. For example, the Family Sup-port Scale (Dunst, Jenkins, & Trivette, 1988) measures the perceived contributions of relatives, agencies, and informal social networks to parent–child relations by asking parents if they are satisfied with the level of support they are receiving.

Disruptions in Attachment   Attachment refers to the strong af-fective bond that typically exists among family members and some-times among other individuals. Attachment between parents and their children appears to develop during very early interactions. For mothers and their infants, attachment may begin to form before birth as vestibular and kinesthetic reflex reactions coordinate the movements of the fetus with the mother's actions. After birth, contact, coordinated movements, and other interactions continue to build the attachment between parents and their children. Harlow's experiments with monkeys (1959) suggested softness and movement were among the critical touch characteristics required by infants; those deprived of these attributes developed behavior symptomatic of severe attachment disruption. Although these laboratory-based experiments were conducted with animals, the results were startlingly similar to the human behavior previously observed in children receiving impersonal institutional care (e.g., Spitz, 1945).

Attachment of young children to their parents is typically measured by the child's response to the parent in stressful situations. Disruptions in attachment between children and their parents have often been associated with child abuse, and healthy attachment is thought to provide protection from abuse (Youngblade & Belsky, 1989). For example, young children from abusive families have been shown to exhibit insecure attachment to their mothers (Browne & Saqi, 1988). Of course, disruptions in attachment could be a symptom of abuse (Lamb, Gaensbauer, Malkin, & Schultz, 1985), rather than the cause of it, and more research needs to be done on this complex relationship. However, many experts consider attachment disruptions and abuse to be two manifestations of an underlying dysfunction in the parent–child relationship (Youngblade & Belsky, 1989), suggesting that disruptions in attachment may signal that abuse is already occurring or, if not, that it is likely to occur in the future.

At least one prospective study dealt with this potential mutual causation by assessing risk for child abuse during pregnancy and then evaluating actual abuse in the following years. The risk assessments proved quite accurate, with 80% correct prediction of abusive parents and 89% correct prediction of nonabusive parents. Of those identified as being at high risk for abusing their children, the child was unwanted or considered at risk for bonding in 80% of the cases (Murphy, Orkow, & Nicola, 1985).

Sadly, parents of children with disabilities sometimes appear to be less attached to their children than other parents (Foley, 1985; Wasserman, Lennon, Allen, & Shilansky, 1987). More work is needed in this area; however, the attachment between children with disabilities and their families appears to be disrupted in at least five ways. First, some children with disabilities have specific impairments that may interfere with the perception or processing of stimulation essential for the development of attachment (Andrew, 1989). For example, a child who is deaf and blind may require extra stimulation through contact and movement to develop attachment with her or his caregivers.

Second, parents may reject children with disabilities because of their own preexisting attitudes toward disability or because similar attitudes of rejection expressed by others influence parental behavior. Brazelton and Cramer (1991) in their discussion of "the disappointing infant" suggest that the child's "imperfection" threatens the image of parents and "attachment may fail to develop because the child, far from being a source of pride, has become the proof of parental failure" (p. 213). Even in their rather pessimistic discussion of parental attachment to children with disabilities, these authors point out that the outcome is largely determined by societal attitudes and expectations communicated to the parent, and they urge intervention to help develop parental bonding.

The attitudes of some professionals and other members of society continue to give parents the message that "they shouldn't let themselves become too attached" to their child with a disability because it will only cause them grief. Professionals may even recommend that parents consider institutionalization or even euthanasia rather than encouraging parents to love their child. Gould (1981) provides a valuable but chilling example of how famed American psychologist Lewis Terman "needed less than an hour to crush the hopes and belittle the efforts of struggling 'well-educated' parents afflicted with a child with an IQ of 75" (p. 179). Terman felt this to be his duty because the mother in his example was encouraged by her child's mastery of reading and might therefore resist institutionalizing her son.

This practice of deliberate professional interference with parental bonding with children with disabilities still continues. Forest (1991), for example, quotes the advice of a physician to one family in 1989: "Don't bond with the baby—she will probably die, or at best be a burden to you for the rest of your life" (p. 400). Hart (1970) provides a disheartening quotation from Thelma Nichols who tried to kill her daughter with a disability by withdrawing life-sustaining care for 2 days, after she was told that her child "wouldn't be any good" and would not survive the year. "I just sat there," the woman said, "alone in the flat, listening to her trying to breathe. It was awful. In the end, I gave up and gave her the drugs" (p. 58).

Third, some parents may have internalized attitudes of rejection toward people with disabilities that they must overcome before they can learn to accept and love their own child. For example, some cultures view a child with a disability as a punishment from God. This view often contributes to resentment and rejection.

Fourth, stress related to the onset or diagnosis of a child's disability may interfere with the development of attachment. This may be particularly true when the diagnosis is made shortly after birth, an important time for the development of family attachments. It is possible that diagnosis at this time is even more threatening to the healthy attachment of fathers than to the attachment of mothers because maternal attachment may develop to a greater extent prior to birth in response to pregnancy. However, this theory remains untested.

Finally, well-intentioned professionals may encourage parents to assume a role as a program coordinator, therapy assistant, teacher's aide, behavior manager, or other quasi-professional for their child. Although this practice is not necessarily harmful, care must be taken to assure that any new role requirements do not overly interfere with parents' primary role. For example, parents who fail to regularly carry out an uncomfortable tendon stretching procedure on their child may be poor therapists, but, the damage done to the parent–child relationship by performing this procedure could be worse than the physical neglect of failing to administer it.

The assessment of attachment in families that include members with disabilities is a complex issue (Blacher, 1984; Blacher & Meyers, 1983), and no single evaluation of attachment is suitable for a precise measure of risk for abuse. Nevertheless, the extent to which other family members seek contact and interaction with the individual with a disability and the extent to which that individual seeks contact and interaction with them provides a good basic indicator. Affectionate physical contact, turn taking, coordinated physical movements, and general responsiveness to each other are also signs of attachment.

Family Member Attributes Personality traits of family members and other caregivers have been found to be associated with increased risk (e.g., Oliver, 1985; Pillemer & Finkelhor, 1989). Unfortunately, the predictive power of personality testing is insufficient to identify potential offenders clearly. Nevertheless, low self-esteem, impulsiveness, and a need to exert authority or control over others are among the traits often observed in abusers (see Chapter 6, Table 1). Abusive mothers were found to be unable to empathize with their children (Melnick & Hurley, 1969). Research suggests that about half of parents who abuse their children have diagnoses of antisocial personality disorder, major depression, or alcoholism. Depression by itself appears to contribute relatively little risk, but this risk becomes much higher when depression is combined with alcohol abuse (Bland & Orn, 1986).

Substance Abuse The use of alcohol and other disinhibiting drugs (e.g., cocaine) is related to all forms of family violence and abuse. The most direct effect of these drugs is to reduce inhibition of aggressive or inappropriate sexual behavior; however, excessive use of these substances can also influence other abuse-related factors such as attachment formation, family isolation, and stress. Conversely, people who have difficulty forming attachments may be more likely to drink (Kwakman, Zuiker, Schippers, & de Wuffel, 1988). Prenatal exposure to drugs has also been associated with problems in development of attachment (Rodning, Beckwith, & Howard, 1989). Oliver (1985) found that alcohol and drug dependence was more common in abusive families than in nonabusive families.

Substance abuse can occur in any family, but the families of some children with disabilities may be more prone. The connection may be most direct for disabilities directly caused by substance abuse, for instance, children with fetal alcohol syndrome (FAS) or "crack-babies" born to mothers using cocaine. While physiological mechanisms have been identified linking substance-abusing mothers to disabilities in their offspring, the effects are confounded by social and environmental factors. For example, mothers who frequently use cocaine often receive little or no prenatal care, have deficiencies in their diet, and are more likely to suffer from infectious diseases in pregnancy (Schutter & Brinker, 1992). The substance abuse of pregnant mothers that causes disabilities in their children typically continues after birth and is likely to be associated with family violence. Infectious diseases associated with intravenous drug abuse, such as HIV/AIDS (Diamond & Cohen, 1992), can also cause disabilities, leading to increased risk for abuse. Violence-induced disabilities (VID) (often undiagnosed) also link substance abuse to disability because substance abuse is likely to have occurred when the initial violence took place, and is likely to continue to be part of later violent episodes. Even accidental forms of trauma-induced disability can be associated with substance abuse. For example, large numbers of people are disabled every year as a result of intoxicated drivers, and the people most likely to be injured are the drivers themselves and their family members.

The use of alcohol or other disinhibiting drugs by family members should be identified as a significant risk factor for abuse. Occasional use of alcohol is seen as socially acceptable in most contemporary cultures, and not every individual becomes violent with the use of alcohol or some other drugs. Furthermore, the amount of alcohol or other drugs required to disinhibit antisocial behavior varies across individuals and depends on a number of other interrelated factors. Therefore, until more precise information becomes available, minimal social use of these drugs should be viewed as being associated with only a small increase in risk. If a family member often exhibits changes in behavior associated with drugs or alcohol (e.g., slurred speech, missed appointments), the risk should be viewed as more significant. If a family member shows signs of disinhibition of aggression or inappropriate sexual behavior associated with drug use, the risk for abuse should be considered high.

Dangerous Attitudes Just as some drugs can reduce inhibition and increase risk for violence and abuse, attitudes and beliefs can also disinhibit violence and provide rationalizations for justifying the offenses in the mind of the offender. A more detailed discussion of these attitudes, how they can unleash violence toward people with disabilities, and steps that can be taken to modify them is presented in Chapter 11. For the present discussion, it should be noted that attitudes of devaluation, dehumanization, and ambivalence (Katz, Glass, Lucido, & Farber, 1977) have often been associated with abuse, and changing such attitudes may be important for reducing risk (Yuker, 1988).

Family History of Violence One of the simplest predictors of family violence is a history of previous family violence. For example, a child who has been abused once by a parent is more likely to be abused again, and a child who lives in a home where a parent or sibling is the victim of family violence is also at higher risk (Sigurdson et al., 1991). The predictive power of a history of violence may reflect the combined effects of a number of other factors (e.g., isolation, attachment disruptions, substance abuse), but it can also be identified as a risk factor regardless of the presence or absence of these other factors. A past history of violence is particularly likely to increase risk if the offender goes unpunished and never receives rehabilitative counseling for the initial transgression. Violence or abuse by one family member also appears to increase the risk that other family members will exhibit similar behavior. For example, a child who is abused by her or his parents is more likely to abuse siblings. The mechanism for the spread of violent behavior across family members is probably related to observational learning and the victim–offender cycle described in Chapter 6.

Most of the implications of a history of family violence for families of people with disabilities are the same as for other families. Families with known or suspected histories of past violence should be considered at greater risk. If an individual's disability was caused by violence to the individual or to her or his mother, that individual is more likely to be abused in the future. Because many violence-induced disabilities are not diagnosed, alleged cases of VID outnumber confirmed cases. Thus, suspected cases of VID or other suspected past family violence must also be considered to be associated with increased risk. Of course, it is important to exercise caution in the assessment of and response to suspected, rather than confirmed, cases of abuse. No parent should be accused of or blamed for family violence or for causing a child's disability unless there is significant evidence.

Perceived Stress   The importance of the role of stress in causing or triggering the abuse of people with disabilities is controversial (see Chapter 6, section on Dependency–Stress Model of Abuse). Nevertheless, it is clear that caregivers who perceive themselves as being severely stressed and as having difficulties coping are more likely to commit abuse. These individuals often see the person whom they abuse as a source of their stress. Families that either report or exhibit difficulty coping with stress, especially those who identify a family member with a disability as the source of their stress, should be considered to be high-risk families. Some researchers believe that children and other family members who are hyperactive or who exhibit behavior problems are more likely to be abused. This may be related to increased stress or inability of family members to manage problematic behavior by appropriate means. As a result, behavior problems in children, combined with poor parenting skills (e.g., overuse of parental punishment and control), can be a particularly dangerous combination. Other factors (e.g., poor parental impulse control, substance abuse) may further compound the risk.

Nevertheless, the relationship between children's behavior problems and their risk of abuse remains complex and is difficult to sort out for several reasons. First, because behavior problems often occur as a response to abuse, the presence of behavior problems in abused children does not provide conclusive evidence that behavior problems are causal factors. Second, much of our evidence regarding the role of behavior problems in causing abuse comes from the abusive parents themselves—who can hardly be considered objective judges. Many parents of abused children with and without disabilities blame their children's behavior for the abuse, but research does not support their perceptions (Sobsey, 1990c). Bugental, Mantyla, and Lewis (1989) suggest that it is how parents perceive the characteristics of their children, and not the actual traits of their children, that often predicts abuse.

Third, *tall poppy syndrome* may influence our perception of the link between child behavior and abuse. This implies that parental traits and ecological traits are the primary determinants of *whether* children are abused, but child behavior determines *when* abuse takes place and in some cases *which* child is abused. For example, an angry parent may intimidate several children, but the one who fights back is likely to be targeted for abuse. Although all these children may be psychologically abused, the one who attempts to fight back is often the one who will be physically abused and identified as an abused child exhibiting "problem behavior." Fourth, many of the studies linking child characteristics or behavior to parental abuse could be explained by other reasons. For example, premature infants have been found more likely to be abused than full-term infants, and this difference has been ascribed to "high-pitched cries [that] are particularly aversive" (Bugental et al., 1989, p. 259). However, increased risk of abuse for premature babies could also be ascribed to attachment disruption associated with increased medical care requirements at birth, common factors that predispose toward prematurity and child abuse (e.g., fetal battery), or a number of other reasons.

Considering these concerns, reports of child behavior problems should not be ignored as a possible predictor of abuse; however, they should be carefully evaluated. Parental reports of behavior problems may indicate that the parents are having difficulty coping, even (perhaps especially) if the parents' perceptions are unfounded. Therefore, these families often need assistance and support. When behavior problems really do occur, they may be signals that the family requires training to better meet their child's needs, or, the "behavior problems" may be symptoms of abuse that is already taking place.

Professionals should be careful to provide support and assistance without overly focusing on the stress experienced by families or the magnitude of parental problems. Overemphasizing the plight of parents may make it harder for them to cope by creating negative expectations and encouraging negative attitudes toward the child whom they view as the source of their problems. Encouraging parents to view their experiences as occurring within a normal continuum and to have positive, but realistic, expectations helps parents to adapt and supports the parental development of positive attitudes toward themselves and their children.

Contemporary research appears to de-emphasize the importance of stress as a causal factor in child abuse and other violence. As more sophisticated models develop, researchers are beginning to view objective or external stress (the sum of outside demands faced by an individual) more as a trigger of abuse than as an underlying cause, and subjective or internal stress (the individual's response to external demands) more as a warning signal. Although subjective stress generally appears to worsen with greater external demands, some people report low stress in spite of high demands, and others report high stress in the absence of increased demands. In addition, stress is increasingly considered to be one of a group of interacting social variables that include coping skills, resources, adaptability, social support, and other social considerations (Zigler & Hall, 1989). In addition, there is good reason to believe that the frequency and amount of stress experienced by families of people with disabilities have been overemphasized due to flaws in research design and interpretation (Glidden, 1993; Sobsey, 1990a). Stress, especially the family's own perception of stress, cannot be ignored. Families that report severe stress, regardless of objective circumstances, may be communicating that they are having difficulty coping and need assistance.

Professional opinion regarding the role of stress in causing abuse is mixed. Most experts believe that stress has at least some role in abuse, and some consider it to be a major causal factor. Dunst, Cooper, and Bolick (1987), for example, view child abuse as *"one of a number of possible conditions that result from the increased responsibilities and demands associated with rearing a handicapped youngster"* (p. 28, italics in original). Considering the differences of opinion regarding the role of stress, more research is needed to help guide abuse prevention programs in dealing with this issue. Nevertheless, helping families to cope with stress should remain among the goals of family-centered abuse prevention programs for three reasons. First, as mentioned above, if stress is not a major causal factor, stress may act to trigger abuse in some families, and stress reduction could therefore help families to avoid some abusive episodes. Second, parental reports of perceived stress may indicate problems such as difficulty coping or general dissatisfaction, which may be important in identification of families at risk. Third, reducing stress can support families in staying together, thus avoiding the need for extrafamilial care along with its associated risks.

Finally, reducing stress in the family has little potential to do harm, except if the method used to attain stress reduction places further restrictions on the family, increases the vulnerability of the child or family member with a disability, or if meeting parental needs for stress reduction becomes the sole focus of the support program. Therefore, stress reduction intervention must be carefully planned to avoid these problems. For example, teaching children to be overly compliant may reduce parental stress, but increase the risk for abuse, and programs that focus only on parental respite and leisure may also reduce parental stress, but fail to address other issues such as fulfilling parental responsibilities.

Testing

In some cases, tests can be used to identify parents who are at high risk for committing physical abuse. The Child Abuse Potential Inventory is a questionnaire with good validation data. It takes about 20 minutes to complete and can be self-administered by any individual with at least a third-grade reading level (Caliso & Milner, 1992). This test can be very helpful, provided that careful attention is paid to the limits of its currently demonstrated validity (Milner, 1989). For example, the test predicts physical abuse, but not necessarily sexual abuse. It differentiates between abusive and nonabusive parents who were abused as children, groups that often are not identified by other tests (Milner, Robertson, & Rogers, 1990). More work needs to be done to determine how social and cultural factors may interact with the test (Miller, Handal, Gilner, & Cross, 1991), and specific research should be undertaken to determine if any special considerations need to be applied to using the test with parents of children with disabilities.

Uncertainty of Risk Assessment

Although this discussion has centered on the identification of high-risk families, the complexity and uncertainty of risk assessment does not allow for a precise prediction. False positives (families that appear to be high risk for violence or abuse, but never actually experience abuse) or false negatives (families that do not appear to be high risk for violence or abuse, but do experience abuse), are common. Regardless of this uncertainty, some elements of abuse prevention are important for all families, regardless of risk, because they support healthy functioning families as well as dysfunctional ones or because they can help to prevent extrafamilial abuse, as well as abuse within the family.

FAMILY ABUSE PREVENTION STRATEGIES

Intervention can reduce the risk of abuse within families in several ways (Altepeter & Walker, 1992). First, parent training can lessen parental dependence on coercion and physical force used in behavior management and improve problem-solving and stress management skills. Second, establishing family networks can help families to become less isolated and may also help to manage stress. Third, counseling can help lower drug and alcohol dependency, which are associated with child abuse and neglect, and, in so doing, address other forms of family violence (e.g., spousal abuse). Fourth, intervention can also assist with the development of strong bonds between family members to help reduce risk for abuse.

Preventing abuse within high-risk families that include a member with a disability is essentially the same as abuse prevention within other high-risk families. Targeting intervention specifically toward high-risk families may be necessary because limited resources make it impossible to provide support services to all families, regardless of the degree of risk. However, singling out high-risk families for intervention is less than ideal because some families that need counseling are inevitably missed. Furthermore, identifying families as "high-risk" may only stigmatize and further isolate them, thus increasing risk, or create an expectation for abuse that also increases risk. Therefore, inclusion of *all* families in as many aspects of prevention as possible is ideal.

Because many people with disabilities are more dependent on their families than other individuals of the same age, family intervention should not be limited to families with children or elderly members. Intervention may be required throughout an individual's lifespan. Every family is unique, and individualizing prevention programs to the needs, interests, strengths, and resources of each is often a key to their effectiveness in preventing abuse. Maximizing family participation in the development of an individualized program also helps to ensure that participants feel they are an active and integral part of the process, rather than a passive (or even unwilling) target of intervention. For example, some parents will indicate that they are having great difficulty coping with the aggressive behavior of their child with a disability. Teaching them appropriate and effective methods for responding to this challenging behavior may be valuable for abuse prevention and will also encourage family participation. Other families, however, may not have to deal with challenging behavior or may already have the necessary skills to respond appropriately. Teaching these other families appropriate responses may have little prevention value and could alienate participants who feel that they are wasting their time.

Training in Parenting Skills

Some success has been demonstrated in training high-risk parents in specific skills that help reduce risk. Wolfe, Sandler, and Kaufman (1981) used classroom and home-based training to teach an 8-week course to parents who had been referred after at least one incident of abuse. Another group of parents on a waiting list for training served as controls. Parents in the course were taught general information about child development, nonabusive behavior management strategies, problem-solving skills, self-control, and relaxation techniques. At the end of the course, parents who received training showed significantly improved child management skills, and none of those completing the program were suspected or reported to have committed abuse during a subsequent 1-year monitoring period. Other similarly structured programs report the same kind of improvements, although some have reported mixed results (Altepeter & Walker, 1992).

Based on their considerable experience with Project 12 Ways in Illinois, Lutzker and Rice (1984) urge that abuse prevention programs be individualized by negotiating with the family to determine which components would be most valuable for them. They generally recommend teaching parents the following:

1. Provide children with simple and clear instructions.
2. Reinforce appropriate behavior.
3. Use less intrusive forms of punishment, such as time out from preferred activities, as a consequence for inappropriate behavior.

Consistent with their ecobehavioral approach, the authors stress the need for training in the actual environments in which abuse is most likely to occur. Program evaluation data suggest that rates of reported abuse have declined in areas where this project has been implemented.

The parental training programs discussed here were undertaken as abuse prevention or treatment initiatives. They were not specifically addressed to families of children with disabilities. However, other similar programs have targeted these specific families in efforts to improve family functioning and reduce overall stress.

Overcoming Isolation

All families require the support of friends and associates. Unfortunately, contemporary social trends (e.g., increased geographical mobility, greater reliance on agencies, smaller families) have weakened traditional family, friendship, neighborhood, and community networks, leaving many individuals and families isolated from natural support systems. This problem is not unique to families with a member with a disability, but these families often have even greater difficulty avoiding isolation.

Families that become isolated may need assistance in building social networks. Help can be provided informally in some cases, or more formal assistance with a family support coordinator and a family support plan might be necessary in others (Dunst, Trivette, & Deal, 1988). The development of ties within generic community networks (e.g., neighbors, church, club members) is desirable for most families; however, disability-based interest and advocacy groups can partially or fully provide support networks for some families. These disability-based groups can serve a variety of functions. First, they offer an opportunity to establish supportive relationships with other families who share some of the same life experiences and who are pursuing similar goals. Second, these groups provide a place for families to share up-to-date information on the availability of special resources and can serve as a springboard for coordinating efforts to achieve some common goals (Dybwad, 1990). Networks of families of a person with a disability also serve as potential vehicles for other prevention methods. For example, they may be useful in building more positive attitudes and self-images, and they can be used to help circulate information on prevention of family violence and abuse.

Facilitating Attachment

Although it is never too late to work toward improving relationships within the family, it is far easier and much more likely to be effective when efforts to support attachment begin early. Professionals working with the family must carefully consider the potential impact of their own behavior and avoid words or actions that might discourage attachment. They should also refrain from placing demands that would increase family members' anxiety levels or from encouraging family interactions that are so structured as to leave little opportunity for enjoying the relationship.

Families must be encouraged to participate in contact and interaction that is reinforcing both to the child with a disability and to other family members. For example, "baby massage" programs might seem largely recreational, but in some cases, massage gives parents a chance to participate in mutually reinforcing contact and interaction with their infant. The resonant and coactive behavior involved in massage could also contribute to the facilitation of more advanced communication in the future, but the simple opportunity to partake in reinforcing contact and interaction with few competing demands may be even more critical for the development of healthy attachment between child and parent.

Including Fathers

Many parental support and training programs primarily or exclusively involve only the mother. From an abuse prevention perspective this is extremely unfortunate. Because fathers may have greater difficulty forming attachments to their children with disabilities, many will need more help than the mothers. Including fathers in abuse prevention programs is vital to their effectiveness because men perpetrate much of the abuse, including most of the severe violence (see Chapter 3, section on Gender of Offenders). Ironically, fathers who are already attached to and involved with their children are probably the easiest to include in family education and support programs. Conversely, fathers who are the hardest to enlist in these programs are often those who need intervention the most. As mothers who raise children without active paternal involvement tend to be more isolated, greater maternal involvement may also help to reduce the risk of maternal abuse.

Exclusion of fathers from parenting programs often sets off a vicious cycle. Programs begin with the intent to include both parents, but shift their focus as more mothers and fewer fathers participate. As the focus shifts to reflect the predominantly maternal participation, it becomes even more difficult to get the fathers involved.

How can male involvement in parental education and support programs be encouraged? The following ideas may be useful:

1. Be sure that invitations are clearly directed toward both parents.
2. Provide models with male staff and volunteers. Fathers who attend programs and find that they are the only male present often feel out of place and drop out.
3. Consider child care. For some families, only one parent can attend because the other must stay with the children. If the program can provide or assist with child care, both parents might be able to participate. Alternatively, providing two or more sets of sessions may allow each parent to attend separately.
4. Allow fathers to help develop the program agenda so that it reflects content that is more gender balanced.

Some groups may benefit from having some sessions strictly for mothers, some for fathers, and some for both. Other sessions may be better organized by topic rather than gender.

Supporting Parental Relationships and Family Bonds

Children from single-parent homes and children from homes with step-parents are more likely to be abused than those from homes with both natural parents (Zigler & Hall, 1989). Children from homes where parents have severe or violent conflicts with each other are also more likely to be abused than children from homes with normal levels of parental conflict. Obviously, these facts suggest that promoting healthy marriages and family bonds helps to keep children safe (Zigler & Hall, 1989). The wide variety of supports and interventions that might be undertaken to accomplish this end goes beyond the scope of this book; however, all programs serving families should pursue two basic goals. First, they should provide general support for family and parental relationships through involving both parents in the program, encouraging opportunities for fathers and mothers to enjoy some leisure time, and reinforcing joint and cooperative efforts of parents. Second, they should attempt to identify families in crisis and refer parents to relationship counseling or other needed services that go beyond the service repertoire of the basic family support and training program.

Helping Families with Substance Abuse Problems

Families with one or more members who are dependent on alcohol, cocaine, or any of a number of other drugs pose special challenges. As previously discussed, these families are both more likely to have children with disabilities and more likely to be abusive (e.g., Zigler & Hall, 1989). Involving families with severe substance abuse problems in family support and training programs is difficult because they often respond with disinterest and sometimes with anger. Furthermore, parents with chronic substance abuse problems may need to address their substance abuse before they can benefit from family support. Professionals working with family training and support programs should be prepared to recognize substance abuse problems and refer these parents to treatment programs or encourage them to seek treatment on their own. However, careful consideration should be given before demanding that parents seek treatment. Substance-abusing parents who feel pressured to seek treatment will often drop out of programs in order to avoid this pressure. Those working with these families will often have to decide when to work with parents, in spite of their problems, and when to risk losing all contact with the family in an effort to get substance-abusing family members into treatment. Unfortunately, no simple guidelines exist for making these decisions and each case must be considered individually.

Supporting Parents with Special Needs

Although a number of studies suggest that parents with low IQ scores are more likely to be inadequate parents who abuse or neglect their children (Greenspan & Budd, 1986; Seagull & Scheurer, 1986), the role of intelligence cannot be separated from other confounding factors (e.g., differences in detection and reporting, increased risk of parental abuse history, increased probability of family isolation, increased likelihood of out-of-family care during the parents' childhoods). In addition, the fact that some parents with mental retardation are excellent child rearers suggests that it would be both incorrect and unfair to view all individuals with mental retardation as potential abusers (e.g., Greenspan & Budd, 1986; Tymchuk & Andron, 1990). Therefore, it is important to remember that "virtually all studies have found a sizeable percentage of mentally retarded parents to be functioning within, or close to, normal limits, especially when compared to parents with similar demographic characteristics" (Greenspan & Budd, 1986, p. 116). The appearance of abuse and parenting inadequacies among these parents may also appear larger than it really is because of the unusually close scrutiny, sometimes associated with expectations of failure, that is applied to parents with mental retardation; therefore, each parent must be considered as an individual. Nevertheless, because many parents with developmental disabilities have been raised in group care or abusive homes, parental training is often helpful.

Research has demonstrated that women with or without disabilities who have been raised in institutional group care have much more frequent and severe parenting difficulties than women raised in natural families (Rutter, 1989a). In one study (Rutter, 1989a), of women who had been admitted to institutional care before the age of 2 and who remained in group care throughout their childhoods, 80% were poor parents compared to only about 10% of noninstitutionalized controls. This outcome should not be surprising because the women raised in institutional care had no opportunity to model their own parenting skills on natural families. Although no similar information is available regarding fathers who were raised in institutional care, there is no reason to expect these men to show better parenting skills. Parents and potential parents raised in group care need family support and training. Including them in groups with other parents is generally recommended because modeling and information sharing may be of use to them. Sometimes the needs of specific parents or of a group of parents may be so different that a separate group may be required.

Individuals with mental retardation who have deficiencies in parenting should be treated like other parents. Children born into these families have a right to reasonable safety, and that right should be protected if and when it is threatened. However, it is essential that no threat to the child's safety is assumed merely because of a parent's disability. If there is real evidence of a threat to the safety or welfare of a child whose parents have disabilities, the evidence must be judged with the same cautious standards as those used for other families. If intervention is required, the same principles must apply. Parents with mental retardation can and do benefit from support and training programs (Greenspan & Budd, 1986). They may require simplified materials and language, but the basic content of training should be the same for all (Tymchuk & Andron, 1990).

Managing Stress in Families

Families that report excessive amounts of stress may be signalling for help. Both acute and chronic stress require consideration. Families indicating acute stress may be in or approaching a state of crisis. Any one of a number of individual, social, economic, or other factors could precipitate such a crisis. Family members are often aware of the cause for this acute stress and know what kind of help is needed. For example, in some families, one parent, typically the mother, provides the great majority of care. A crisis may arise when she becomes ill and the family has no adequate caregiving alternatives available. This is a real problem that requires a practical solution. Helping the family to achieve that solution is the best way to address their stress.

Chronic stress is less directly related to one or a few causes. It may be associated with isolation, lack of support and resources, poor coping skills, or some combination of these and many other factors (Zigler & Hall, 1989). The interventions previously described in this section can help many families cope with stress. Developing support networks, facilitating attachment among all family members, combating substance abuse within families, and supporting healthy family functioning can all aid in minimizing stress. Providing respite care to families who have few caregiving alternatives can also be helpful.

EXTRAFAMILIAL CAREGIVERS

Supporting and training natural families is an important element of abuse prevention because it reduces the chance of abuse within families; however, perhaps more importantly, it reduces the need for care by extrafamilial caregivers by keeping vulnerable individuals in their natural homes. In spite of intervention efforts, for the present, many individuals with disabilities require services from paid caregivers for all or at least some essential services. As long as this remains true, abuse prevention programs will need to focus on making these services as safe as possible through screening, supervision, and training of extrafamilial caregivers.

Paid staff and volunteers who care for people with disabilities require careful consideration. Conscientious selection and screening when hiring staff can eliminate a significant number of likely offenders from contact with vulnerable people, and the rest of this chapter focuses on this aspect of abuse prevention. Training and supervision can reduce the likelihood of abuse by some staff and help to deter abuse by others. These aspects are addressed in Chapter 9, which discusses methods of building a safer service environment.

The Importance of Careful Caregiver Selection

Two important facts should become clear to anyone who carefully examines the human services industry. First, some people are attracted to human services because they provide abundant opportunities for abuse. Second, in the vast majority of instances, service agencies do little to prevent access to these predators and often act to protect them. The screening procedures routinely employed by banks and retailers to protect their cash are far more stringent than the procedures that most human services use to protect our children and other vulnerable people.

The need for careful selection of caregivers has been recognized as an essential component of abuse prevention programs for some time (e.g., Gil, 1979). Sobsey and Mansell (1990) point to evidence that offenders are often drawn to caregiving professions because of the easy access to vulnerable, potential victims. The history of Robert Noyes provides a typical example (Marshall & Barrett, 1990). Noyes, a high school principal, was arrested in 1985 for child sexual abuse. He later pleaded guilty to sexually assaulting 18 boys and one girl over a 15-year period.

Before his 1985 arrest, Noyes was caught molesting children on a number of occasions, but was allowed to continue working with children. As an education student in 1968, he was caught molesting children on a camping trip, but was not prevented from continuing his preparation for a career in childhood education. Two years later he took a break from his teacher education program and was employed by the Children's Aid Society to supervise troubled children. He was discharged from that job after he apparently attempted to rape a young boy who ran screaming from the dormitory. Remarkably, Noyes was not charged, and within 2 weeks he was working at a camp where he was again discovered molesting boys and asked to resign. He then returned to college, and in 1971 he was asked to resign as a volunteer at a boys' club because of further sexual misconduct. Shortly thereafter, Noyes began his formal career as a teacher in an elementary school. In 1978, when mothers complained that he had molested their sons, the principal of the school asked them not to involve the police and promised that Noyes would never teach again. He was teaching in another elementary school by 1982, however, when another mother complained of his possible sexual misconduct with her son. When she complained to the principal of that school, she was told to discuss the matter directly with Mr. Noyes who suggested that her son was the one with the sexual problems. By 1985, Noyes had been promoted to high school principal when he sexually abused a female student. The student told her social worker who contacted police. Noyes was subsequently arrested, convicted, and sentenced after a 17-year career of child abuse on the public payroll.

Clearly Noyes is personally responsible for these offenses; nonetheless, the people who facilitated his career knowing the danger that he posed share his responsibility. Robert Noyes and the people who protected him are not unique. Similar behavior characterizes many other abusers and the people who cover up their abuse. Reasonable precautions must be followed to limit the access of such offenders to the human services, and steps must be taken to detect and remove those offenders who have already gained access.

MacNamara (1988) suggests that in providing human services to vulnerable people, "no setting can be abuse-free over time" (p. 77). He also provides powerful evidence of the inadequacies of disciplinary procedures to eliminate abuse. In reviewing 10 years of reports of abuse from a central institution serving 1,100 residents and its smaller nursing facilities that served another 300 individuals, MacNamara found 511 abuse allegations in spite of a code of silence that severely restricted reporting. Four major scandals during that decade had revealed multiple incidents of abuse by caregivers in collusion with each other and many others who knew of, but failed to report, the abuse. Although 85 caregivers were known to have committed more than one instance of abuse (an average of 3.2 incidents per caregiver), only 22 (26%) of these offenders were terminated or forced to retire. The remaining 63 (74%) continued employment in this agency. Most of these (37) received only brief suspensions or reprimands. Because these 85 abusive caregivers had committed 271(53%) of the 511 known cases of abuse, excluding all or even some of them from the agency would have been likely to substantially limit the problem.

As a supervisor and administrator in a large institution, my experience was very consistent with MacNamara's findings. (See Chapter 4, A Personal Comment, and Chapter 1, A Personal Ethnography of Abuse, for more on the author's own personal experiences at an American institution.) Unexplained injuries, fearful residents, staff innuendos, and hundreds of other signs clearly told me that the abuse incidents that were reported or disclosed were only a tiny tip of the iceberg. Even the detection of incidents did not promise that much could be done. Institutional policy and the collective bargaining agreement made firing almost impossible unless a long history of previous charges had been substantiated leading to a series of gradually escalating disciplinary actions (e.g., reprimands, fines, suspensions). Because only the most frequent and flagrant violators, the least vigilant, and the most unlucky were likely to be caught, dismissals of abusers were rare. The fact that the dismissals that did occur often seemed unrelated to the severity of the offense was perhaps even more unfortunate. For example, employees who had not yet completed their 6-month probationary period could be and sometimes were terminated for minor infractions, while "permanent employees" were protected by an elaborate bureaucratic process. Fellow employees who saw a few unfortunate peers get fired for relatively minor misconduct, while others received only minor penalties for serious assaults, were unlikely to see any consistency or logic in the administration of discipline that could have served as a deterrent to abuse. Although disciplinary action and criminal prosecution has a significant role in abuse prevention, punishment alone has been ineffective in deterring abuse in human services; other approaches are needed.

Screening Employees

Although there is no known means of ensuring that potentially abusive employees can be screened out of the human services, several screening procedures are potentially useful in selecting nonabusive new employees. These include criminal record checks, careful evaluation of references, interview methods, and psychological testing.

Police Checks Police checks are used in some states and provinces for people who run a bingo, operate a bowling alley, do plumbing, sell cigarettes, work as undertakers, practice as a clairvoyant, work in a casino, or drive a taxi. Yet the people who care for children and for people with disabilities can often do so without a review of their criminal records. Perhaps the fact that some people considered too dangerous to work in a casino are easily hired into positions caring for children and vulnerable adults is a reflection of society's priorities.

Some caregivers have previous convictions for physical violence or sexual assault or abuse that should exclude them from providing care to vulnerable people. For example, one study of 325 children who were sexually abused by extrafamilial caregivers revealed that in 29 (9%) cases the parents were aware of the caregiver's previous record of child molestation or related offenses, and in an additional 44 (14%) cases, the regular caregiver "handed children over to relatives and friends who were sexually abusive. In many cases these relatives and friends had a record of child molestation" (Margolin, 1991, p. 220). It is likely that there were other abusers in this group who had conviction records that were not known of because there was no evidence of routine screening. A review of screening programs for those working with vulnerable people found that 5%–8% of screened employees have some kind of criminal record (Ombudsman of British Columbia, 1987). Because chronic abusers working as care providers often have access to many potential victims, the percentage of abuse that may be attributed to these individuals may be much higher than the reported 5%–8%. In a study of abuse in out-of-home placements, 27% of perpetrators had prior allegations of abuse (Rosenthal, Motz, Edmonson, & Groze, 1991). New York City requires checks of people seeking employment in childcare centers and these checks have revealed relevant convictions in about 1% of those screened (Ombudsman of British Columbia, 1987). This relatively low rate suggests that these police checks are acting as a deterrent, discouraging those who know that they cannot pass screening from applying for these jobs. This deterrent effect may be even more valuable to abuse prevention than the elimination of those who are directly rejected through screening.

Screening procedures must strike a delicate balance between protecting vulnerable people and protecting the rights of individuals to work in jobs of their own choosing. Eliminating potential abusers through police checks, reference checks, interview procedures, and testing is a valid objective. Arbitrary rejection of potentially productive employees, however, does nothing to ensure quality of care. Failure to take reasonable measures to protect social service recipients against abuse has been found in court to constitute negligence, but overly zealous efforts to check the records of applicants may intrude on their right to privacy (Baas, 1990).

The best time to conduct police checks is before the individual is employed because it is typically much more difficult to dismiss pay-rolled employees than it is to refuse employment to applicants. If an employee is found to have falsified information on his or her application, there may be grounds for dismissal. However, firing someone because initial screening procedures were inadequate may be impossible and could even lead to legal action against the employer (Baas, 1990).

Laws and procedures regarding criminal record checks and other screening procedures, as well as access to personal information, vary across states and provinces, so it is important to learn the specific standards of your own locality. The National Association of State Directors of Teacher Education and Certification (NASDTEC) maintains the Teacher Identification Clearinghouse, a United States database on teachers who have had their certificates revoked or suspended. The database includes names, known aliases, social security numbers, and birthdates (Baas, 1990). NASDTEC reports this information to each state's Department of Education (Washington, D.C., also participates), and schools can check their list of applicants against the NASDTEC list by contacting their state agency.

The Ombudsman of British Columbia (1987) recommends the following principles to ensure thorough, but fair, screening of potential employees. First, all those currently employed in or seeking employment in jobs working with vulnerable people must undergo security checks. This requires careful attention to defining who is a vulnerable person and what positions are included. Checks should be mandated for private as well as public employees. Second, there must be a mechanism in place to monitor agency compliance and ensure that checks are being carried out. Third, information must be given both to the applicant or employee and to the employer, so that employees know exactly what information has been given out. This allows them to explain any information that might be misleading and to challenge any information given in error. Fourth, the nature of relevant information should be clearly defined and only such relevant information provided to employers. For example, employers do have a right to know if a potential employee has committed a violent crime or sexual assault, but they may not have a right to know that an employee was arrested in a sit-in as a union activist. Fifth, employees have a right to provide supplementary information that they believe should also be considered. Sixth, the employee's privacy must be maintained. Seventh, consent forms should specify the information sought, how it will be used, and how this information will be made available to the applicant as well as the prospective employer.

The Ombudsman of British Columbia's (1987) report stresses that these procedures must be recognized as limited and should not be expected to replace other safeguards, including other screening procedures. Police checks cannot reveal information about offenses that were never discovered or never reported; nor can they provide information about charges that were unsubstantiated. Furthermore, police checks do not always provide information about juvenile offenses or those offenses that were pardoned. The Ombudsman's report also suggests that checks be implemented at admission to training programs to avoid preparing people for jobs that will not be open to them when they complete their training.

Usually information from abuse registries such as child welfare or adult protective services that is unsubstantiated by criminal convictions is unavailable for police checks that are limited to criminal records. The use of such unconfirmed allegations might be seen as an infringement on the rights of the accused. Nevertheless, in some cases, limited use of this information is allowable. For example, when placing a child in foster care, some social service agencies review their own child abuse report records and consider any information about previous allegations.

The issue of if and to whom such information can be made available, as well as how it can be used, is not a simple one. The legal basis for establishing and maintaining child abuse and other similar registries is based on safeguards that limit the potential for misuse of such information. The rights of all individuals to due process of the law must be carefully weighed against the rights of vulnerable people to be free of abuse. Cases of abuse, such as the case of Jason Carpenter (see chapter introduction) whose abuse-induced disabilities can never be treated, make a strong argument for at least the restricted use of such information. A strong pattern of suspected abuse should have eliminated Jason's abusers as potential foster-parents. Although this pattern was not supported by previous convictions, consideration of such suspected abuse was justifiable because of the predominating right of the child to safety, and because the potential caregivers' desire to provide care is not a basic right, but a privilege, and therefore subject to less protection. Because the privacy of individuals whose names appear in these registries is a legitimate right, procedures for checks of child and adult-protective abuse registries generally require that applicants for a particular position waive this right after having the screening procedure thoroughly explained to them.

Reference Checks   Most job application procedures request letters of reference or at least require the names and addresses of people who might be contacted. Often references reveal little useful information to the prospective employer. Nevertheless, references can sometimes be very helpful. The following suggestions may be useful when considering an applicant's references.

Consider the source of the applicant's references. Employers, especially recent employers in human services settings, should be included. If not, be certain that there is a good explanation. If the references seem questionable, request permission to contact recent employer(s). In doing so, ask for a few names of people who might be familiar with the applicant's work. Reluctance to allow contact with former employers or limited willingness to allow contact with only one or two individuals in the previously employing agencies are bad signs. If the applicant is completely unwilling or appears obviously uncomfortable about allowing contact with the former employer, ask why and evaluate the explanation carefully. For example, some applicants might say that they haven't resigned from their previous job yet and do not want their current employer to know that they are seeking other employment. The potential employer in such a case may want to consider whether this level of honesty and openness is acceptable. If it is, explain why this information is critical to the hiring decision. If an applicant is a good prospect in all other respects, he or she might be told that a tentative decision has been made to hire, contingent on acceptable references. Thus, they will not have to let their old employer know they are job seeking unless they are a serious candidate for the new job.

Beware of missing information and faint praise. It is a bad sign when previous employers seem to have difficulty finding positive things to say. Statements like "no serious difficulties" could be signs of problems on the job. Letters that comment on punctuality, reliability, and industriousness, but say nothing about human interaction skills, should be a cause for concern in human services professions. Some letters of reference communicate a subtle level of discomfort with the applicant. This sometimes occurs when the person giving the reference has suspicions of problems with the employee, but few real facts to back up the feelings of uneasiness. Such situations can be hard to differentiate from simple personality conflicts or a reference who has a hard time saying anything good about anybody. Sometimes a private conversation with the past employer can help to sort out what the actual source of concern is and how much weight to give to it.

Establish specific procedures for obtaining references. Generally, it's better to have letters of reference go directly to the prospective employer from the person supplying the reference and not to have them transmitted via the applicant. Letters that go to applicants first are more likely to be eliminated, altered, or forged if the applicant is unsatisfied with what they say. References will not be as honest or direct if it is known that the applicant will be the first person to read the letter. For this reason, some agencies use forms that require applicants to sign a statement waiving their rights to see the letters before forwarding the form to the past employer(s). In some cases, individual letters of reference written to each prospective employer may be impractical, especially when the competition for jobs is fierce and the applicant may be applying for many different jobs. In such cases, copies of general letters of reference to prospective employers may be useful for initial consideration, if there is an opportunity for follow-up contact with the previous employer by phone or letter before a final decision to hire is made. Even when letters go directly to potential employers, forged letters are still occasionally found, although obtaining letterhead is usually a difficult task. Calling the reference is generally the best defense against such forgeries.

The greatest limitation of letters of reference is the frequent lack of honesty of many of the authors. For example, some employers are so anxious to get problem employees out of their agency that they are willing to write decent letters of reference. In other cases, previous employers are afraid of personal confrontation or legal action if they write an unflattering letter. As a result, many wonderful letters are written for people who are bad risks. Three things can be done to help reduce this risk. First, each of us must take personal responsibility for our own behavior in writing letters. We need to think about what we would want to know if we were the prospective employer and communicate both negative and positive information clearly. Second, personnel departments and administrators should do exit reviews of employees, especially those who commit abuse or misconduct. Part of those reviews should include looking at the employee's old letters of reference, and informing those writing new letters of reference of the outcome. This kind of feedback may prove revealing. Third, legal action should be taken against past employers who knowingly falsify information in letters of reference. People who withhold or falsify information about abuse to help offenders get jobs with vulnerable people logically bear part of the responsibility for any offenses that these people later commit in their new employment. Legal action based on that responsibility could serve as a powerful deterrent.

Interviews Interviews can also be useful to screen out problem employees. Poor impulse control, unrealistic expectations, problems with authority, low self-esteem, and negative attitudes about vulnerable people are among some of the traits that may be uncovered in job interviews that warn of future problems. Of course, job applicants will attempt to be on their best behavior during an interview and will naturally try to conceal any traits or behavior that they feel might hurt their chances of getting the job. Some job applicants who are potential abusers may be practiced or clever enough to avoid any chance of detection; however, in many cases, potential problems do become clear. Poor impulse control is probably the easiest to detect because these individuals may have difficulty suppressing negative behavior and attitudes even when they know that expressing them is against their best interest. Hasty answers that show little thought may indicate difficulty controlling impulsive behavior.

For applicants who have prior experience working with clients similar to those served by the potential employer, interview questions might focus on how the applicant dealt with work situations in the past (Rodriguez & Hignett, 1976). For example, the employer might ask how the employee would respond to an attack by a client. Obviously, an applicant who indicates that he or she would respond with violence is a cause for concern, but other responses may also alert the interviewer to potential problems. For example, an unrealistic response such as an applicant insisting that he would just talk quietly and not try to defend himself may be a demonstration of unrealistic expectations or an attempt to conceal fear. An applicant who never considers requesting help from another worker may be a poor team member.

Sometimes questions that are more hypothetical generate more honest and spontaneous answers because the individual's defenses are less likely to be on guard. Instead of asking "what would you do if . . ." or "what did you do when . . . ," the interviewer might ask "how do you think a staff member would respond if . . . ." In some cases, a parallel situation might be discussed to elicit a more candid response. For example, few applicants for childcare positions will advocate harsh punishment, but when asked what they would do to someone who committed abuse, some will advocate very severe punishment including torture or mutilation. While this may appear to express the applicant's commitment to children, it may be a clearer indication of his or her underlying aggression and rationalization of violence.

The style of the applicants' interactions may communicate a great deal more about their attitudes toward clients and authority than the actual verbal content of their responses. Almost anyone will be a little nervous during a job interview, but the applicant who is too deferential or fearful may have difficulties coping with authority. Interviews should rarely, if ever, be conducted solely in offices. Create opportunities for applicants to actually see and interact with the people they will be serving. Attitudes may become apparent in these interactions, but the interviewer should also later ask applicants what they thought about the clients in open-ended questions, providing further opportunity for evaluation. For foster parents, respite care providers, and others who provide services in their own homes, at least part of the interview should take place there, along with a home safety inspection.

Psychological Testing   Psychological testing of potential staff remains a controversial issue. However, testing has demonstrated strong potential for identifying abusive and nonabusive staff. Haddock and McQueen (1983), for example, administered a series of questionnaires to 21 abusive and 21 nonabusive institutional attendants. These questionnaires were then blindly scored. The two groups were matched for age, gender, ethnic origin, marital status, and job responsibilities. All but 3 of the 21 abusive employees were identified as abusive through testing. Of equal importance, none of the 21 nonabusive employees were incorrectly identified as an abuser. The tests employed included the Child Abuse Potential Inventory (CAP-I), the Minnesota Satisfaction Questionnaire (MSQ), and a General Information Form designed by the authors. Multiple regression analysis of the results found that a combination of eight variables provided the best prediction of abuse. These eight variables in order of importance were as follows:

1. The CAP-I score (estimated risk for child abuse)
2. The MSQ Independence score (dissatisfaction with the opportunity to work alone)
3. The number of children the employee had (employees with more than one child were more likely to abuse)
4. The MSQ Advancement score (dissatisfaction with chances for promotion)
5. The MSQ Achievement score (dissatisfaction with one's own achievements)
6. The employee's report of severe discipline used by his or her parents
7. The amount of alcohol used by the employee (employees who consumed more alcohol were more likely to abuse)
8. The marital status of the employee (married employees abused more than single employees)

The CAP-I was originally developed to be used with parents to assess likelihood of abuse, but it has also been used with foster-care providers and human services employees (Milner, 1989). In this study, the CAP-I was useful by itself to predict abuse, but was not as accurate as the combined questionnaires. In spite of the apparent accuracy of the combined measures, Haddock and McQueen (1983) argue for caution before administering these tests as premployment screening methods. They note that more research is needed on predictive validity, particularly through longitudinal research, rather than a relatively quick comparison of abusive and nonabusive caregivers. Additional research is also needed to determine how cultural and socioeconomic bias can be avoided in such testing; whether the same predictors are valid for people working with children and those working with adults; whether the same tests can predict neglect, physical, sexual, and psychological abuse or whether separate scales might be needed; whether there are any unique factors that must be considered in applying these tests to individuals working with people with disabilities; and whether some categories of offenders (e.g., those most likely to offend in group rather than isolated settings) may require different evaluation strategies. Considering all these factors, psychological testing has great potential for screening out potential offenders, but until better refinement of testing can be achieved, tests should only be used with great caution. The further refinement of existing tests and the development of new tests should be a research priority for preventing abuse in paid care settings.

CONCLUSION

Abuse prevention programs must consider caregivers. While caregivers are often among those who abuse people with disabilities, they can also provide the best known protection against abuse. Risk reduction can be achieved by ensuring that people with disabilities who require care receive it from those who are most likely to protect them, not abuse them. Risk reduction can also be achieved by providing support networks for families and other caregivers that will encourage the best possible relationships between them and the individuals in their care.

In-home care with natural families is typically the safest living alternative. In-home care can be made even safer through training and support programs. When children and vulnerable adults require care from nonfamilial caregivers, those caregivers must be carefully screened. Supervision, support, and training for paid and volunteer caregivers are also important components of risk reduction. These strategies are discussed in Chapter 9.

9

Building Safer Environments

Conditions at the institution in Fojnica had never been good, but when civil war engulfed Bosnia, they deteriorated. As Muslim forces overran Croatian positions, three-quarters of the population hurriedly evacuated the town. The doctors, nurses, and attendants responsible for the facility were among those that fled leaving 230 people, mostly children with mental retardation, locked in the institution without food or water ("Canadians rescue," 1993). There was no evidence of any attempt to provide for their needs; they had simply been left to die. The doctor who gave the order for the staff to leave indicated that he was concerned that Muslim troops would capture them, but "would not say why the children were considered expendable when the staff had to be saved ("Shame of Fojnica," 1993, p. A14). Fortunately, United Nations Peacekeepers discovered the institution a few days after it was abandoned and only six (four young children and two adolescents) had died (Jimenez, 1993).

The staff who chose to abandon these people did not do so with malicious intent. There was a war going on, they had other important concerns, and inmates of the institution were simply not a high priority. After United Nations Peacekeeping forces took control of the institution, they asked the staff to return, but in the midst of uncertainty about getting paid and the continuing chaos of the surrounding countryside, only two staff members returned.

The United Nations forces had not been the first to arrive at the institution; other soldiers (it remains uncertain which warring faction they represented) had been there after it was abandoned. They had looted and vandalized the offices and kitchens, using their automatic weapons to blast through locked doors. Empty vodka bottles and other

remains of a party indicated that they had spent considerable time celebrating within a few feet of the dying inmates. They must have heard
the crying, but when they had taken everything of value to them and
finished celebrating, they too left without making any effort to help
("Shame of Fojnica," 1993). The Canadian government was proud of
the role of its forces acting as United Nations Peacekeepers in saving
the lives of the children and adults living in the institution and pledged
to provide all the aid it could to these children ("Canadians rescue,"
1993). However, they clearly indicated that this did not include accepting them into Canada (Jimenez, 1993).

The situation in Fojnica has been compared with the fall of Berlin
in World War II. As Allied forces moved in from both sides, residents
of Berlin were thrown into a panic and many attempted to flee ("Shame
of Fojnica," 1993). The zookeepers in Berlin were also facing the chaos,
but their feelings of responsibility for and attachment to their animals
were strong. They stayed with their animals, cared for them, and protected them throughout the pandemonium. It is sad that no similar
sense of responsibility or attachment was demonstrated for fellow human beings in Fojnica.

The situation at Fojnica was unusual, perhaps even unique in
some aspects, but it also shares some essential characteristics with the
situations that many other people with disabilities encounter in institutional living. Neither the people who directly provide their care, nor
the administrators who run the institutions, appear to place a high priority on the quality or continued existence of the residents' lives. Neglect, in a variety of forms, is the most direct result of this apathy. Physical and sexual abuse commonly follow.

Schwier's (1990) collection of autobiographical accounts of people
with developmental disabilities provides rare insights into the realities
of institutional life. All of these accounts relate stories of social and
emotional neglect in environments where every aspect of the lives of
the inhabitants was ruled unforgivingly by institutional convenience.
Most of the accounts provide examples of the abuse that thrives under
these circumstances. Levine (1990), for example, compares two of the
institutions where he lived. Of one institution where he spent 5 years in
the early 1970s, Levine relates, they "punished 'em when they had to,
but they didn't beat you like and they also did nice things" (p. 75). He
provides clear descriptions of the isolation and coldpack procedures
used in this institution to ensure the obedient compliance of residents.
The coldpack procedure involves strapping a resident to a mattress
filled with ice water and then wrapping ice water–soaked sheets
around the individual resulting in rapid loss of body heat. The procedure was used "to make you know who's boss and who isn't boss"

(p. 77). Incredibly, this relatively sophisticated approach to social control seemed kind compared to the beatings with straps and broomsticks at the other institution where Levine had spent 15 years of his life.

Each individual in Schwier's collection is unique, yet each of their stories echoes a similar account of institutional neglect and abuse and of a better life in the community. Many of those who speak out about institutional life in Schwier's book also tell us that they were the lucky ones. They were among the elite class of institutional residents who could speak for themselves and who could do useful work in exchange for modest privileges. Those who could not do these things were treated more harshly.

Much of the discussion of the previous chapters suggests that some environments encountered by people with disabilities are riskier than others. This chapter is about ways for people with disabilities to remain in the safest environments, while making all the environments that they currently live in as safe as possible. The fact that some environments are safer than others is consistent with most people's general experiences. For example, some neighborhoods are safer than others, and most of us would feel insecure if we were isolated from potential sources of assistance and placed under the control of potential offenders.

Environmental approaches to crime prevention are based on two simple principles. First, minimize exposure to high-risk environments and maximize exposure to low-risk environments. Second, alter environmental characteristics associated with increased risk to lower the danger associated with these settings. For example, isolated parking lots outside bars at night are often the scenes of physical or sexual violence. Applying the first principle, simply avoiding these areas, reduces risk. Applying the second principle, lighting the area more brightly or patrolling the area regularly, might reduce the number of violent episodes that could occur there.

These same principles can be applied to risk management for people with disabilities. Applying the first principle, moving people out of high-risk environments to those associated with less danger, increases their personal safety. For example, Schwier's (1990) collection of personal accounts confirms that people's lives improved and problems of violence and abuse were diminished simply by moving people out of institutions and into community settings. As another example of the use of these principles, segregated services have been shown to be associated with greater risk of violence and abuse (e.g., Rindfleisch & Rabb, 1984; Sullivan et al., 1991); applying the second principle, altering environmental characteristics (e.g., making these services more inclusive by reducing overall isolation from the rest of society), can make even these segregated settings less prone to violence.

Of course, some people may wonder, "Why bother with the second principle of altering the environment when the first principle of removing people from dangerous environments provides a simpler solution?" The answer to this question is twofold. First, the simple truth is that in spite of past and current efforts to move every individual with disabilities to less restrictive environments, many people continue to live in segregated settings and have a right to reasonable safety while living in them. Second, in reality, every environment falls into some continuum of risk and safety. None are entirely free of risk, and different individuals may have different levels of vulnerability in the same environment. Consequently, identifying and controlling risks is a useful prevention strategy across all environments.

Chapter 8 suggests two major strategies that can help to control environmental risks. First, supporting and training parents helps to reduce risk in family living environments. Second, screening out paid caregivers with high potential to abuse helps make service environments safer. This chapter discusses other environmental measures to control risks such as the normalization of risks; the design and organization of safer human services environments; the development of clear policies and procedures that reduce risk; and the recruitment, support, training, and supervision of competent staff.

NORMALIZING RISKS

Normalization of the Environment

Normalization, integration, inclusion, and *deinstitutionalization* are interrelated and overlapping concepts that, if used effectively, can help to reduce risk of abuse for people with disabilities. Nirje (1969) defined normalization as "making available to the mentally retarded patterns and conditions of everyday life which are as close as possible to the norms and patterns of the mainstream of society" (p. 181). Wolfensberger (1972) further refined the concept as the "utilization of means which are as culturally normal as possible, in order to establish and maintain personal behaviors and characteristics which are as culturally normative as possible" (p. 28). Wolfensberger asserted that making the living conditions of people with mental retardation "at least as good as that of average citizens" (Wolfensberger, 1980) would tend to support behavior typical of others of the same age. This assertion has been confirmed by observations that many individuals develop functional skills, even without specific training, and require less medication to control behavior when they move to more natural environments (e.g., Lord & Pedlar, 1991).

A related benefit of normalizing the environment appears to be the normalization of risk. People living in more natural environments appear to experience lower levels of risk more typical of the rest of society (e.g., Rindfleisch & Rabb, 1984; Sullivan et al., 1991). This risk reduction probably occurs through three different mechanisms. First, the natural environments appear to have fewer inherent risks. For example, they are less likely to cluster together large numbers of both vulnerable and aggressive individuals. Second, natural environments are less likely to teach skills that are dysfunctional for personal safety. For example, institutional environments frequently teach generalized compliance to achieve the management and control functions of the facility; yet those who learn generalized compliance become more vulnerable to abuse. Third, natural environments provide better opportunities to learn skills and behavior that help reduce risk. For example, people living in natural environments learn about asserting their personal space through modeling and imitation, but few appropriate models are available in most institutional settings.

Integration and Inclusion

Integration and inclusion are two primary means for achieving normalization. Integration refers to the process of returning someone to the natural environment who has previously been segregated. Inclusion refers to maintaining the individual in the natural environment; thus, by avoiding the initial segregation, inclusion makes integration unnecessary. Integration is almost always more difficult to achieve than inclusion. It requires individuals to make more transitions because they first must readjust to segregated environments and then adjust back to the natural environment. Nevertheless, the power of integration to curb abuse has been recognized by the courts. Nevada County California schools in a court-approved settlement agreed to work to increase integration as a remedy for the abuse of children with disabilities that occurred in segregated schools. As part of the settlement, The California Department of Education agreed to strengthen and step up its monitoring and enforcement procedures to assure that special education students are appropriately integrated ("Settlement in case," 1991).

Because there are few opportunities to learn the functional skills of the natural environment while segregated, those who have been included since birth have more time to learn these necessary skills. Samuel Gridly Howe may have been among the first to express the value of inclusion in a speech given in 1866: "Beware how you needlessly sever any of those ties of family, of friendship, of neighborhood, during the period of their strongest growth, lest you make a homeless man, a wanderer and a stranger" (quoted in Wetherow, 1992, p. 63). Ironically, this speech was given at the laying of a cornerstone for the building of a new institution.

Deinstitutionalization

Deinstitutionalization generally refers to the move of people out of institutions and into communities. Although this concept may appear to be relatively simple to bring into practice, it is actually a long, complex, and poorly understood process that has had limited success. Since the 1960s, many people with mental retardation have, indeed, left large state-funded institutions. The number of people with mental retardation living in these institutions was over 194,000 in 1967, but declined to less than 90,000 by 1988 (Taylor, Bogdan, & Racino, 1991). However, many of these people have been moved to nursing homes, private group-care facilities, group homes, and other forms of institutional or quasi-institutional residential care. For example, about 45,000 people with mental retardation live in private residential facilities with more than 15 beds and another 54,000 live in nursing homes (Taylor et al., 1991).

Does this movement represent real deinstitutionalization and progress toward community living? Have the risks of abuse been reduced by this change? The answers to these questions remain unclear. Defenders of the deinstitutionalization process might argue that the settings that characterize the new system are smaller, more homelike, and less geographically isolated. Critics might argue that these new settings are no more socially integrated than the traditional institution and may even be more difficult to supervise.

One study of nursing homes set up to serve deinstitutionalized children with severe and multiple disabilities in Massachusetts suggested little reason to hope that these children were better off (Glick, Guyer, Burr, & Gorbach, 1983). Low standards of care and financial disincentives (e.g., a fixed daily rate of payment regardless of the amount of services provided) were blamed for poor educational and rehabilitative services. Approximately 4% of the children studied died each year.

Other studies of deinstitutionalization, however, provide a better rationale for optimism. They suggest that many people leaving institutions have more enjoyable lives, become more independent, and have greater opportunities for learning as they move from institution to community placements (e.g., Larson & Lakin, 1989; O'Neill, Brown, Gordon, & Schonhorn, 1985). These two contradictory impressions of deinstitutionalization are not actually in conflict with each other; rather they describe different aspects of a vast, complex, and heterogeneous process. For example, one study of 18 individuals who had been deinstitutionalized (Lord & Pedlar, 1991) found that 13 of the 18 (72%) had significantly better lives as was indicated by increased skill development, less dependence on medication, more visits from families, and a greater number of subjective reports of happiness by staff and families observing this transition. However, the same study found that insufficient planning led to frustration and incompatible groupings, a custodial approach resulting from a lack of leadership in some homes, superficial integration only with other members of the community, and general failure in the development of meaningful outside social networks.

Considering these complexities, deinstitutionalization cannot be considered merely as movement through a continuum from larger to smaller institutions, then private intermediate care facilities, group homes, foster care, and so on. Rather, it must be seen as the combined result of movement along a number of interrelated yet independent continua (e.g., larger to smaller, regimented to individualized). For example, while foster care would typically be considered a more natural and less institutional setting than a group home, a foster care setting that includes several foster children and is very regimented and depersonalized may be more institutional than many larger group homes. Some of these continua are listed in Table 1.

Deinstitutionalization of residential, educational, vocational, leisure, and other settings institutional in nature can occur through at least three distinct mechanisms. First, the most common mechanism is for people to be moved from settings with a great many institutional characteristics and integrated into those with fewer institutional

Table 1. Deinstitutionalization

Institutional care	Family and community care
Large	Small
Isolated from community	Integrated into community
Impersonal	Personal
Hierarchical	Egalitarian
Few choices for residents	Many choices for residents
Dependency	Independence
Special	General
Artificial	Natural
Agency ownership and control	Resident ownership and control
Bureaucratic	Informal
Regimentation	Individualization
Many caregivers	Few caregivers
Caregivers motivated by pay	Caregivers motivated by attachment
Depersonalized relationships	Strong interpersonal bonds
Transient relationships	Enduring relationships
Emphasis on control	Emphasis on development

characteristics. Second, attrition and inclusion can be used to differentially place individuals new to the service system in the least institutional setting, while limiting or halting admissions to more institutional settings. Finally, although often difficult to achieve, existing services can be modified to make them less institutional.

Integration and inclusion are the preferred methods for deinstitutionalization and normalization of behavior and risks. The goal of these processes should always be to keep each individual as close as possible to generic community settings and normal patterns of interaction while meeting their specific needs. Methods for achieving this goal have been well described in a number of other texts and articles (e.g., Johnson & Johnson, 1989; Lakin & Bruininks, 1985; Pearpoint, Forest, & Snow, 1992). Unless and until full inclusion is achieved for all individuals, however, it is essential to consider how existing service environments can be made safer.

ABUSIVE SERVICE ENVIRONMENTS

Underreporting of Abuse

Abuse continues to be endemic to most, if not all, service environments. Reported abuse is all too frequent; yet most abuse goes unreported. Of course, the number of unreported cases can never be known, but the evidence of underreporting is powerful. Marchetti and McCartney (1990) suggest that verbal and psychological abuse is almost never reported; abuse reports appear to be limited to serious instances of physical and sexual abuse. They also point out that direct care staff, who make up the largest percentage of workers in most agencies and who have the best opportunity to observe abuse, report much less than would be expected. Furthermore, the longer employees work in an agency, the less likely they are to report abuse. They also found that most administrators are aware of underreporting problems, with over 70% believing that less than 50% of abuse is reported. According to Rindfleisch and Bean (1988), the actual percentage of abuse reported in institutional care is only 20% of reportable offenses, and even this estimate may prove to be optimistic.

Why Abuse Occurs

There are many known causes of abuse in service environments, and more causes are likely to be identified in the future. Some abuse can be expected to occur in any setting where people interact. The inherent vulnerability of many people with disabilities also contributes some additional risk. Many service environments are isolated from the community, and isolation increases risk. The depersonalization and dehumanization of the people whom agencies are intended to serve reduces inhibition against abuse. Service environments cluster people with disabilities and staff, so that once abuse occurs, the abusive model is likely to be imitated by other residents and staff. Many service agencies have hierarchical authoritarian structures that emphasize power and control, which are fundamental components of abuse. Despite the frequency of abuse in human services, most agencies fail to acknowledge the full extent of the problem and thus render it impossible to implement effective prevention programs.

Rindfleisch (1984) describes the typical administrative structure of institutions that foster sexual abuse as: 1) being authoritarian, 2) placing stress on control and management of clients at all costs, 3) relying on theoretical or ideological models that depersonalize and devalue residents, and 4) displaying an oppressor mentality that tolerates or encourages hostility and aggression toward minorities. In such settings, workers who feel frustrated, powerless, and dissatisfied with their own treatment by more powerful administrators and supervisors may redirect their anger toward more vulnerable residents.

Abusive Caregivers

They key to building safer service environments is in staffing. Staff who commit abuse may do so for a great variety of reasons and exhibit a great variety of abusive patterns. Some measures to reduce risk appear to be most effective against some specific patterns of abuse; other measures are better suited to different patterns. Archetypes of abusive caregivers are useful for exploring these relationships.

MacNamara (1992) described different types of abusive caregivers based on his extensive experience working in institutions. These include:

- Predatory abusers (who may exhibit psychopathic and sociopathic character disorders)
- Anticaregiving abusers (who harbor negative attitudes and resentment toward the people whom they are supposed to be serving), indifferent abusers (who simply don't care and will take the path of least resistance)
- Contrite abusers (who feel guilty, but continue to abuse)
- Chemically dependent abusers (who have little control over their own behavior)
- Negligent abusers (who cannot or simply do not give the attention or effort required)
- Ineffectual caregivers (who try, but lack basic competency in caregiving)

- Superiority-obsessed abusers (who will do anything required to bolster their self-esteem and assert their superiority)
- Frightened caregivers (who become dangerous when confronted with challenging behavior or other potential emergencies)
- Heroic caregivers (who use their exploits to gain status or manipulate their situations)
- Disintegrating abusers (who were formerly good caregivers, but are deteriorating as a result of personal or institutional influences)
- Mosaic abusers (who exhibit some elements of various categories)

Additional categories considered here are:

- Corrupted abusers (who lack internal control to inhibit abuse when external safeguards are inadequate)
- Pathologically eroticized abusers (whose thoughts and behavior are dominated by sexuality)
- Saboteur abusers (who commit abuse as a form of sabotage against the caregiving system)
- Social abusers (who abuse others because it is an expectation of the abusive subculture in which they take part)

Table 2 provides further information about these archetypes and also suggests some primary approaches to environmental risk management. For example, predatory abusers must be screened out prior to hiring or eliminated through disciplinary action leading to termination whenever possible because they are unlikely to benefit from other forms of intervention. Frightened abusers, however, often have the potential to be transformed and become excellent caregivers as a result of training and counseling.

The great majority of people who commit abuse within the human services are mosaics. For example, Sister Godfrida, a Roman Catholic nun as well as a nurse, was suspected to have taken part in the deaths of 21 of her patients and was convicted of killing three. Godfrida indicated that she killed these individuals because they were difficult at night, a motivation associated with an indifferent abuser, but the discovery that she was addicted to morphine also suggested that chemical dependence may have played a role (Segrave, 1992). In another example of a mosaic abuser, Waltrud Wagner, a nurse's aide, killed, in collaboration with her coworkers, at least 49 and perhaps as many as 300 of her patients. Wagner indicated that she had murdered them because "they had irritated her during the night shift or had been unpleasant" (Segrave, 1992, p. 297). This might suggest that Wagner was an indifferent caregiver motivated simply by institutional or personal convenience. Nevertheless, her systematic murder of at first one, than up to

Table 2. Archetypes of abusive caregivers and recommended primary approaches to environmental risk management

Abusive caregiver types	Predominant abuse	Disability attitudes	Impulse control	Coworker relations	Management relations	Primary risk management
Predatory abusers	Mixed	Negative	Variable	Shallow	Mixed	Screening, discipline
Eroticized abusers	Sexual	Negative	Variable	Mixed	Mixed	Screening, discipline
Anticaregiving abusers	Mixed	Negative	Variable	Mixed	Negative	Screening, discipline
Indifferent abusers	Neglect	Variable	Variable	Shallow	Mixed	Training, support
Negligent abusers	Neglect	Variable	Variable	Shallow	Strained	Training, counseling
Ineffectual caregivers	Neglect/mixed	Variable	Variable	Mixed	Strained	Training
Contrite abusers	Mixed	Positive	Poor	Strained	Strained	Support
Chemically dependent abusers	Mixed	Variable	Poor	Mixed	Strained	Counseling, screening
Superiority-obsessed abusers	Emotional/mixed	Negative	Variable	Strained	Negative	Counseling
Frightened caregivers	Physical	Variable	Poor	Mixed	Mixed	Training, discipline
Heroic caregivers	Physical/mixed	Variable	Variable	Strained	Mixed	Counseling, discipline
Disintegrating abusers	Mixed	Variable	Variable	Mixed	Mixed	Counseling, discipline
Corrupted abusers	Mixed	Variable	Poor	Positive	Mixed	System change
Saboteur abusers	Mixed	Negative	Poor	Strained	Negative	Counseling
Social abusers	Mixed	Variable	Variable	Positive	Mixed	System change, supervision
Mosaic abusers	Mixed	Variable	Variable	Mixed	Mixed	Mixed

three, patients a month infers some deeper predatory tendencies. The group involvement indicates a social abuser component, and dissatisfaction with the demands of the job while money and respect went to licensed nurses suggests the displaced anger of the saboteur caregiver. The socialized saboteur mosaic was perhaps most apparent in Wagner's training sessions for other nurse's aides, in which she used modeling and direct instruction in teaching them to prepare lethal injections, strangle patients, or drown them by forcing a hose down their throats. While these examples may be extreme in regard to their deadly nature, they are typical in their complexity.

ENVIRONMENTAL RISK MANAGEMENT STRATEGIES

A service system with good resistance to abuse must not depend on a single risk-management approach for controlling a single type of abuser. It must incorporate a variety of safeguards and protections into the following strategies:

- Design and organization
- Policies and procedures
- Recruitment and screening
- Orientation and inservice training for staff
- Counseling and support programs
- Supervision and leadership

Design and Organization

Abuse prevention must begin at the earliest stages of planning of any human services system and remain in the forefront of all decision making throughout the life of the agency. The prevention of abuse can often be better achieved through focus on the cultivation of good relationships and positive practices than through focus solely on the elimination of undesirable relationships and practices. A positive focus suggests positive expectations, but it does not imply denial of the problem. Acknowledging the reality of the constant potential for and frequent occurrence of abuse in human services is critical to any effort to ensure safety.

Surprisingly, although a great deal has been written about quality assurance for programs serving people with disabilities, the issue of violence is rarely addressed. For example, Knoll (1990) reviewed 17 different quality of life measurement instruments for the presence or absence of content in 96 topical areas. Many were relevant to abuse (e.g., employment of nonaversive intervention, respect, privacy), but the simple freedom from sexual or physical violence was not even included as a criterion. Whereas the right to personal safety may be considered so basic and obvious that it should not require a definitive statement, other basic rights (e.g., rights to religious expression, due process, privacy, assembly) were specifically included in Knoll's review. The frequency of violence and abuse in the lives of people with disabilities, especially those in institutional care, makes this omission particularly serious. Knoll (1990), however, should not be faulted for this omission, as it is merely a reflection of the instruments he surveyed and the general state of the field.

Agency Responsibilities To Set and Maintain Safety Standards The lack of reasonable measures to ensure personal safety in institutional care has led to legal challenges to mandate agency responsibility for creating safer environments (LeGrand, 1984). These cases have established the general rules of responsibility for: 1) a level of safety consistent with community standards and 2) reasonable efforts to manage known risks. The first criterion suggests that those living in institutional care have a right to a level of safety that is no worse than the level available in the community where they resided before entering institutional care. The second implies that agency administrators must develop plans to manage known risks. For example, if some residents are known to be assaultive and others are known to be vulnerable, administrators are required to develop a reasonable plan for ensuring the safety of the vulnerable residents.

These standards recognize that while no agency can guarantee complete safety, all human services have clear responsibilities for risk management that should be incorporated into the design and organization of all human services agencies. These responsibilities should certainly be clearly stated in field standards for quality of care. The potential misapplication of personal safety standards requires some caution and suggests the need for a third standard to accompany these two—the protection of personal safety must *not* be interpreted to mean the restriction of the rights or liberties of those protected or their rights to assume reasonable risks. The purpose of such a standard would be to prevent intrusions such as locking people in isolation or denying rights to personal, social, and sexual expression under the guise of protection.

Failure To Confront Issues Most service agencies and the instruments that assure their quality control fail to directly confront issues of abuse. This failure makes agencies and the people they serve more prone to abuse for several reasons. First, it broadcasts the message to potential abusers that the agency is unwilling to take a strong stand and suggests that abuse may be tolerated in order to keep the issue buried. Second, it suggests to residents and employees who report abuse that discussion of the topic is unwelcome, and they are unlikely to be supported if they continue to bring it up. Finally, it sends a strong message to everyone involved that the people who make the rules and design the programs have little concept of the realities of day-to-day life in the service setting.

Making Human Services Less Institutional The potential for abuse can also be minimized by designing human services systems and agencies that are less institutional. They should generally be smaller, better integrated into the community, egalitarian in structure with real choices for residents, supportive of independence, informal and unregimented, and structured to foster strong and enduring interpersonal bonds between caregivers and service consumers.

Realistic Expectations of Staff Realistic expectations of staff are essential. For example, placing a single, poorly trained staff member in charge of highly aggressive and highly dependent individuals may be a recipe for abuse. The staff person is neglectful if he or she allows the residents to harm each other, but may have to be physically abusive in order to control any aggressive acts without adequate assistance. Under such circumstances, telling staff that they cannot use physical force, but still must maintain order, may really be telling them to threaten or assault residents, but not to get caught doing it.

Working with Labor Unions Unions and professional organizations have often been blamed for the failure of management to address problems of abuse effectively. Some of the blame may be deserved in some cases, but in many cases, such blame only provides a rationale for supervisory or administrative inaction. These organizations have the potential to be powerful allies in the battle against abuse, but before this potential can be realized they must be convinced that it is in their best interest to do so.

Some initiatives might be of common interest both to human services administration and to labor unions. For example, counseling and support programs that staff with chemical dependency or emotional problems can confidentially obtain may be a valuable benefit for employees and also help reduce risk. Better training and clearer policies and procedures for staff who have to deal with violent clients would be beneficial to unions because these can help reduce the exposure of their members to injuries and disciplinary actions, while reducing the risk of abuse for those being served. Improved living conditions for service recipients generally translates into improved working conditions for staff. Both help eliminate abuse in at least two ways. First, the deplorable conditions in many institutional settings depersonalize and dehumanize clients and numb any feelings that workers might have about residents' suffering. Second, those whose feelings are not numbed by these appalling conditions are typically driven out because of them, leaving only the most insensitive staff (generally those most prone to abuse) to provide care.

Other areas of abuse prevention may be harder to agree upon, and these may become subjects for legitimate negotiations. For example, job security and protection from termination are fundamental goals for unions. Therefore, they have a basic interest in protecting their members from termination regardless of what charges have been made against them. Unions might be more flexible, however, about solutions that involve maintenance of income and benefits while moving a union employee out of a job. Furthermore, it is important to remember that unions play an important role in protecting people from charges that are unfounded. The best time for unions and management to explore common interests in abuse issues is typically before (or at least outside of) a conflict over a particular case. Administrators and union officials often see the worst side of each other in such conflicts. Under these circumstances, it is easy to forget that unions and professional organizations represent vast numbers of well motivated and hardworking human services workers and not just some of the worst exceptions that they are often called upon to defend. Finding common ground for union and management in abuse prevention is indeed a challenging task, but it is not one without great potential.

Integration into the Community   Human services that are well integrated into the communities that they serve are more resistant to abuse. Therefore, consideration of such factors as physical location within the community, use of generic community services and resources, and policies that encourage interaction with community members can help reduce risk associated with isolation (Sobsey, in press; see also Chapter 4, section on Isolation). The mere physical presence of a group home within the community does not constitute integration or eliminate isolation. Other members of the community need to actually enter the home and interact with residents and staff. Of course, it is important to know who these visitors are and why they are visiting, and some control must be maintained over their access—just as one would expect to maintain control over access to her or his own home. Sometimes it may be difficult to strike a good balance between controlling access and fostering integration, but in practice the gray areas are generally small. The common sense rules that most people apply to their own homes typically represent the best balance. For example, more caution is generally applied with strangers and casual acquaintances than with people we know well. In most circumstances, we expect people to knock or ring the bell, not just wander in, and while we might invite casual acquaintances into our kitchen or living room, we would not expect them to enter other areas of the house without a specific invitation to do so.

Personal privacy may also have to be balanced with isolation. Reasonable privacy is a right everyone should share that protects us from intrusion. Too much or inappropriate privacy, however, may be a risk factor and could be a sign of abuse. Again, community standards typically provide the best guide. Residents have a right to privacy, especially during bathing, dressing, and other personal activities; however, in general, common areas should be more open. Staff who bolt or chain doors from the inside without any apparent need, obsessively draw curtains, or cover windows with pictures or schedules are sometimes hiding inappropriate interactions. Creating open areas for social exchanges, meals, leisure activities, and other group interactions helps to limit isolation and discourage abuse.

Locked-door policies are sometimes rationalized as necessary measures to prevent one or more residents from running away or wandering off and possibly becoming lost or injured. Clearly, some people with disabilities do need to be protected from such dangers, but it is essential that protection be provided with minimal intrusion. Larmer and Webb (1989), discussing security provision for adult care facilities, recommend that exits be within easy sight of areas frequented by staff, and, if necessary, that chimes or a shopkeeper's bell be placed on the door to ensure that staff will be alerted whenever the door is opened. In some cases, residents who frequently wander off might be given alert bracelets that activate a sensor panel in the doorway to alert staff when these individuals are leaving the facility. Even these methods can be intrusive if used with residents who do not really require them; however, if actually necessary, they represent a less intrusive alternative to simply locking the doors.

Policies and Procedures

MacNamara (1992) points out that in spite of all of the heightened concern about abuse in human services, no clear and generally accepted definition has been put forward. Nevertheless, it is essential that each agency have clear policies and procedures regarding abuse that minimize the potential for ambiguity or misinterpretation. Several approaches exist for determining what constitutes abuse. First, lists can be generated on specific types of physical, mental, sexual, or neglectful acts or omissions that constitute abuse. Second, broader conceptual definitions can be generated. For example, MacNamara (1992) recommends that two basic principles concerning residents may be all that is required of staff. These are: 1) to protect from harm, and 2) to refrain from doing harm. A third approach involves the application of typical community standards. For example, child abuse, assault, harassment, and many other forms of violence or abuse are already defined by criminal statutes, and simple enforcement of these may offer significant protection to individuals assisted by human services.

A combination of these three approaches is generally recommended. Enforcement of existing community statutes actually provides very significant protection, and this enforcement has often been lacking in community services. The application of community standards and the involvement of community-based law enforcement when required facilitates integration and helps to normalize service environments to reduce risk.

Additional measures are usually required in human services settings that serve vulnerable people because of the potential for control and exploitation. For example, belittling a client or exerting excessive control would rarely be enforceable as criminal offenses, but are nonetheless abusive, and therefore should be controlled by administrative procedures. Sexual exploitation and coercion of adults in care also requires careful definition. Typically, agency policy should prohibit any sexual interaction between staff and service consumers because of the potential for abusive interactions. If there are any exceptions (e.g., some clients might be considered capable of making their own informed choices), these conditions must be clearly defined.

Reporting Abuse policies and procedures must also mandate reporting and provide protection for residents or staff who report incidences of abuse. Of course, such policies and procedures are only of value if staff are clearly informed of policy and well-trained in procedures. Mandated reporting is often codified in child protection statutes and dependent adult protection acts, but should also be clearly stated in institutional guidelines.

Control and Intervention Policies and procedures must also be explicit in the areas of control and intervention. For example, if a resident wants to leave the facility, do staff members have a right to lock her or him in? If one service consumer attacks a staff member or another client, what type of restraint can be used to respond to the attack? Such situations frequently occur, and without clear guidelines can result in serious problems. Some staff may fail to take appropriate action because they fear that it will be viewed as abusive. Others will take inappropriate intrusive actions that constitute abuse either because they lack the guidance or knowledge to handle the situation or because they will use the opportunity to rationalize intentional abuse.

MacNamara (1992) recommends that caregivers take a formal oath acknowledging all their responsibilities, and presents a lengthy example of what this might entail. This approach is certainly worthy of consideration. However, the underlying principles of clearly stated administrative rules and the assumption of personal responsibility might also be achieved through other means of communicating policy.

Managing Challenging Behavior One of the most complex areas in providing nonabusive human services to people with developmental disabilities is the management of aggressive, self-injurious, or disruptive behavior. Fortunately, considerable progress has been made in controling this type of behavior through nonaversive procedures; however, specific policies and guidelines need to be clearly defined in order to eliminate procedures that leave the person exhibiting the aggressive behavior vulnerable to abuse.

Physical Intervention When people with disabilities engage in behavior that is potentially threatening to themselves or to others, a number of different control strategies are advisable. Minimal protective intervention involves using only the amount of force or control necessary to stop the individual from doing harm and nothing more. Sometimes very little force is required and the behavior does not recur. Often, however, the behavior does recur, and it is sometimes difficult to prevent the aggression without hurting the individual exhibiting it. If the behavior is recurrent, it will sometimes be impossible to stop it before harm is done. Furthermore, the frequent need for physical intervention increases the risk for abuse. For example, the frightened caregiver may overreact, believing the threat to be greater than it actually is. The negligent or ineffectual caregiver may fail to act entirely, thus allowing harm to take place. Therefore, although physical intervention is sometimes appropriate, it is often ineffective.

Physical Restraints and Isolation Physical restraints (e.g., restraint nets, straight jackets) or isolation rooms are rarely, if ever, appropriate. The individual is usually prevented from doing harm while restrained, but once released from restraints or isolation, the behavior often recurs. Therefore, unless the individual spends a great deal of time restrained, the challenging behavior will only be postponed, not eliminated. Restraints are intrusions against individual liberty and prevent participation in appropriate, as well as inappropriate, behavior. Isolated or restrained individuals have no opportunities for learning positive alternatives to their harmful behavior. Furthermore, physical restraints can be dangerous because people often struggle against their application and can be hurt in the process. Sometimes people in restraints themselves become victims of aggression by others. Use of restraints leaves the individual vulnerable to abuse, and some staff who may be predatory or anticaregiving abusers are likely to use restraint in particularly abusive ways.

Chemical Intervention Tranquilizers and other drugs have been widely used as chemical restraints to prevent behavior problems in people with developmental disabilities (see Chapter 5, section on Psychoactive Drugs). In many cases, however, even when given in massive doses they fail to produce any clear improvement in behavior. In some cases, such as in behavior problems associated with posttraumatic stress disorder, chemical restraints may actually worsen the problem. These drugs, especially when given in large doses over a long period of time, often produce serious side effects such as cataracts and liver damage. Like physical restraints, they also interfere with learning and participation in appropriate, positive activities. In spite of these problems, tranquilizers and other drugs may have some limited use. They are likely to be most useful for managing acute emotional crises while a more appropriate program is being put into place to specifically address the behavior problem itself. Behavior must be carefully monitored during a baseline measurement period and during application of the drugs to ensure that the medication is producing the desired result (Orelove & Sobsey, 1991).

Punishment Programs   The use of punishment programs to control challenging behavior should be eliminated whenever possible and carefully controlled if used at all. Many of these programs are inherently abusive and would never be allowed in prisons or other environments without informed consent of the individual receiving the treatment. They also provide opportunities for abusers to act out their aggressions under the cover of "treatment," and provide models of coercion for others to follow. In addition to these disadvantages, the record of punishment to effect lasting change has not been demonstrated (Sobsey, 1990b).

Nonaversive Approaches   Nonaversive approaches to behavior management are typically the best alternative to managing aggressive behavior. The following practices are recommended:

1. Alter the environmental conditions (e.g., if two residents fight when they sit together at lunch, it may be possible to change their seating arrangements).
2. Involve the client in positive activities (e.g., involving the individual in more educational and recreational activities may redirect some of the energy being channeled into aggression).
3. Determine the function of the inappropriate behavior and teach the individual an appropriate alternative for achieving that function (e.g., if a client is attacking others in order to get others to leave him alone, teaching him an appropriate method of requesting privacy may reduce the need for the inappropriate behavior).

Readers who would like a fuller description of nonaversive behavior management and how to train staff in this area may wish to read Evans (1990).

Recruitment and Screening of Staff

Careful recruitment and screening of staff are essential to creating a safer service environment. Screening procedures such as checking police records, requesting letters of reference, and interviewing techniques are addressed in Chapter 8. This discussion focuses on ways to recruit competent, nonabusive service providers to the human services industry.

Staff recruitment should be conducted with two major goals. First, it is desirable to recruit large enough numbers of candidates to fill open positions and to allow for thorough screening and selection to take place. Second, recruitment efforts should be directed toward those candidates with the greatest potential. The best method for achieving both of these goals is to make the job, if properly done, attractive to potential workers. This is best accomplished through creating environments that are supportive of both service consumers and service providers.

Improving Working Conditions Improved working conditions result in greater job satisfaction, which is an important element of attracting good candidates to the human services. This is true for several reasons. First, it is difficult, if not impossible, to attract good workers into bad jobs. The smaller the pool of candidates for a job, the greater the need to hire questionable or undesirable candidates becomes, thereby making screening and even termination of unsatisfactory or abusive workers less easy to enforce. Second, the risk for abuse increases when unattractive jobs create staff shortages that make the work for remaining employees even more difficult and demanding. Third, when staff are chronically dissatisfied, especially in a system that is rigidly managed, dissatisfaction and anger are frequently displaced from the more powerful management to the more vulnerable service consumers.

For these reasons, administrative efforts toward increasing job satisfaction for those staff providing decent services may be better spent than on efforts to inhibit or punish inappropriate behavior. Nevertheless, care should be taken in the types of incentives and rewards that are offered to new recruits. Offering good pay and benefits for a job with unpleasant working conditions creates a particular problem because of its potential to trap those dependent upon their paycheck into jobs that are not suited to them. This problem may be particularly apparent with indifferent or chemically dependent abusers. Good pay attracts good staff, but it can also attract abusers.

Pillemer's (1985) finding that caregivers who are financially dependent on contact with elders are more likely to abuse them suggests that too much dependence on monetary rewards may be dangerous. Nevertheless, there is no reason to believe that poorly paid workers will do better than well paid workers, only that monetary concerns have limited value unless they are combined with methods to enhance the staff's sense of accomplishment and personal satisfaction in doing a good job. Staff should share in decision making and responsibility for outcomes; the administrator who assumes credit for good results "in spite of" his or her staff is inviting sabotage.

Accurate Job Descriptions   Accurate job descriptions that emphasize desirable employee attributes and skills need to be developed and circulated by the hiring agency (Pecora, Whittaker, & Maluccio, 1992). These can help attract the kind of staff that is desired and discourage those least suited to the work. For example, two advertisements and job descriptions might be prepared: one stressing routine care and maintenance of order and the other stressing the facilitation of growth and development. The job really requires some elements of each, and an honest job description must indicate this, yet emphasizing one or the other will typically attract different groups of job applicants. Preparing job descriptions may also be useful in determining real administrative mandates and agency priorities. For example, it may require those involved with preparation to decide whether clean floors or human development and social interaction is the agency's higher priority.

Community Integration   Community integration also has potential benefits for recruiting staff. Smaller service units based in communities typically have a larger labor pool to draw on than large facilities in isolated settings; this generally results in a greater number of job candidates and, consequently, greater opportunity to be selective in hiring. When human services are provided in isolated settings, potential employees have no opportunity to observe and consider whether a career in human services is appealing to them. When a facility is based in the community, it is easier for those considering this career to actually see the human services in action.

The opportunity to interact with people with disabilities has often had a powerful impact on people's lives and career decisions. Many of the best service providers indicate that they became interested in the field after meeting someone with a disability through their school, church, friends, or family. Such introductions to the field are increasing in number as more and more people with disabilities are fully included in community activities. People who have positive interactions with people with disabilities during these meetings are more likely to be attracted into human services than those who have had neutral or negative interactions. Some individuals will be attracted to the field for the wrong reasons (e.g., predatory abusers who see people with disabilities as vulnerable). These job candidates will typically be a small minority, but they must be carefully screened out.

Exemplary Employees   If an agency already has some exemplary employees, these staff can help recruiting efforts in two ways. First, they should be asked if they know of any other people who might be interested in the job whom they believe would make good employees. Second, they should be asked how they heard about or were recruited for the job. Their answers may point out good recruitment strategies for attracting future workers.

Staff Training

Staff training has the potential to be a critical element in preventing abuse. Brookhouser (1987) points out that every study of abuse in residential care agrees that staff training is essential to prevention. Unfortunately, training often fails to meet this potential. The topic of abuse is often too uncomfortable to be given much attention. In addition to denying staff members vital information, avoiding discussion of abuse may cause staff members to feel that the whole topic is taboo and could inhibit them from speaking out if they observe abusive incidents inside their agency.

Teaching staff about abuse and how to confront it in their own behavior and in others is an essential part of orientation and staff training. Training must be explicit and frank. Employees should be informed that abuse is common in human services and that they are likely to encounter it during their careers. They must learn the definitions, policies, and procedures that will help them to respond when they encounter abuse. Although it is important to address abuse directly, it may be helpful to focus on positive elements rather than merely providing a long list of negatives. For example, emphasis on the role of caregivers in providing beneficial services and protecting the rights of service consumers may be more useful than presenting only negative examples of violations of those rights. Gardner and Chapman (1985) provide a good discussion of teaching these rights to staff. Information on basic civil rights such as "equal protection of the law" and "freedom from cruel and unusual punishment" can be easily extended to discussion of abuse of people with disabilities. (See Chapter 1, section on Rights and Realities for People with Disabilities, for further information on this subject.)

Coping with Potentially Abusive Feelings   Staff should be taught to acknowledge, recognize, and cope with their own potentially abusive feelings. Most new employees do not anticipate that they may feel frustrated and angry toward some of the people they serve or that they may feel sexually attracted to some of them. Nevertheless, these feelings are very common amongst human services workers. Staff who are unprepared for such feelings may have more difficulty in dealing with them. Staff should learn that they are responsible for their actions, rather than their feelings. Some individuals, especially those with low self-esteem and unrealistically high self-expectations, may have problems differentiating between feelings and actions. They may feel that because they are tempted to commit physical and sexual aggression, they are already guilty. These individuals often become corrupted abusers or saboteur abusers. One of the strategies that could be taught to those having difficulty coping with their feelings is to seek help from friends, employee support programs, or other sources.

Responding to Difficult Behavior Staff training should include discussion of how they might feel and react if one of the individuals with disabilities who is in their care is verbally, physically, or sexually aggressive toward them. The development of potential response plans that are nonabusive during training may help staff if and when they encounter these situations in their work. In addition to learning about nonaversive behavior management strategies, staff working with clients who have a high probability for aggression requiring physical intervention should be well-trained in nonviolent self-defense strategies (MacNamara, 1992). These are designed to reduce the need for physical confrontation as much as possible, but if such confrontation becomes necessary, they allow physical control to be exerted with minimal risk to the client, as well as the staff member. It also allows staff to handle these confrontations with less fear and anxiety, which reduces risk of abuse by a frightened or saboteur caregiver.

Sexuality Staff should be made aware of the range of sexual behavior that they can expect to encounter on the job, what their own reactions might be, what actions and interventions are acceptable on their part, and what may be signs of sexual abuse or exploitation. Brown and Craft (1992) provide a number of useful materials for training related to sexuality and the sexual abuse of people with mental retardation. For example, one suggested activity presents a number of real-life events (e.g., "a mother pulls back the foreskin on her adult son's penis to wash him," p. 38; "a young man with severe learning difficulties has an erection when hugging a female staff," p. 39) and invites groups of staff to discuss how concerned they would feel about each situation.

Developing Positive Attitudes Cultivating positive attitudes about people with disabilities and about the ability of individual employees to do a good job should be a part of every staff training program. As presented in Chapter 12, this may be best accomplished by allowing opportunities for successful interactions in a supportive environment and by providing the appropriate models. Nevertheless, specific discussion of attitudes and beliefs during orientation and training can be useful, particularly to help staff understand how socially pervasive beliefs and attitudes about people with disabilities may influence their own behavior.

Communication and Teamwork Skills Staff need to be trained in communication and teamwork skills to help ensure that the agency runs relatively smoothly. Reading, lecture, and audiovisual materials can be helpful, but role playing and other forms of student participation activities may be particularly critical for producing solid results. In fact, effective teamwork and communication styles may be more clearly understood by *how* these skills are taught than by *what* is being taught. For example, lecture material may include content that tells staff that they should express their opinions and actively participate in team decision making; however, this material should not be taught through a lecture in which questions are discouraged or ignored because this will send a contradictory message to the students. Most will learn to say that their input is valued (as they have been told), but their behavior will be influenced far more strongly by the way they have actually been treated in the training. Differing verbal and behavioral messages may have the added disadvantage of developing in the students a sense of fundamental dishonesty in the agency that will make them less secure and less willing to be honest with others.

Participation of Clients Whenever possible, people with disabilities, particularly those served by the agency, should participate directly in the planning and delivery of staff training. This should not merely be a token gesture, but a real effort to include the content that they consider to be most relevant. Clients' views on what they feel would be desirable in staff behavior and what kinds of positive contributions that they believe staff can make to their lives is essential information. Teaching staff that the service consumers are important and that they should be respected, while at the same time totally ignoring their potential input in training or using them as props for the agency's own agenda also suggests a serious discrepancy between course content and administrative behavior. Demonstrating sincere respect for service consumers through meaningful inclusion in staff training provides an excellent model that is likely to be far more effective than any strictly verbal or written communications.

Modeling Training should not be considered an activity that is solely relegated to the classroom. Modeling of positive interactions and good work habits by other staff or trainers in the actual work environment is probably far more effective. Of course, it is important to ensure that new staff are exposed to appropriate, not inappropriate, models. Sundram (1986) suggests that agencies identify exemplary employees and pair these employees with new recruits during their training to create a kind of apprenticeship system.

Staff training cannot be expected to solve all problems. Validation of staff training as an effective method for preventing abuse of people in human services settings still requires demonstration. Nevertheless, staff training appears to be one of the most potentially productive strategies for risk reduction.

Support Programs

Employee counseling and support programs can aid in reducing the risk of abuse by helping troubled employees to confront personal issues that could potentially lead to abuse. Employees who have substance abuse problems or who are having difficulty coping with their jobs for a variety of reasons can benefit from these kinds of programs. For example, employees who are not dealing well with feelings of resentment toward the agency or their superiors may find that counseling will help them to learn how to handle their anger without directing it toward the vulnerable people they are serving.

Unions and professional organizations can assist employers in the development and implementation of staff support programs. People who voluntarily seek the assistance of these programs should be able to do so in confidence. Unless reasonable assurances of confidentiality can be made, many people who could benefit from this type of service will choose not to use it.

Supervision and Leadership

Good supervision and genuine leadership are important elements of abuse prevention, but ineffective or misguided attempts at supervision may actually increase risk. Positive approaches to supervision should be pursued whenever possible. Providing rewards for good caregiving is just as effective (perhaps even more effective) for reducing risk than simply punishing infractions. The successful use of nonaversive supervisory techniques by superiors provides employees with appropriate models to imitate in their own interactions with clients. It also reduces the risk of saboteur abuse by reducing staff anger toward management. If supervisors cannot use positive approaches to eliciting desirable behavior from their employees, it is difficult to understand how they can expect to demand that their staff succeed in using methods that are nonaversive.

Good supervision should be present in the workplace, not isolated from it. Supervisors who spend little time interacting with their staff or the people they serve are unlikely to exert much beneficial influence. In the worst examples of poor supervision, supervisors spend most of their time doing paperwork in offices that are well removed from the actual service environment. Supervisors who participate in and model good caregiving are more likely to have the respect of their workers and to be in a position to influence them in a positive way.

Sometimes supervisors must play the role of adversaries who discipline staff. When abuse occurs, they must remember that their first responsibility is to the service consumers, and authorities should be notified without hesitation if there is a serious allegation or suspicion of abuse. They must investigate carefully and without bias. When disciplinary action is appropriate, the required steps must be taken, even if it will prove to be unpopular with others.

Good supervisors are good communicators. They must be sensitive to both staff and service consumers and should listen and respond appropriately. For example, if staff members tell their supervisor that they cannot cope with the behavior of a particular resident without potentially hurting the resident, the supervisor must determine an appropriate response based on all relevant information. Failing to acknowledge the concern or to take meaningful action toward solving the problem is likely to lead to abuse. In some cases where no simple solution is available to address the concerns of everyone involved, the supervisor must explain the situation to higher-level decision makers and request their further assistance.

CONCLUSION

This chapter suggests some strategies for developing safer human services environments for people with disabilities. The first and simplest strategy is to work toward the inclusion of all people with disabilities in the mainstream of society, thereby eliminating (or at least limiting) the need for specialized service environments that are associated with increased risks. A second strategy must also be employed. Because many people with disabilities continue to be served in artificial human services environments (e.g., group homes, institutions), these environments must be made more natural and less institutional. This can be achieved through the development and implementation of sound organization and planning; efficient and thoughtful policies and procedures; careful recruitment, screening, and training; support programs; and supervisory leadership.

10

Law and Law Enforcement

Sometimes it is difficult to know whom to believe. On the afternoon of August 7, 1991, Daniel William Brennan asked a young man, David P., to cut his lawn. That same day, the young man, a 22-year-old with mental retardation, complained to a social worker that Mr. Brennan had whipped him, forced him to perform fellatio, and sodomized him (Webber, 1993). Mr. Brennan indicated that he was only trying to be kind when he asked the young man to visit him. David P. was ruled incompetent to testify in court, and several witnesses pointed out that David P. often masturbated in public and had made previous unsubstantiated allegations against others of similar sexual offenses. The court had a difficult job sorting out the case; however, two pieces of evidence tipped the scale of justice toward a conviction and a 7-year sentence. First, there were deep red welts on David P.'s back that were consistent with his accusation of being whipped. Second, a videotape was confiscated from Mr. Brennan's house showing David P. lying naked on a bed, while the camera zoomed in on his genitals.

With this evidence, conviction might have been simple, but, in fact, it was not. Because David P. himself was not allowed to testify, his allegations to the social worker were considered hearsay evidence, and the defense argued for their exclusion. Although the videotape was surrendered voluntarily, the defense argued it too should be excluded because Mr. Brennan was not properly informed of his right to refuse a search of his home. Mr. Brennan indicated that he would appeal his conviction (Webber, 1993).

This case raises a number of important questions. Would a conviction have been possible without the videotape? If conviction was difficult to achieve in this case, even with the corroborating physical evidence, how difficult is it in other cases, probably the vast majority, where corroboration is unavailable? If victims of crime can be barred from the witness stand because of their disabilities and their statements made outside of court can be excluded as hearsay, how can these people be protected by enforcement of the law?

The integrated ecological model of abuse presented in Chapter 6 indicates that abuse occurs when large power inequities exist between individuals or groups. Laws and the mechanisms for their enforcement exist as society's means for narrowing or, ideally, eliminating these inequities. When individuals do harm against those who are less powerful than themselves, the greater powers of society must be brought to bear against the aggressor. However, the legal system remains imperfect, and much abuse continues to be hidden. Some power inequities are tolerated and sometimes even encouraged.

This chapter explores the role of law and law enforcement in responding to the abuse of people with disabilities and deterring further abuses against them. Although some specific legislation and court decisions are addressed, more general issues and principles are the primary focus of this chapter for three reasons. First, comprehensive discussion of all of the specific laws and court decisions would require far more space than is available here. Second, laws differ from country to country, and even from state to state, making it impossible to focus on specific laws without localizing the discussion to a particular jurisdiction. Third, court decisions and legislation change rapidly, and an in-depth discussion of specific laws would soon become outdated.

LAW ENFORCEMENT AND CRIMES AGAINST PEOPLE WITH DISABILITIES

Whenever a crime is committed, the police are responsible for investigating and enforcing the law. Most abuse, at least in its more severe forms, legally constitutes a criminal offense. Although little clear information is available that compares criminal offenses against people with disabilities with crimes against people without disabilities, an Australian study shows that the overall rate for personal offenses against adults with mild to severe mental retardation who attended sheltered workshops was 2.7 times as high as the rate of offenses against other Australians (Wilson & Brewer, 1992). As shown in Table 1, the rates for personal offenses against victims with mental retardation were particularly elevated in the categories of robbery (12.7 times as high), sexual assault (10.7 times as high), and assault (2.9 times as high). Only auto theft was lower for the group with disabilities and that was likely due to the fact that only a few had cars to be stolen.

Wilson and Brewer (1992) point out that greater severity of mental retardation was associated with greater risk for personal offenses and

Table 1. Crimes against people with mental retardation compared with crimes against other citizens as reported by Wilson and Brewer (1992)

Crime	Victims with mental retardation	Other victims	Elevation of rate
Personal offenses			
Robbery	5.1%	0.4%	12.7 times higher
Sexual assault	3.2%[a]	0.3%[a]	10.7 times higher[a]
Assault	11.4%	4.0%	2.9 times higher
Theft (other than auto)	7.6%	6.4%	1.2 times higher
Auto theft	0.6%	0.7%	0.9 times higher
Household offenses			
Break and enter	11.4%	6.4%	1.8 times higher
Household theft	4.4%	3.7%	1.2 times higher

[a]Based on female respondents only.

lesser risk for household offenses. For both groups of offenses, those living with natural families had the lowest rates of victimization, whereas those living in institutions, group homes, or living alone had the highest rates of victimization. A survey of people with physical disabilities who use attendant care (Ulicny, White, Bradford, & Mathews, 1990) indicated similar elevation of crime risk. The authors found that 10% of those surveyed were physically assaulted by their attendants, and 40% had been victims of theft or robbery by their attendants.

Despite this elevated risk, many crimes against people with disabilities never come to the attention of police (Sobsey & Doe, 1991). In the Wilson and Brewer (1992) study, 40% of the crimes against people with mild and moderate mental retardation went unreported to police, and 71% of crimes against people with more severe mental retardation went unreported. Sometimes, even when crimes against people with disabilities are reported, police demonstrate a reluctance to become involved. This reluctance could stem from a variety of reasons. The police may have negative attitudes or a lack of experience with people with disabilities (Yuker, 1986). They may believe that the prosecutor will reject the case because of the victim's disability (Gunn, 1989), or they may see the case as complex and therefore likely to create a large demand on the time and resources. As suggested in Chapter 1, police are sometimes directed by higher-level officials to stay out of the affairs of other government agencies (e.g., departments of mental health, hygiene, or retardation). Often, a combination of these factors results in assigning low priority to these kinds of cases.

Police Investigation

Police investigations of alleged crimes against people with disabilities or crimes that involve witnesses with disabilities must follow the same principles of thorough investigation as are required in other cases. In fact, these basic principles may be even more important in cases involving people with disabilities. For example, interviewing witnesses promptly is important in any case, but when a witness has a disability that may impair his or her long-term memory, immediate follow-up is even more critical. Even if the witness has a clear recollection, the presence of a disability that could impair memory weakens the case because questions about the person's capacity to remember are likely to be raised during the trial, and any delay prior to the police interview will strengthen this sense of doubt. In addition, conducting a formally recorded interview promptly helps reduce the chance that others will discuss the matter with the victim before a statement is taken. This helps lessen the vulnerability of the case to arguments that the witness has been unduly influenced.

Several good sources suggest additional principles to be applied and specific measures to be taken in cases involving crimes against people with disabilities. Some of these recommendations include:

1. Providing better training to police officers to help them prepare for handling these cases (California Attorney General's Commission on Disability, 1989; Skoog & O'Sullivan, 1993)
2. Ensuring equal access to justice and equal protection of the law (California Attorney General's Commission on Disability, 1989; Coles, 1990; Nova Scotia, 1991)
3. Compensating to the greatest extent possible for any special needs related to the witness's disabilities (e.g., witness cannot speak) and to related social disadvantages (e.g., witness has few social skills because he or she has been segregated from others) (Nova Scotia, 1991)
4. Making every reasonable effort to provide assistance or equipment to aid and support the witness (Nova Scotia, 1991)
5. Involving law enforcement, people with disabilities, advocates, and service providers in consultation and teamwork (California Attorney General's Commission on Disability, 1989; Coles, 1990; Nova Scotia, 1991; Skoog & O'Sullivan, 1993)
6. Ensuring that all police officers, particularly those involved in working with witnesses with disabilities, have positive attitudes toward those in this population (Skoog & O'Sullivan, 1993)

Community-Based Law Enforcement

Since the 1970s, there has been increasing recognition that effective law enforcement must be rooted in the communities that it serves (Sobsey, in press). The move toward community-based law enforcement was prompted (at least in part) by the recognition that centralized police services, with their technologically advanced methods (e.g., computerized information processing, radio dispatched police cruisers) were in some ways unable to compete successfully with the local neighborhood police officers whom they were replacing (e.g., Trojanowicz et al., 1975). These neighborhood foot patrolmen often knew every inch of the beats that they walked and every face in the neighborhood. They had a perspective on the communities that they served that was difficult to develop by merely driving through the community in a police car.

The move away from foot patrols to modern police services was necessitated by economic factors, changes in the nature of criminal activity, and other social factors. Nevertheless, law enforcement from outside the community often receives poor support from community members and lacks the necessary local knowledge to be effective. As a result of these concerns, modern law enforcement has worked to reestablish community-based services. Community-based law enforcement agencies work cooperatively with other community agencies, meet with groups and individuals to establish mutual goals, develop direct relationships between individual police officers and the people in the neighborhoods they serve, and work at establishing local community offices. The goal of these activities is not to return to the past, but rather to find new ways to establish links with the community. This is achieved by consulting with community members in setting law enforcement priorities, making efforts to hire individuals who represent the communities that they serve, participating in community-initiated crime prevention efforts (e.g., block parents, neighborhood watch), supporting joint police and community efforts to apprehend criminals through the use of media coverage and reward programs, and undertaking a variety of other activities to help link police with the community.

One emerging priority, as currently identified by police in consultation with communities, is family violence prevention and intervention. To establish a more effective role in preventing and responding to family violence, police require specific training and resources for dealing with this type of crime (Skoog & O'Sullivan, 1993). Skoog and O'Sullivan (1993) recommend that this training should address at least four areas of criminal activity involving violence against: 1) children, 2) women, 3) seniors, and 4) people with disabilities.

During the same time that modern community-based law enforcement has been developing, many other social changes have taken place, particularly for people with disabilities. Many individuals who were formerly isolated in institutions are now reentering the community, and many more who might have been institutionalized in the past are staying in the community. In addition, many people with disabilities have established advocacy networks and are making their needs and aspirations known.

Chapters 2, 3, and 4 of this book are largely devoted to a discussion of how people with disabilities have been much more frequently victimized by violent crime than have other members of society. The great majority of these crimes have often been "invisible," hidden behind institutional walls from the remainder of society and from the police. Only a tiny fraction of these crimes are ever reported. Sundram (1984), for example, reports 53 settled abuse charges for a total institutional resident population of 24,000 over a 9-month period. Of these charges, 44 resulted in a guilty verdict or arbitrated penalty. These figures correspond to a victimization rate of about 244–294 per 100,000 people. In the same year as Sundram's report, the reported violent crime victimization rate for New York State was about 1,035 per 100,000 (Nelson A. Rockefeller Institute of Government, 1983) or about four times as high as would be expected according to Sundram's figures. The obvious discrepancy becomes even higher when one considers that research suggests that people with disabilities are about twice as likely as others to be victimized (e.g., Sobsey & Doe, 1991; Wilson & Brewer, 1992), and people with disabilities living in institutions appear twice as likely to be victimized as those living inside the community.

Taken together, these factors suggest that the expected rate of victimization in institutions should be three times higher, rather than four times lower, and suggests that crime committed in the community is 12–15 times as likely to be reported as crime occurring in institutional settings. It must be emphasized, however, that such estimates are rough, as they are based on figures from various studies that measure related, but distinctly different, phenomena. Nevertheless, these figures probably *underestimate* the extent of the discrepancy between institutional and community settings because the definition of abuse employed in New York State facilities includes all of the violent crime categories as well as other behavior that might not legally constitute a crime.

Even when abuse is reported to institutional administrators, police are often kept out of the investigations (Sundram, 1984). Although the rate of victimization appears to be significantly lower in the community (e.g., Sullivan et al., 1991), it is also more difficult to conceal. The higher rate of reporting in the community means that as more people with disabilities return to or remain in the community, more of the victimization of this population will become visible to others, including the police. As more voices are raised to stop this abuse, the more difficult it becomes to ignore the problem.

Preparing Police

Modern community-based law enforcement is attempting to better respond to crimes against people with disabilities (e.g., Coles, 1990). They recognize the need for commitment on the part of all police services and officers, the necessity of additional preparation and training for all police officers, and the desirability of more intensive training for some law enforcement specialists (e.g., Skoog & O'Sullivan, 1993). While the full parameters for required training and resources are still being established, some basic guidelines have emerged. Skoog and O'Sullivan (1993), summarizing the findings of a Canadian national police trainers' workshop, identify five areas of police competencies related to people with disabilities:

1. *Attitudes*—The attitudes of law enforcement personnel toward people with disabilities and the crimes that are committed against them are seen as critical to improving services. "Officers must be open-minded and empathetic with respect to persons with disabilities. Officers must understand why persons with disabilities are particularly vulnerable, and why they may be more reluctant to report incidents of family violence to the police" (Skoog & O'Sullivan, 1993, p. 22). Although little is known about the attitudes of law enforcement officers toward people with disabilities, preliminary research suggests that attitudes need careful study and require some modification (Yuker, 1986). (Chapter 11 provides further information specific to attitude change.)

2. *Awareness of issues*—Police officers should be aware of the medical and legal issues associated with disability. They must be educated about various disabilities, especially those that affect understanding and memory, and what can be done to compensate for, rather than compound, the effects of these impairments.

3. *Multidisciplinary teamwork*—Police officers should know about available resources (e.g., child protection workers, teachers, physicians) who can work with police as a team to assist them in investigating cases involving victims with disabilities and in preparing these cases for court. They need to understand when and how to seek consultation and assistance from these other team members. All team members, including police officers, need to learn from and teach one another, in order to ensure that they are supportive of others' efforts toward reaching a common goal.

4. *Court orientation*—Police officers must recognize the complexities involved when cases with victims with disabilities are brought to court. They need to be able to help in preparing witnesses with

disabilities for court and to anticipate any problems that may arise (e.g., prime witnesses being excluded) by providing a careful and thorough investigation of the alleged crime.

5. *Specialist versus generalist training*—Some law enforcement personnel require comprehensive training in investigating cases that involve people with disabilities. They should understand the physical, social, and psychological aspects of disability and be prepared to interact with people with a variety of individual needs. These specialists might provide consultation to other police officers and respond to referrals of cases that require their expertise. It would be impractical to train all law enforcement personnel with these skills, but all should possess more general "gatekeeper" skills that enable law enforcement to make appropriate responses in initial interactions with complainants and to know what steps should be taken most immediately.

These five considerations for training and service delivery provide important directions for law enforcement. They also suggest two interrelated areas of concern. First, these five stated considerations arise from the perspective of family violence; however, many people with disabilities are victims of institutional violence, which has its own unique considerations. Therefore, police need training relevant to institutional, as well as to family, violence. Second, successful police work will require an understanding of the nature and dynamics of human services systems and the social realities encountered by people with disabilities, as much as an understanding of disabilities themselves. Law enforcement must be prepared to address the special needs of people immersed in the service system and the unique features of conducting an investigation in service environments.

For example, an investigation of 29 highly suspicious infant deaths in Toronto's Hospital for Sick Children led to the quick arrest of a registered nurse for the murder of the most recent apparent victim (Bissland, 1984). The nurse was charged because she had been assigned one-to-one supervision of an infant whom the police felt certain had been murdered, and they believed that she was the only one who had the opportunity to commit the crime. However, more thorough investigation revealed that the nurse who had been charged was not working on the dates of some of the most highly suspicious deaths and had been relieved for lunch and breaks by other staff on nights that children in her care had died. The murder charges were dropped, and a civil suit for wrongful arrest soon followed. In the end, the probable murder of at least 8, and probably as many as 29, children by Digoxin poisoning went unpunished.

According to Bissland (1984), some of the complexities that thwarted police were a lack of knowledge of hospital procedures, apparent pressure to make a quick arrest so that the hospital could return to its normal routine, and an apparent lack of full cooperation on the part of some hospital staff. For example, police were told that critical records of nursing assignments at the time of the deaths had been destroyed, but the missing records resurfaced long after the investigation had gone astray. This pattern of less than enthusiastic cooperation from within institutions is not unique.

Police in Grand Rapids, Michigan, were more successful in securing the conviction of two nurses in the suffocation of six nursing home patients; however, a similar pattern of institutional resistance plagued their investigation (Cauffiel, 1992). Available evidence indicates that similar serial murders in hospitals and nursing homes are likely to be as common, if not more common, than serial sex slayings or thrill killings (e.g., Hickey, 1991) that are typically given widespread public and professional attention. Despite this fact, little research has been conducted on the part of law enforcement to develop profiles of these medical murderers or specific investigative procedures for the institutional settings where these offenses occur.

Better success in policing institutional offenses can only occur when the principles of community-based law enforcement are adequately applied to the ethnographically distinct communities and cultures of hospitals, residential schools, group homes, and other service delivery systems. Police must understand the internal dynamics of service institutions to perform their job effectively within these environments. Before this can be accomplished, police, and society in general, must identify this as a law enforcement priority.

Often this commitment appears to be lacking, and abuse and violence in institutions remain hidden or are rationalized. For example, in the case of the Grand Rapids nursing home murders described above. Cauffiel (1992) quotes Ken Wood, the estranged husband of one of the convicted killers, as saying:

> How much life did she really take? All of the victims weren't even living. They enjoyed nothing, experienced nothing and were going to die. The families at the time of death were relieved at the end of the suffering. . . . I know they had no right to play God . . . but when you decide how much of her life should be taken or lost to prison, shouldn't it be equal to what was taken from their victims? (p. 485)

Although these were the words of a husband pleading for leniency for his wife, Cauffiel (1992) suggests that this was "a view not uncommon in Grand Rapids, in Michigan, in America among those who became familiar with the coverage of the Alpine Manor murder case"

(p. 485). This view contrasts sharply with the reality that most of the patients killed were not particularly debilitated and perpetrator Cathy Wood's own statement that "we did it because it was fun" (quoted in Cauffiel, 1992, p. 254). Such rationalizations that trivialize serious crimes against people with disabilities can only be seen as denying their right to equal justice. Progress toward reducing risk of violence and abuse for people with disabilities requires that equal protection of the law is applied to *all* members of society.

ENSURING EQUAL PROTECTION

Equal protection of the law is a fundamental principle of all democratic states, but the concept of equal protection of the law can be difficult to realize in practice. For example, Ray Walker was a 28-year-old man with mental retardation who lived in a licensed residential care home in California until he was reported as missing. After 7 days, his body was found in a box that had been nailed shut after he was placed inside alive by a residential care provider. The care provider responsible was found in Las Vegas, returned to California for trial, and convicted of manslaughter; however, he received no jail time. Instead, the man was placed on probation and prohibited from working as residential care provider for only 2 years (Baladerian, 1990).

This case raises questions of fundamental equality under the law. If such a crime were committed against an individual without a disability, would the same sentence have been imposed? Other cases involving light sentences for serious offenses against people with disabilities that are discussed throughout the first half of this book suggest that our legal system provides less protection for the personal security of people with disabilities than it does for other citizens. When such apparent inequities exist, the role of government should be to intercede to restore equality. This is generally accomplished through specific legislation to protect the rights of people who are disadvantaged and court decisions that establish responsibility for protecting the rights of these individuals.

Legislative Initiatives and Legal Precedents Toward Equal Protection

Legislation has often been enacted to help protect people with disabilities from violence and abuse. Specific legislated protection is somewhat controversial because it could be perceived as paternalistic and stigmatizing or as perpetuating the stereotype of people with disabilities as being incompetent and denying them their natural right to experience legitimate risks by restricting them in order to protect them. For example, denying people with disabilities the right to a normal sex life has sometimes been rationalized as a means of protecting them from sexual abuse. This kind of restrictive overprotection has been appropriately criticized as denying people the human dignity of risk (Perske, 1972). These are not frivolous concerns; careful consideration must be taken to ensure that the benefits of protective legislation outweigh the potential costs and that methods of legislative protection are cautiously chosen to avoid unnecessary restrictions or other negative consequences.

Generic legislation can provide significant protection for people with disabilities that is not specifically based upon disability itself. For example, between 1962 and 1967, all 50 states passed legislation mandating that child abuse be reported (Reppucci & Aber, 1992). Since that time, most states have amended their statutes to provide additional protection. Many have also modified their rules of evidence to provide greater accommodation of children as witnesses. This legislation is intended for all children, with or without disabilities, and it has indeed provided significant protection for some children with disabilities.

Unfortunately, several problems seem to have emerged from this legislation that raise questions about the adequacy of these laws. First, many adults with disabilities require this protection for the same reasons that it has been extended to children. For example, many adults remain dependent on caregivers and have limited communication skills that make it difficult for them to disclose abuse. Second, research suggests that in spite of mandated reporting laws for all children, abuse of children with disabilities remains much less likely to be reported (Schilling et al., 1986). Although mandated reporting laws have been far less effective for children with disabilities, evidence suggests that they have substantially helped the general population. The fact that 84% of child protection workers reported that they had never served even a single child with a developmental disability (Schilling et al., 1986) suggests that these laws are simply inadequate for ensuring the protection of all children. Finally, these laws are not well-suited to the needs of people with disabilities who do not live with their natural families. Protection is typically legislated under child welfare statutes that are primarily designed for dealing with family problems and are poorly suited for addressing problems that occur in foster-care, group homes, and institutions.

These limitations do not necessarily imply that legislation providing generic protection is of no use to people with disabilities. These protective laws have significant value, and with better application and enforcement, there is the potential for even greater effectiveness. At the same time, however, some additional protection may be specifically required for people with disabilities.

People with disabilities may be protected in various ways. In the United States, the Developmental Disabilities Assistance and Bill of Rights Act of 1975 required states to set up protection and advocacy systems in order to qualify for federal funds. These systems were to be responsible for: 1) protection and advocacy and 2) pursuit of legal remedies. These organizations were also to remain independent of any service-providing institution and to provide information and referrals. However, neither the law nor its subsequent guidelines provided a clear definition as to how these agencies should be set up or the scope of their activities (Sales, Powell, & Van Duizend, 1982).

The Developmental Disabilities Assistance and Bill of Rights Act of 1975 was amended (42 U.S.C. 6042) along with the Protection and Advocacy for Mentally Ill Individuals Act of 1986 (42 U.S.C. 10801) to provide a clearer description of the kind of protection required. With these new legislative initiatives, each state is specifically required to enact legislation for people with disabilities. Several Canadian provinces also have protective legislation (e.g., Prince Edward Island's Adult Protection Act, 1988), and others have introduced legislation; however, some provinces remain without mandated protection. Although specific legislation varies from state to state, most include similar provisions (Furey & Haber, 1989). These general provisions include:

- Definitions of abuse
- Mandated reporting of abuse
- Complainant protection
- Independent investigations
- Agency responsibilities
- Protective intervention services

Definitions of Abuse   Legislated definitions of abuse under a particular statute may be either broad or very narrow. These definitions may limit abuse for the purpose of the particular statute to the maltreatment of a certain category of individual or to maltreatment that occurs in particular environments. For example, statutes aimed at curbing institutional abuse may limit their scope to group residential facilities that are run, funded, or regulated by federal, state, or municipal agencies. On the one hand, a very narrow definition of abuse can limit the ability of a law to control particular forms of victimization that fall outside the definition. For example, restricting the definition of abuse to assault, sexual assault, and other criminal offenses may limit the power of the law to address verbal or psychological abuse. On the other hand, defining abuse too broadly may create ambiguities that render the law unenforceable.

Mandated Reporting The legal requirement to report child abuse now exists in all 50 states. Some states require reporting of child abuse by any citizen who has knowledge of its occurrence; other states only require human services professionals to report suspected abuse. With the introduction of adult protective legislation, most states are now also beginning to mandate reporting of abuse of adults with disabilities. The increasing number of reports after the introduction of this legislation demonstrates the value of these laws. In Connecticut, for instance, the number of cases of reported abuse more than doubled from 30 per month in 1985 when the law requiring professionals to report became effective to 73 per month by 1987 (Furey & Haber, 1989).

Nevertheless, critics of mandated reporting have sometimes suggested that some professionals should be exempt from this mandate because offenders who might seek counseling only if confidentiality were assured might be deterred. There is some evidence to support this assertion. For example, Berlin, Malin, and Dean (1991) found that patient disclosures to psychiatrists of child sexual abuse dropped from about 21 per year to zero per year in Maryland, after psychiatrists were mandated to report such disclosures.

Complainant Protection In May 1992, an arsonist set fire to the bunkhouse on a rural property near New Orleans. The fire destroyed files and documents related to allegations of abuse in nursing homes, and it almost claimed the life of Sue Harang's daughter who was sleeping in the building when the fire was set (Beck & Miller, 1992) Harang, an advocate involved in investigations of abuse and maltreatment in nursing homes in many parts of the United States, indicated that the files were to be used in an FBI investigation that was aimed toward assessing the possible wrongdoing of a Massachusetts-based chain of nursing homes. Harang stated that the fire scared her and the loss of her documents was a significant setback, but she vowed to continue her work.

When a social worker in a Louisiana institution reported directly to police that the staff were trading drugs for sex with residents, he was reprimanded by his superiors for failing to follow institutional procedures, requiring that reports be made only to them. When he witnessed other criminal activities, including the beating of patients, he again reported the incidents to the F.B.I., claiming that he had already reported the abuse to his superiors, but no action had been taken. Investigation showed that he had also assisted patients in filing complaints with the Department of Justice. He was fired by his employers for spreading rumors and breaching confidentiality. He claimed wrongful dismissal, but the American Fifth Circuit court affirmed the right of the institution to fire him, upholding "the employer's authority to discipline employees for making disruptive statements" ("No private right of action," 1989, p. 471).

Complainant protection is a vital component of any act designed to protect people with disabilities. It should specifically protect professionals, and any other individual, from civil action or administrative harassment. It must also protect service consumers from service interruptions, restrictions, and all other forms of retaliation.

Independent Investigations   One of the chief obstacles to effective investigation of abuse in human services delivery systems is that the agencies themselves are often directly responsible for conducting their own investigations of abuse. This results in three specific problems. First, investigators face a conflict of interest because a finding of abuse creates bad publicity for the agency and often results in the disruption of agency policy and practices. There are few rewards and many frustrations for those who attempt to address abuse problems in their own agencies. In the end, most administrators simply place a low priority on dealing with the problem, by only handling the individual incidents that occasionally surface and force them to respond. The Chairman of the New York State Commission on Quality of Care, Clarence Sundram (1986), referred to this tendency as "benign neglect of the problem by institution managers and professional staff whose duty it is to protect patients from harm" (p. 20). Although Sundram is probably generous in characterizing the neglect of institutional administrators as "benign," he goes on to say that

> the reality of their world is that the other demands of running an institution on a day to day basis—of dealing with the articulated priorities set by the agency head, the governor, or the legislature, and of dealing with more visible problems—simply result in pushing the problem of patient abuse from the foreground. (p. 21)

Second, agency investigators typically lack the skills of trained police investigators. In some institutions, for example, the employee relations department is responsible for investigating assaults and other alleged criminal offenses. Often these allegations are never reported to police; if they are, the report is usually made only after a long delay and the completion of an internal investigation. As a result, police often have a much more difficult time conducting their own investigation.

Third, internal investigations typically trivialize the offense and minimalize the penalties by replacing criminal law enforcement with administrative discipline. Repackaging a criminal offense as a mere administrative infraction reduces the perceived severity as well as the resulting penalty. For example, an act that if investigated by police might be labeled as an aggravated assault and punished with a significant jail sentence, might be called abuse or misconduct and be punished with a $500 fine as a result of internal investigation and "discipline."

Legislation should mandate that all allegations of abuse within human services agencies are reported to external protection and advocacy organizations immediately after their disclosure. These organizations have primary responsibility to investigate the safety of the individual who may have been abused and to take action, if necessary, to ensure the person's future safety. The mandate should also specify that those allegations that would constitute criminal offenses, if proven, be reported to the appropriate law enforcement agencies. This would not preclude internal action by the human services agency involved. When outside investigations are needed, as is often the case, law enforcement and protective agencies should coordinate separate investigations. External advocacy and protection agencies can also provide a useful function by monitoring internal investigations and disciplinary practices.

As greater responsibility for investigation of specific allegations is given to external agencies, the focus of internal investigations may become more focused on identifying the underlying causes that contribute to institutional abuse and less focused on individual incidents of abuse. The involvement of external agencies in abuse investigations also has the potential to make the "invisible" problem of abuse in service agencies become visible, thus helping to raise the priority of dealing appropriately with abuse at every level of supervision and administration.

Agency Responsibilities Amy's school district contracted with a taxi company to provide her with transportation to her special school. For 3 months, from December 1984 to February 1985, the taxi driver drove her to his home and sexually assaulted her. A lawsuit was launched against the school district and the driver, but the judge directed a verdict absolving the school district of any responsibility under *sovereign immunity* ("Sexual assault, transportation," 1993), a legal principle that protects governments from responsibility for negligence associated with carrying out properly appointed duties. The court considered the decision to contract transportation with the taxi company to be within the normal discretion of school boards. Although an Ohio Court of Appeals found for the school district (*Tinkham v. Groveport-Madison Local School District*, 1991), the case raises two important questions. Is abuse by cab drivers against students with disabilities a rare and unpredictable occurrence that school boards cannot be expected to consider, or is there a pattern of such offenses that they should recognize and respond to with protective measures? Is it discriminatory for school boards to contract transportation with taxi companies only for students with disabilities?

In another case, the trial of six executives of the Autumn Hills Convalescent Care Center ended in a mistrial as a result of a hung jury (Long, 1987). Of the 12 jurors, 9 had voted to convict, but the 3 remaining jurors disagreed. The six executives and the corporation itself had been on trial for the murder of one of the nursing home residents. Also named in the indictment were 60 other nursing home residents who were allegedly abused and neglected. Although this trial did not end in a conviction, it clearly demonstrated how administrators who contribute to and tolerate abuse can be held criminally, as well as civilly, responsible for the consequences of their behavior.

Legislation can strengthen this protection by mandating that service providers have a positive duty to protect service consumers. Establishment of this duty would be particularly useful in cases where direct responsibility may be difficult to determine. For example, when residents of an institution are abused by other residents, the institution and its management could be held responsible for failing to take reasonable prevention measures.

Part of the responsibility given to service providers should include the establishment of policies and procedures for abuse prevention, reporting, and intervention. Minimum standards and guidelines for policies and procedures should be provided. Of course, agencies must also be held responsible for the actual implementation and enforcement of their own regulations.

Protective Intervention Services   If investigation shows that abuse has occurred and that the individual is at risk for continued or future abuse, some action must be taken to help ensure the person's safety. This is accomplished through the development and implementation of a protective services plan. The nature of the plan will depend on the risk that must be controlled. In some cases, it may mean a change of residence or program; in other cases, closer supervision of the facility or an order that the offender will not be allowed access to the victim may be deemed necessary. The implementation of the plan must be monitored by protection and advocacy workers. Failure to comply with the plan may be cause for criminal charges or may result in removal of the individual from the abusive setting altogether.

THE COURTS

The courts serve two vital functions that are meant to protect members of our society. They mete out punishment to offenders, and in so doing, deter potential future offenders. Second, they provide due process of law to ensure that allegations are well-founded before punishment can be handed out. Thus, courts are intended to provide protection for potential victims of crime, and for people who have been accused of criminal behavior. These two interacting duties must be carefully balanced. If courts are too lenient on offenders or too reluctant to convict them, they may lose their power to deter criminal behavior. However, if they are too strict or they convict people arbitrarily, they may also lose their ability to deter crime because punishment is only an effective deterrent if it is contingent upon behavior. If innocent people are punished along with guilty ones, there is very little incentive for innocence.

For example, in considering seven landmark child abuse cases, the U.S. Supreme Court attempted to balance the inherent conflict between the constitutional rights of the defendant and the best interests of the child. In four of these cases, the Court found that the interests of the children were more important than the rights of the accused. In three cases, the Court gave more weight to the constitutional rights of the defendants (Kermani, 1991).

In order to achieve the balance between protecting victims of crime and protecting accused individuals, a complex set of rules and legal procedures have been developed regarding the ways in which judges and juries arrive at their decisions. Rules of evidence govern the kind of information that can be brought before the courts, how it can be presented, and who can present it. Oral testimony and cross-examination of witnesses are fundamental elements of the Anglo-American system of justice. Any evidence may be presented to the court that is: 1) relevant to the matter at hand; 2) probative, tending to prove or disprove the fact under dispute; and 3) not excluded under any of a long list of specific exceptions.

The right to appear as a witness in court has changed over time. In post-revolutionary America, for example, anyone was allowed to give testimony, as long as he was a free adult property owner. Slaves, children, women, and the poor were not considered trustworthy enough to participate in the justice system. Gradually, participation has been broadened to recognize the fundamental equality of all men, women, and, increasingly, even children before the law.

Witnesses with Disabilities

Clearly, equal protection of the law for all members of society is desirable, and much progress has been made toward this goal in the 2 centuries that have followed the American revolution. Nevertheless, it remains equally clear that significant progress has yet to be achieved. People with disabilities remain one of the groups least well-served by the justice system. While the principle of full participation in the justice system by people with disabilities is now generally recognized, the realization of this principle has often been restricted by problems with physical and social access to the courts, rules of evidence, and court-room procedures that unfairly impinge on the rights of people with disabilities, and a lack of willingness to make reasonable accommodations to individual differences. Access to the justice system is one of the most fundamental rights of all citizens because without this access, individuals cannot legally defend any of their rights and are forced to become dependent on others to advocate on their behalf. Ensuring access and reasonable accommodations required by people with disabilities helps to ensure a balance of power that reduces their risk for abuse.

Physical Access to the Courtroom   People with disabilities often experience barriers to courtroom participation. These barriers may be obvious or subtle. For example, the Architectural Barriers Act of 1968 required that obvious architectural barriers to all United States federal and most other courtrooms be eliminated. However, many courtrooms remain less than fully accessible (California Attorney General's Commission on Disability, 1989). Witnesses in wheelchairs are often physically unable to enter the witness box, and they are therefore required to give testimony from another part of the courtroom. Whether this affects the judges' and juries' perceptions of their testimony remains uncertain.

False Allegations   No research data are available that describe how common false allegations are among people with disabilities. Undeniably, some allegations of abuse are false, but the actual percentage of false allegations is difficult to determine. As indicated in Chapter 3, false allegations are rare. Most studies suggest that they only occur in about 2% of child sexual abuse cases (Westcott, 1992). Jones and McGraw (1987), for example, found that 2% were shown to be false, while 53% were substantiated. The remaining cases could not be clearly proven or disproven. Older children appear more likely to fabricate (Westcott, 1992). No allegation of abuse should be arbitrarily dismissed, and all allegations should be treated seriously and investigated thoroughly.

Issues of Competency   People with mental retardation or other disabilities that affect memory of communication are often disadvantaged as witnesses. To serve as a witness, individuals must: 1) have seen, heard, or otherwise perceived relevant events; 2) possess sufficient memories of these events to assist the courts; 3) demonstrate the ability to communicate a recounting of these events; 4) know the difference between the truth and fabrication; and 5) understand their obligation to tell the truth (Perry & Wrightsman, 1991). Whereas most witnesses are presumed competent in each of these five areas, competency is often questioned in the case of children and people with disabilities of all ages. People with mental retardation are often among those whose competency is most likely to be questioned. As Perry and Wrightsman (1991) point out, many people with mental retardation "have the capacity to be witnesses. However, it is necessary to convince the trier of fact that the [individual] is competent and credible" (p. 91).

No clear and uniform criteria exist to determine exactly what an individual must do to demonstrate competency. Some states require that witnesses understand an oath and are fully aware of the penalties for giving false testimony because these provide some assurances of truthfulness. However, the failure of oaths or the penalties for perjury to curtail false testimony casts considerable doubt on the value and effectiveness of these measures. For this reason, some have argued that people with disabilities be allowed to give testimony without having to take an oath or deliver a promise to tell the truth (Department of Justice Canada, 1993). Others have argued that oaths should be eliminated for all witnesses and that witnesses should simply be informed of their statutory duty to tell the truth (e.g., Robb, 1992). This last approach has the additional advantage of eliminating problems regarding other witnesses who may have ethical or religious objections to swearing an oath.

Although elimination of oaths may seem drastic, it is important to recognize that it only allows individuals the right to be heard; it does not guarantee that they will be believed. Determining credibility remains one of the primary tasks of the courts. Allowing testimony from all potential witnesses lets the court weigh each piece of evidence as they see fit. For people with disabilities who would be excluded under more restrictive rules, elimination of oaths provides greater opportunities for participation in the justice system and allows at least the chance for equal justice.

Broadened Access The general trend throughout the 1980s and 1990s has been to allow greater latitude in presuming the competence of witnesses and to leave judgment concerning the value of their testimonies to the juries and judges hearing their cases. Fifteen states now follow the lead of U.S. federal rules of evidence and have passed laws that presume every person to be competent to testify regardless of age or disability (Whitcomb, 1992). These laws should make competency hearings unnecessary; however, many judges in these states continue to hold these hearings and to exclude witnesses even where there is no legal basis for the practice (Perry & Wrightsman, 1991). Some states have added exceptions to this type of legislation (Perry & Wrightsman, 1991). Fourteen states have legislation that asserts that anyone, regardless of age, who meets certain requirements (e.g., ability to communicate with or without a translator, understanding of the duty to tell the truth) is competent to testify. Twenty states have laws that specifically address competency standards for child witnesses. Only one state, Virginia, lacks a specific statute to guide the courts regarding children's competency (Whitcomb, 1992). The general trend toward broadening access to the courts is useful to people with disabilities, but the practice of basing greater access on age, rather than on demonstrated necessity, fails to fully apply the underlying logic of broadened access and fails to provide people with disabilities equal protection of the law. The principle of presumed competency should be fully applied to allow all citizens, especially those who allege that crimes have been committed against them, full and equal access to the courts.

Credibility, Memory, and Suggestibility   Three issues closely tied to competency are the issues of credibility, memory, and suggestibility. In some cases, potential witnesses who lack credibility are often challenged on the basis of having a poor memory or of being too vulnerable to suggestion, and they may be found incompetent to give testimony. The rationale for this may be a lack of relevance or the lack of probative value (e.g., the witness who remembers nothing related to the alleged facts of a case can ordinarily do little to prove or disprove those facts).

It has often been implied that young children and people with developmental disabilities are inappropriate as witnesses because they have poor memories and can easily develop false memories through the process of suggestion before or during the trial. Research shows that people with mental retardation typically recall fewer details of events than people without disabilities, but it does not suggest that they are more likely to fabricate false memories or distort what they do recall. In fact, people with mental retardation are probably less likely to fabricate believable lies that stand up to cross-examination because this requires sophisticated abstract reasoning skills.

Perlman and Ericson (1992), for example, found no significant difference between adults with and without mild developmental disabilities in the number of structured recall questions that they answered correctly after watching a videotape. Adults with developmental disabilities actually did better than those without disabilities in answering questions that were contrary to expectation. However, they did not do as well on short answer questions, especially those that were presented in a manner deliberately designed to be confusing. Overall, these findings suggest that people with developmental disabilities may be better witnesses than is generally expected. Some people with disabilities have particular difficulty with dates and times and even the sequencing of events, but they know what happened and who did it. It is important for the courts to recognize and identify these limitations in order to prevent valuable testimony from being contaminated with confused responses to questions that are poorly understood.

Often, lawyers who are cross-examining someone with a developmental disability will purposefully try to confuse the witness by focusing on dates, times, and other relatively abstract features in an attempt to create confusion and damage the witness's credibility. Judges will sometimes intervene to protect a witness from this kind of attack, but the amount of latitude given to lawyers in cross-examination varies greatly. Usually solid preparation of the witness can prevent some of these problems.

Preparing Witnesses for Court

All witnesses should be prepared for the courtroom before entering to give testimony. Preparation is designed to meet two primary objectives: 1) to make the witness more effective in persuading the judge or jury, and 2) to minimize the potential trauma of a court appearance. A study of children who have testified in court found that their experiences were typically associated with negative emotional reactions and dissatisfaction with the process by the children as well as their primary caregivers. However, the authors suggest that systematic preparation of the children was rare, but, when provided, appeared to make their participation less uncomfortable (Goodman et al., 1992).

People with developmental disabilities typically require thorough preparation even more strongly than other individuals for several reasons. First, they are less likely to have gained previous knowledge about courtroom behavior through incidental learning. Second, they are more likely to exhibit atypical communication or behavior that can disadvantage them in the courtroom. Third, their behavior is sometimes scrutinized more closely in the courts than the behavior of other witnesses because there is less presumption of competence. Finally, some people with disabilities find appearing in court to be particularly traumatic, and good pretrial preparation can reduce that trauma.

Whereas little has been written that specifically addresses the preparation of individuals with disabilities for participating in the courtroom, a considerable amount of material has been written regarding the preparation of children for court testimony (e.g., Bauer, 1983). Many of the same general principles can be applied. In preparing individuals for court appearances, it is important to differentiate between teaching people about the courtroom process and telling them exactly what to say. Preparing witnesses regarding what they should say is normally viewed as inappropriate influencing and could result in grounds for a mistrial or appeal. However, preparing witnesses to know what to expect and how to conduct themselves in the courtroom is very acceptable. It is important that witnesses are familiar with the physical environment itself, who will be present at the trial, and the process in which they will be expected to take part. They need to know that they can take their time in answering a question, and that it is okay for them to say that they do not understand a question or do not know the answer. Many of these principles have been applied in curriculum materials for preparing children for the courtroom (e.g, Harvey & Watson-Russell, 1986) and can also be used with many children with disabilities. Although geared toward children, these materials could also be adapted for use with adults with or without disabilities.

Bauer (1983) describes how a child who has been sexually abused can be prepared for court appearances in order to reduce the child's risk for psychiatric damage that could be caused by the courtroom procedure. Topics include the use of detailed descriptions of courtroom procedures for preschool and primary grade children, visiting the courtroom before appearing in court, the need for the child to understand sexual terms that might be used in cross-examination, and role playing for latency-age and adolescent children. The author argues that it is unlikely that these techniques will interfere with the course of justice and that they are needed to protect children from procedural assault in the courtroom.

Facilitated Communication in the Courtroom

Carla was a 29-year-old Australian woman with significant disabilities who apparently disclosed incest and other forms of abuse through *facilitated communication*, a process that typically provides physical assistance through guidance of the hand or arm of a person with autism, cerebral palsy, or other developmental disability, while that person types out messages on a computer, typewriter, or other similar device. Although her parents claimed innocence, she was removed from her parents' home after apparently using facilitation to make such statements as:

> Dad is having sex with me. . . . He touches me inside and puts his prick in me [and mom] nestles me out of the way or tortures me in her own way by not looking when dad hits me in the mouth. (Heinrichs, 1992a, p. 9)

Experts argued that Carla lacked the internal language to produce such statements. Furthermore, Carla clearly spoke the word, "No," as social services workers forceably removed her from her home. If these allegations were true, Carla was being abused at home and needed protection from her parents. If these allegations were false, and, as suggested by the experts, did not originate from Carla herself, then she was being abused by the people who were wrongfully removing her from a loving home against her will on the basis of a counterfeit disclosure.

Carla's parents went to court to demand her return and that the validity of her facilitated communication be tested with a double-blind test. In this test, both Carla and her facilitator wore headphones, and each was given a series of simple questions for Carla to answer. Sometimes, both Carla and her facilitator heard similar questions; sometimes they heard different questions. Carla answered none of the questions correctly when her facilitator did not hear the same questions. Even more troubling, she answered several questions correctly that the facilitator heard, but Carla did not hear. The results clearly showed that at least some communication actually originated with the facilitator and not with Carla. With no corroborating evidence and considerable reason to doubt the validity of the allegation, the court awarded guardianship to Carla's mother, and Carla was returned to her home. Ironically, her facilitators suggested that Carla herself was responsible for the false charges and stated that Carla had admitted (through further facilitation) that she had lied when she made the original allegations (Heinrichs, 1992b).

Questions Concerning Its Use Although this series of events illustrates the need for great caution in considering any allegations arising through facilitated communication, it is important to note that other allegations of abuse made through facilitated communication disclosures have been corroborated by other witnesses, physical evidence, and confessions. Therefore, rejecting all allegations that arise in this manner cannot be justifiable. Since 1990 more than 100 similar allegations made by children and adults with disabilities of physical and sexual abuse have been communicated in this fashion. The facilitated communication procedure itself remains controversial. Traditional scientific tests of the validity of the method have generally failed. One summary of scientific studies (Green, 1993) lists 21 different controlled studies that involved 187 tests of the validity of facilitated communication. Facilitated communication failed to be validated in 184 (98.4%) of these tests.

Nevertheless, advocates of the technique point to remarkable results that are obvious to teachers, families, therapists, and many others working closely with people using facilitation. Detractors suggest that these results are so remarkable that they must be regarded with suspicion. In many cases, people with mental retardation requiring high levels of assistance who were formerly believed incapable of using or understanding even the simplest language are typing out high school or college level English in just a few weeks or months. Advocates respond by saying that it is our stigmatizing attitudes about these people that make it difficult to accept that they are capable of such behavior.

Indeed, the apparent ability of some people diagnosed with autism or mental retardation to communicate through facilitation challenges our previous notions of mental or cognitive disabilities and suggests that these individuals simply lack the ability to communicate. In fact, some controlled studies have demonstrated that at least some people with disabilities are able to communicate using this procedure. For example, a study conducted by the Intellectual Disability Review Panel (1989) in Victoria, Australia, demonstrated that some users of facilitated communication conveyed information that could not have originated with the facilitator. However, some of these same subjects also communicated information that could only have originated with the facilitator. Thus, although facilitated communication has been demonstrated to be a valid form of communication, there are still some disturbing questions regarding the influence of the facilitator.

Crossley (1991), the originator of the technique, suggests that this method should be considered a means of teaching independent communication. She acknowledges that until the learner demonstrates independence, it may be difficult to evaluate if or how much of the communication is originating with the learner. The general controversy over the validity of facilitated communication has intensified greatly as the stakes are raised by allegations of abuse. There is potential for great harm if legitimate disclosures are ignored. Yet, there is also strong potential for harm if false disclosures result in traumatic intrusions into the lives of people with disabilities, disruptions of healthy and supportive families, lost jobs for nonabusive caregivers, and ruined reputations of all those falsely accused. In addition, if allegations of abuse are proven to be false, or even if well-founded allegations appear to be false, there is some danger of a backlash. Police, prosecutors, and the public may develop skeptical attitudes that could result in the dismissal of future allegations of abuse of people with disabilities, no matter how they are communicated and regardless of how well-founded and well-corroborated they may be.

Acceptance by the Courts   The courts have been mixed in their acceptance of testimony or hearsay evidence originally communicated through facilitated communication. Some have rejected facilitated communication due to its lack of scientific acceptance as determined by the Frye test (*Frye v. United States*, 1923), a legal principle that requires general acceptance of a scientific technique before an expert witness can provide evidence based on that technique (e.g., lie detector tests are generally inadmissible because they do not pass the Frye test). A recent U.S. Supreme Court decision, however, limits the application of the Frye test in many jurisdictions; even before this ruling, some judges did not feel that the Frye test should be applied to facilitated communication.

Some judges have suggested individual tests for validating the testimonies of individual witnesses. This is probably the most reasonable approach, as the general value of facilitated communication need not be an issue. Even if it is valid in 99% of cases, it may not be valid in the case of the particular witness in question. If it is invalid in 99% of cases, but it is legitimate for the witness at hand, he or she should be allowed to use it. The nature of the validation test required by the judge may vary. In a case where independence seems clear (e.g., a witness with no physical contact with his or her facilitator or only the facilitator's hand on the witness's back), no such test may be necessary. In a case where the facilitator's hand is on the witness's hand or arm, raising questions about guidance, a simple test may be useful. Such tests may include asking the facilitator to leave the room while the witness views some event, then asking the witness to report the event through facilitation once the facilitator has returned; employing a second facilitator who knows nothing about the allegations that have been made; or a more formal test such as the double-blind question test using headphones that was previously described.

Caution Advisable Because of the concerns discussed here, police, prosecutors, and caregivers should be extremely cautious in considering abuse charges made on the basis of facilitated communication disclosures. The extent of influence that has been demonstrated in some tests of facilitated communication suggest that whether or not the individual communicates spontaneously, allegations of abuse could actually originate with the facilitator, rather than the apparent communicator. The motivations for a facilitator to influence such allegations remains a subject for speculation. They might include conscious efforts to blame a parent or caregiver whom the facilitator may suspect of abuse for other reasons, or an unconscious manifestation of Münchaussen syndrome by proxy (a syndrome discussed in Chapter 2). Münchaussen syndrome by proxy is sometimes characterized by caregivers who believe that the individuals in their care are victims of abuse as a result of a similar abuse experience in the caregiver's life that they may or may not consciously remember. For this reason, law enforcement personnel, prosecutors, and advocates should be very certain of their facts and attempt to corroborate them in every way possible before laying charges on the basis of complaints made through facilitated communication. In spite of these cautions, however, if there are good reasons to believe that abuse has really occurred, all involved parties have the responsibility to act on these allegations.

Civil Courts

The primary protective value of criminal proceedings is their deterrence of potential future crimes. Civil suits may have similar deterrent effects, and in some cases, complaints that cannot be addressed in criminal court can be addressed in civil court. These courts operate slightly differently. For example, in civil court, it may only be necessary to determine that the preponderance of evidence supports the allegation, rather than the stricter "beyond a reasonable doubt" standard of criminal court. In addition, civil liability does not necessarily require that a criminal statute has been violated, only that an individual bears responsibility for the outcome of his or her behavior.

Civil proceedings might be considered in cases where criminal conviction seems unlikely. It may be particularly worth pursuing in cases where monetary damages might be awarded to compensate the victim for physical injury or psychological harm (e.g., to pay the cost of therapy). In addition, civil suits may deter individuals and organizations from future behavior that leaves them open to future litigation.

LEGISLATIVE ISSUES AND PROCEDURES

Consent

In cases of sexual assault against people with disabilities that affect their communication, the issue of consent often becomes critical. Sexual behavior involving two consenting adults is not a crime, so sexual assault only exists if one individual initiates sexual interaction without the consent of the other. Defining exactly what constitutes consent, or the measures that must be taken by one party to ensure that consent has been voluntarily given by the other, is the central issue in many sexual assault trials.

Although the laws regarding consent to sexual relations differ in their details from jurisdiction to jurisdiction, some general principles typically apply. Consent can be explicit or implied. Explicit consent involves literally saying, "Yes." Implied consent is communicated through one's actions. There is often a great deal of dispute over exactly what type of behavior is an adequate demonstration of implied consent. For example, some defense attorneys have argued that if a woman goes home with a man and drinks alcohol with him, her behavior constitutes implied consent (Marshall & Barrett, 1990). Consent is not normally considered a simple matter of acquiescence. For example, if a person is unconscious or otherwise impaired, consent cannot be assumed simply because she or he fails to resist or to articulate her or his refusal.

Consent cannot be the result of coercion. For example, if one man tells another that he will expose the person's confidential homosexual behavior unless he agrees to sex between the two of them, it would not constitute consent because a threat has been made. Sexual participation based on false pretenses, for example, a false promise of marriage or sexual contact that has been misrepresented as being a necessary part of a medical procedure, also does not constitute consent. Even if no true consent was actually given, it would not be considered a crime if an individual honestly and reasonably believed that he or she was given consent. For example, if a couple has had regular consensual sexual interactions and then one partner decides that she or he no longer wishes to participate, but does not communicate this change to the partner and acquiesces to sexual interaction, the partner may honestly and reasonably believe that voluntary consent was given.

Principles of consent are reasonable when properly applied, yet each principle can also create legal loopholes that permit offenders to go free when interpreted too broadly or too narrowly. These principles are often interpreted along with a great deal of other historical and contextual information. For example, acquiescence would not typically be considered an adequate demonstration of consent, but under some circumstances (such as the one described below), it may be interpreted that way.

Disabilities can have important implications concerning the principles behind the determination of consent. The complexities of how disability affects the interpretation of these principles are illustrated in the following case example, which involved a young man with cerebral palsy who accused his home care provider of sexual assault (Hebert, 1986). This young man notified police that he had been sexually assaulted by his home care provider while he was being given a bath. Investigation revealed that the home care provider had previous convictions for sexual offenses. The main issue at the trial was the issue of consent. The judge ruled that in view of the facts that the young man's speech was not clear, that he did not vigorously struggle to protect himself, and that he sometimes laughed when under stress, the caregiver may have honestly believed that the young man was consenting.

The caregiver was acquitted of charges. However, the victim's impaired speech and his laughter under stress were direct outcomes of his hypertonic cerebral palsy. His dependence on the caregiver for assistance getting in and out of the bath and the real danger of his drowning if he attempted to struggle were powerful reasons for avoiding a violent confrontation. As a professional caregiver and a licensed vocational nurse, the home care provider should certainly have been aware of these facts. In applying the principle of honest belief too broadly, the judge failed to acknowledge the history or context of the relationship or the role of disability.

In this case, and many others involving an individual with a disability, implied consent should be narrowly defined. Implied consent must never be assumed on the basis of the failure to exhibit a behavior that is rendered difficult or impossible because of an individual's disability. Honest and reasonable belief in consent must also be considered in view of any impairments to an individual's abilities that are obvious, known to the alleged offender, or should be known to the alleged offender through training or experience. Failure of the courts to apply common sense in recognizing that a person who is mute cannot be expected to say no, that a person who is paralyzed cannot be expected to run away, or that people with other types of disabilities will be limited in their abilities to deter unwanted sex fails to provide people with disabilities equal protection of the law and makes them easy prey for abusers.

Coercion and false pretenses may also require broader definitions for some people with disabilities. For example, people who have been taught to obey institutional staff all their lives through aversive consequences for disobedience will probably feel coerced into doing whatever they are told, even when no direct threat is presented. Similarly, many people with mental retardation may be more susceptible to misrepresentation of sexual contact by offenders. For example, as described in Chapter 3, in Glenn Ridge, New Jersey, four former high school students were convicted of sexual assault based on the premise that the young woman they assaulted was incapable of consenting due to her mental retardation ("Four found guilty," 1993). However, the case might have been prosecuted without portraying the victim as incompetent. It might have been argued that the inducements offered her by the young men to gain her consent (e.g., the promise of a date with the brother of one of the young men involved) constituted invalid consent gained under false pretenses. The standards for false pretenses should have been considered very broadly in this case in view of the offenders' knowledge of their victim's disability and their associated responsibility to make a legitimate attempt to make her options clear, rather than to manipulate her into consenting. Conviction under this principle may have been more difficult to obtain, but it would have reduced the necessity for portraying the young woman as incompetent and unable to consent to sexual interaction under any circumstances.

Hearsay Evidence

Hearsay evidence refers to second-hand statements given to the court. A witness presenting hearsay evidence tells the court what someone else had told the witness that the person had done or observed. Normally, hearsay evidence is not allowed in the courtroom because direct testimony about one's own actions or observations is considered to be better, more solid evidence (Perry & Wrightsman, 1991). Because the person who made the original statement to the witness is typically not under oath, the repeated statements are considered less trustworthy, and because the originator of the statement is unavailable for cross-examination, the right of the defendant to face and confront his or her accuser may be seen as being violated in some cases. Nevertheless, there are many exceptions to the admission of hearsay evidence based on necessity. The most obvious and dramatic exception might be a murder victim who names his assailant before succumbing to his injury. Thus, although the originators of such deathbed accusations are not under oath and unavailable for cross-examination, they obviously cannot be expected to appear in court. However, the information given through hearsay evidence may be vital to the case and remains subject to corroboration or refutation from other sources.

Other common exceptions to the disallowance of hearsay evidence include:

1. Statements of young children alleging sexual abuse (typically because the only potential witnesses are the child and the perpetrator, and sometimes young children are excluded from court, are unable to remember after an extended delay before trial, or would be severely traumatized by the courtroom experience)
2. Present sense impressions (descriptions of events made while the originator is observing them, such as the description of abductors breaking into a home made to a friend by telephone)
3. Excited utterances (spontaneous statements made under stress are considered less likely to be fabricated)
4. Statements regarding the originator's state of mind at the time of an event (because state of mind is not directly observable, statements regarding one's state of mind are treated as an acceptable source of evidence)
5. Statements made to a healthcare provider for the purpose of medical diagnosis and treatment (considered to be reliable because the originator has a personal interest in ensuring that his or her health needs are properly met)
6. Residual exceptions to other statements that bear circumstantial reasons for trustworthiness (these may be acceptable to the court based on a variety of criteria, including any valid reasons for accepting the trustworthiness of the statement, the availability of other sources of evidence, the potential motivation of the originator, and the time the original statement was made in relation to the event being described)

During the 1980s and 1990s, courts have tended to be more liberal in allowing hearsay evidence. This trend is probably related to a healthy recognition that courts should respond to society's need for justice and not solely to the strict adherence to legal procedure. Legal procedures are intended to ensure fairness, and the role of the court is to help make certain that the actual facts of the case are heard. Arbitrary application of legal procedures is contrary to fairness and only serves to conceal the truth. In fact, even defense attorneys are often willing to accept hearsay evidence. A study by Leippe, Brigham, Cousins, and Romanczyk (1989) found that 19% of defense attorneys considered the hearsay evidence of a physician to be somewhat or completely acceptable, 16% considered hearsay from a psychologist as acceptable, 10% considered hearsay from a teacher acceptable, 7% considered hearsay from parents acceptable, and 5% considered hearsay from other children acceptable.

Not surprisingly, the great majority of prosecutors in the study found all of these categories acceptable. However, allowing such hearsay may not be entirely to the disadvantage of the defense. Placing alleged victims on the stand, especially children and people with disabilities, and subjecting them to merciless cross-examination is risky for the defense. Unless the testimony of a vulnerable witness can be totally discredited, cross-examination may alienate the judge or jury and allowing hearsay evidence lets the defense avoid taking this risk.

Age should not be an arbitrary criterion for accepting hearsay in lieu of direct testimony. Some children are able to testify effectively in court without experiencing excessive trauma. While young children have been given special status under the exceptions listed above, there is no reason why this protection should not be extended to vulnerable adults including, but not necessarily limited to, those with disabilities. Any time a witness is particularly vulnerable to trauma, has difficulty with memory, is under a threat, or is unable to appear in court for other reasons, the court may make an exception. Disability, in and of itself, should not necessarily be a reason for substituting hearsay for direct testimony. Many people with developmental or physical disabilities can testify under the same conditions as anyone else or require only minimal accommodations. These individuals should be encouraged to do so, consistent with the goal of full participation in the community. Categorizing everyone with disabilities as too vulnerable to participate in court will limit the access of people with disabilities to the legal system and encourage an unrealistic and potentially dangerous stereotype of all people with disabilities as being inherently vulnerable. Thus, the fundamental guideline should be necessity, based upon the individual and the situation.

Videotaped Interviews, Screening, and Closed-Circuit Television

This same rule of necessity should govern the use of videotaped interviews as evidence. Videotaped statements by or interviews with victims of crimes have sometimes been allowed to be introduced as evidence.

These have frequently been used in the case of children alleging abuse. Typically, the child is still expected to appear in court to affirm the statements made on the tape and to be cross-examined. These same procedures have sometimes been used with adults when necessity can be shown (e.g., an adult with impaired memory), but courts remain inconsistent regarding adult witnesses and videotape.

Certain rules should be followed in making and presenting interview tapes. Everyone present at the interview should have clearly identified roles. The entire taped interview should be made available without editing. Taped interviews should be made as early in the investigation as possible for two reasons. First, if impaired memory is a legitimate rationale, making the tape as soon after the alleged crime as possible is likely to procure the most detailed information and provide the best demonstration of necessity to the court. Second, in many abuse cases, especially those involving vulnerable victims, the defense will allege that the victim's statements arose from the influence of various people involved, such as police, therapists, or social workers, rather than from the person's actual memories. Making the videotape early in an investigation reduces the risk of influence and the potential that influence will be alleged by the defense. Interviews should be carefully conducted by a member of the investigative team who is well aware of the legal requirements for such interviews. Often, a social worker, communication specialist, or other individual who knows the interviewee personally and is aware of any special needs that he or she has is also an essential member of the interview team. Parents or other supportive caregivers may also participate to help ensure that the witness feels more secure.

Sometimes witnesses are allowed to testify via closed-circuit television or from behind a covered screen. This measure is intended to reduce the trauma of the courtroom appearance, while still providing the opportunity for cross-examination. Again, these accommodations have generally been used with children, but are sometimes extended to adults when necessity can be demonstrated.

While hearsay or videotaped interview typically accomplish the goal of reducing trauma for the witness more effectively, sometimes the court will allow screening or closed-circuit television instead of the other alternatives to preserve the right to cross-examination. In such cases, screening or closed-circuit television should be considered, but only if there is clear reason to believe that they will really have a positive advantage for the witness. For many individuals, testifying from behind a screen or via closed-circuit television can be just as traumatic, if not even more traumatic, than testifying in an open courtroom. For some, including many individuals with disabilities, it may be confusing or distracting, and could lead to greater difficulties in answering questions. It may also contribute to the stigma that is associated with disability by emphasizing the deviance of the witness who is isolated from the court. These potential disadvantages must be considered carefully. Nevertheless, screening or closed-circuit television may be the best available alternative in cases where an appearance in an open courtroom would be particularly disturbing.

Corroborating Evidence

Corroborating evidence is any evidence that helps to strengthen or confirm the validity of given testimony. For example, the videotape seized by police and the welts on the victim's back helped corroborate the story told by the young man discussed in the beginning of this chapter. The amount of corroborating evidence available and how much of it is actually presented in court varies from case to case.

When little or no corroboration is available to support allegations, courts are rightfully reluctant to convict. Such cases must be totally decided upon whom the jury ultimately believes—the defendant or the accuser. Because our system of justice protects people from false accusation by requiring proof beyond a reasonable doubt, uncorroborated allegations rarely result in convictions.

Investigators and prosecutors have a responsibility to prepare their cases with enough corroborating evidence to ensure a conviction. This might include testimony from other witnesses or other types of evidence that support the allegation. For example, after the abuse of one individual is disclosed in a group care setting, careful investigation often results in the finding of more victims of abuse by the same perpetrator. Several victims making similar allegations are generally more persuasive than a single individual acting alone (Coles, 1990). Thorough investigation may also identify other supporting witnesses who have seen or heard something that supports the story of the victim.

Physical evidence can also corroborate allegations. It is important that any injuries to the victim be carefully documented through medical examination and high-quality photography. Examination should be conducted as soon as possible after an assault has taken place by professionals skilled in forensic examination. Police and other investigators should keep a list of physicians who are trained in this type of examination. In many cases of sexual assault and some cases of physical assault, no strong evidence will be found in a medical examination; however, it is important to recognize that in some cases, medical examination can produce the most powerful evidence. In conducting these examinations (as in all aspects of the investigation), the victim's rights must be protected and all possible steps must be taken to minimize further trauma (Furniss, 1991).

Practical limits on time and resources can restrict the length of any investigation. Therefore, police and prosecutors must determine when they feel enough evidence has been gathered to ensure a conviction. Because the victim with a disability may be considered less credible or even be barred from giving testimony, it is particularly important that high standards for gathering supporting evidence be firmly established (Coles, 1990; Gunn, 1989).

Expert Witnesses

Rule 702 of the Federal Rules of Evidence states:

> If scientific, technical, or other specialized knowledge will assist the trier of fact to understand the evidence or to determine a fact of issue, a witness qualified as an expert by knowledge, skill, experience, training, or education, may testify thereto in the form of an opinion or otherwise. (Bureau of National Affairs, 1975, p. 55)

The role filled by these experts is different from that of other witnesses because their testimony is not about direct observations of the alleged offense. Their role is to help judges and juries understand the evidence that is brought forward. The role of experts should not be to make conclusions for a judge or jury. For example, if fiber samples found at a crime scene match those found in an alleged perpetrator's home, an expert might be called to testify about how common these fibers are and what the chances are of finding similar fibers elsewhere. The expert, however, cannot testify that these fibers prove the accused's guilt or innocence.

The use of expert witnesses in court can be a powerful asset for the prosecution or for the defense. However, frequently many questions arise about who is and who is not an expert, whether the evidence presented is really scientific, and whether the information presented helps to clarify the case for the court. For example, two groups of experts often testify at child sexual abuse trials. One group presents a wide range of behavior as being symptomatic of child abuse; the other interprets the same behavior as being unrelated to abuse and appears to attribute all, or at least the great majority, of disclosures by children to fantasy. Experts are typically paid both for their preparation and for their courtroom time, and frequently both the prosecution and the defense hire experts because they assume that the other side will employ one (Whitcomb, 1992).

In some cases, expert witnesses may prove necessary for successful prosecution; three types of expert testimony may be of assistance to the court in clarifying certain issues. First, medical experts can be very helpful to express the probability that the medical findings in the case are the result of violence. In allegations of physical or sexual violence, the medical expert might be asked to explain how any injuries that were noted would have been likely to occur and to provide useful information about the time of the injury. In cases of sexual abuse or assault, this sometimes means indicating how likely the injuries, or other findings described, could have resulted from the kind of activity charged, and how likely they could have been the result of other causes.

In other cases of sexual abuse or assault, the primary role of the medical expert may be to explain that examination findings of little or no physical injury are often typical following sexual violence (Doctors for Sexual Abuse Care, 1991). This is even more frequently true when disclosure is delayed. In such cases, medical findings are only present in 10%–20% of examinations of children (Whitcomb, 1992) and are probably even less apparent with adults. Medical experts are sometimes allowed to express their opinions about the victim's medical history or make statements in addition to discussing medical findings, but these may be restricted or disallowed by the court. The medical expert is often a different physician from the one who conducted the examination immediately after the alleged violence. It may be necessary to have both testify, one to indicate what was found on examination and the other to provide expert opinion on the interpretation of those findings.

Second, expert testimony might aid the court in assessing the credibility of the person making the allegations. Some countries (e.g., Israel, West Germany) do allow expert witnesses in the area of sexual abuse. These witnesses are normally appointed by the court rather than hired by the prosecution or defense (Whitcomb, 1992). In most countries, however, because the determination of credibility is one of the primary responsibilities of the jury or the judge, courts are typically reluctant to allow experts to directly suggest whether or not witnesses are to be believed (Perry & Wrightsman, 1991). Experts may be allowed to testify less directly on how people who have been victimized typically respond, and this may aid the court in assessing credibility. For example, many children who are sexually abused report the abuse only after significant delay, and many recant their disclosures at some time during the investigation (Furniss, 1991). Without this knowledge, judges and juries might be likely to interpret such behavior as suggesting false allegations. Knowing this is a common pattern of behavior does not prove whether any specific child is telling the truth, but may help prevent a juror from reaching a conclusion based on a false assumption.

Third, experts may assist the court in interpreting patterns of behavior of an alleged victim or perpetrator. Courts have been inconsistent in determining if this type of testimony will be allowed. They have typically been very reluctant to admit evidence on whether the accused fits the profile of an offender. Sometimes experts have been allowed to testify regarding the general patterns of behavior that are typical of crime victims, but not about whether the alleged victim in the case fits these patterns. Some courts allow testimony regarding these personality and behavior patterns or syndromes only if they are necessitated by an attack on the witness's credibility.

The use of expert witnesses in cases involving abuse of people with disabilities is a relatively new and unexplored field; most court precedents in this area have been established in cases of child abuse. For the most part, similar rules would be expected to apply, but some additional considerations may be needed in cases involving alleged victims with disabilities. Experts in communication or specific disorders may be called to describe behavior or communication patterns typical of individuals with a particular type of disability. For example, it may be important for the court to know whether a particular behavior pattern would be likely in an individual with autism who had not been abused or to know that some people with cerebral palsy may appear to smile or laugh involuntarily when talking about things that have been very stressful for them.

When abuse is alleged within a service delivery system, it may be necessary to call upon experts to express opinions on what is considered normal or acceptable procedure. For example, if a male caregiver was accused of fondling a female client but claimed that this was part of normal care, an expert might be called to discuss normal standards of care and personal privacy. Similarly, if caregivers were accused of a physical assault but claimed that they were only trying to restrain the client from hurting himself or herself, an expert might be called to discuss the appropriate and inappropriate conditions and methods for applying physical restraint.

CONCLUSION

This chapter has described some of the procedures of law enforcement and prosecution and discussed some issues relevant to criminal offenses committed against people with disabilities. Although law enforcement is only beginning to address the unique issues of investigating cases involving violence against people with disabilities, thorough application of established generic principles of investigation is generally appropriate in these cases. Some specialized knowledge on the part of law enforcement about people with disabilities and the service systems that they encounter can improve the application of these principles.

Successful prosecution of these cases also depends on good application of generic legal principles with a few accommodations to the individual needs of the person with a disability involved in the case. Protective legislation can help make convictions possible by mandating that human services agencies report abuse, protect those who do report, and take other related measures to help overcome the disadvantages that are typically faced by abused people with disabilities. Such legislation now exists in all American states and some Canadian provinces.

11

Changing Attitudes that Disinhibit Violence

Throughout this book, people's attitudes and beliefs are identified as important factors in allowing and encouraging abuse against people with disabilities. Cultural attitudes and beliefs make up the outer ring of the integrated ecological model of abuse introduced in Chapter 6. Of course, beliefs are held by individuals, and to some extent, attitudes of a culture or society simply reflect the sum of the attitudes of its individual members. However, the individualistic view that considers the whole merely as the sum of its parts is too simplistic. It ignores the important fact that individuals interact with and have influence upon the thinking of others. Individual attitudes are constantly being shaped by these interactions. Government, law, religion, literature, and tradition are some of the mechanisms used by cultures and societies to ensure that individual members share in and are affected by culturally endorsed ways of thinking and behaving. A few of the many attitudes and beliefs that are influenced or regulated by society include:

1. The values placed on various groups of people (e.g., children, women, racial minorities, immigrants, people with disabilities)
2. The conditions under which violence is acceptable
3. The degree to which various groups are either integrated or segregated
4. The power held by the individual members of various groups
5. The kinds of human services that are available

The effects produced by societal attitudes and beliefs are often subtle, deeply layered, and difficult to measure, but these effects are also far too powerful to be ignored. In fact, most researchers who have given serious consideration to the abuse of people with disabilities be-

303

lieve that societal impressions are of enormous importance. Mac-Namara (1992), for example, suggests that "abuse begins with an attitude" (p. 41). Much of this book illuminates a problem that has existed for many years and urges its readers to take action to address that problem. Yet, before this problem can be successfully managed, society must adopt attitudes that allow all of its members to see the problem, recognize that it must be addressed, and believe that meaningful change is possible. This chapter analyzes how some of the common attitudes and beliefs that are held about people with disabilities contribute to their abuse and suggests strategies for changing such perceptions.

DANGEROUS IDEAS

An attitude is a manner of acting or disposition expressed by an individual about someone or something or about some larger category of people or things. Attitudes can be very general or very specific and are typically considered to have several different dimensions (Kahle, 1984):

1. The evaluative dimension determines a general response to some class of things (e.g., good or bad).
2. The potency dimension determines the strength of the affect (e.g., strong or weak).
3. The behavioral dimension determines whether and how the attitude may influence actions (e.g., active or passive).
4. The social dimension determines the commonality of an attitude across all members of a society (e.g., universal or individualistic).
5. The contextual dimension determines the effect of environments and situations (e.g., situation-specific or contextually stable).
6. The cognitive dimension determines if the attitude is influenced by or influences specific ideas or beliefs (e.g., rational or irrational).

A belief can refer to anything accepted as true or to an expectation or judgment. Attitudes and beliefs reinforce each other. People typically develop attitudes that are consistent with their beliefs and believe in things that are consistent with their attitudes. For example, people are more likely to believe accusations of misconduct against people they don't like than similar allegations against their friends. For this reason, beliefs that reinforce preexisting attitudes are often easily established despite little real evidence and are typically difficult to eradicate. Beliefs that are inconsistent with preexisting attitudes are generally established only with great difficulty and are easily discarded.

Attitudes and beliefs can be highly individual, but people usually learn many or most of these from others. This education takes place both formally and informally through interactions with families, friends, schools, communities, the mass media, and a variety of other people and agencies. Some degree of consistency in attitudes and beliefs is essential to the development and maintenance of any culture or society. Of course, some cultures permit greater individualism than others, but even this is related to cultural perceptions regarding the relationship of the individual to the society.

Beliefs can be evaluated on the basis of whether or not they are supported by so-called "objective reality." While there is some utility in this type of evaluation of one's beliefs, there are also some limitations. Whether or not such objective reality exists remains a topic of some philosophical controversy (i.e., "beliefs about beliefs"). If objective reality does not exist, there is much more uncertainty as to whether human beings can accurately observe and understand it because our perceptions are inevitably influenced by our attitudes and beliefs.

Science has attempted to steer clear of this debate by avoiding the concepts of reality and truth altogether and focusing instead on reliability (agreement among observers) and theories (simple explanations for a set of observations). Thus, theories and models are not considered to be either right or wrong, but rather as more or less useful tools (e.g., Hawking, 1988). For example, in physics, Einstein's theory of general relativity is not necessarily considered to be "true" and Newton's theory of gravity "false," rather Einstein's theory is viewed as being consistent with a greater number of observations (e.g., the orbit of Mercury) than is Newton's.

In a similar manner, attitudes and beliefs about people can be compared to observations of their behavior. Beliefs about the behavior of women, Asians, octogenarians, or any other group of people can be tested against one's observations; however, there is an important difference. There is little reason to believe that one's attitudes and expectations have a significant effect on planetary orbits, but every reason to believe that they have a strong influence on human behavior. For example, if a dominant social belief portrays a particular group of people as poor educational achievers, they are likely to be denied educational resources and encouraged to fail. As a result, educational achievement is likely to be below average, thus confirming the original expectation. Because observers are already expecting this result, they are unlikely to question the cause of the outcome and will simply record yet another observation that is consistent with their initial beliefs. Self-fulfilling prophecies produce self-perpetuating myths as beliefs influence actions, actions influence outcomes, and outcomes influence observations that confirm initial beliefs.

Attitudes Toward Abuse and Violence

Attitudes and beliefs play an important role in determining people's behavior, particularly in encouraging or discouraging abuse and violence and in predicting social responses to their occurrence. Most offenders blame their victims for provoking the abuse. Mothers who abuse their children, for example, typically see their child's behavior as being more deviant than it actually is. They often use this belief to justify their own abusive behavior (Bradley & Peters, 1991).

Many popular books, movies, and television shows seem to illustrate a similar message through plots that appear to follow the same basic scenario. The hero is a simple, unassuming human being who is the victim of various horrors (e.g., his home is burned, his wife is raped and murdered, his children are abducted and tortured, he himself is violently beaten but refuses to defend himself because he abhors violence). Police and other authorities fail to help because they are incompetent, corrupt, or both. Eventually the hero is forced to fight back. The remainder of the story details how the hero brutalizes and violently defeats the evil ones who forced him into violence. Superficially, the lesson is that the villains receive their just desserts. More subtly, the message implied is that violence is acceptable, even noble, when it is justifiably provoked. Such mixed messages can be dangerous and their ultimate effects may be hard to predict.

Similarly, this mixed message is presented by the abused child and abused spouse defenses that are now being presented to the courts with increasing frequency. In these cases, parents or spouses (usually husbands) have been killed by their children or surviving spouses who claim that because of a long history of abuse they feared for their lives and so were forced to kill in self-defense, even when no threat was imminent at the time of the murder. On one level, the willingness of the courts in such cases to consider acquittals may be sending the message that victims of crime have a right to defend themselves, which would help to create greater equality of power between potential perpetrators and their victims. On another level, this willingness may also be communicating that provocation justifies violence—a message that is likely to increase rather than reduce power inequities. A similarly complex issue surrounds the effects of capital punishment. Superficially, capital punishment sends the message that society will not tolerate murder, but at the same time, it also communicates that killing people is the only way to solve some of society's problems.

The relationships among perceived attributes, attitudes, and acts of violence appear to be strong. For example, Hunter, Stringer, and Watson (1991) examined the effect of group identity on blame and found that both Irish Protestants and Irish Catholics felt that violence was justified when committed by a member of their own group against a member of the other group, but felt that it was unjustified when committed by a member of the other group against a member of their own group. This suggests that group membership and social distance influence our attitudes about the acceptability of violence. Attitudes about individuals or groups that tend to depersonalize, dehumanize, or distance them appear to make violence against them more acceptable. This justification may act directly to decrease the inhibition of violence and indirectly to reduce counter-controls, as society tends to view crimes against "nonmembers" as being less serious.

Society's view that offenses against outsiders are less serious is well documented in studies of sentencing patterns. These studies ask individuals to determine the appropriate sentences for real or hypothetical crimes and measure the effects of various attributes of the crime vignette on the subjects' views of appropriate sentencing. One study (Miller, Rossi, & Simpson, 1986), for example, examined the ratings by groups of black men, black women, white men, and white women regarding the appropriateness of sentences for various crimes. The results revealed that each group felt crimes were most serious when committed against someone similar to themselves and least serious when committed against someone who was different. This may help to explain (as discussed in Chapter 2) how a judge could describe the torture and beating to death of a young man with a developmental disability as "not serious" (Engman, 1992, p. A1).

Perhaps the strongest implication for considering the effects of attitudes and attitude change on justice for crime victims with disabilities is the role of perception. Miller et al. (1986) found that "perceived or subjective proximity to crime has stronger implications than objective proximity" (p. 313). It is people's attitudes and beliefs about how similar or different they are compared to the perpetrators or victims of a crime that influence how serious the crime appears to them. Therefore, encouraging people to see similarities between themselves and actual or potential victims of crime can be expected both to inhibit crime and to facilitate a concerned response to offenses that do occur. Conversely, encouraging people to see differences between themselves and actual or potential victims of crime can be expected both to reduce inhibition to crime and to impede vigorous societal responses to its occurrence.

Social distance or differences have significant influence on the way that people view violence, regardless of the values placed on group identity. People may feel as socially distant from people whom they consider to be members of groups they perceive as being of greater value as they do from those they consider to be of lesser value. Stigma and ambivalence also appear to interact with social distance. Ambivalence theory suggests that members of stigmatized groups, such as African-Americans and people with disabilities, are considered both disadvantaged and deviant (Katz, Glass, Lucido, & Farber, 1979). Under ideal conditions, most people who do not belong to these stigmatized groups will treat members of these groups fairly similarly to the way they would treat others. In situations of threat or conflict, however, they will blame and denigrate stigmatized group members more than they would nonmembers as a means of resolving their own conflicting feelings.

The relationship of victim blaming to actual criminal behavior has also been illustrated through research. Sundberg, Barbaree, and Marshall (1991) measured the sexual responses of male university students to scenes representing consenting and nonconsenting heterosexual interactions. The subjects all showed arousal response to nonconsenting sex that indicated their sexual responses were inhibited, but when they were given scenarios that implied that the victim was to blame, their inhibition decreased and their arousal increased.

The effects of stigma on victims of crime appear to be strongest in cases where the evidence is weak or ambiguous. If the evidence presented at a trial is compelling, offender and victim attributes (e.g., attractiveness, disability, gender, race) appear to have little effect on juries' decisions, but when the evidence leaves some room for doubt, these attributes become far more influential (Reskin & Visher, 1986). This finding may also have particular implications for crimes against people with disabilities because of individual (e.g., an individual with impaired communication may not be able to provide testimony) and ecological (e.g., the large number of caregivers in group-care facilities makes it difficult to determine individual responsibility) factors that often contribute to the complexity of these cases.

Taken together, these studies suggest that attitudes are powerful forces in the facilitation or inhibition of violence. Perceived differences, social distance, stigma, ambivalence, and blame contribute substantially to violence and likely reinforce each other. Because of the stigma associated with disability, society has often segregated this population, thereby increasing social distance and encouraging greater perception of differences. In turn, social distance and perceived differences have encouraged abuse and have led to victim blaming and denigration in response to society's need to resolve its ambivalence toward violence. Segregationist policy has also led to increased perception of differences by enlarging, rather than diminishing, commonalties of experience between people with and without disabilities.

Often, "statutes tend to exaggerate the differences between disabled and nondisabled people" (Melton & Garrison, 1987, p. 1008), and gross mistreatment, often associated with institutional care, encourages the belief that people with disabilities are fundamentally different and that they are responsible for their own suffering. The depth of the stigma against people with disabilities is communicated by some of the few legal victories that suggest "that they cannot be treated under conditions that, if applied to prisoners would constitute cruel and unusual punishment" (Melton & Garrison, 1987, p. 1008). The following section describes how this stigma persists in general public perceptions of this specific group of people.

Attitudes Toward People with Disabilities

The constellation of attitudes and beliefs associated with violence and abuse of people with disabilities is complex, and analysis is difficult because it can never be entirely objective when evaluating culturally pervasive ways of thinking. Historically, a variety of beliefs have been expressed about people with disabilities that may continue to influence current conceptions. For example, St. Augustine identified "fools" as punishment that mankind must endure because of the sins that it has committed (Ryan & Thomas, 1987). In the Middle Ages, children with disabilities were considered to be "changelings" that supernatural beings traded for the parents' real child. Martin Luther further developed this idea suggesting that it was Satan who replaced parents' children with devils who should be killed. A closely related belief was that children with developmental or physical disabilities were born as a result of sexual intercourse between the mother and the devil.

Although such antiquated beliefs may appear to be outdated in view of current scientific knowledge, they may still be expressed in other ways. For example, the "changeling" belief may be reflected in the current assumption that parents of a child with disabilities are grieving for the "healthy, normal child" that they had anticipated before the diagnosis of their child's disability (Bogdan, Brown, & Foster, 1992). Thus, the "fairies and devils" of the past are replaced with the "psychological science" of the current generation, but the fundamental notion that a "changeling" has replaced the parents' legitimate child remains intact.

Literature regarding attitudes toward people with disabilities is typically generalized to all types of disability. The findings from studies employing a wide variety of general and specific labels to people with mental retardation or developmental disabilities appear to be justified by research suggesting that attitudes are usually similar toward a variety of disabilities and that labels associated with mental retardation are among the most heavily stigmatized (Gething, 1991).

QUESTIONING WHY NEGATIVE ATTITUDES EXIST

It will probably never be fully understood why, throughout history, attitudes toward people with disabilities have been so pervasively negative. Livneh (1988) suggests a multitude of conscious and unconscious, social, emotional, and cognitive sources for this bias (e.g., social demand for aesthetics, group pressure for conformity, fear of ostracism by association, concept of disability as a punishment for sin, minority identification). Many of these appear to be related to human competition and the need to believe that individuals control their own destinies. The philosophy of competition preaches the common notion that all good things come to people as a result of their own sincere efforts and all misfortune comes as a result of their personal failures. It tells us that if one is more fortunate than another, it is because of one's own merit; if others experience misfortune, they have somehow been less deserving.

To believe that someone has disabilities through no fault of their own threatens this basic belief that is so closely associated with human competitive nature. However, cooperation is as much a part of human nature as is competition. Human progress has always been achieved through the interaction between cooperation and competition. Morgan (1987) stresses this idea, pointing out that while many societies permit and encourage abuse of people with disabilities, others strictly prohibit abuse and ensure care for those who require it. She points out that even in the animal kingdom, these same differences exist (e.g., sharks and baboons attack members of their own groups who are disabled, while wolves and chimpanzees provide care for their disabled members).

HOW NEGATIVE ATTITUDES ARE REINFORCED

Wolfensberger (1975) has written extensively about the role of societal attitudes in the mass institutionalization, sterilization, and murder of people with disabilities. Waxman (1991) provides a discussion of general assumptions that permit and encourage sexual violence against people with disabilities. The following sections discuss the ways in which these dangerous notions about people with disabilities are reinforced.

Dehumanization

Dehumanization encompasses the actions, attitudes, and beliefs associated with treating a person or group of people as less than human. For people with mental retardation, these attitudes have been frequently expressed—both implicitly and explicitly. As indicated in Table 1, three interrelated forms of dehumanization can occur: 1) conceptual dehumanization, 2) ecobehavioral dehumanization, and 3) reactive dehumanization. Conceptual dehumanization occurs when attitudes, beliefs, labels, or language accentuate differences between an individual or group and the rest of humanity. For example, attempting to explain abnormal behavior by labeling someone as a "retardate" does nothing to help gain a better understanding of the behavior itself. Instead, it merely encourages the belief that such behavior emerges from inherent differences between the individual (or people with mental retardation in general) and her or his (their) fellow human beings.

Ecobehavioral dehumanization moves beyond the mental process. It translates dehumanizing concepts into reality through alteration of the individual's environment and of behavior toward the individual so that the circumstances conform to the dehumanizing notions. For example, uniforms worn by "patients" in some facilities help to reinforce the assumption of differences between them and the staff. Such real and tangible differences arise from the underlying conceptual dehumanization and, in turn, help create a reality consistent with the initial belief. In other words, because society views an individual as less than human, it puts that individual in a uniform and in an isolated institution. These real society-created differences in the ways in which these individuals live subsequently increase the differences that society perceives and feeds the concept that created the disparities.

Reactive dehumanization adds to the harm that is done when the behavior and appearance of people who are dehumanized deteriorate

Table 1. Levels of dehumanization

Level	Expressions
Level I: Conceptual Dehumanization A category of individuals is viewed as less than human.	Attitudes Expectations Beliefs Labels and language Propaganda
Level II: Ecobehavioral Dehumanization People are treated differently based on their dehumanized status.	Uniforms Brutalization Segregation Humiliation Denial of necessities
Level III: Reactive Dehumanization People's behavior and appearance become more deviant as a result of dehumanizing treatment.	Regression Inappropriate behavior Learned helplessness Physical deterioration

to conform to their societal status. This occurs when an individual who has been isolated, abused, and disempowered responds with behavioral changes that further feed the dehumanization process. All three of these stages interact in a vicious cycle as the increasingly deviant behavior reinforces the dehumanizing concepts and "justifies" further maltreatment, which, in turn, produces greater deviance. Thus, as institutionalized individuals learn to act atypically, their behavior becomes further evidence that justifies the original dehumanizing concepts that led to their institutionalization.

Fuller's (1949) article, "Operant Conditioning of a Human Vegetative Organism," provides a good example of dehumanization. Considering the age of the article, the term *vegetative organism* might be considered simply an example of obsolete terminology, yet Fuller's rationale for choosing this subject reveals a more conceptual view of the subject as being less than human. He suggested that because operant conditioning had been entirely dependent on animal research and human research in the subject was lacking, choosing a subject that is partially human represented a good starting place.

Self-Perpetuating Nature   The self-perpetuating nature of dehumanization has often been apparent in the inhumane treatment of people with disabilities. Dehumanization supplies the rationale for the inhumane treatment provided because these individuals are viewed as less than human, they are not entitled to be treated like other human beings. Warehoused in overcrowded institutions without the appropriate care or education, many individuals with disabilities develop behavior that is increasingly atypical. This behavior is consistent with the belief that they are not really human and serves to reinforce it. Thus, as illustrated in Figure 1, the behavior produced by inhumane treatment confirms the preexisting belief that these individuals are less than human and deserve to be treated in this fashion.

The behavior that abused people exhibit in response to their maltreatment is often used as further proof of their subhuman status, providing additional rationale for the offenses committed against them and increasing social distance to disinhibit abuse. For example, Wolfensberger (1991) recounts the story of a boy with mental retardation from an impoverished family who was neglected, starved, and abandoned in the early 17th century. Deprived of human care, he survived by killing and eating dogs, and on several occasions, by cannibalizing small children. Stories of these events were confounded with stories of the boy being transformed into a wolf. Accounts of this and similar "subhuman" behavior tended to focus on the relationship between the disability and the behavior, but ignored the central role of abuse.

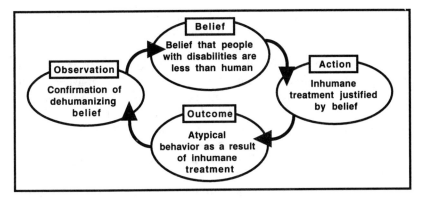

Figure 1. Dehumanizing beliefs are self-perpetuated by the inhumane treatment of people with disabilities.

Facilitation of Violence A number of researchers believe that dehumanization contributes substantially to the abuse of people with disabilities. Sullivan, Vernon, and Scanlan (1987) assert that the view of children with disabilities as less than human permits them to be abused. Garbarino (1987) suggests that stigmatization associated with disability licenses and validates abuse in the minds of offenders. Senn (1988) points out that similar myths are common among sex offenders regarding their victims and that stigmatized views of people with disabilities aggravate these myths; "the process of dehumanization in which the person with a disability is made into an object or something less than fully human would reduce inhibitions against aggressing against them" (p. 12).

Some of the most chilling evidence on the role of dehumanization comes from death row interviews with the infamous serial killer Ted Bundy (Michaud & Aynesworthy, 1989), who stressed the need to "depersonalize" his victims in order to overcome his inhibitions and brutally murder them. He describes a number of methods (e.g., the use of pornography and alcohol, avoiding conversation with his victims) that he employed to avoid thinking of the women that he murdered as human beings, and he compares the process to the training of soldiers:

> We sent men to Viet Nam and they were able to kill, because the tactic taken by their leaders was to depersonalize the enemy. You're not killing a man; you're killing a 'gook,' a Viet Cong. Under those conditions men kill very easily. (Bundy, as quoted in Michaud & Aynesworthy, 1989, p. 63)

Franz Stangl, a prominent member of the T-4 euthanasia program and later Commandant of Treblinka, the most productive extermination camp of Nazi Germany, expressed similar ideas suggesting that institutional depersonalization, cruelty, and humiliation were deliberately employed in the death camps to increase the social distance between staff and prisoners. The intention behind these strategies was "to condition those who actually had to carry out the policies . . . to make it possible for them to do what they did" (quoted in Sereney, 1974, p. 101). Efficient mass murder could only be accomplished if staff no longer viewed their victims as human. In this way, people with disabilities were the tinder that kindled the holocaust. They had already been segregated, depersonalized, and stripped of their defenses long before the euthanasia program began. Their deaths were easy to arrange, and the process of their extermination provided the blueprint for the "ethnic cleansing" genocide centers that followed. (See Chapter 5, section on Efforts to Eliminate People with Disabilities, for more on this subject.)

Similar depersonalization has been reported among staff of neonatal units who use terms such as *nonviables* or *fetuses* to describe newborns with severe disabilities in danger of dying and *chronics* for those with disabilities whom they believe will survive, while reserving terms such as *babies* or *good babies* to describe infants without any apparent disabilities (Bogdan et al., 1992). These labels and the attitudes associated with them may have significant effects on parental attachment to children and can influence the quality and quantity of future parent–child interactions.

Myth of Insensitivity to Pain　One particular myth of the dehumanization process is the belief that people with mental retardation are incapable of suffering or experiencing pain in the same way as other people. Ryan and Thomas (1987) provide an interesting historical reference to this belief from a traveler's 1779 account of Swiss "cretins" who were "deaf, dumb, imbecile, [and] almost insensitive to blows" (p. 89). Couston's (1954) collection of seven single-paragraph case studies supplies an excellent example from more recent history. These anecdotal reports describe seven individuals who seemed to demonstrate little indication of pain in spite of serious illnesses and injuries. However, Couston's own descriptions include classic signs of pain. One with a fractured hip "showed some resentment on movement," another with an ulcer made "little complaint of pain except on deep palpation," another "was deeply shocked," another showed "annoyance" (p. 1128). These responses were simply not interpreted as signs of pain because of the preexisting belief that these patients were incapable of experiencing it. Couston's description also tells us that at least one individual was sutured without the benefit of anesthetic, an action rationalized by the belief that such people are incapable of experiencing pain like other human beings. Ironically, it is precisely this kind of treatment that leads to a state of learned helplessness where the person learns to suppress any overt responses to pain (e.g., Miller, Rosellini, & Seligman, 1977).

Biersdorff's (1991) article, largely based on Couston's earlier findings, provides strong evidence that such myths do not die easily. She rejects more contemporary empirical studies involving many more subjects that contradict the pain insensitivity and pain indifference theories as lacking in scientific rigor, and revives Couston's anecdotal reports as "research support." It appears that strict standards are applied to the evaluation of information that contradicts preexisting beliefs, while the same standards are drastically cut for evaluating the information that supports such beliefs.

The myth of insensitivity to pain is not the only dehumanizing belief applied to people with disabilities, but it provides an example that is particularly dangerous for disinhibiting violence toward them. Because the victim is viewed as being incapable of suffering, the burden of guilt is removed from the offender. This "feeling no pain" myth takes on a special form in sexual offenses against people with mental retardation (Sobsey & Mansell, 1990). The victim is sometimes considered incapable of understanding the sexual assault or sexual abuse that has been committed against them, and because he or she does not fully understand what has happened, he or she is thought to suffer less than someone without mental retardation. In the mind of an offender, this helps to justify his or her actions and disinhibits the inappropriate behavior. Equally distressing, this myth is often shared by the remainder of society who may trivialize such crimes by sentencing offenders less severely in cases involving victims with disabilities. This myth has absolutely no basis in reality; the physical and emotional harm done to people with disabilities as a result of abuse is well documented (e.g., Sobsey & Doe, 1991).

Devaluation

Devaluation is a general term that encompasses those actions, attitudes, and beliefs that place a reduced value on a particular person or group of people, in this case, people with disabilities. There are many specific manifestations of this attitude. One example of devaluation is related to the concept of *quality of life*, a term frequently used in debates regarding euthanasia. Quality of life is a vague term that refers to the enjoyment of the life experience and the freedom from suffering. Many people can at least imagine a life so filled with suffering, so empty of pleasure, and so unlikely to change that there would be little point in living. Some of us would probably want our lives to end under such conditions. However, the evaluation of an individual's quality of life is totally subjective. Attempting to apply one's own criteria for quality of life to the experience of another person simply becomes a very subjective view of the potential value of that person's life. The fact that "poor potential quality of life" has been suggested and sometimes accepted as a rationale for killing people with disabilities simply reflects the low value that society places on these lives (Schaffer & Sobsey, 1991).

This myth is also self-perpetuating. Because the lives of people with disabilities are considered to have less value, they are often denied essential treatment and are more likely to be abused and mistreated. As a result, the quality of their lives is damaged and the devaluation is confirmed. As a result, the perpetuation of devaluation leads to further mistreatment as illustrated in Figure 2.

Defamation

People with disabilities are often blamed for their own problems and for the problems of the people around them. These sentiments are reflected in the popular literature that commonly portrays victims and villains as having disabilities (Zola, 1992). This notion is also expressed in many "scientific and professional" publications, and it is probably most dangerous in this scientific form. Gould (1981) provides a comprehensive discussion of how the development of educational psychology was warped by the compulsive need to entrench aristocratic, racist, sexist, and ethnocentric myths into scientific theory. Advocates of social Darwinism like H.H. Goddard and Lewis Terman suggested that IQ scores were not only a precise and immutable measure of intellectual ability, but also of moral development and industriousness. This view was supported not only by weak and spurious arguments, but also, in many cases, by scientific fraud perpetrated by "scientists" intent on

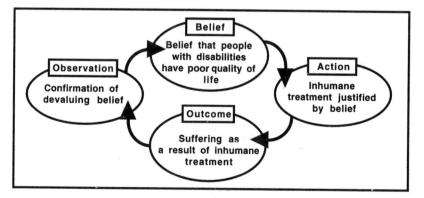

Figure 2. Devaluing beliefs are self-perpetuated by the inhumane treatment of people with disabilities.

supporting the idea of the inherited superiority of the upper classes. Science began to replace religion as the predominant mode for justifying the power of those who controlled the majority of society's resources. This new scientific chauvinism declared that people with developmental disabilities were not only intellectually inferior, they were also morally unfit and a threat to the "better" classes of people. As such, they deserved whatever ill treatment they received. While current psychology has clearly softened its stand on the inherited nature of intelligence and its relationship to moral superiority, it has not denounced this position completely, and the spectre of the "handicapped menace" continues to haunt popular belief.

A particularly insidious form of defamation takes place when children with disabilities are viewed as "abominations," a form of divine retribution for parental sins. For example, when Victor Wahlström (1992), president of the International League of Societies for Persons with Mental Handicap, addressed the United Nations General Assembly, he brought this message from an unnamed African mother:

> Profoundly handicapped persons get absolutely nothing. Most people consider that our children are useless and a burden. Many of them seem to think that the reason for getting a mentally handicapped child is that we parents have committed sins. (p. 1)

The concept of parental punishment is not exclusively African. Similar concepts can be traced to Chinese, Native American, Judeo-Christian, and a variety of other cultures. According to the mythology of some South American Indians, for example, infants with deformities

> cannot have been conceived in a natural way; they must have come into being through the operation of a demon. Such a monster is looked upon with horror and regarded as a most ominous thing not only for the family concerned but for the whole village. (Karsten, 1932, p. 77)

Beliefs such as these help to explain why, in many cultures, disability is more acceptable as a rationale for infanticide than any other reason (Daly & Wilson, 1988).

The effects of such beliefs can be deleterious in several ways. First, and most obvious, by portraying the child with a disability as a punishment for the parents, the child is immediately cast into an extremely negative role. The expectation is created that such a child will inevitably bring suffering to the parents, encouraging all parent–child interactions to be viewed in the most negative possible light and ensuring that the parents will feel some resentment. Second, because the child with a disability is viewed as a form of divine punishment, there is no moral imperative for other members of the community to support the family. In fact, anyone who attempts to help them might be seen as thwarting the will of God. Third, within this conceptual framework, stigma is not restricted to the individual with the disability, but is extended to the entire family because their sins are seen as the source of the "abomination."

The dual derivations of the word *abominations* as applied to imperfect children born to punish their parents encompasses these negative attitudes well. Its original roots (*ab* + *hominate*) imply away from man or not fully human, but these appear to have been confounded with the related definition (*abominari*) meaning an ill omen, worthy of hatred (*The Oxford English Dictionary*, 1971). Thus, dehumanization is combined with defamation in a single concept.

Through this concept of abomination, the individual with a disability is transformed into a burden of guilt and shame that the family must wear like Coleridge's mariner in *The Rime of the Ancient Mariner* (cited in Richards [1980]) was forced to wear the albatross around his neck. This analogy may provide insight that goes beyond the albatross image. Coleridge's ancient mariner suffered because of his attitude of contempt and rejection. He was freed from his burden of guilt only when he changed those ways of thinking and learned to see the natural beauty and grace of all creation. The poem suggests that the burden of guilt and stigma are inevitably intertwined and that this condition can only be transcended when people learn to accept and respect all others. Some professionals may be unknowingly supporting defamation by encouraging the assumption that all people with disabilities are burdens and sources of stress for their families. Failure to accept and respect these individuals for who they are, or an unreasonable preoccupation with transforming them into someone society would consider more acceptable, may be subtler manifestations of the defamation process.

The complex mechanisms that allow such cultural and religious myths to encourage rejection of people with disabilities may seem abstract, but the effects are very real. In a 1992 seminar of the Pan-African Federation of Associations for Persons with Mental Handicap, representatives from 16 African countries identified such "social prejudice" as a pressing problem that "results in mistreatment, such as starvation, and in some societies even murder" ("Social Prejudice," 1992, p. 16).

Disempowerment and Disenfranchisement

The disempowerment of people with disabilities is a reality that can also be a self-fulfilling expectation. Recognizing the problem can be an essential step toward empowerment, but care must be taken not to dwell on vulnerability or to imply that helplessness is an inherent outcome of disability. The mere recognition that people with disabilities are vulnerable to abuse may actually increase their risk because potential offenders seek out this quality in their selection of potential victims. Ticoll (1992a,) provides the example of a major men's magazine, Hustler, that "once instructed its readers that 'mentally retarded girls' were ideal subjects for sexual abuse as they would not be able to identify their attacker" (p. 25). The notion of pervasive vulnerability can also be dangerous in the minds of family members and professionals who may respond by assuming the inevitability of disempowerment and disenfranchisement rather than acting to prevent or eliminate these injustices.

Distancing and Detachment

Distancing and detachment refer to the isolation of people with disabilities from normal human relationships and affective bonds. Physical segregation provides one example. Although the squalid and abusive conditions that exist in some human services institutions are periodically brought to society's attention, they are generally well hidden, and therefore, confrontation with these conditions is easily avoided.

Detachment creates an emotional distancing. As discussed in Chapter 8, parental attachment to children supports the inhibition of abuse and disruptions in attachment are frequently associated with the disinhibition of abuse. Segregation and isolation of people with disabilities represents the social embodiment of the most extreme form of detachment—the physical removal of people with disabilities from their homes and communities. The objectification of people with disabilities in various forms also results in distancing. For example, a computer bulletin board named *alt.sex.fetish.amputee* allows those interested in obtaining erotic or pornographic materials featuring people with various disabilities to exchange information. The requirements of at least 100 more "yes" votes than "no" votes and that at least 2/3 of all voters must be in favor to create this group on Internet (Kehoe, 1993) suggests that quite a few people are interested in this topic.

Language and Stigma

Language often contributes to stigma, but whether certain labels are inherently stigmatic or become stigmatic over time is difficult to resolve. For example, words such as *idiot, imbecile,* and *moron* were once used to describe various levels of mental retardation, but they are now simply used as insults. Sometimes people's awkward efforts to avoid labels through euphemisms or vagueness implies as much discomfort and ambivalence as do the original labels. For example, it seems odd that the legal term *persons* is frequently used to describe a group of individuals with disabilities, when the common term *people* would be satisfactory to describe any other group. While such linguistic oddities are undoubtedly well-intended, they probably serve to increase social distance and perceived deviance rather than to diminish it.

Similarly, many now consider it important to identify people as *individuals with disabilities* rather than *disabled individuals*. The apparent motive is to put the individual first and de-emphasize the disability, but the result is often awkward and may actually increase emphasis on disability when the phrase runs contrary to standard usage. For example, if we would describe an individual as a *tall man* or a *blond man*, why not describe an individual as a *disabled man*? The use of a special rule for this class may emphasize, rather than minimize, differences.

Context is also important in considering the use of language. When it is relevant to the topic under discussion, mentioning a disability makes sense. However, mentioning disability when it should be irrelevant may indicate a preoccupation with the issue or suggest that the speaker views disability as an all-pervasive trait that is relevant to every aspect of a person's life.

Consideration of individual preferences is also important. Terms such as *mental deficiency* and *mental retardation* may not be intended in a negative sense; however, many people with disabilities consider these terms insulting. Often their discomfort is derived from a long personal and social history associating the term with rejection, abuse, and denigration. Dudley (1983) found that 16 of the 27 individuals who informed him about the stigma of labeling in their life rejected the term *mental retardation*, and 8 others were ambivalent in their acceptance. Only 3 out of the 27 felt the label was appropriate. Similarly, some people with disabilities do not like the person-first rule. One physically disabled woman told the author that she is not a *woman with a disability*, she is a *disabled woman*. She feels strongly that her life-long disability is as essential a part of her as her gender or heritage, and she feels that the person-first rule fails to recognize this critical aspect of her identity. People should have a right to reject any labels that they do not like and forcing an unwanted label on anyone is abusive.

The term *mental retardation* is one of the most stigmatized disability labels. Carroll and Repucci (1978), for example, found that professionals associated more stigma with this term than with *delinquency* or *emotional disturbance*. When compared to the other groups, professionals had the lowest expectations of progress and the highest expectations of deviance for children with mental retardation. Similarly, Gething (1991) found that people associated greater discomfort with hypothetical interactions with people with Down syndrome than with people with drug dependency, AIDS, blindness, cerebral palsy, Alzheimer's disease, or paraplegia. Only the label *schizophrenia* was more negatively rated than Down syndrome.

ATTITUDES OF CAREGIVERS

The attitudes of human services professionals and other caregivers toward people with disabilities are particularly critical for several reasons (Geskie & Salesek, 1988). Because caregivers have frequent contact with people with disabilities, they have a high potential to either abuse or assist them. Thus, caregivers' attitudes are likely to have the most direct effect on the lives of those in their care. Caregivers are also likely to play central roles in setting the course of human services systems and in setting program priorities. Because they are viewed as experts, they also help to shape the attitudes of the general public, as well as of other service providers.

Perhaps most importantly, service professionals often provide guidance directly to people with disabilities and their families, and therefore have the potential for influencing family attitudes and decisions. For example, negative sentiments expressed by diagnosing physicians may encourage parental rejection of a child. This rejection could lead to a secondary disability (e.g., behavioral disability) that could be even more incapacitating than the primary disability. Some children with average or near-average intelligence have been rejected by their families, institutionalized, sterilized, or refused medical treatment because of negative attitudes expressed by physicians.

Medical models often depersonalize the life experiences of human beings. Thus, "'life' [itself] appears as an object of medical, professional and administrative management" (Illich, 1992, p. 233). This professional detachment from the lives of others creates social distance, and the "patient" or "consumer" is objectified as a mere commodity of the system.

The authoritarian stance of service providers appears to be of particular concern for three reasons. First, it is considered to be countertherapeutic (Geskie & Salesek, 1988). Second, it has been shown to be combined with negative attitudes toward people with disabilities (Canter, 1963). Third, it is associated with excessive control and coercive handling (Geskie & Salesek, 1988). As suggested in Chapter 6, authoritarian attitudes and controlling behavior are also connected with cases of overt abuse.

Nursing and attendant care providers, as groups, have been identified as occupational categories associated with authoritarian attitudes toward people with disabilities (Geskie & Salesek, 1988). Of course, such group characteristics summarize large numbers of individual opinions, and therefore may reflect a larger number of people with authoritarian attitudes in the group and not necessarily the inherent traits of every individual involved. Furthermore, some dispute remains as to whether the authoritarian attitudes found in these groups represent fundamental attributes of the group members themselves or a mere reflection of the requirements of the job. Some have argued that because the job demands of attendants and nurses commonly involve some element of control, authoritarian attitudes in these groups are situational rather than inherent. Others have pointed out that even as students, nurses tend to have more authoritarian attitudes (Meyer, 1973), and that because these attitudes presuppose their exposure to the workplace, they cannot have resulted from it.

It is likely that situational as well as individual personality factors are involved and that each reinforces the other. Some people with authoritarian personalities are probably attracted to human services because of the ample opportunities to exert control over others; others probably become more authoritarian as a result of the job environment. The presence of those with controlling tendencies increases the overall authoritarianism in the environment, which in turn, reinforces the controlling tendencies of those who inhabit it, making it more attractive to new members with this type of personality.

ATTITUDES OF POLICE AND LEGAL PROFESSIONALS

The attitudes of the people who enforce society's laws and prosecute offenses are of critical interest to abuse prevention. Yuker (1986) suggests that most lawyers and police possess little knowledge of people with disabilities and that many harbor negative sentiments, but points out the lack of current information on this subject. In one of the few available studies, only 3% of a group comprised of police, judges, and lawyers indicated that they had experienced any previous contact with people with mental retardation, and less than 10% had received any formal or informal training in this area (Schilit, 1979). Lawyers are generally unaware of the rights of people with mental retardation, even when they are representing them as clients (Yuker, 1986). Nevertheless, research suggests that even brief educational intervention can produce positive changes in the attitudes of lawyers and law enforcement personnel. Yuker (1986) points out that police and courts often call on psychiatrists, psychologists, and other human services professionals to guide them when working with people with mental retardation or other disabilities. These consulting professionals bring their own attitudes along with them that often influence the points of view of the police and lawyers with whom they consult. Although the attitudes of these consultants are generally positive, they can sometimes communicate negative images of people with disabilities.

CHANGING ATTITUDES

Can attitudes toward people with mental retardation ever be changed? Research suggests that these attitudes can change, and, more importantly, that attitudes already appear to be changing for the better. Rees, Spreen, and Harnadek (1991) tested university students and found that their mean ratings on 17 out of 22 attributes of people with mental retardation improved significantly between testing done in 1975 and 1988. In addition, they point out that specific instruction made a positive change in ratings for those among the 1975 group who received it. Although ratings improved among the 1988 group following specific instruction, the control group who received no specific instruction also showed improved ratings over the same year. The authors suggest that instruction made less difference in 1988 because the deinstitutionalization, integration, and positive media attention of the 1980s reduced the need for specific education. Other studies (e.g., Ojanen, 1992) lend support to the idea that sentiments toward people with disabilities are becoming more positive as younger generations with more enlightened attitudes replace older generations. However, some studies have shown little or no improvement in negative thinking over time (e.g., Trute, Teft, & Segall, 1989).

Strategies

The following is a list of useful strategies for improving attitudes toward people with disabilities:

1. Ensure contact between people with and without disabilities.
2. Educate others specifically about people with disabilities.
3. Improve education in general.
4. Provide positive models.
5. Intervene early.
6. Target key groups and individuals.
7. Emphasize positive approaches to changing negative points of view.
8. When necessary, challenge negative attitudes and behavior.
9. Be realistic.
10. Listen to others' concerns.
11. Recognize one's own imperfections.
12. Personalize and humanize interactions.
13. Enlist allies.

Ensure Contact Simply ensuring contact between people with disabilities and other members of society has been shown to improve attitudes; however, some caution is needed regarding the nature of the interaction. Gething (1991) found that people who experienced more frequent contact with people with disabilities experienced less discomfort with them as a result. Yuker (1988) found that while effects on attitudes were positive in 51% of cases studied, contact made no significant differences in 39% of cases and actually led to an increase in negative attitudes in the remaining 10% of cases. The fact that contact led to more positive attitudes five times as frequently as it did to an increase in negative attitudes suggests that contact is a powerful tool for attitude improvement. The 10% of cases where interaction did more harm than good, however, suggests that contact can produce complex results. One simple explanation for the higher number of improved attitudes is that impressions prior to interaction are generally negative, and people often find that contact with people with disabilities is not as uncomfortable as they had expected it to be. However, Yuker (1988) presents another important variable, suggesting that contact must take place under favorable conditions in order to produce positive results; unfavorable conditions are likely to produce negative results.

For example, consider the following hypothetical scenarios of the integration of two different classrooms—1 with 26 students and 1 general education teacher, the other with 6 students with multiple disabilities, a special education teacher, and 2 teaching assistants. In the first scenario, the 6 students with multiple disabilities are placed in the general classroom, creating a new total of 32 children. The special education teacher and the two assistants are reassigned to other duties. Under such conditions, one teacher is now expected to teach and carry out related services that were previously assigned to four different adults. The classroom is overcrowded, the children with disabilities are still clustered in a group much larger than their natural ratio in society, and the teacher has not been appropriately trained.

Such conditions are programmed for failure. The teacher is likely to feel that the demands upon her or him are excessive. Some students are likely to feel neglected. Parents of both the students with and without disabilities will probably feel that their children are receiving inferior educational services. The students with disabilities are likely to be blamed for most or all of these circumstances because the problems will be associated with their inclusion. The real causes of the problem (e.g., the dwindling away of resources during integration, continued clustering beyond natural proportions, inadequate teacher preparation) will be less obvious and are likely to be ignored. Contact under these kinds of unfavorable conditions can lead to a worsening, rather than an improvement, of attitudes toward the students with disabilities.

In the second scenario, these same two classrooms could have been integrated sharing all the resources that were already available to them separately. Two smaller classes could have been created, each with a teacher and an aide, and a smaller number of students with disabilities (perhaps still higher than ideal or natural proportions). Under these more favorable conditions, success is encouraged, and interaction between the two groups generally improves overall impressions.

As the above example suggests, efforts to improve attitudes through increased contact must consider the nature and context of the interaction itself. Even under the most difficult conditions, efforts to integrate students that trade off valuable resources in order to achieve inclusion can result in failure, backlash, and worsened opinions regarding people with disabilities. Planning will help ensure successful interactions. If attitudes are extremely negative prior to contact, further education may be desirable before and/or during interaction. Cooperative activities that involve benefits for all participants, not just those with disabilities, are recommended. Take measures to minimize stress and decrease pressure for competition for all involved. Make certain that resources are adequate for the activities undertaken. These and other related measures to ensure positive outcomes can make interaction between people with disabilities and other community members one of the best strategies for improving attitudes.

Some investigators of attitudes toward people with disabilities have made a critical distinction between opinions regarding social relations and those concerning social responsibility (Trute et al., 1989). They suggest that social relations attitudes are connected to direct personal interactions with people with disabilities (e.g., friendships, marriages), but that opinions regarding social responsibility are related to less direct relationships (e.g., employer–employee, landlord–tenant). This distinction is important for two reasons. First, attitudes could change in one area, but not the other. For example, parents may learn to feel comfortable about students with disabilities being placed in their child's classroom, but remain uncomfortable about these same children with disabilities forming close friendships with their own children. Second, these distinct attitudes may require different interventions. For instance, whereas direct contact may be the best method of affecting thinking about social relations, education may be more effective for influencing attitudes about social responsibility.

Improve Education Increased acceptance of others is typically associated with higher levels of education, so efforts toward improving education in general appear to be useful in improving attitudes about people with disabilities (Geskie & Salesek, 1988). Specific education about people with disabilities has also been shown to be effective. Although research has produced some contradictory findings, most studies suggest that accurate information about people with disabilities helps to overcome the effects of negative myths and generally improves overall perceptions. Educational intervention appears to be most effective when it is combined with some kind of interactive activity (Horne, 1988). Simulations, cooperative-learning, or role-playing activities are useful for this purpose. Best results seem to occur when educational intervention and increased contact take place at the same time.

Provide Positive Models   This book frequently makes use of social learning theory with regard to how models can contribute to abuse; however, models can also lead to positive attitudes and abuse prevention. Human services often send mixed messages by espousing one point of view while modeling the other. For example, many contemporary teacher education institutions now advocate for the inclusion of people with disabilities in the classroom, yet exclude these individuals from their own classes. Involving people with disabilities in a wide variety of settings and activities and respecting the contributions that they make models positive attitudes and successful inclusion. Providing nonpunitive and nonviolent models is also important. Demonstrating that such methods can and do succeed increases the chance that others will imitate them.

Intervene Early   Many of a person's most persistent attitudes develop early in life, and it is generally easier to influence the development of a person's attitudes than to try to change them once they've become firmly entrenched (Zimbardo & Leippe, 1991). Therefore, intervening as early as possible has the greatest potential for producing the most positive results with the least required effort. Teaching young children to accept diversity and reject violence is best accomplished within families at an early age, but should also be part of the childcare and preschool curriculum. Teaching the acceptance of all kinds of human diversity, not just acceptance of people with disabilities, tends to encourage nonprejudicial ways of thinking.

Target Key Groups and Individuals   Although it is important to promote positive attitudes toward people with disabilities in all members of society, targeting key groups and individuals can produce the most immediate results for abuse prevention. Those providing services for people with disabilities need to be focused on because their attitudes and behavior have the most direct effects on the lives of their clients. Targeting administrators in highly visible roles can be useful because these individuals can serve as positive or negative models for other staff to imitate. Often natural leaders can be identified within groups and organizations whose attitudes and behavior strongly influence those around them. Identifying these individuals and supporting them to treat people with disabilities in a positive fashion often ensures that others will respond in the same way (Zimbardo & Leippe, 1991).

Emphasize Positive Approaches There are several reasons why positive approaches to improving attitudes are generally more effective. First, as suggested above, they present a nonpunitive model. Second, confrontation can result in angry or defensive responses that can lead to greater inflexibility. Third, optimism appears to be one of the most decisive tools for persuasion. For example, Martin Luther King, Jr., one of the most powerful and effective orators of our time, frequently inspired people with visual imagery of his dream of a better world and invited his listeners to share that vision with him (Zimbardo & Leippe, 1991). Similarly, negative attitudes toward and violence against people with disabilities are long-standing and potentially overwhelming problems. The first step toward meaningful change is encouraging others to believe that change is possible.

Challenge Negative Attitudes and Behavior While accentuating positive change and minimizing confrontation remain important goals, violence and abuse cannot go unchallenged, and hatred and injustice cannot be ignored. The balance between using positive approaches whenever possible and challenging when necessary is difficult to achieve, and no simple rule allows easy decisions to be made about how to deal with each particular situation. Often, however, confrontation is less incompatible with positive approaches than it might initially appear. Using the following principles may help to ensure that directly confronting others' negative attitudes produces the best possible results:

1. Choose areas of confrontation carefully—consider both the importance of the issue and the realistic possibility of making a difference.
2. Determine who should address the issue—consider whether it is an issue for advocates, child welfare, law enforcement, and so on, and then turn it over to the appropriate agency.
3. If acting as an advocate, be certain to propose an acceptable solution rather than simply state the problem.
4. Whenever possible, offer something in return for what is being requested. For example, if one section of proposed legislation would segregate students with disabilities, one might let the legislator who sponsored the bill know that one would support and actively work for its passage if amended to remove that specific section.

This gives the legislator a reason to make the requested change. If he or she thinks the person will oppose the bill regardless of the amendment, there is no reason to carry out the suggestion.

5. Avoid personal conflict and animosity; it is easier to negotiate change within a positive relationship than within a negative one.

Be Realistic Unrealistically positive views of people with disabilities may be almost as dangerous as unrealistically negative ones. False information and insincere feelings are usually identified as such sooner or later and could lead to even greater negative views of people with disabilities as the false information is rejected. They may also betray hidden negative feelings in the person who disseminates the false information because if that individual sincerely believed that people with disabilities are acceptable as they really are, there would be no need to misrepresent them. In addition, realistic views of other people with or without disabilities, including all their human frailties and imperfections, can be expected to have the greatest impact on inhibiting violence and abuse. Presenting people as being overly perfect can result in the same depersonalization and objectification as results from presenting them as being too imperfect.

Listen to Others Attitude change is best accomplished as an interactive process. It is important to listen to the views and concerns of others and to address these directly, rather than simply telling people what to think and how things should be. Often negative attitudes and inappropriate behavior are rooted in genuine concerns, and changing such attitudes and behavior requires an understanding of those issues. For example, teachers may have negative attitudes toward integration of students with disabilities for a wide variety of reasons. Some may feel insecure regarding their own abilities, others may lack confidence because they feel unprepared to serve these students, and still others may feel that they are already overworked and will be asked to take on additional work without the necessary resources. Understanding the reasoning behind each individual's concerns and addressing those concerns directly can be critical in changing attitudes.

Recognize One's Own Imperfections Often, people lack insight into their own beliefs, even though they are trying to change the beliefs of others. It is important for everyone to understand that no one is perfect and that no single point of view represents total enlightenment. Attitudes toward violence and disability are deeply enmeshed in the culture and everyone is affected to some extent. Recognizing one's own imperfections and limitations can be very helpful for understanding similar imperfections and limitations in other people. Failing to recognize one's shortcomings tends to create unrealistic expectations of others.

Personalize and Humanize Interactions Attitudes that discourage abuse must strengthen the bonds and decrease the social distance between individuals and groups. Bogdan and Taylor (1992) emphasize the need for accepting relationships. Honest acceptance is based on a positive view of the real person including his or her differences and disabilities—not on denial of these traits. They suggest that humanizing relationships are characterized by the following: 1) attribution of feelings and thinking to the person, 2) recognition of personal individuality, 3) conceptualization of the person as a reciprocating partner in interactions, and 4) definition of social roles for the person. These traits should be emphasized in portrayals of people with disabilities to personalize individuals and prevent dehumanization of the group as a whole.

Enlist Allies Attitude change and advocacy are very demanding pursuits. To accomplish them it is important to request assistance from every possible resource. Many organizations, agencies, and individuals are potential allies and helping them to see areas of mutual interest is critical to bringing them on one's side. For example, many organizations work for the preservation of human rights of various groups. These organizations can be much more effective when they work together than when they are fragmented. People with disabilities and their advocates can provide a valuable service to the community by working for the human rights of all disempowered people. In return, a coalition of minorities working for the rights of people with disabilities may be more effective than people with disabilities and their advocates working by themselves.

Using Mass Media

Radio, television, newspapers, and magazines are important influences on public opinion and perception. They can be extremely useful for increasing public awareness of social problems and in encouraging constructive change. Therefore, valuable allies for those interested in changing attitudes about abuse and disability can be found in the mass media (McCall & Gregory, 1987). To take advantage of these alliances, however, it is necessary to understand certain principles, limitations, and dangers that must be considered.

First, it is important to remember that while these agencies can be valuable, they typically remain fiercely independent, and they each have their own goals and objectives to meet. Advertisers, readers, viewers, or listeners can exert strong influences. Finding common interests with the media often provides the best assurance that they will represent one's own interests and concerns. Patience is often required. Human interest stories are usually presented by the media on a space available basis and may be delayed or eliminated when war, natural disasters, or any other headline arises.

Second, as suggested by McCall and Gregory (1987), the media are often effective at creating or building upon preexisting public sentiment, but less proficient at changing these points of view. As a result, direct confrontation with inappropriate attitudes or practices is rarely the most successful style. For example, it may be more successful to counter negative stereotypes of people with disabilities in the media by trying to present more positive images than it would be to try to argue against the negative ones. Although there are times when confrontation is necessary, particularly to provide a public display of rejection of inappropriate behavior, reserving its use for the rare occasions when it is absolutely required generally yields the best results.

Third, the mass media are inherently limited by time, space, and background knowledge of their audience to only superficial treatment of most issues. This is especially true for electronic media, but newspapers and magazines also have this limitation. Hours of interview are often compressed into a few seconds of information, often presented without critical context. Therefore, it is better to attempt to put across a few important points using simple language. Attempting to address the many subtleties and complexities that surround most issues often makes the presentation too muddled to be truly effective.

CONCLUSION

This chapter presented methods for improving attitudes toward people with disabilities as a means of reducing their risk for violence and abuse. Attitudes can have powerful effects on the encouragement or inhibition of violence. Although there is some indication in contemporary society of perceptions becoming more positive regarding people with disabilities, public sentiment generally remains negative. Many societies have a long history of such attitudes toward this population. A number of strategies exist for changing ways of acting toward people with disabilities. Contact under favorable conditions between people with and without disabilities, as well as educational intervention have been shown to be effective strategies, particularly when used in combination. Using the mass media to present positive images of people with disabilities can also influence general public thinking. Improving attitudes toward people with disabilities is a critical consideration for abuse prevention.

12

Healing the Consequences of Abuse

Sheila Mansell & Dick Sobsey

Because this book is about abuse prevention, a chapter on therapeutic services for abuse victims may seem out of place. Nevertheless, treatment of victims of abuse and the offenders who commit abuse is an essential component of prevention. Survivors of abuse who do not receive counseling and other therapies may be left more vulnerable to further abuse as a result of processes such as learned helplessness or an internalized cycle of victimization (see *multiple-victimization cycle*, p. 154). Offenders are likely to commit more offenses without the aid of rehabilitative counseling. Furthermore, in a significant number of cases, people who were previously victimized go on to victimize others in an externalized cycle of victimization (see *victim–offender cycle*, p. 154), and successful treatment can help to break that cycle. In addition, intervention can help to minimize the severity of harm caused by abuse that has already taken place, preventing some of the potential damage of abuse even after abuse occurs.

Many of the strategies discussed in this chapter are based on work done with people who have been sexually abused or sexually assaulted because more information is currently available regarding the treatment of this particular form of abuse. Graziano and Mills (1992) point out that counseling for children who have been physically or psychologically abused or neglected has generally been ignored in professional practice as well as in the professional literature. In spite of a clear

Sheila Mansell, M.Ed., is a Research Associate with the University of Alberta Abuse & Disability Project in Edmonton, Alberta, Canada.

indication of physically abused children's need for counseling, greater emphasis has been placed on protective services, counseling of abusive parents, and medical treatment of the physical harm resulting from the abuse. Nevertheless, since the 1970s there has been general recognition within the profession of the need for interventions such as play therapy, group therapy, and therapeutic education with children who have been physically abused or neglected, or have suffered psychological trauma (Kempe & Kempe, 1978).

Fortunately, treatment strategies can be generalized across various forms of abuse. For example, Ryan (1992) reported on a group of 51 people with developmental disabilities who met the technical criteria for posttraumatic stress disorder (PTSD), indicating that "trauma in this sample included sexual abuse by multiple assailants (starting in childhood), physical abuse that was commonly the cause of the person's cognitive deficits, or life-threatening neglect combined with some other active abuse or trauma" (p. 8). In spite of this diversity of etiology, all 23 individuals in this sample who received treatment based on the same six-point protocol improved as a result of the intervention. This finding suggests that the same principles of treatment can be successully applied to various forms of abuse.

Little information has been written specific to the needs of victims of abuse with disabilities. Therefore, most support programs for these individuals are based on programs for victims of abuse without disabilities, but are individualized to suit the needs and skills of the persons being served (e.g., Sullivan, 1993). The assumption is that the same basic principles of intervention apply until and unless a strong need for accommodation arises. It also facilitates integration of services for people with disabilities with services for other members of the community, which tends to encourage future personal safety.

In fact, our understanding of effective treatment is further limited by the relatively small number of well-designed studies to validate treatment strategies for abuse victims without disabilities. For example, Thomlison (1991) reported only nine separate evaluation studies of treatment programs for child sexual abuse, although more than 2,200 such programs were identified in the United States alone. He also found that the nine available evaluation studies were methodologically weak and that effective evaluation of such programs is still in its infancy. All of the studies reviewed suggested that treatment was associated with improvement, but because common criteria were lacking, nothing definite could be determined concerning the relative value of various procedures.

It is important to note that the word *treatment* is used here in a broad sense to include counseling, education, support, and a variety of other interventions. It is not intended to be regarded in its medical sense as a "cure" for some pathological condition because we cannot assume that all abuse victims have such a condition. By making victimization a condition of disease, we risk increasing the harm done to those abused, encouraging individuals to assume a passive role, and adopting negative expectations regarding their own resources for coping. The conceptualization of abused people as "sick" can also add to the stigma already associated with victimization.

EFFECTS OF ABUSE

The growing recognition of abuse and violence in our society has been reflected in considerable research addressing incidence, psychological effects, prevention strategies, and therapeutic interventions. Although acknowledgment of sexual abuse is relatively recent, a wide variety of sexual abuse treatment strategies have been developed to address the psychological and behavioral effects of abuse on the victim. Finkelhor and Browne's (1985) review of the child sexual abuse literature suggested that the initial effects of child abuse include fear, anxiety, depression, anger, and inappropriate behavior. Long-term effects include depression, self-destructive behavior, feelings of isolation and stigmatization, poor self-esteem, tendencies toward revictimization, substance abuse, sexual maladjustment, and difficulty establishing trust (Finkelhor & Browne, 1985).

To explain the effects of child sexual abuse, Finkelhor and Browne (1985) created a model of the traumagenic dynamics of abusive sexualization, betrayal, powerlessness, and stigmatization. Study of these dynamics is essential for trauma assessment and the development of treatment goals. Physical and psychological abuse produce similar effects on the victim's emotional development. Although there has been little research that specifically describes the effects of abuse on people with disabilities, the research that is available suggests that victims of abuse with disabilities experience effects similar to those experienced by other victims (e.g., Sobsey & Doe, 1991). It is essential that practitioners understand the total impact of abuse in order to address its psychological and behavioral effects (Porter et al., 1982).

SEXUAL ABUSE SUPPORT SERVICES
AND PEOPLE WITH DISABILITIES

Since the 1980s, there has been mounting evidence to suggest that there is an increased risk of both sexual assault and sexual abuse for people with disabilities (Sobsey, Gray, Wells, Pyper, & Reimer-Heck,

1991). In fact, some research suggests that about 70% of people with disabilities experience sexual assault (e.g., Stimpson & Best, 1991). A few studies have documented incidence patterns (Sobsey & Doe, 1991) and abuse prevention strategies (Sobsey & Mansell, 1990), yet very little is known about the specific effects of abuse on people with developmental disabilities or about appropriate therapeutic adaptations to support those who have been abused. Recent research by the University of Alberta Abuse & Disability Project (e.g., Sobsey & Doe, 1991; Mansell, Sobsey, & Calder, 1992) included a survey of sexually abused people with disabilities. In this survey, a variety of sexual abuse issues were addressed including attributes of offenders and victims; offenders' relationship to the victims; the number and nature of abuse episodes, charges, reports, and convictions; the impact of abuse on victims; and victim support services. Results from this study suggest that for many people with developmental disabilities who have been sexually abused, therapy is generally inaccessible, unavailable, or ineffectively adapted to their specific needs (Mansell, Sobsey, & Calder, 1992; see also Chapter 3, Figure 5, this volume). This chapter discusses some of the reasons for the inadequate state of sexual abuse support services for people with disabilities, as well as some of the issues that practitioners need to consider in providing more effective services for this population.

Difficulties in Providing Treatment

Providing available and accessible support services for people with developmental disabilities who have been sexually abused is clearly important in view of their heightened risk for abuse; however, a number of barriers have prevented the development of these necessary services. These barriers include a prolonged denial of their abuse, low research priority in the development of appropriate intervention methods, inadequate accessibility to existing sexual abuse therapy services, and a paucity of professionals trained in counseling this particular population. Differential attitudes toward people with developmental disabilities are evident and suggest the influence of devaluing beliefs and ignorance about disability (Cushna, Szymanski, & Tanguay, 1980; Spackman, Grigel, & MacFarlane, 1990). These same negative attitudes increase their risk for abuse as well as limit their access to treatment (Baladerian, 1993). For example, the belief that people with mental retardation are insensitive to abuse was mentioned in Chapter 6 as one of the factors that disinhibit violence toward them. This same myth can make intervention appear to be unnecessary, as there would be no logical reason to treat someone who does not really feel any pain or suffer any psychological harm.

Treatment Accessibility Obtaining treatment for people with disabilities can be problematic because of insufficient accommodations in providing basic needs such as physical accessibility and appropriate resource materials. For example, not all sexual assault centers have ramps or elevators for physical access, nor do all centers possess resources such as alternative telephone devices, translation services, or nonprint alternatives for reading materials. Despite resource and physical accessibility problems, a recent survey of experts in the areas of sexual abuse and/or disability suggested that sexual abuse treatment centers have made considerable progress in providing these accommodations (Sobsey, Mansell, & Wells, 1991). Nevertheless, ensuring that sexual abuse treatment programs for people with developmental disabilities are both accessible and appropriate is a complicated task.

Treatment Availability Increased accessibility of sexual abuse treatment centers does not, however, suggest that well-adapted therapies are widely available. A lack of appropriate intervention programs persists because many of the professionals who work with people with developmental disabilities possess insufficient experience or training in the abilities, special needs, and limitations of this high-risk population (Tanguay & Szymanski, 1980). Lack of confidence prevents many of these professionals from providing sexual abuse treatment services to their clients.

Availability of services will continue to be problematic as long as professionals in sexual abuse treatment are isolated from people with developmental disabilities in their training and practice. Providing sexual abuse counselors, therapists, and other professionals with the necessary experience and training may give them the confidence, knowledge, and skills they will need to work with this population. It could also improve professionals' attitudes toward people with disabilities (Talbot & Shaul, 1987) and heighten awareness of their equal need for intervention services to deal with their abuse.

Despite the growing recognition of the increased risk of sexual abuse for people with developmental disabilities and the potential for adapting therapies to accommodate the needs of those who have been abused, the provision of sexual abuse treatment for this population has not become a widespread practice (Tharinger, Horton, & Millea, 1990). Nevertheless, a few researchers and practitioners have adapted some specific therapy techniques to meet these needs. These suggested methods of treatment are discussed below.

Effective Treatment Programs

Development of therapy approaches for abused individuals with developmental disabilities has been a low priority of professional research.

Many proponents of early psychotherapy assumed that people with developmental disabilities were unsuitable candidates for traditional insight-oriented therapies because of their limited language and abstract-conceptual abilities (Monfils & Menolascino, 1984). Level of intelligence was considered an important determinant of success in and suitability for insight-oriented therapies. Professionals' ignorance of and exaggerated pessimism about both disability (Rubin, 1983) and the efficacy of therapy for people with developmental disabilities (Spackman et al., 1990) probably prevented many practitioners and researchers from questioning these assumptions. The emphasis on intelligence may also have hindered the development of more appropriate approaches to treatment.

A few researchers and practitioners challenged the importance of intelligence in determining the suitability of therapy by adapting existing techniques and using other more relevant indicators of a person's ability to benefit from a particular form of therapy or counseling. Therapy techniques adapted for people with developmental disabilities are similar to conventional approaches used with people without disabilities. Assessing developmental level, ability to form relationships, social adaptability, and family or other living situations provides more relevant information to the practitioner about suitability for therapy than does intelligence alone. Consideration of these factors may help practitioners to choose appropriate techniques for adaptation (Rubin, 1983). Researchers have reported success in adapting a variety of existing therapies for people with developmental disabilities including individual counseling and psychotherapy (Godschalz, 1983; Rubin, 1983; Spackman et al., 1990; Szymanski, 1980) and group therapy (Downes, 1982; Laterza, 1979; Monfils, 1985; Monfils & Menolascino, 1984; Szymanski & Rosefsky, 1980). Below are examples of some of these techniques.

Individual Psychoanalysis Sinason (1990) has employed individual psychoanalytic treatment with people with developmental disabilities and argues that it can be effectively applied even to those requiring the highest level of assistance. She identifies three main stages of treatment. The first stage deals with removing the abused individual's secondary psychogenic impairments to improve communication between therapist and client. Sinason suggests that apparent impairments of communication and thinking associated with mental retardation are often partially (and sometimes entirely) the symptoms of traumatic experiences and are not direct results of the primary disability. Through the development of trust and a communicative relationship, many of these secondary impairments can be reduced or eliminated. The second stage involves the client's experience of sorrow and deep feelings of anger or shame about their abuse and trauma. Once communication has been optimized, the client can develop a trusting relationship with the therapist that allows the individual to confront her or his feelings about being victimized. In the third stage, the client begins to establish control over her or his own life. Support and communication between therapist and client continues to be important, but the focus of the interaction moves toward decision making and other more practical issues. The therapist must also help the individual work toward her or his own independence during this stage.

Group Therapy Tomasulo (1990) suggests strategies for counseling groups of people with developmental disabilities who require lower levels of assistance. His method of group counseling is not exclusive to abuse victims, but can be applied to addressing other relevant issues as well. Often, it may be helpful to establish mixed groups that include members specifically dealing with abuse in addition to members addressing other life issues (e.g., social relationships, vocational concerns). However, some individuals coping with highly traumatic abuse might benefit from being grouped with others who share similar concerns. Issues of abuse frequently arise in group counseling of people with disabilities, even when abuse was not the original reason for referral. The author stresses the importance of the group process, suggesting that the interaction of members is more beneficial than the actual content of the group discussion. He emphasizes that the therapist's role must be to facilitate interactions among the group members themselves, as opposed to the therapist being the central focus of all group discussions.

Tomasulo (1990) recommends establishing four stages within each group session:

- Stage 1: *Orientation*—Make group members aware of who is present and the purpose of the group.
- Stage 2: *Warm-up and sharing*—Encourage disclosure of feelings and experiences. These may range from simple disclosures of something that a group member did since the last session took place to the discussion of abuse or other traumatic subjects.
- Stage 3: *Enactment*—Utilize role playing and other related techniques to recreate the traumatic experience. Tomasulo recommends that this stage be kept relatively brief because of its highly demanding nature.
- Stage 4: *Affirmation*—Stage 4 should occur at the end of each session. Group members are praised individually and collectively for their participation. This stage allows group members to wind down their intense emotions before terminating the session.

Hyman (1993) recommends similar group strategies and some additional ideas for effective group counseling of sexually abused individuals with disabilities. Coleaders can be useful in many groups, she suggests, especially if some members occasionally need individual support or assistance to participate. The use of coleaders allows for inclusion of individuals with more severe disabilities and provides additional modeling when needed. She has a different group member bring food to each session to encourage bonding within the group and runs parallel groups for families and significant others to aid them in providing support in the home and other settings. Hyman warns against using words such as *sexual abuse* in early sessions because they may inhibit or otherwise influence members' personal perceptions of their experiences.

Adapted Therapy Techniques Spackman et al. (1990) suggest that individualized adaptations to therapy for people with developmental disabilities might include psychodynamic techniques such as direct and indirect suggestion; therapeutic metaphor; paradoxical and experiential interventions; behavioral techniques; cognitive approaches; nonverbal techniques similar to play and art therapies; and verbal techniques such as reassurance, support, directed discussion, reflection and clarification of feelings, and interpretation. Downes (1982) suggests that the majority of people with developmental disabilities (i.e., those who do not require maximum levels of assistance) have sufficient verbal skills for action and play therapies as well as for conversational and behavioral therapies. Spackman et al. (1990) point out that there are a wider range of therapeutic approaches available to those practitioners willing to learn how to use their clients' receptive language, symbolic communication, visual imagery, and tactile and kinesthetic interactions in their own communication with clients.

There are also many adaptations specific to group therapy. Laterza (1979) recommends the use of eclectic group therapy adaptations such as action-oriented group work, adapted modeling techniques, transactional analysis techniques, and behavior contracts. Monfils (1985) recommends theme-centered group work that utilizes relaxation techniques, modeling, and role playing. Potential group members should be individually assessed to determine their motivation for change, abilities to express themselves verbally, and the degree to which they will benefit from the group structure. For any of these suggested individual or group therapy techniques to be successful, they must be appropriately adapted to each individual's level of understanding, social adaptability, and developmental level. Abuse and assault are among the issues that are frequently discussed in these groups.

The diversity of possible adaptations to therapy does not necessarily suggest that these adaptations are widely used or even currently available. Professionals' negative perceptions of the ineffectiveness of adapted therapy with people with developmental disabilities may be a product of their own unrealistic goals and may prevent more wide-spread use of these techniques. Some may feel that there is little reason to try to treat the effects of abuse or other such problems if they cannot cure the individual's underlying disability. In addition, many of the studies of therapeutic adaptations have methodological problems such as varying diagnosis, lack of control groups, lack of standardized treatment techniques, and inadequate measures of evaluating therapy outcome (Szymanski & Rosefsky, 1980) that could contribute to professionals' negative perceptions. Better evaluative research to determine the efficacy of adapted therapies for people with developmental disabilities is required to ameliorate this problem.

Currently Available Treatment Programs   A few practitioners and researchers have adapted sexual abuse therapies for people with disabilities by using conventional sexual abuse treatment approaches. Cruz et al. (1988) noted that women with developmental disabilities who had suffered intrafamilial sexual abuse as children experienced significant issues surrounding guilt, needs for intimacy, lack of self-esteem, feelings of isolation, difficulty handling and expressing anger (due to fears of retaliation and abandonment exacerbated by their dependency on others), concern and confusion about their own sexuality, and feelings about being "damaged goods." Cruz and colleagues used a cotherapy approach to work with these women, where one therapist with expertise in sexual abuse was paired with another therapist with expertise in developmental disability. The cotherapy approach was used in conjunction with adapted group therapy techniques such as role playing and group discussion. Cruz et al. (1988) present a promising example of a sexual abuse treatment program for people with developmental disabilities. The professional liaison of a cotherapist approach, combined with the application of adapted therapy techniques to sexual abuse treatment, may help to ensure that sexual abuse intervention is both available and appropriate for people with developmental disabilities.

Sullivan and colleagues (1990) reviewed literature on sexual abuse and combined it with their expertise about children with disabilities to adapt sexual abuse treatment for this population of children. Treatment goals included alleviating feelings of guilt, regaining the ability to trust, treating depression, helping children express anger, teaching about sexuality and interpersonal relationships, teaching self-protection techniques, teaching an effective vocabulary with which to label feelings, teaching sexual preference and sexual abuse issues when appropriate, and treating secondary behavior characteristics (Sullivan, Vernon, & Scanlan, 1987). Therapy techniques included directed and nondirected counseling, play and reality therapy, psychodrama and role playing, transactional analysis, behavior therapy, didactic counseling, and generalization training (Sullivan et al., 1987).

Sullivan, Scanlan, Knutson, Brookhouser, and Schulte (1992) studied the efficacy of these therapy adaptations by using The Child Behavior Checklist (Achenbach & Edelbrock, 1988) before and after therapy on a sample of 72 sexually abused subjects from a residential school for the deaf. The sample included 51 boys and 21 girls between 12 and 16 years old. Therapy was conducted by a therapist fluent in sign language. The study included a nontreatment control group because half of the parents refused the offer of free psychotherapy services for their child. Before therapy, both the treatment and nontreatment groups had elevated CBC scores showing a high number of behavior problems. The children who received therapy had significantly fewer behavior problems following treatment. The research of Sullivan and colleagues shows considerable promise in developing adapted sexual abuse treatment for children with disabilities and determining its efficacy.

Sullivan (1993) offers a good description of the Therapeutic Education for Abused Children with Handicaps (TEACH) at the Center for Abused Handicapped Children at the Boys Town National Research Hospital in Omaha. The program includes nonoffending parents and siblings of abused children with a variety of disabilities. It has served more than 100 sexually abused children (ages 3–21). Validation data are available on 72 of these children, half of whom were treated, that indicates a significant reduction in problem behavior as a result of therapy. The program is eclectic, using elements of cognitive-behavioral psychotherapy, communication training, play and art therapy, behavioral procedures (e.g., desensitization to stimuli associated with trauma, gentle teaching, role playing, and in vivo generalization training). Each child's program is individualized to meet a structured set of psychotherapeutic goals.

Ryan (1992) describes a protocol used at the University of Colorado Dual Diagnosis Program with 51 adults and children with developmental disabilities who exhibited posttraumatic stress disorder after a variety of abuse experiences including sexual abuse by multiple assailants, severe physical abuse, and life-threatening neglect. The protocol had six essential elements. First, medication was judiciously used only to treat specific symptoms. Sedation was not used because it was considered to interfere with therapy. Second, careful physical examination was performed to identify and treat concurrent medical problems (2/3 of this group were found to have medical problems that exacerbated their psychological difficulties). Third, iatrogenic complications were minimized. For example, the use of tranquilizers was reduced or discontinued, as they often interfered with treatment and aggravated symptoms. Fourth, psychotherapy was employed using any available means of communication (half of the group were nonverbal). Fifth, environmental alterations were made to reduce contact with disassociative triggers. For example, the smell of a perfumed powder worn by the parent who abused him needed to be eliminated from one individual's environment because it triggered episodes of psychotic behavior. Careful observation of behavioral antecedents was required for identifying these stimuli. Sixth, support staff were trained to create a general atmosphere of safety in the environment. Although Ryan stresses the need for more systematic evaluation, current results suggest that the program is effective.

While much more needs to be learned about effective treatment programs for abused people with disabilities, six criteria have been suggested (Sobsey, 1993):

1. Programs must be tailored to meet each individual's needs and abilities.
2. Programs must be eclectic, utilizing the most suitable elements of all available treatment methods.
3. Programs should be as generic as possible, taking advantage of what has been shown to be effective with people without disabilities, and leading toward social integration, rather than toward increasing isolation.
4. Programs must be ecologically grounded, issues within the physical and social environment need to be addressed, and focus should not be limited to the abused individual.
5. Programs must be concrete and explicit. Because many people with disabilities have difficulty with complex communication and abstraction, communication must be simple, direct, and suited to each individual's modalities.
6. Programs must be evaluative. Specific goals should be identified and criteria set in order to judge whether the program has been effective.

Considerations

Practitioners providing sexual abuse treatment must carefully consider the impact of clients' combined issues surrounding developmental disability and sexual abuse (Cruz et al., 1988). Although these findings may result from social or educational experience, people with developmental disabilities have typically exhibited poor coping skills, weak problem-solving skills, and poor communication skills that are often accompanied by low self-esteem, feelings of inadequacy, and social isolation (Spackman et al., 1990). Therefore, sexual abuse issues for this population may be exacerbated and more complicated than for sexually abused people without developmental disabilities.

In addition, practitioners need to examine their own attitudes toward disability and be aware both of their prejudices about working with people with developmental disability (Monfils, 1983) and of their attitudes toward victims of sexual abuse. Positive attitudes toward mental retardation that promote personal rights and emphasize acceptance and potential for continued learning and growth are essential (Monfils & Menolascino, 1984). Effective therapy requires that practitioners possess considerable knowledge about and sensitivity to disability and sexual abuse issues and show creativity and flexibility when adapting therapy. These attributes will help practitioners to develop attainable goals for their clients. As mentioned earlier, many therapists have rejected clients with developmental disability because of their own frustration that therapy could not cure the client's mental retardation (Cushna et al., 1980). It is essential that practitioners have patience with clients' rate of progress and realistic expectations of their therapy.

Treatment of Offenders

The first half of this chapter addressed methods of therapy for people with disabilities who have suffered abuse. This concluding section provides information about those who commit this abuse and methods of intervention for aiding these offenders to understand and overcome their need to perpetrate these crimes. Therapy services for victims as well as offenders are essential components of abuse prevention.

General Offender Characteristics People who commit offenses against people with disabilities are discussed in detail in earlier chapters (particularly Chapters 3 and 6). However, a brief description of general offender characteristics is required here in terms of intervention and rehabilitation counseling. The majority of these offenders are male (see Chapter 3, section on Gender). Most are in positions of authority over their victims. Some appear to deliberately seek out these positions in order to exercise control; others become corrupted after entering this type of relationship, where there is a grossly inequitable distribution of power and theirs is the advantaged position. In some cases, sadism seems to motivate offenders, however, more often it is the need to control those they perceive as being more vulnerable than themselves, combined with their own extremely low self-esteem, that appears to motivate those who commit abuse against people with disabilities. (See Chapter 6, section on Abusers of People with Disabilities, for more on the underlying motivational factors behind abuse.)

Need for Treatment Effective treatment of victims of abuse can not only help the persons abused, but can decrease the chances of some victims becoming future offenders (Stenson & Anderson, 1987). In fact, many offenders have their own histories of victimization, including being themselves abused as children (e.g., Finkelhor, 1984; Langevin, Wright, & Handy, 1989). Therefore, in many cases, treatment for offenders should address any possible histories of victimization, as well as their own destructive behaviors.

Regardless of their past, offenders who abuse people with disabilities will benefit from counseling, and counseling could also decrease the chances that they might abuse in the future. Because one offender can produce many (sometimes hundreds) of victims, successful treatment of a single offender can prevent many instances of abuse. Increasing evidence indicates that offenders who receive treatment are less likely to reoffend than those who do not receive treatment (Barbaree & Marshall, 1988). Unfortunately, offenders often have even less access to treatment than do victims, partially due to the fact that their crimes are rarely admitted, nor do offenders typically request counseling. As Marshall and Barrett (1990) point out, when offenders do volunteer for counseling, they are often required to spend more time in jail than those who refuse treatment.

In most cases, only those offenders who have been apprehended and charged have access to limited intervention services. Paid service providers who commit abuse may also be prevented from receiving rehabilitative counseling because of administrative policies that dismiss offenders from their jobs without charging them for their crimes (see Chapter 4, section on Administrative Structures). Such dismissal policies do not prevent these offenders from continuing to abuse vulnerable people, as most are eventually reemployed in human services where they will continue to have access to potential victims.

Prevention of abuse requires that offenders are adequately treated or that they are removed from situations that allow them to reoffend. In many cases, even the best treatment programs fail; therefore, removal of opportunities to reoffend is usually necessary. However, it is rarely possible to eliminate all opportunities to reoffend for any extended period of time. For example, offenders who do go to jail for committing abuse are typically released sooner or later, and many of them continue to commit sexual and violent offenses (particularly against people with developmental disabilities) while still in prison.

As suggested in Chapters 8 and 9, some potential offenders can be screened out or isolated from potential victims. Others may not continue to offend if given adequate preventive education and training.

Offenders who appear asocial and predatory or who have long histories of abusing others may be extremely difficult to treat. For these individuals, isolation or strict supervision may be the most effective methods for controlling their behavior.

Suggested Treatment Goals Marshall and Barrett (1990) point out several suggested treatment goals for those who commit physical or sexual aggression against others:

1. Control impulsivity.
2. Manage anger.
3. Learn appropriate social behavior.
4. Develop empathy for those who are victimized.
5. Enhance self-regulation of behavior through avoidance of potential situations for further abuse.

Treatment for sexual aggression often includes intervention to increase sexual response to appropriate partners, while weakening sexual response to inappropriate partners (e.g., children). These treatment components may be used individually or in combination (Marshall & Barrett, 1990).

People with Disabilities Who Commit Abuse

Treatment of the wide variety of offenders who commit psychological, sexual, and physical abuse against people with disabilities goes beyond the scope of this book. However, one group of offenders does require specific consideration. People with disabilities who commit abuse constitute a significant proportion of those who offend against this population (see Chapter 3, section on Offender Relationships).

Although people with disabilities sometimes perpetrate abuse, caution must be applied in considering the precise relationship between disability and the commission of offenses. For example, many studies suggest that parents with developmental disabilities are over-represented in neglect and maltreatment studies (Seagull & Scheurer, 1986). However, because many parents with developmental disabilities do not abuse, and those with lower IQ scores actually seem less likely to abuse than those with higher IQs, the relationship does not appear to be a direct one. While families that include parents with developmental disabilities have been identified as having increased risk for abuse and violence, the reasons for the increased risk remain unclear. This is especially true because studies of these families typically do not control for other risk factors. For example, parents with disabilities are more likely to have been abused as children and more likely to have been raised in group care. Factors such as these, rather than level of intelligence, are likely to be the real contributors to increased risk.

Some of the factors that may contribute to the overrepresentation of people with developmental disabilities among abusive parents include:

1. The association between poverty and disability
2. The risk for disruptions in bonding with their own parents
3. The likelihood that they themselves experienced abuse
4. The potential discrepancies between criteria used for judging child abuse by these parents and the criteria exercised with parents without disabilities
5. The decreased skills for concealing abuse among parents with disabilities

Similarly, extrafamilial abusers with developmental disabilities may be overrepresented because they may be more likely to be caught and convicted for their offenses (Perske, 1991). In fact, they may be blamed for significant numbers of offenses that they did not commit in order to cover for the offenses of those who will use their intellectual superiority to shift blame to those less capable of defending themselves.

Specific treatment programs for offenders with developmental disabilities have been rare and are typically more restrictive than rehabilitative in nature (Griffiths et al., 1989). Some researchers suggest that existing offender treatment programs may be useful if individually tailored to the needs of offenders with developmental disabilities (Murphy, Coleman, & Haynes, 1983). Griffiths et al. (1989) developed a community-based approach for people with developmental disabilities who commit sexual offenses that emphasizes teaching, environmental change, and positive counseling to develop appropriate social skills and relationships.

Like other offenders, individuals with disabilities who commit abuse are rarely charged, and treatment for these offenders is typically inaccessible, even within institutional settings. Often, existing offender treatment programs are viewed as being ineffective for offenders with developmental disabilities. Offending by people with disabilities is likely to continue when they are denied treatment and remain clustered in institutions with potential victims (see Chapter 4, section on Clustering). More research is needed to develop adapted forms of treatment for these offenders.

Ironically, almost all the offenders with developmental disabilities described in the professional literature have been previous victims of abuse. It is largely through being abused themselves, or through observing abusive models, that they have learned to abuse others. For this reason, many offenders also require counseling regarding their own victimization issues and to enhance empathy with those whom they might otherwise abuse.

CONCLUSION

Research from the University of Alberta Abuse & Disability Project suggests that people with developmental disabilities who had been sexually abused had considerable difficulty obtaining accessible, available, and appropriate sexual abuse treatment (see Chapter 3, Figure 5). Greater recognition by human services professionals of the need for accessible, effective treatment could have significant impact on addressing this issue. For example, professional training in developmental disability and sexual abuse education could serve to heighten awareness of sexual abuse treatment needs and encourage research on sexual abuse treatment adaptations. Sexual abuse education is strongly urged in order to improve professionals' abilities to detect signs of abuse, encourage sexual abuse reporting, and promote the implementation of sexual abuse prevention strategies (Sobsey & Mansell, 1990). Finally, greater advocacy for funding of sexual abuse treatment programs, as well as professional liaisons in the areas of sexual abuse and developmental disability, are also needed to help ensure that sexual abuse treatment for abused individuals with disabilities is both available and appropriate.

Treatment for offenders is necessary because many offenders have their own histories of victimization. This is especially true of offenders with disabilities who need carefully structured treatment programs that emphasize the development of more appropriate behavior. Rehabilitation counseling for offenders is an essential component of abuse prevention because it can help to prevent offenders from committing further abuse.

13

Abuse Prevention and Intervention Teams

_____

Half a century ago, "collaboration" was a charge of treason, a sign of absolute disloyalty to "our" values. It is ironic that today "collaboration," along with the other "C" words—cooperative, community-based, culturally competent—is one of the banners of the reform movement in child welfare. (Weber, 1992, p. 3)

As Weber (1992) suggests, most of the positive changes in dealing with child abuse and other forms of family violence have been achieved through cooperative efforts among a variety of individuals, organizations, and disciplines. As he also implies, this cooperation has often been difficult to secure and has sometimes been viewed with considerable suspicion by potential collaborators. Since the first multidisciplinary child protection team was formed in 1958, the value of the team approach has been widely recognized in the prevention and intervention of family violence (Untalan & Mills, 1992). These child protection teams, often called *action systems* (Pincus & Minahan, 1973), may include various combinations of professional and nonprofessional members and are considered important for effective social intervention. Nevertheless, the team approach remains underutilized.

Achieving meaningful reductions in violence and abuse in the lives of people with disabilities requires even greater collaborative efforts for four reasons. First, most of the current systems and program structures associated with violence prevention developed with little consideration for the needs of people with disabilities. For example, although the categories of child abuse and elder abuse have been established, many individuals with disabilities remain dependent on caregivers and vulnerable to abuse throughout their entire lives. These vulnerable adults do not fit into child or elder abuse categories. Similarly, family violence prevention has become the goal and focus of many programs, but many people with disabilities are victims of institutional violence by nonfamilial caregivers. These institution-related problems are not easily addressed within the framework of family violence.

Second, the long history of segregated services for people with disabilities has meant that many generic community agencies have been allowed and even encouraged to believe that people with disabilities are someone else's responsibility. The most extreme example of this is when institutions investigate and provide discipline from within the agency for criminal offenses against residents, and outside law enforcement is expected not to participate in these internal investigations, despite the possibility that the law may have been broken by the offenders.

Third, many people with disabilities are already involved with a multidisciplinary support team. Existing teams should include a focus on violence and abuse prevention as part of their work. All team members need "gatekeeper" skills to recognize risks, report suspected abuse, and help ensure that services are abuse resistant. New members with specific training in abuse prevention and investigation should be added to some of these existing teams, or current members may be trained to fill all or part of this specialist role.

Fourth, individual needs of people with disabilities and specialized features of service systems require that members of abuse prevention and intervention teams have access to consultation with specialists in these areas. For example, investigating an assault within an institution necessitates some skills that are different from those required for investigating an assault within a family; interviewing an alleged victim of violence who has severely impaired speech may call for strategies and tactics that are not likely to be part of standard police training.

Sgroi (1989) points out that the abuse of people with mental retardation that often occurs in service environments frequently requires three separate but interrelated investigations. First, a criminal investigation by law enforcement personnel is needed to determine if a crime has been committed, by whom, and what charges, if any, should be laid. Second, a civil investigation by child protection, mental retardation or mental health advocates, or other authorities responsible for ensuring the safety of vulnerable populations is required. This investigation should determine if legal intervention is necessary to protect the victim against further abuse. Third, an internal investigation by the service agency is needed to determine if changes in policies, procedures, or supervision could help reduce the risk for similar instances of abuse in the future. The coordination of these separate investigations is highly desirable for achieving the best results with minimal duplication of efforts and to minimize the risk that the activities of one investigation will interfere with either of the others.

TEAM STRUCTURE AND INTERACTION

Team structure and team member relationships need to be determined by the current task demands. Sometimes a formally structured team with regular meetings is necessary for addressing a specific task (e.g., the development of policies and procedures regarding the reporting or investigation of allegations of abuse within a service agency). Abuse prevention and intervention teams often include the same core members as other educational or support services teams, but are extended to include other formal or informal members. For example, all school-based teams that plan education-related services need to consider the inclusion of specific training in personal safety skills, as well as an evaluation of how other training and services could create risks that require management. If current team members have the skills and resources required for these tasks, no additional team members may be needed at this stage. If, however, current team members feel that additional assistance is needed in certain areas, individuals trained in these areas must be added to the team. Their role can range from informal consultation to full team membership, depending on the nature and extent of assistance that is required. This approach of integrating abuse prevention and intervention teams with existing service teams is advisable in the majority of situations where personal safety is one among a constellation of functional skill areas to be considered.

Formal abuse prevention and intervention teams focused solely on the issue of abuse may be required in some circumstances. For example, all states now require that advocacy teams remain in place to report allegations of institutional abuse and to control risk for abuse in institutional care. Such teams may have separate headquarters from the institutions with whom they are working, but team members need to regularly visit the actual institutional settings where the people whom they are intended to protect spend their time.

Leadership

Team leadership must also change on the basis of particular task demands. For example, if abuse is alleged to have occurred, it is important that the investigative team be led by someone specifically skilled in investigation. This may be a police officer (if a criminal offense is alleged), a child welfare worker (if the current or future safety of a child is in potential jeopardy), an adult protection and advocacy worker (if abuse of a vulnerable adult supported by state protection and advocacy laws may have occurred), or an agency administrator responsible for altering policies and procedures to limit potential future risks (in cases where no specific laws have been violated).

Coordination of Efforts

In some cases, several concurrent investigations may be initiated by police, child welfare or adult protection authorities, and agency staff. When this occurs, it is helpful to coordinate the efforts of investigators from the three teams. Failure to coordinate efforts adequately is likely to produce poor results for all three investigations and increased demands on the victim and other witnesses who may be submitted to repeated interviews unnecessarily. A conjoint interview by a police officer and a social worker may eliminate the need for an additional interview and often proves to be of greater value to both interviewers because each has the benefit of hearing the other's questions. By avoiding repeated interviews, investigators can also minimize concerns over whether interactions in earlier interviews have influenced the individual's responses to later interviews.

If a major inquiry into criminal allegations is taking place, law enforcement personnel may have to take charge of the case and be responsible for coordinating with other investigations. Often staff from child welfare or adult protection agencies are ideal for coordinating investigations because their primary responsibility is protection of the victim, and they are thus less likely to face issues of actual or apparent conflicts of interest that often arise when administrators investigate their own services. Regardless of who coordinates the investigations, two major responsibilities must be considered: 1) protecting the abused individual from further abuse and from severe or unnecessary secondary trauma associated with the investigation and 2) determining how the individual objectives of all the investigations can be met or which objectives should be given the highest priority.

Even when the efforts of various investigations are coordinated, conflicts may develop between those involved in investigation and those involved in intervention. For example, investigators and prosecutors may prefer that counseling for the victim of abuse be delayed until after the trial is completed because they fear that the defense will claim that the individual's testimony was influenced by the counselor during therapy. However, postponing therapy until the end of a trial often entails a delay of a year or more, and therapists often recommend that the immediate initiation of counseling is essential to the alleged victim's recovery, even if this creates some risk of damaging the victim's credibility. To some degree, conflicts of this sort are inevitable, but good coordination can minimize the difficulty.

Two principles can be useful in resolving such conflicts. First, the principle of personal empowerment and advocacy suggests that decisions regarding therapy be made by the person most directly affected, that is, the individual who was allegedly offended against. If that person needs assistance, every effort should be made to ensure that the advocate represents the individual interests of that person to the best extent possible. The person offended against must not be deprived of counseling, even if it makes prosecution more difficult. Every victim of violence has a right to the support or treatment that he or she feels is necessary to healing. Nevertheless, it is important to recognize that if and when people seek counseling, it is their decision, and for many people who experience violence, supporting efforts for prosecution is of paramount importance and may even have therapeutic value.

Second, the principle of coordination suggests that threat to prosecution imposed by counseling can be greatly reduced through carefully coordinated efforts. Investigators can reduce the threat of a challenge to the victim's credibility by getting a full and complete statement early in the investigation, prior to the initiation of therapy, and by keeping careful records (ideally including tapes of this statement). If later statements or testimony are challenged, consistency with earlier statements can be demonstrated to refute the challenge of undue influence. Therapists can also support the witness's credibility by carefully avoiding the use of therapeutic methods that might be open to the challenge of influence and by keeping thorough records of their counseling sessions.

Transdisciplinary Teamwork

Coordination efforts require well-functioning interdisciplinary and sometimes transdisciplinary teams. All teams need to be interdisciplinary; they should include representatives from the relevant disciplines and instill good working relationships and sound communication among all team members. Teams become transdisciplinary when at least some of the team members release various traditional duties, allowing and enabling other team members to assume these responsibilities (Orelove & Sobsey, 1991). In order for this process to succeed, team members need to trust one another and overcome any administrative or interpersonal obstacles that might interfere with the process. The following strategies can be useful in developing transdisciplinary teamwork:

1. Develop administrative structures that make members primarily responsible to the team, rather than to external authorities.

2. Acknowledge and periodically reaffirm the team's responsibility to the individual or group being served.
3. Develop a mission statement as a team.
4. Use terminology that all team members share whenever possible.
5. Take time to discuss and resolve conflicts that occur between team members.
6. Respect members' diversity and differences.
7. Determine who has the primary responsibility for each task or objective.
8. Create opportunities and allow time for communication.

Readers interested in further information on teamwork should consult other texts (e.g., Furniss, 1991; Orelove & Sobsey, 1991; Rainforth, York, & Macdonald, 1992; Wasson, 1984) for additional ideas and more detailed information on the development and maintenance of effective interdisciplinary and multidisciplinary teams.

TEAM MEMBERS

Most of the abuse prevention and intervention team members are the same people already involved with other aspects of services and care for people with disabilities. Ironically, these individuals occupy positions associated with the greatest potential for abusing people with disabilities (see Chapter 5, Caregiving or Abuse?). Therefore, the first responsibility of every team member is to refrain from being abusive in any way and to provide the best possible quality of interaction with others, particularly the individual with disabilities whom the team has been brought together to assist. The idea that abuse prevention team members need to seriously reflect upon their own behavior seems obvious. However, this introspection is often avoided because abusive behavior carries such great stigma that it is generally much easier to discuss it in terms of its being other people's problem, rather than one's own. This is often complicated by questions concerning one's own behavior and discomfort with discussing these feelings of uncertainty. To avoid this discomfort, it is often easier to think of abuse and violence as absolute issues, rather than as behavior that exists along a continuum.

Although some team members may actually be concealing severe abusive behavior of their own, more often it is relatively minor uncertainties about their own behavior that creates the discomfort that some team members will experience when dealing with issues of abuse. Team members need a safe and supportive environment in which to discuss their concerns. They need to recognize that we all have weaknesses and imperfections and that we all can continue to learn and to develop more compassionate responses.

All team members must have an absolute commitment that the welfare of the people they serve comes first and a clear recognition of their own responsibility to confront these issues. They must realize that those who fail to take appropriate action to confront abuse problems are morally, and sometimes legally, responsible for the abuse that takes place. Cover-up tactics must never be tolerated and should be viewed with the same disdain as the offenses themselves. Inherent conflicts often appear when institutional staff investigate possible abuse within their own institutions because the acknowledgment of a problem not only reflects poorly on the individual committing the offense, but on the agency as well. Under such conditions, it is essential that investigators remain objective and impartial.

The following is an example of the necessity for impartial investigation. When Genene Jones, a licensed vocational nurse (LVN), was connected with a large number of unexplained deaths and medical crises in a San Antonio pediatric intensive care unit, the hospital conducted an internal investigation (Moore & Reed, 1988). Although there were strong reasons for the investigative team to suspect Jones of murdering the children, the board did not notify child protection services of suspected child abuse, nor did they notify the medical examiner of suspicious deaths as they were required to do by law. They did not inform either the police or the parents of the children who had been murdered or abused of their suspicions. Instead they avoided confrontation and bad publicity by laying off all LVNs assigned to the pediatric intensive care unit. In this fashion, Jones was removed from the hospital without creating a furor. Jones, however, quickly resumed her deadly activities in a new job as the nurse in a pediatrician's office. Even after the police became involved as a result of the new deaths in the pediatrician's office, hospital administrators continued to withhold information from the police and grand jury, eventually resulting in citations of contempt of court. Such behavior is never acceptable in the human services. In the meantime, Jones was fired by the pediatrician under suspicion that Jones had murdered her patients. Jones moved to new employment as a nurse working with adults at the state school for people with mental retardation (Elkind, 1989).

The pediatrician for whom Jones had worked after leaving the hospital also refused to provide much help during the first round of grand jury hearings (Moore & Reed, 1988). On the advice of her lawyer, the doctor pleaded the fifth amendment in response to questions about the murders of her patients. This tactic may have been considered best for protecting the doctor and her malpractice insurance company from legal action, but one could only assume that such considerations were more important to her than addressing the wrong done to her patients or to their families. However, to the credit of this pediatrician, she eventually went against the advice of her lawyer and cooperated in answering questions at a second grand jury hearing. Because she and a few others were willing to speak out, Jones was convicted, and her deadly assaults against children were stopped (Moore & Reed, 1988).

The hospital committee investigating 10 of the most suspicious deaths of children in the intensive care unit found that Genene Jones was present when suspicious events began in all 10 cases. However, the committee concluded that this was probably only a coincidence, although they also reported that "negligence or wrongdoing cannot be excluded" (quoted in Elkind, 1989, p. 210). The committee went on to point out that their investigation had "revealed absolutely nothing for which the hospital district could be held liable . . ." and recommended "judicious silence on the issue" (quoted in Elkind, 1989, p. 210).

While Jones's presence at each of these events may have been merely a coincidence, the probability of random occurrence would have been very small. For example, assuming that Jones worked 40 hours out of the 168 hours in each week, the probability of her presence at any one event would have been 40/168 or $p = .24$, substantially greater than the $p = .05$ (1 in 20) or $p = .01$ (1 in 100) standards commonly used as research probability criteria. For 10 of these events, however, the probability of her being present at each one would have been $(40/168)^{10}$ or $p = .00000059$, substantially less than a one in a million chance.

Did the conclusion of internal hospital investigations represent a deliberate attempt to cover up these murders, a failure to recognize the nature and extent of the problem, or a legitimate attempt to investigate and take appropriate action? A complete answer will probably never be known. Jones was eventually convicted and sentenced to more than 150 years in prison. One hospital administrator was fined $100 for his part in obstructing the criminal investigation (Moore & Reed, 1988). Some of the apparent difficulties faced by this hospital in responding to a serious problem can be averted by having clear missions, policies, and procedures in place based on a firm commitment to the welfare of the people an agency serves. A team approach is essential to the development, implementation, and maintenance of such policies and procedures.

The following discussion presents some of the different members that should be involved as part of a multidisciplinary abuse prevention and intervention team. The long list of team members described here is rarely available to any one team. Often the core team may start with only one or two individuals. It is generally advisable to start with the resources that are available and do the best job possible, rather than to wait indefinitely for resources that may become available at some undetermined point in the future. Outside organizations can help with the development of an effective team through providing examples, consultation, support, or materials for the job to be done. The appendix at the end of this volume provides a list of individuals and agencies that may be useful in such efforts.

People with Disabilities and Their Families

People with Disabilities People with disabilities can and must play an active role on a violence and abuse prevention team. Attempts to protect these individuals, while failing to fully include them, ignores their individual definitions of what is or is not abusive in their lives and denies them the human dignity of taking reasonable risks. Their exclusion from team efforts can only be expected to perpetuate the paternalistic system that is currently responsible for putting them at risk. Human services providers, especially those concerned about abuse of people with disabilities, must see one of their primary roles as supporting individuals to take control of their own lives. The success of service providers should be measured in terms of the degree of control that their clients exert over their own lives; the failure of service providers should be measured in terms of the control that they themselves exert over their clients.

People with disabilities must be encouraged to take responsibility for their own lives. They can determine what they want and pursue these goals. This is the only way for them to achieve true empowerment. Others can only make it easier or harder for them to do this. They can advise and urge them to take control to the maximum extent possible, and they can support their efforts, but the decision to take control of one's life must come from within.

People with disabilities should be included in meaningful ways in every aspect of violence and abuse prevention. Failure to do so can only perpetuate the very power inequities and paternalistic systems that have left people with disabilities vulnerable in the past. The extent and nature of that participation must be individualized based on the person's age, environment, abilities, and various other factors. For example, a very young child with severe mental retardation may not be able to make complex planning decisions, but may be able to indicate that he or she does not like a particular caregiver or caregiving setting. Such preferences should be explored and respected whenever possible, encouraging the child to express preferences rather than forcing the child to endure an uncomfortable situation. As children grow into adolescents and young adults, they should be encouraged to make their own decisions whenever possible. Parental guidance along the way helps to prepare them for independence and increases the prospects that the transition to adult life will be made successfully.

If abuse occurs, parents, caregivers, and advocates sometimes exclude the person who has been abused from participation in decisions regarding the action to be taken. This may happen because they become overzealous in their efforts to protect the individual or because they feel that the individual who has been abused has failed to protect himself or herself, so it has to be done for them. Nevertheless, it is particularly important to allow someone who has been victimized to control or participate in decisions regarding response to the abuse to the maximum extent possible. This is essential to recovery and adjustment following victimization. Depriving a person of control at such a time can only increase his or her feelings of disempowerment and helplessness. Sometimes it may be justifiable to intrude on other people's decisions, whether they have a disability or not, but such intrusions should be extremely rare and limited. For example, after being abused, some individuals may become extremely self-destructive, perhaps even suicidal, and it may be deemed necessary to protect them until they can work through this stage of reaction.

Decisions regarding reporting and future precautions are often the most difficult to determine. As stated throughout this book, reporting of criminal offenses is strongly encouraged; however, many victims of violence and abuse choose not to report for various reasons. Adults usually make that decision for themselves, and people with disabilities generally should have the same right. If the individual is reluctant, it is typically better for friends, family, or other caregivers and advocates to encourage and assist the individual to report, but not to force the person into taking that action. Exceptions may occur on the basis of apparent danger, but should be based on circumstance, not disability.

Some individuals cannot or do not indicate a choice about reporting, and some may not understand what reporting is or even that they have a right to protection from abuse. These situations should not be interpreted as a decision not to report. If an individual really cannot make this choice independently, the choice must be made by someone else, and if there is any uncertainty about the best course of action for the person who has been abused, a report should be made.

Parents and Families Family members play vital roles on abuse prevention and intervention teams. Parents are often the first to suspect that their child is being abused because of subtle changes in the child's behavior. They, along with teachers and other team members, play a central role in teaching the child personal safety and social skills and appropriate sexual behavior. Usually, parents are the primary decision makers regarding program alternatives, and they are typically called upon to determine what constitutes reasonable and legitimate risks.

Many of the examples cited and issues raised in this book are frightening to concerned families and others who care about people with disabilities. There is good reason for concern, and active measures need to be taken to manage risks. However, it is also important to place these concerns in perspective and to avoid preoccupation with fears that may immobilize any useful risk reduction measures or overly restrict the people whom they are intended to protect. Wilgosh (1990) explored parents' concerns about sexual abuse of their children with developmental disabilities. Some of the parents in the study had children who had already been abused. Others were uncertain as to whether abuse had taken place, and all were worried that abuse would occur in the future. In some cases, fears of abuse had led to restrictions on the children and increased demands on the parents. For example, some parents drove their children to school every day or would not use relief services because of their potential for abuse. Some of these parents described their fears of abuse as "paranoia," and some expressed difficulty in finding a balance between providing reasonable protection and accepting legitimate risks.

Family members can do a lot to protect one another from abuse. Parents, especially, play an important role in the lives of infants and young children. Forming healthy bonds with the child helps to reduce the risk of abuse within the family, reduces the chance that the child will leave the family for more risky living environments, and also contributes to the development of higher levels of self-esteem and more advanced communication skills that can help protect the child from abuse throughout his or her lifespan. Parents should recognize their unique parental roles and place the highest priority on fulfilling them, rather than sacrifice their parental responsibilities to the paraprofessional roles that are often thrust upon parents. This statement should not be viewed as challenging the transdisciplinary approach (e.g., Orelove & Sobsey, 1991) that often encourages parents to act as therapist or behavior manager, but rather as emphasizing the need to exercise caution in its application. Parents also need to recognize the risks being faced by their children, particularly those risks that are associated with specialized services. Parents must learn to walk a fine line by allowing their offspring to face legitimate risks, while avoiding those risks that are unnecessary or unacceptable.

Parents should recognize that providing a safe home for their child with a disability is a primary responsibility and one of the most valuable things that they as parents can do for every member of their family. All family members should also recognize that building and supporting healthy community relationships helps strengthen family well-being and increases future prospects for a safe and successful transition to greater independence in the community for young adults with disabilities.

Family perspectives on violence and abuse can enhance or detract from the child's risk. Table 1 contrasts a healthy and balanced family perspective on violence and abuse with two potentially dangerous perspectives. In spite of the best efforts and intentions, it is impossible to prevent all instances of abuse. It is important for families to recognize that abuse can occur and that it could happen to any member of the family. Healthy attitudes toward abuse neither trivialize nor overly exaggerate its potential. Family members should acknowledge that some forms of abuse are more severe than others and that each situation should be evaluated individually.

For example, a single instance of a child's hair being pulled by another child in a childcare situation is very different from either one of the childcare staff pulling the child's hair or chronic aggression from another child. A perspective that trivializes abuse may lead to the ignoring of any actual risk and the failure to intervene appropriately if abuse does occur. A fatalistic perspective on abuse could also lead to inaction in some situations because the abuse might be seen as inevitable, and action to prevent it may seem futile. In other cases, a fatalistic attitude toward abuse may lead to compulsive and unwarranted attempts at prevention that restrict the individual from normal social interactions. A balanced family perspective helps ensure that reasonable precautions are taken and that, if abuse does occur, reasonable action is taken to minimize any harmful effects. This kind of perspective helps to provide children with protection, while allowing them to develop self-confidence by taking reasonable risks.

If abuse does occur, it usually disrupts the entire family. Wilgosh (1990) quotes a parent who describes the extent of this damage by comparing it to a ship striking an iceberg: "You think you are aware of the

Table 1. Contrasting family perspectives on violence and abuse

	Trivialized	Healthy	Fatalistic
Risk	Can't happen	Genuine possibility	Inevitable
Prevention	No need for prevention	Management of risk	No prevention/ compulsive prevention
Harm	No real harm done	Range of effects	Devastation
Investigation	Unnecessary	Potentially useful	Worthless
Treatment	Unnecessary	Might be helpful	Useless
Recovery	Not required	Reasonable goal	Impossible

immediate extensive damage to your ship, but the true size of the iceberg is hidden below the waterline" (p. 44). It is important for parents and other family members to recognize and respond to their own feelings regarding the abuse, but at the same time, they also need to separate their responses from those of the individual who has been abused (Furniss, 1991). In some cases, family members may need their own counseling or support. In this way, family members can address their own issues and may be more able to provide support to the individual abused as well as to one another.

Parents and other family members should be encouraged to participate on the transdisciplinary team to the maximum extent possible. Perhaps the greatest challenge to including family members on the team is when abuse occurs within the family itself. In severe cases, it may be necessary to remove children from their families and sometimes even to disallow all parental contact whatsoever. In such extreme cases, parental participation may be counterproductive. However, in milder cases of abuse where the interests of the child may still be best served by keeping the family intact, the participation of both abusive and nonabusive family members on the team remains desirable.

Social Workers and Teachers

Child Protection Workers   Child protection or child welfare workers are social workers or professionals from other related disciplines whose specific responsibility is protecting children from abuse and neglect. They can be important members of any abuse prevention team serving children with disabilities and should become central members of the team when abuse of any child is suspected. They are typically charged with ensuring safety for children, which often leaves them responsible for such difficult decisions as whether children should stay in their own homes or be removed to protective care.

Several interrelated issues need to be considered regarding the role of child protection workers in serving children with disabilities. First, although children with disabilities appear to be overrepresented among abuse victims, they appear to be significantly underrepresented in the caseloads of child protection workers (Schilling et al., 1986). Second, because child welfare acts have mostly been developed to address abuse within families by removing children from abusive families, they generally are not well-suited to addressing the needs of children in institutional care or other living alternatives. Walter (1993), in a review of one child protection system, concludes that children in institutional or other alternative care are largely ignored by the system. Third, the combination of the heavy, sometimes overwhelming, demands on child welfare staff and resources and the belief that children with disabilities, especially those in institutional care, and their caregivers are being served by other social services agencies often results in a reluctance to take on any additional responsibility for this underserved population.

Sometimes child welfare agencies discourage other forms of protection that might compensate for deficiencies in their design or application. In Alberta, for example, the Child Welfare Act has special provisions for "Handicapped Children's Services" intended to support the efforts of families to keep their children at home. These intentions are good, and the support provided to families is extremely valuable. However, because social workers assigned to this area have different mandates than do those assigned to child protection work, it is often assumed that children with disabilities are already receiving the benefits of child protection, when, in fact, some of them are in need of both services. Ironically, because child welfare acts are supposed to protect all children, there is sometimes reluctance to include children with disabilities in other types of legislation because of the belief that they are already protected under child welfare laws.

The failure of many child protection systems to adequately serve children with disabilities, however, should not be a reason for excluding child protection workers from the team. Their training and experience helps them to understand risk factors, recognize and evaluate signs of abuse, and formulate plans for responding to known and/or suspected abuse. They typically have essential knowledge about helping children through a complex maze of social and legal services, and their experience with the system often allows them to predict the potential benefits and risks of pursuing a particular course of action. These factors make them ideal members of teams serving children with disabilities.

Child protection workers can provide consultation and advisement to the team on abuse prevention planning. However, when abuse is suspected they should assume a leadership role in determining the best course of action to ensure the safety of any child who may already have been abused, as well as those who may be at risk. For example, if a child protection worker suspects abuse of a child by a foster parent caring for several foster children, removing the child thought to have been abused from the home does nothing to protect the other children living there who are also at risk or to protect children who might be sent to the same foster home in the future. Action should be taken to carefully evaluate the truth of the suspicion and any risk that it implies for other children.

There is another important reason for including child protection workers on teams protecting children with disabilities from abuse. The integrated ecological model presented in Chapter 6 suggests that integrating children with disabilities as fully as possible into generic community-based systems minimizes risk, and segregating children into disability-based services appears to increase risk. Whenever possible, this principle should be extended into child protection services, as well as educational, health care, and other social services.

Adult Protection Workers Since the 1980s, protection and advocacy services that include adult protection workers have been developed in response to the passage of legislation to combat institutional abuse (Weicker, 1987). Their roles differ from state to state, but generally these individuals have responsibility for protecting adults in institutional care from abuse. In this capacity, they may visit and inspect institutions, initiate investigations, notify law enforcement of allegations, ensure that investigations are conducted properly, and take other necessary actions to make certain that the adults for whom they are responsible are safe.

Naturally, adult protection workers should play a central role on prevention and intervention teams for the adults in their care. Often their role should be to lead the team, especially when allegations arise. In determining the role of adult protection workers, however, it is also important to consider their mandate for independence. Because of the potential conflicts of interest that can arise when advocates are employees of the same agencies implicated in abuse allegations, adult protection systems have been set up to carefully preserve the independence of protection and advocacy workers. The need to preserve this independence may limit the role of these individuals on abuse prevention teams largely comprised of agency staff. This independence must be respected, even if it means that the protection and advocacy worker's participation on the team is limited, and other individuals on the team must play a more central role.

The extent of appropriate team participation and of independence for adult protection and advocacy workers differs across states, agencies, and situations, but these workers are generally well aware of their roles and know when they must assert their independence. Therefore, while their participation should always be invited and encouraged, their independence should always be respected. Even when they cannot play a leadership role on the team, adult protection workers should be consulted because typically they are experts on law and procedures for protecting adults with disabilities in institutional care.

Social Workers People with disabilities are often served by various social workers responsible for determining residential, educational, health care, and other program options for individuals with disabilities and their families. These social workers serve children and adults with disabilities and their families in both community and residential service programs. They should be active members of both prevention and intervention teams, particularly in decisions regarding the safest placement and program alternatives or when potential abuse requires specific protective action (e.g., change of placement, consultation with child protection or adult protection worker).

Often social workers are among the first to recognize emerging or potential problems. For example, families may express great difficulty coping with current demands or describe changes in behavior that could be signs of abuse. They can also help identify family strengths and resources that protect people from abuse and help the team develop a balanced picture of positive as well as negative factors that may influence risk.

Teachers Teachers also have an important role to fill. They typically spend more time with children and young adults than anyone else, except for parents or residential caregivers. They are often among the first to detect physical or behavioral signs of abuse. They have important roles to play in avoiding educational methods that increase generalized compliance, teaching appropriate assertiveness skills, providing social and sex education, and training personal safety skills.

Physicians, Nurses, and Other Health Care Workers

Health care workers are also among the first to observe evidence of abuse. They need to recognize signs of abuse and report them if they are adequate to form the basis of suspicion. Recognizing signs of abuse can be more difficult when the patients being seen have disabilities because symptoms of abuse are sometimes masked by the disability itself or are ascribed to other causes. Health care workers need to be aware that abuse often takes place in the health care system; thus, workers should be alert for signs of abuse in healthcare, as well as in families. Perhaps the most difficult suspicions to report are those that involve colleagues, but it is essential that these be reported with the same vigilance that should be applied to other suspicions of abuse.

Skilled health care staff can be useful in the investigation of abuse by interpreting physical signs to suggest or rule out possible causes. Physicians who care for abused children should be familiar with the principles and techniques of clinical photography or have someone available who is skilled in this area. Good equipment and lighting are needed for recording physical evidence (Ricci, 1991). Photographic records of injuries are valuable both to refresh the memory of witnesses and to present to police as evidence of abuse. They can often be useful in reassuring others that what may seem like a sign of abuse is a normal physical finding (e.g., what appears to be chronic bruising of the lower back in a child may be a simple birthmark).

Health care personnel have a particular responsibility with regard to the attitudes they convey about people with disabilities and the potential effects of these attitudes on the families and significant others in the lives of their patients with disabilities. Of course, all team members share this responsibility, but health care personnel, especially physicians, seem to be particularly influential in this regard, perhaps because they are usually among the first to discuss a child's disability with the child's family. Negative and discouraging attitudes on the part of the physician can interfere with the bonds between parents and their children, and in doing so, increase the child's risk for abuse. In contrast, positive and encouraging attitudes on the part of health care professionals may increase opportunities for healthy attachment to develop between infants with intensive needs and their parents (Gennaro, 1991). All health care personnel should make every effort to support the development of positive bonds between parents and their children, regardless of whether or not the children have disabilities.

Legislative and Law Enforcement Personnel

Police   As discussed in Chapter 10, law enforcement has an obvious role in abuse prevention and an essential and central role in intervention when violence occurs. With the development of community-based crime prevention and law enforcement programs, police have become more sensitive to the needs of communities and various minority groups including people with disabilities (Roeher Institute, 1993). The generic crime prevention and law enforcement skills of police are important resources for the team. Consultation between police and other team members is essential to the best application of these skills to meeting the needs of people with disabilities. For example, the police know how to conduct interviews to get needed information and to avoid leading witnesses into statements that they would not spontaneously make. Most police officers, however, need help in applying these interview skills to people with disabilities who have significant differences in communication abilities, styles, and methods. Other team members (e.g., direct service providers, communication therapists, social workers) can work with police to assist in this area. In many cases, these specialists may actually participate in the police interviews, but in others they may simply provide advice as to how the interview should be conducted or interpreted.

Lawyers, Prosecutors, Judges   Everyone involved with the legal system should recognize their responsibility to make reasonable accommodations to individual differences, including disabilities. They should be aware of legal precedents and procedures that may influence judicial outcomes in cases related to disability. Prosecutors need to work closely with other team members to ensure that crime victims with disabilities are properly prepared for court. Lawyers representing individuals with mental retardation and other disabilities must be careful to ensure that they are representing the interests of their clients and not the interests of caregivers who may appear to speak for these clients. Judges should recognize their underlying responsibility to ensure fairness and to facilitate justice rather than to allow a focus on procedural details that is so narrow it obscures these more important issues.

Legislators Although progress has been made in legislation to protect people with disabilities through adult protection statutes in most of the United States, some Canadian Provinces and many other countries have yet to enact similar laws. Similarly, some American states have enacted *hate crimes* laws that provide for stiffer sentences when crimes are committed against people with disabilities, but other states and U.S. federal law itself still do not specifically recognize disability in their hate crimes laws. Providing adult protection laws where they do not already exist and including disability as a category covered in all hate crimes laws could significantly improve protection for people with disabilities. Consultation among legislators and other team members is needed to help develop and pass the appropriate legislation.

Therapists, Counselors, and Advocates

Therapists Speech-language, occupational, physical, play, and other therapists are also important team members. They are sometimes the first to learn about abuse through a disclosure or other occurrence, and they should know how to respond if such an event takes place. Occupational therapists can often provide counseling and education in the area of sexuality. As people with disabilities reach adolescence and adulthood, these therapists can help guide them toward a full, safe, and rewarding expression of their sexuality. People with physical disabilities that affect their posture and movement may need special help to identify sexual alternatives that they can employ successfully. Such guidance toward appropriate sexual and social expression helps to protect people with disabilities from sexual abuse and exploitation by educating them about healthy alternatives and attitudes toward sex. Sex education also helps protect people with disabilities from sexual and other forms of abuse by reducing their social isolation and promoting positive, loving relationships with others.

Speech-language therapists help people to develop functional communication skills. Communication skills are essential to abuse prevention because individuals with restricted communication are often identified by offenders as vulnerable prey. Aggression against those limited in their ability to communicate what has happened to them often goes unnoticed. The abuse is therefore likely to be repeated, often with increasing severity. Experts in communication can also be important to the team in helping to clarify disclosures made by people with impaired communication. Speech-language therapists may be called upon by the courts to help in assessing the validity of statements made by individuals using atypical forms of communication. For example, some witnesses may use a communication board in court and require an assistant to translate their responses into spoken language. The court may require professional assurances from a speech-language therapist that the assistant can reliably translate messages originating with the witness. If the witness's statements are critical to the case, investigators and prosecutors should initiate such an assessment before charges are laid and the courts become involved.

Physiotherapists often concentrate on improving gross motor skills, particularly those required for mobility. Improving these skills can also reduce vulnerability. In some situations, being able to walk or run may be critical to avoiding or escaping danger. Developing strength and agility may be prerequisites to learning self-defense skills. Because the nature and extent of physical limitations varies significantly among people with disabilities, physical goals and objectives should be individualized. The assessment skills of the physical therapist may be essential for developing goals that are suitable to the individual involved.

Play therapists can be helpful during assessment and treatment, especially for people with limited formal communication skills who are either known or suspected to have been abused (Marvasti, 1989). During assessment, play therapy is generally nondirective with reinforcement and nonintrusive support for participation. It is designed to allow and encourage the individual to reenact his or her own experiences, and, in doing so, to communicate about them. During the treatment phase, the therapist gradually takes a more active role in encouraging the individual to play out successful resolutions of potentially abusive scenarios. Through play therapy, the individual can work on resolving his or her anger and frustration, while learning adaptive responses that help reduce the risk of further abuse.

Counselors Psychologists, social workers, and other counselors have primary responsibility for designing and implementing programs to help victims of abuse to overcome the negative effects of their experiences. Counselors can assist all team members to work together to promote the recovery of an individual who has been abused. Abuse affects different individuals in different ways. Although such concepts as posttraumatic stress disorder and traumatic sexualization can provide useful guidelines for treatment, it is important to recognize that each person reacts differently to abuse depending on her or his previous life experiences, constitution, the nature of the abusive experience, and various other factors. Although some kind of emotional distress appears to be common to all abuse victims, the nature and extent of the effects vary substantially. Some individuals may require treatment for pathological reactions to their victimization, but others may only need emotional support. Assuming that all victims have catastrophic responses to abuse may actually increase the harm done and interfere with recovery by transferring this expectation to the individual who has been victimized. Therefore, the counseling process must be carefully individualized and guided by the particular needs of the individual whom it is intended to assist.

As previously discussed, sometimes the family of the victim and other involved caregivers will also need counseling after abuse occurs. In some cases, the same counselor who provides support for the victim of abuse can also counsel other family members and caregivers. In other cases, however, it is essential that these people are counseled by a separate and independent therapist. This is particularly necessary when the needs of the other people involved are substantial or when significant conflict exists or is likely to occur between the individual abused and his or her family. For example, after a young woman has been sexually assaulted, her parents might feel that she should move back into their house because they believe she would be safer there. She may feel, however, that she wants to remain independent and that being forced to move to her parents' home would feel like further punishment for being abused. If the counselor who works with this young woman also attempts to counsel her parents, and the conflict among them is not easily resolved, the counselor may lose the trust of either the young woman, her parents, or all three individuals being counseled.

Similarly, it may sometimes be desirable for an offender and a victim to be involved in the same counseling process. However, even in circumstances where this is desirable, it may be important that each has his or her own separate counselor whose primary responsibility is either the victim or the offender, as it may be impossible to represent the best interests of both parties. For example, some offender treatment programs involve crime victims and attempt to develop empathy in offenders for these victims. While this may be valuable for some offenders, it should only occur if it is consistent with the best interests of the crime victims to be involved.

Although counseling is typically discussed as an intervention for people who have already been victimized, it can also be an essential part of prevention for people who have not been abused. For example, counseling related to sexuality, lifestyles, relationships, and conflict resolution is useful to various people, particularly to many people with disabilities who may encounter difficulties in these areas for a variety of reasons (e.g., institutional care, lack of education). Team members can help identify counseling needs and may need to assist or at least cooperate in the counseling process for some kinds of interventions. For example, if the counselor is trying to encourage an individual to be more assertive and make more decisions for himself or herself, it may be necessary for residential and program staff to be informed of this goal and to support and encourage the individual in developing this kind of behavior.

Advocates Advocates, including self-advocates, have an important role to play in working for the availability of better services and legislation to help prevent violence and abuse of people with disabilities and to provide accessible treatment for those who have experienced abuse. Individual advocacy to help meet the needs of one individual, and group advocacy to help improve the lives of many or all people with disabilities, is needed. Although some issues require advocacy specific to the needs of people with disabilities (e.g., accessible services), joining forces with generic advocacy groups that seek to deal with social issues of interest to all citizens (e.g., crime prevention, community building) could prove beneficial for all groups represented. For example, Victims of Violence, an organization that advocates for the rights of all crime victims and their families, also includes a subdivision, Disabled Victims of Violence, that focuses on issues of primary concern to people with disabilities (see the appendix at the end of this book).

Good communication between advocates and other team members is essential. While it is important for some advocacy groups to remain independent of service providers and government agencies, service providers and agency staff can often suggest areas that require more funding or reorganization, and external advocates can sometimes be more effective in demanding that such changes be made than can people from within the agency itself. Good communication also allows for the identification of common goals and minimizes unnecessary confrontations that can deplete energy and resources on both sides that might otherwise be used more productively.

Service Agency Personnel

Service Planners and Administrators This book provides many examples of administrative failures (e.g., cover-ups of abuse, failure to screen employees, helping known abusers to find employment in other service agencies) that contribute to the vulnerability of people with disabilities within service systems. Such examples suggest that some administrators place a higher priority on protecting their agency than the clients that the agency is intended to serve. Despite these problems, however, many administrators and service planners also contribute to the development of safer service systems by taking their duties very seriously, recognizing that the ultimate goal of their work is the welfare of the people they serve, and striving to improve their services. Such individuals are important members of an abuse prevention and intervention team. These individuals must play a central role in planning and implementing services and coordinating team efforts and resources. In addition to their own staff, service planners and administrators must communicate with other team members, including researchers, consultants, family members, people with disabilities, law enforcement, and child protection experts in order to determine how to provide services that empower and protect the individuals being served.

Direct Service Providers All direct service staff should take part in prevention and should report any suspected abuse. They need to take an active role in prevention and intervention efforts, especially when it involves any individual whom the staff member serves as a key worker. It is important that staff also support each other in their right to be free of harassment if they report abuse. Peer support groups can sometimes be formed to help formalize the support network.

Staff Development Professionals

Staff training is an important element of violence and abuse prevention, detection, reporting, and intervention services. Although much more needs to be learned in order to guide future staff development work, current knowledge is adequate to allow for reasonable efforts. Some useful materials for training staff can be obtained by contacting some of the sources listed in the appendix.

It is imperative that staff trainers be knowledgeable about vulnerability and abuse prevention and that they directly confront the reality of these issues during training. Failure to acknowledge the reality of known or potential abuse problems by staff provides a model of secrecy and blocked communication that may discourage reporting of abuse by staff later on. External experts can be useful in certain aspects of training; however, members of the abuse prevention and intervention team should have a direct role not only in the planning of staff development, but in the actual training of staff as well. For example, direct services staff telling new peers what, how, and when to report abuse may be more effective than supervisors trying to convey the same message. Failure to involve direct services staff and people with disabilities in the abuse prevention and intervention aspect of training may reinforce the idea that the topic of abuse is taboo and contribute to an atmosphere of apprehension with regard to confronting abuse problems directly.

Outside Advisers

Consultants Consultants are people who may not be regular members of the team, but who occasionally take part in team activities to provide assistance with particular issues or tasks. This may be because the consultant has some specific expertise needed by the team or because the individual has had previous experience with a similar task or concern. Sometimes an external perspective can be useful because extra staff are needed on a temporary basis for a demanding, but time-limited task, or some combination of these reasons.

One example of a consultant might be an expert witness (see Chapter 10, Law and Law Enforcement). Expert witnesses may work with police, prosecutors, and other team members, but their primary role is to assist the court in an area of specialized knowledge. They should not give opinions outside their areas of expertise and they should not draw conclusions, but rather they should supply information that assists the judge or jury in reaching their own conclusions (McCormick, 1992). For example, an expert witness should not say that a child has been sexually abused, but may say (providing of course that it is true) that in his or her expert opinion the child's behavior is consistent with that of children who have been sexually abused and that such behavior is extremely rare in children who have not been sexually abused.

Cultural Advisers In some settings, ethnic or cultural advisers are essential members of the team. For example, in trying to include families in support networks, failure to recognize and respect cultural differences will inevitably exclude many families and create problems for others. Occasionally, substantive issues may interfere with cultural adaptation. For example, some cultures may seriously devalue women or people with disabilities, and such attitudes may be incompatible with the work of the team. However, when the team makes good faith efforts at finding common ground, major problems are uncommon and rarely insurmountable. Recognizing and supporting other aspects of a family's culture generally results in greater willingness on their part to consider different perspectives on such issues.

Offenders

This book chronicles many examples of offenders who commit horrific abuse. The suggestion to include such people on abuse prevention teams might seem like consorting with the enemy, yet these individuals may have the capacity to play a vital role, providing that limits are clearly set and safeguards securely put in place. There are several reasons why the participation of offenders may prove helpful.

First, it is important to recognize that there is a continuum between supportive and abusive interactions. Whereas some offenders are so abusive that they are beyond rehabilitation, others still have the potential to make a positive contribution. Any attempt to eliminate everyone who has ever done an unkind thing or uttered a harsh word would inevitably fail because no one is completely exempt from such behavior. However, it may be possible to greatly reduce the number of unkind deeds and harsh words. Supporting people in their efforts to control their abusive behavior may be as important, and possibly more effective, than battling against them.

Second, offenders who should be removed from contact with vulnerable people may help us to better understand the nature of offenders and the conditions that make offenses more likely. Obviously, their perspective must be carefully scrutinized because sometimes it may be manipulative or irrational. However, even these perspectives might provide valuable clues to understanding and preventing offenses.

Third, sole reliance on enforcement and punishment to achieve a kinder and gentler society is an inherent contradiction with practical disadvantages. As an example, the Victims of Violence organization (see the appendix) has often employed young offenders, sometimes as part of community service sentences, to work in their organization. Obviously, care must be taken not to allow predatory offenders to use such services as another means of manipulating the system to reach potential victims; however, many of these young offenders appear to benefit from the experience. Some have even remained involved in community service long after completing any court requirement to do so. When this kind of inclusion produces meaningful change, everyone benefits.

Researchers

Research on violence and abuse in the lives of people with disabilities is rapidly evolving, but there is still much work to be done. Increased risk for people with disabilities is well established, and the integrated ecological model presented in Chapter 6 provides a good start toward understanding some of the mechanisms that lead to increased risk. However, many of the details remain uncertain.

Researchers need to help clarify the conditions that increase risk and the conditions that improve safety. This information is essential to guiding future prevention programs. Research to validate prevention and intervention programs is also required. Emerging information suggests that some offenders are particularly likely to offend against people with disabilities, and more information is needed about how common this group of offenders is and how to identify them. Once this has been accomplished, subsequent research should aim at determining how screening, sentencing, or intervention might best be used to reduce the harm done by this particular group. In addition to conducting research and disseminating the results, researchers should be available for consultation to prevention and intervention teams, legislators, police, and the courts. This consultation is essential to translating research into practical results.

CONCLUSION

This book has described the disturbing reality of violence and abuse in the lives of people with disabilities, and it has attempted to outline some of the solutions to this complex problem. A number of conclusions appear reasonable based on what is currently known. Children and adults with disability experience increased risk for physical, sexual, and other forms of abuse. They are not only more likely to be abused, but when they are abused, the abuse is particularly likely to be chronic and severe. Many factors contribute to this increased risk including: impairments of mobility, communication, and judgment; lack of counter-controls; disruptions to family bonding; institutional care and clustering; social isolation; abusive models; and negative attitudes toward disability. Historical and cross-cultural information suggests that violence against people with disabilities is often more acceptable than violence toward people without disabilities.

Recent developments in legislation and law enforcement suggest that progress toward promoting the personal safety and well-being of people with disabilities is taking place. Prevention and intervention programs are developing and evolving. Research is rapidly expanding, and new information is becoming available almost every week.

This book provides a foundation for an emerging field of research and practice. However, there is much more work to be done, and future progress depends on the continued commitment of those who are currently involved and new commitment from those who have not yet become involved. As author of this book, I invite readers to make that commitment.

Appendix

A number of individuals, organizations, and companies provide useful information on and materials for the development and implementation of programs dealing with abuse of people with disabilities. The list provided here is not comprehensive, but it does suggest a number of potentially helpful contacts. Every effort has been made to ensure that information provided is current at the time of publication and accurately reflects the agencies and individuals described.

Advisory & Coordinating Committee on Child Abuse (ACCCA)
91 Hensman Road
Subiaco, WESTERN AUSTRALIA 6008
Telephone: (09) 388-2466   Fax: (09) 388-2405
ACCCA distributes a bibliography on child sexual abuse and children with disabilities. They also maintain a library with a wide selection of child protection materials.

Advocacy Resources Centre for the Handicapped (ARCH)
40 Orchard View Boulevard, Suite 255
Toronto, ON M4R 1B9 CANADA
Telephone: (416) 482-8255   Fax: (416) 482-2981   TDD: (416) 482-1254
ARCH provides a wide range of legal and advocacy services for people with disabilities. They have been actively involved in advocating for legislative changes to protect people with disabilities living in institutional care from abuse and many other related concerns.

Allied Therapeutic Services
P.O. Box 2103
Summerville, SC 29484
Contact: Rosalyn Kramer Monat-Haller
Telephone: (803) 873-6935

Allied Therapeutic Services offers direct therapy for individuals, couples, and families and consultation to agencies and professionals on sexuality issues for people with developmental disabilities. They also provide training workshops for agencies, parents, teachers, and other professionals. Therapy, training, and consultation are available on a fee for service basis.

Alternatives to Fear
2811 E. Madison Street, Suite 208
Seattle, WA 98112
Contact: Jennifer Nelson
Telephone: (206) 328-5347
This organization teaches self-protection and rape prevention to women with visual impairments over age 16 on a small fee for service basis.

**British Association for the Study & Prevention
of Child Abuse and Neglect (BASPCAN)**
10 Priory Street
York, YO1 1EZ ENGLAND
Telephone: (0904) 621-133   Fax: (0904) 642-239
BASPCAN has a working party concerned with child abuse and disabilities and runs seminars based on this theme. They also publish Child Abuse Review, including the 1992 special issue (edited by Margaret Kennedy) on abuse and children with disabilities.

British Columbia Ministry of Education
844 Courtney Street
Victoria, BC V8V 1X4 CANADA
Contact: Bonnie Spence-Vinge
Telephone: (604) 356-2333   Fax: (604) 356-7631
The ministry maintains a registry of certified therapists who specialize in treating people with disabilities who have been abused. They distribute an interministerial protocol that addresses disability issues for the prevention and intervention of child abuse. The ministry also implements and evaluates abuse prevention curricula, including curricula for students with developmental disabilities.

Paul H. Brookes Publishing Co.
P.O. Box 10624
Baltimore, MD 21285-0624
Telephone: (800) 638-3775 or (410) 337-9580   Fax: (410) 337-8539
This company publishes a variety of books on topics related to people with disabilities, including service quality assurance, sex educa-

tion, nonaversive approaches to challenging behavior, abuse, the justice system, employment, and other related subjects. Catalog available upon request.

Caparulo Associates
793 Orange Center Road
Orange, CT 06477-1712
Contact: Frank Caparulo
Telephone: (203) 349-3467 Fax: (203) 349-1382
Caparulo Associates offer counseling for both sexual offense victims and offenders with disabilities. They investigate and provide expert witnesses. They train staff in the prevention of and response to actual offenses. Services are available to families, human services agencies, and the courts, on a sliding fee scale.

Center for Abused Handicapped Children
Boys Town National Institute
   for Communication Disorders in Children
555 North Thirtieth Street
Omaha, NE 68131
Telephone: (402) 498-6600
The center provides treatment services and consultation, conducts assessment, and carries out research related to abuse of children with disabilities.

Center on Human Policy
200 Huntington Hall, 2nd Floor
Syracuse, NY 13244-2340
Contact: Rachel A. Zubal
Telephone: (315) 443-3851 Fax: (315) 443-4338
This organization publishes materials on the community integration of people with disabilities and advocacy for equal treatment and nondiscriminatory attitudes. Catalog available upon request. Many materials are relevant to abuse prevention.

Centre for Applied Psychology of Social Care
University of Kent, Beverley Farm
Canterbury CT2 7LZ UNITED KINGDOM
Contact: Hilary Brown
Telephone: (0227) 764-000 Fax: (0227) 763-674
This organization conducts academic research in the area of abuse and disability and provides consultation and staff training related to these issues. Fees for consultation and training are negotiable.

Clearinghouse on Child Abuse and Neglect
P.O. Box 1182
Washington, DC 20013-1182
Telephone: (800) FYI-3366 or (703) 385-7565   Fax: (703) 385-3206

A service of the National Center on Child Abuse and Neglect, the clearinghouse organizes and supplies information from its extensive library and data base on all aspects of child abuse, including a wealth of materials related to children with disabilities.

DAWN CANADA: DisAbled Women's Network Canada
776 East Georgia Street
Vancouver, BC V6A 2A3 CANADA
Telephone/TDD: (604) 254-3585

DAWN CANADA is an organization of and for women with disabilities that carries out advocacy, research, and a number of other functions relevant to women with disabilities.

Deaf, Hard of Hearing, and Deaf-Blind Well Being Project
601 West Broadway, Suite 800
Vancouver, BC V52 4C2 CANADA
Contact: Lori Dalecki
Telephone: (604) 877-7626   Fax: (604) 874-7661 TDD: (604) 874-2566
E-Mail: DISC—LDALECKI

This organization provides specialized treatment services for children and adults with hearing and visual impairments who have experienced abuse. They are also developing comprehensive mental health services.

Disability, Abuse & Personal Rights Program
P.O. Box T
Culver City, CA 90230-0090
Contact: Nora Baladerian
Telephone: (310) 391-2420   Fax: (310) 390-6994

This program offers training and consultation to professionals, conducts research, treats abuse survivors with disabilities, maintains and provides access to training resources and materials, furnishes expert witness services, and conducts prevention training for people with disabilities. Training, consultation, and treatment services are provided for a fee. Suggested donations are accepted for materials. Order forms are available upon request.

Family Planning Association
27-35 Mortimer Street
London, W1N 7RJ ENGLAND
Contacts: Jackie Taylor (training)   Melissa Dear (materials)
Telephone: (071) 636-7866   Fax: (071) 436-5723 (training) or (071) 436-3288 (materials)

The association offers a 3-day–training course on sexual abuse and learning difficulties for £150 per person (fees negotiable for groups). They publish relevant training materials, including *Working with the unthinkable: A trainer's manual on sexual abuse of adults with learning difficulties.* Catalog available upon request.

I Contact: Education & Consultation
BM 272, 33 Des Floralies
Eastman, Québec J0E 1P0 CANADA
Contact: Dave Hingsburger
Telephone/Fax: (514) 297-3080

Contact provides education and consultation on sex education, sexual behavior, and abuse issues for people with developmental and other disabilities.

International Coalition on Abuse & Disability (ICAD)
Abuse & Disability Project, 6-102 Education North
University of Alberta
Edmonton, AB T6G 2G5 CANADA
Telephone: (403) 492-1142   Fax: (403) 492-1318
E-Mail: ICAD_Editors@psych.educ.ualberta.ca

ICAD is an electronic computer network of people around the world interested in the subject of abuse and disability. To belong to ICAD, a person must have access to an electronic mailing address with a gateway to Internet. This would include users of Internet, America On-Line, Compuserve, and most other similar networks. There is no cost for the ICAD service. Services include a listserver, ICAD-L, and an ICAD file transfer protocol, (ftp) server. To join, send an e-mail message to: "listserv@ualtavm.bitnet" that reads "SUBscribe icad-1" followed by one space, your e-mail address and your first and last name (e.g., SUBscribe icad-1 Dick_Sobsey@psych.educ.ualberta.ca Dick Sobsey). Acknowledgment of your list membership and full instructions will be returned to you by e-mail. Any list member can post messages to the list that will be received by all other members. This includes information about conferences, books, articles, requests for information, and other related short communications. Longer documents (e.g., project reports, conference presentations, and so forth) are kept on the ftp server. Interested list members may download these documents to their own computers.

International League of Societies for Persons with Mental Handicap
248 Avenue Louise
B-1050 Brussels, BELGIUM
Contact: Mme. Paule Renoir, Administrative Director
Telephone: (32-2) 647-6180   Fax: (32-2) 647-2969
This organization identifies abusive situations throughout the world and works along with national societies, individual governments, and agencies of the United Nations to correct abuses.

Journal of Sexuality and Disability
Human Services Press, Inc., 233 Spring Street
New York, NY 10013-1578
Fax: (212) 807-1047
The journal publishes articles on sexuality topics, including sexual abuse and sexual assault of people with disabilities, including their 1991 special topic issue, edited by Sandra Cole, on sexual exploitation.

Keep Deaf Children Safe Project
National Deaf Children's Society
Nuffield Hearing & Speech Centre, Gray's Inn Road
London WC1X ODA ENGLAND
Contact: Margaret Kennedy
Telephone/TDD: (071) 833-5627   Fax: (053) 282-4113
The project offers counseling to and advocacy for deaf children who are abused and their families; provides consultation and training to professionals regarding abuse prevention and intervention; develops and publishes relevant training resources for deaf children, including materials on sexual abuse prevention; and conducts research relevant to abuse and disability. Children with disabilities and their families are generally provided with free services; there are fees for services to agencies.

LDA
Abbegate House, East Road
Cambridge CB1 1DB UNITED KINGDOM
Contact: Mr. Dennis Blackmore
Telephone: (0223) 357-744   Fax: (0223) 460-557

LDA markets *Living Your Life: A Sex Education and Personal Development Programme for Students with Severe Learning Difficulties* and *A Chance to Choose.* Both programs teach assertiveness, positive self-concept, and personal safety skills.

Lexington Center for Mental Health Services, Inc.
The Child Abuse Project, 25–02 75th Street
Jackson Heights, NY 11370
Contact: Michael Crocker, Program Director
Telephone/TDD: (718) 899-8800 ext. 272   Fax: (718) 899-9846
The center offers a variety of child abuse prevention and intervention training programs for teachers, social workers, child protection workers, law enforcement personnel, counselors, and nurses. Some of the programs focus directly on accommodating the needs of children with specific disabilities (e.g., mental retardation, sensory impairments). The center also distributes some curricula and materials. Training is provided on a fee for service basis. Materials are distributed within New York State at a reduced cost.

Maine Department of Mental Health and Mental Retardation
Office of Advocacy, State House Station 40
Augusta, ME 04333
Contact: Richard Estabrook, Chief Advocate
Telephone: (207) 289-4273 TDD: (207) 289-2000 Fax: (207) 289-4268
This agency investigates allegations of physical, sexual, and institutional abuse. It advocates "in any matter pertaining to the rights and dignity" of service consumers. Maine citizens receiving or eligible to receive services from the department are entitled to advocacy services free of charge.

Metropolitan Organization to Counter Sexual Assault
3515 Broadway, Suite 301
Kansas City, MO 64111
Contact: Jeanie Schiefelbusch, Developmental Disabilities Program Director
Telephone: (816) 931-4527   Fax: (816) 931-4532
This organization provides training and information related to sexual abuse prevention to people with disabilities, caregivers, and other service providers. A lending library is available with relevant books, curricula, brochures, audio-visuals, and other relevant materials. They also offer some counseling for people with disabilities who have been abused. Training and counseling are provided at low cost or

on a sliding scale. Library membership is $25 for agencies and free to people with disabilities, their family members, and students.

Midwest Center for Sex Therapy
9 Odana Court, Suite 202
Madison, WI 53719
Contact: Patricia Miles Patterson
Telephone: (608) 271-2673

This center offers workshops to staff, case managers, support providers, and policy makers on abuse prevention, intervention, and assessment. Evaluation and intervention services are available for offenders and survivors of sexual assault or abuse with or without disabilities. The center provides sex education, assertiveness training, and other areas of counseling to people with disabilities, and it has published *Doubly Silenced: Sexuality, Sexual Abuse, and People with Disabilities* (available from the Wisconsin Council on Developmental Disabilities, P.O. Box 7851, Madison, WI 53707). Services are furnished for a fee, with a sliding scale for assessment and intervention services.

National Assault Prevention Center
Box 02005
Columbus, OH 43202
Contact: Neal Semel
Telephone/TDD: (614) 291-2450   Fax: (614) 291-9206

This center provides training workshops and materials on assault and assault prevention in residential settings for people with a variety of disabilities, service providers, and members of the general community on a fee for service basis.

National Association for the Dually Diagnosed
110 Prince Street
Kingston, NY 12401
Contact: Robert Fletcher, Executive Director
Telephone: (914) 331-5362   Fax: (914) 331-4336

This association publishes a newsletter, as well as occasional monographs, and conducts an annual conference and other educational events for professionals. The focus of the group is on services for people with mental illness and mental retardation. Much of the work discussed by the group is related to behavioral, medical, and therapeutic approaches to behavior problems in people with disabilities, including the assessment and treatment of the effects of trauma resulting from violence and abuse.

National Association for the Protection From Sexual Abuse of Adults and Children with Learning Disabilities (NAPSAC)
Department of Mental Handicap, Queens Medical Centre
Nottingham NG7 2UH UNITED KINGDOM
Contact: Mrs. Pam Cooke
Telephone: (0602) 421-421
NAPSAC maintains an information network for professionals, service managers, and people with learning disabilities.

National Center for Missing and Exploited Children
2101 Wilson Boulevard
Arlington, VA 22201-3052
Hotline: (800) 843-5678   Telephone: (703) 235-3900
TDD: (800) 826-7653   Fax: (703) 235-4067
This agency organizes and makes available information on all aspects of missing and exploited children, including information related to children with disabilities. They supply educational materials and offer individual help to families of missing children.

National Center for Youth with Disabilities (NCYD)
University of Minnesota, Box 721
420 Delaware Street, S.E.
Minneapolis, MN 55455
Contact: Elizabeth Latts, Information Specialist
Telephone: (800) 333-6298 or (612) 626-2825
TDD: (612) 624-3939   Fax: (612) 626-2134
NCYD publishes a newsletter and annotated topical bibliographies (e.g., issues in sexuality) relevant to youth with disabilities. They also maintain a directory of relevant agencies and organizations and conduct customized database searches for a small fee.

National Clearinghouse on Family Violence
Family Violence Prevention Division
Social Services Programs Branch, Health and Welfare Canada
Ottawa, ON K1A 1B5 CANADA
Telephone: (800) 267-1291 or (613) 957-2938
TDD: (800) 561-5643 or (613) 952-6396   Fax: (613) 941-8930
This organization distributes articles, fact sheets, project reports, and information kits on family violence and related topics. They also house a reference collection of approximately 6,000 books, periodicals, and articles on the topic in both French and English, as well as maintaining a referral and resource directory. Many items are directly relevant to the abuse of people with disabilities.

National Coalition on Abuse and Disabilities (NCAD)
Spectrum Institute, P.O. Box T
Culver City, CA 90030-0090
Contact: Nora Baladerian
Telephone: (310) 391-2420   Fax: (310) 390-6994
NCAD supplies a communication link among individuals and organizations working on prevention and treatment of abuse of children and adults with disabilities. They publish a newsletter and work closely with other national and international organizations to plan conference agendas covering information on abuse and disability.

National Committee for Prevention of Child Abuse (NCPCA)
332 S. Michigan Avenue, Suite 1600
Chicago, IL 60604
Telephone: (312) 663-3520   TDD: (312) 663-3540
NCPCA coordinates information and resources in generic child abuse prevention. They have developed a plan to work with the National Coalition on Abuse and Disabilities to ensure that children with disabilities are included in NCPCA and that their services are accessible. They publish a number of valuable resources, including the *Selected Child Abuse Information and Resources Directory*. The organization also conducts a large, national conference on child abuse, which often includes a variety of presentations on abuse and disability.

National Information Clearinghouse for Infants
with Disabilities and Life-Threatening Conditions
University of South Carolina
Benson Building, First Floor
Columbia, SC 29208
Telephone: (803) 777-4425 or (800) 922-9234 ext. 201
or (800) 922-1107 (in South Carolina)   Fax: (803) 777-6058
This clearinghouse organizes and supplies information regarding advocacy and services for infants and young children with disabilities, their families, and other interested parties. Counselors work with families to locate resources in their geographic area.

National Resource Center on Child Sexual Abuse
107 Lincoln Street
Huntsville, AL 35801
Telephone: (205) 534-6868   Fax: (205) 534-6883
This agency collects and distributes information and materials related to child sexual abuse. They publish a bimonthly newsletter and conduct an annual conference, which often includes a number of pre-

sentations related to children with disabilities, and they distribute a variety of materials that focus on their particular needs.

National Society for the Prevention of Cruelty to Children (NSPCC)
67 Saffron Hill
London EC1N 8RS ENGLAND
Telephone: (071) 242-1626   Fax: (071) 831-9562
Free Helpline: (0800) 800-500
The NSPCC offers prevention and protection services to any child in need. Child protection officers are increasingly providing services, including assessment and counseling, to children with physical disabilities or learning difficulties. A literature review and research report on abuse and disability is available through contacting Helen Westcott.

Nia Comprehensive Center for Developmental Disabilities, Inc.
155 West 75th Street
Chicago, IL 60620
Contacts: Sharon Moore or Patricia Burke
Telephone: (312) 873-7354   Fax: (312) 873-9766
Nia provides in-home assessment, individual and group counseling, abuse and neglect prevention training, and court advocacy to families who have at least one member with a developmental delay who has committed abuse, has been abused, or is at risk for abuse. Nia's SAFIT (Save A Family In Time) abuse and neglect services program serves families in the Chicago area for an annual fee of $10.00.

Ontario Women's Directorate Distribution Centre
2 Carlton Street, 12th Floor
Toronto, ON M5B 2M9 CANADA
Telephone: (416) 314-0300 Fax: (416) 314-0254 TDD: (413) 314-0248
This organization publishes the results of studies on service needs relating to violence against women with disabilities in community settings. Large print, audiocassette, English, and French versions are available.

Parent Advocacy Coalition for Educational Rights (PACER) Center
Let's Prevent Abuse, 4826 Chicago Avenue South
Minneapolis, MN 55417-1055
Contact: Deb Jones, Coordinator
Telephone/TDD: (612) 827-2966   Fax: (612) 827-3065
PACER provides inservice training on preventing and detecting abuse of children with disabilities to professionals working with children from birth through elementary school age. They also furnish

abuse prevention training using puppets for elementary-school (kindergarten–Grade 4) children with or without disabilities. A range of materials for use in abuse prevention programs may be rented or bought. Many materials are free to parents of children and young adults with disabilities living in Minnesota. Catalog available upon request. Training is provided on a fee for service basis.

Pavilion Publishing
42 Lansdowne Place
Brighton, East Sussex BN3 1HH ENGLAND
Contact: Jan Alcoe
Telephone: (0273) 821-650   Fax: (0273) 722-040
This company publishes training materials relevant to abuse prevention, disability, and other related topics. Catalog available upon request.

Red Flag/Green Flag Resources
Box 2984
Fargo, ND 58108
Contact: Beth Haseltine
Telephone: (800) 627-3675 or (701) 293-7298
This organization distributes a personal safety skills and sexual abuse prevention curriculum (25-minute videotape and facilitator's manual) for people with developmental disabilities requiring lower levels of assistance. They also provide training to professionals on implementing sexual abuse prevention programs for people with developmental disabilities.

Respond
49 Forest Road
London E11 1JT GREAT BRITAIN
Contacts: Tamsin Cottis or Steve Morris
Telephone: (071) 267-6578
Respond offers individual and group counseling and support to survivors of abuse with disabilities. They furnish training for service providers. Fees are negotiable for training and flexible for counseling.

The Roeher Institute
Kinsmen Building, York University
4700 Keele Street
North York, ON M3J 1P3 CANADA
Contact: Miriam Ticoll
Telephone: (416) 661-9611   Fax: (416) 661-5701

The Roeher Institute conducts, sponsors, and publishes research related to public policy affecting persons with mental retardation. Publications are available in both French and English and include such topics as advocacy, freedom from intrusive treatment, gender issues, integration, service quality assurance, sexual abuse, sexuality, and social devaluation. They also publish and distribute materials on sexual abuse prevention that are appropriate for people with disabilities, caregivers, police, social workers, lawyers, counselors, and researchers.

Seattle Rape Relief
Project Action, 1905 South Jackson
Seattle, WA 98114
Contact: Carolyn Paige, Coordinator
Telephone/TTD: (206) 325-5531   Fax: (206) 632-5536
Crisis Line: (206) 632-7273
The Seattle Rape Relief center was among the first organizations to recognize the unique needs of sexual abuse and sexual assault victims with disabilities and was a leader in pioneering accessible and appropriate services as early as 1977. The current Project Action provides assessment, counseling, education, and advocacy for people with developmental disabilities. They also distribute curricula and training materials.

Sex Information & Education Council of Canada (SIECCAN)
850 Coxwell Avenue
East York, ON M4C 5R1 CANADA
Telephone: (416) 466-5304   Fax: (416) 778-0785
SIECCAN is a nonprofit educational organization that produces and distributes a wide array of sex education information, including some useful, low-cost materials specifically intended for people with developmental disabilities. They also distribute the *Canadian Journal of Human Sexuality*, which sometimes includes relevant articles; maintain a resource library; and organize workshops.

Sex Information & Education Council of the United States (SIECUS)
130 West 42nd Street, Suite 2500
New York, NY 10036
Telephone: (212) 819-9770   Fax: (212) 819-9776
SIECUS maintains a research library on a large number of topics related to sexuality, including sexual abuse. They distribute bibliographies on sexual abuse prevention, education, and treatment, as well as sexuality and disability.

Sexual Abuse Interventions Program
Ministry of Health, Child and Youth Mental Health Services
910 View Street, Main Floor
Victoria, BC V8W 3C8 CANADA
Contact: Peggy Mahoney, Manager
Telephone: (604) 952-1601   Fax: (604) 952-1495
This organization acts as a provincial resource center on disabilities, sexual abuse, and sexuality. It provides access to articles, audiovisual materials and other training resources and maintains a registry of professionals with expertise in assessment, counseling, treatment, preventive education, and other training relevant to sexuality and sexual abuse of people with disabilities.

Sexual Abuse and Young People with Disabilities Project
McCreary Centre Society, 401 N. Esmond Avenue
Burnaby, BC V5C 1S4 CANADA
Telephone: (604) 291-1996   Fax: (604) 291-7308
The Sexual Abuse and Young People with Disabilities Project maintains a resource library related to sexual abuse of children and young adults with disabilities, and a registry of professionals working in this area. They also develop guidelines for investigation. The project has completed much of its developmental work and hopes to establish a permanent resource center.

Sexual Assault Services
The Queen Elizabeth Hospital
Woodville, South Australia 5001
Contact: Dr. M.C. Moody
Telephone: (08) 243-6836   Fax: (08) 243-6806
Sexual Assault Services offers comprehensive care for all victims of sexual assault, age 15 and over, regardless of disability. Individuals with disabilities are accommodated into generic services through the use of consultants, facilitators, and interpreters. Services are free of charge.

James Stanfield Publishing Company
2060 Alameda Padre Serra, P.O. Box 41058
Santa Barbara, CA 93140
Contacts: Garilynn Stanfield or Ann Rhine
Telephone: (805) 897-1185 or (800) 421-6534   Fax: (805) 897-1187
This company markets training materials for teaching sex education, abuse prevention, self-advocacy, personal safety, and social skills to people with disabilities. Catalog available upon request.

University of Alberta Abuse & Disability Project
University of Alberta, 6-102 Education North
Edmonton, AB T6G 2G5 CANADA
Contact: Dick Sobsey
Telephone: (403) 492-3755   Fax: (403) 492-1318
E-Mail: "Dick_Sobsey@psych.educ.ualberta.ca"
   This project conducts research on the abuse of people with disabilities and effective methods of prevention and intervention. It also provides a limited amount of consultation and training on a negotiated fee for service basis. Fees are sometimes reduced or eliminated when such activities fall within mandated initiatives of the project.

Leslie Walker-Hirsch
RD 1 Box 37, Hanover Street
Yorktown Heights, NY 10598
Telephone: (914) 245-3384
   Leslie Walker-Hirsch extends sexuality and sexual abuse prevention training on a fee for service basis for people with mental retardation and emotional disabilities and for human services agency staff, using the Circles Programs (available from James Stanfield Publishing Co.).

VOICE
P.O. Box 238
Derby, ENGLAND DE1 9JN
Contact: Julie Boniface
Telephone: (0332) 519-872
   VOICE is a support and action group for people with mental disabilities who have been sexually abused. VOICE is aimed at supporting families, gaining public awareness, and advocating for law reform.

Western Pennsylvania School for the Blind
201 N. Bellefield Avenue
Pittsburgh, PA 15213-1499
Contact: Robert T. Ammerman, Ph.D.
Telephone: (412) 683-5960 or (412) 681-1736
   This school conducts research on abuse and disability, in addition to other areas of family violence, and provides evaluation of behavioral interventions for parents of children with disabilities who are involved with physical abuse and neglect.

Wisconsin Coalition for Advocacy
16 North Carrol Street, Suite 400
Madison, Wisconsin 53703
Telephone: (608) 267-0214   Fax: (608) 257-6733

The coalition provides advocacy and counseling on legal protections and protective services to people with developmental, physical, or mental disabilities. The coalition also prepares and distributes a number of publications on sexuality, sexual abuse, legal issues, and assertiveness for people with disabilities.

References

Achenbach, T.M., & Edelbrock, C. (1988). *Child Behavior Checklist.* Burlington: Thomas Achenbach/University of Vermont.

Adams, J.A. (1992). Significance of medical findings in sexual abuse: Moving toward consensus. *Journal of Child Sexual Abuse, 1*(3), 91–100.

Adelson, L. (1991). Pedicide revisited. The slaughter continues. *American Journal of Forensic Medicine and Pathology, 12*(1), 16–26.

Adult Protection Act. (1988). *The Acts of The General Assembly of Prince Edward Island.* 57th General Assembly, 37 Elizabeth II, Bill 39. (1988).

Aikenhead, S. (1993, January 29). Disabled removed as abuse alleged. *Edmonton Journal,* p. A7.

Altepeter, T.S., & Walker, C.E. (1992). Prevention of physical abuse of children through parent training. In D.J. Willis, E.W. Holden, & M. Rosenberg (Eds.), *Prevention of child maltreatment: Developmental and ecological perspectives* (pp. 226–248). New York: John Wiley & Sons.

Aman, M.G., & Singh, N.N. (1988). Patterns of drug use. Methodological considerations, measurement techniques, and future trends. In M.G. Aman & N.N. Singh (Eds.), *Psychopharmacology of the developmental disabilities* (pp. 1–28). New York: Springer-Verlag.

Amaro, H., Fried, L.E., Cabral, H., & Zuckerman, B. (1990). Violence during pregnancy and substance abuse. *American Journal of Public Health, 80,* 575–579.

American Humane Association. (1951). *Standards for child protective agencies.* Albany, NY: Author.

Americans with Disabilities Act of 1990 (ADA), PL 101-336. (July 26, 1990). Title 42, U.S.C. § 12101 et seq. (a)(7) *U.S. Statutes at Large, 104.*

Amethya. (1992, February/March). The reality of ritual abuse: A survivor's experience. *Transition,* pp. 17, 20.

Ammerman, R.T. (1991). The role of the child in physical abuse: A reappraisal. *Violence & Victims, 6*(2), 87–101.

Ammerman, R.T., Van Haslett, V.B., Hersen, M., McGonigle, J.J., & Lubetsky, M.J. (1989). Abuse and neglect in psychiatrically hospitalized multihandicapped children. *Child Abuse & Neglect, 13,* 335–343.

Anderson, C., & McGhee, S. (1991). *Bodies of evidence.* New York: St. Martin's Press.

Andre, C.E. (1985). Child maltreatment and handicapped children: An examination of family characteristics and service provision. *Dissertation Abstracts International, 46*(3), 792A.

Andrew, A.K. (1989). Meeting the needs of young deaf-blind children and their parents: I. *Child Care, Health and Development, 15*(3), 195–206.

Antler, S. (1981). The rediscovery of child abuse. In L.H. Pelton (Ed.), *The social context of child abuse and neglect* (pp. 39–54). New York: Human Sciences Press.

Arad, Y. (1987). *From Belzec, Sobibor, Treblinka: The operation Reinhard death camps.* Bloomington: Indiana University Press.

Arad, Y., Gutman, Y., & Margaliot, A. (1981). *Documents on the holocaust.* Jerusalem: Yad Vashem.

Architectural Barriers Act of 1968, 42 U.S.C. §§ 4151–4157.

Armstrong, K.L., & Wood, D. (1991). Can infant death from child abuse be prevented? *Medical Journal of Australia, 155*(9), 593–596.

Baas, A. (1990). *Background checks on school personnel.* Seattle: National Association of State Directors of Teacher Education and Certification. (ERIC Document Reproduction Service No. 324767)

Bagley, C.R. (1991). Preventing child sexual abuse: The state of knowledge and future research. In C. Bagley & R.J. Thomlinson (Eds.), *Child sexual abuse: Critical perspectives on prevention, intervention, and treatment* (pp. 9–26). Toronto, Ontario, Canada: Wall and Emerson.

Bajt, T.R., & Pope, K.S. (1989). Therapist-patient sexual intimacy involving children and adolescents. Special Issue: Children and their development: Knowledge base, research agenda, and social policy application. *American Psychologist, 44*(2), 455.

Baladerian, N.J. (1990). *Sexual and physical abuse of developmentally disabled people.* Culver City, CA: Mental Health Consultants.

Baladerian, N.J. (1993, March). *Identification of abuse in children with disabilities: Barriers, solutions, attitudes and blinding beliefs.* Paper presented at the Ninth National Symposium on Child Sexual Abuse, Huntsville, AL.

Bandura, A., Ross, D., & Ross, S.A. (1963). Vicarious reinforcement and imitative learning. *Journal of Abnormal and Social Psychology, 67*, 601–607.

Barbaree, H.E., & Marshall, W.L. (1988). *Treatment of the adult male child molester: Methodological issues in evaluating treatment outcome.* Kingston, Ontario, Canada: Queen's University.

Barker, D. (1983). How to curb the fertility of the unfit: The feeble minded in Edwardian Britian. *Oxford Review of Education, 9*(3), 197–211. (ERIC Document Reproduction No. EJ 293 955)

Barowsky, E.I. (1976). The abuse and neglect of handicapped children by professionals and parents. *Journal of Pediatric Psychology, 1*(2), 44–46.

Barron, D. [Assisted by E. Banks]. (1981). *A price to be born. Twenty years in a mental institution.* Leeds, England: Leeds University Printing.

Bartlett, J. (1980). *Familiar quotations: A collection of passages, phrases, and proverbs traced to their sources in ancient and modern literature* (15th rev. ed.). Toronto, Canada: Little, Brown & Company.

Bauer, H. (1983). Preparation of the sexually abused child for court testimony. *Bulletin of the American Academy of Psychiatry & the Law, 11*(3), 287–289.

Beck, M., & Long, L. (1986). Gynecologist-patient sexual abuse: I. A medical board's view. In A.W. Burgess (Ed.), *Sexual exploitation of patients by health professionals* (pp. 66–73). New York: Praeger.

Beck, M., & Miller, S. (1992, October 19). The flames of a crusader. *Newsweek,* p. 58.

Bellamy, G., Clark, G.M., Hamre-Nietupski, S., & Williams, W. (1977). Implementation of selected sex education and social skills to severely handicapped students. *Education and Training of the Mentally Retarded, 12*(4), 364–372.

Belsky, J. (1980). Child maltreatment: An ecological integration. *American Psychologist, 35*(4), 320–335.

Benedict, M., White, R.B., Wulff, L.M., & Hall, B.J. (1990). Reported maltreatment in children with multiple disabilities. *Child Abuse & Neglect, 14*, 207–217.

Benedict, M., Wulff, L.M., & White, R.B. (1992). Current parental stress in maltreating and nonmaltreating families of children with multiple disabilities. *Child Abuse & Neglect, 16*, 155–163.

Benenson, A.S. (Ed.). (1990). *Control of communicable diseases in man* (15th ed.). Washington, DC: American Public Health Association.

Berlin, F.S., Malin, H.M., & Dean, S. (1991). Effects of statutes requiring psychiatrists to report suspected child sexual abuse. *American Journal of Psychiatry, 148*(4), 449–453.

Beyer, H.A. (1988). Litigation in the use of psychoactive drugs in developmental disabilities. In M.G. Aman & N.N. Singh (Eds.), *Psychopharmacology of the developmental disabilities* (pp. 29–58). New York: Springer-Verlag.

Biersdorff, K. (1991). Pain insensitivity and indifference: Alternative explanations for some medical catastrophes. *Mental Retardation, 29*, 359–362.

Bigge, J. (1991). *Teaching individuals with physical and multiple disabilities* (3rd ed.). New York: Macmillan.

Billmire, M.E., & Myers, P.A. (1985). Serious head injury in infants: Accident or abuse? *Pediatrics, 75*, 340–342.

Birrell, R., & Birrell, J. (1968). The maltreatment syndrome in children: A hospital survey. *Medical Journal of Australia, 2*, 1023–1029.

Bissland, T. (1984). *Death shift: The digoxin murders at "Sick Kids."* Toronto, Ontario, Canada: Methuen.

Blacher, J. (1984). Attachment and severely handicapped children: Implications for intervention. *Journal of Developmental and Behavioral Pediatrics, 5*(4), 178–183.

Blacher, J., & Bromley, B. (1987). Attachment and responsivity in children with severe handicaps: Mother and teacher comparison. *Child Study Journal, 17*(2), 121–132.

Blacher, J., & Meyers, C.E. (1983). A review of attachment formation and disorder of handicapped children. *American Journal of Mental Deficiency, 87*(4), 359–371.

Bland, R., & Orn, H. (1986). Family violence and psychiatric disorder. *Canadian Journal of Psychiatry, 31*, 129–137.

Blashfield, J. (1990). *Why they killed.* New York: Popular Library Books.

Blatt, B. (1980). The pariah industry. A diary from purgatory and other places. In G. Gerbner, C.J. Ross, & E. Zigler (Eds.), *Child abuse: An agenda for action* (pp. 185–203). New York: Oxford University Press.

Blatt, B., & Kaplan, F. (1966). *Christmas in pugatory: A photographic essay on mental retardation.* Boston: Allyn and Bacon.

Blatt, E.R., & Brown, S.W. (1986). Environmental influences on incidents of alleged child abuse and neglect in New York State psychiatric facilities: Toward an etiology of institutional child maltreatment. *Child Abuse & Neglect, 10*(2), 171–180.

Bogdan, R., Brown, M.A., & Foster, S.B. (1992). Be honest, but not cruel: Staff/

parent communication in a neonatal unit. In P.M. Ferguson, D.L. Ferguson, & S.J. Taylor (Eds.), *Interpreting disability: A qualitative reader* (pp. 19–37). New York: Teacher's College Press.

Bogdan, R., & Taylor, S.J. (1992). The social construction of humanness: Relationships with severely disabled people. In P.M. Ferguson, D.L. Ferguson, & S.J. Taylor (Eds.), *Interpreting disability: A qualitative reader* (pp. 275–294). New York: Teacher's College Press.

Bogdan, R., Taylor, S., deGrandpre, B., & Haynes, S. (1974). Let them eat programs: Attendants' perspectives and programming on wards in state schools. *Journal of Health & Social Behavior, 15*, 142–151.

Braceland, F.J. (1967). In memoriam: D. Ewen Cameron, 1901–1967. *American Journal of Psychiatry, 124*, 860–861.

Bradbury, J. (1983). *Violent offending and drinking patterns.* Wellington, New Zealand: Institute of Criminology, Victoria University.

Bradley, E.J., & Peters, R.D. (1991). Physically abusive and nonabusive mothers' perceptions of parenting and child behavior. *American Journal of Orthopsychiatry, 61*(3), 455–460.

Brazelton, T.B., & Cramer, T.B. (1991). *The earliest relationship: Parents, infants and the drama of early attachment.* London: Karnac Books.

Breggin, P.R. (1991). *Toxic psychiatry.* New York: St. Martin's Press.

Bregman, S. (1984). Assertiveness training for mentally retarded adults. *Mental Retardation, 22*(1), 12–16.

Bremner, R.H. (Ed.). (1971a). *Children and youth in America: A documentary history. Vol. II. 1866–1932.* Cambridge, MA: Harvard University Press.

Bremner, R.H. (Ed.). (1971b). *Children and youth in America: A documentary history. Vol. III. 1933–1973.* Cambridge, MA: Harvard University Press.

Brinker, R.P., & Thorpe, M.E. (1984). Integration of severely handicapped students and the number of IEP objectives achieved. *Exceptional Children, 51*, 168–175.

Bristol, M.M., Gallagher, J.J., & Schloper, E. (1988). Mothers and fathers of young developmentally disabled and nondisabled boys: Adaptation and spousal support. *Developmental Psychology, 24*, 441–451.

Bronfenbrenner, U. (1977). Toward an experimental ecology of human development. *American Psychologist, 32*, 513–531.

Bronfenbrenner, U. (1979). *The ecology of human development: Experiments by nature and design.* Cambridge, MA: Harvard University Press.

Brookhouser, P.E. (1987). Ensuring the safety of deaf children in residential schools. *Otolaryngology–Head and Neck Surgery, 97*(4), 361–368.

Brooks, B., & Gowers, C. (1993). *Assessment of needs for disabled victims of crime in Edmonton, Alberta.* Edmonton, Alberta, Canada: Victims' Programs and Services, Law Enforcement Division.

Brown, H., & Craft, A. (1992). *Working with the unthinkable.* London: Family Planning Association.

Browne, K., & Saqi, S. (1988). Mother-infant interaction and attachment in physically abusing families. *Special Issue: Early child maltreatment. Journal of Reproductive and Infant Psychology, 6*(3), 163–182.

Brownmiller, S. (1974). *Against our will: Men, women, and rape.* New York: Simon and Schuster.

Buchanan, A., & Oliver, J.E. (1977). Abuse and neglect as a cause of mental retardation: A study of 140 children admitted to subnormality hospitals in Wiltshire. *British Journal of Psychiatry, 131*, 458–467.

Bugental, D.B., Mantyla, S.M., & Lewis, J. (1989). Parental attributions as moderators of affective communication. In D. Cicchetti & V. Carlson (Eds.), *Child maltreatment: Theory and research on the causes and consequences of child abuse and neglect* (pp. 254–279). New York: Cambridge University Press.

Bullock, L.F., & McFarlane, J. (1989). The birth-weight battering connection. *American Journal of Nursing, 9*, 1153–1155.

Bureau of National Affairs. (1975). *New federal rules of evidence.* Washington, DC: Author.

Burgdorf, K. (1980). *Recognition and reporting of child maltreatment: Findings from the national study of the incidence and severity of child abuse and neglect.* Washington, DC: National Center on Child Abuse and Neglect.

Burgdorf, R.L., Jr., & Falcon, B.J. (1980). Employment. In R.L. Burgdorf, Jr. (Ed.), *The legal rights of handicapped persons: Cases, materials, and text* (pp. 317–438). Baltimore: Paul H. Brookes Publishing Co.

Caffey, J. (1946). Multiple fractures in the long-bones of infants suffering from chronic subdural hematoma. *American Journal of Roentgenology, 56*, 163–173.

California Attorney General's Commission on Disability. (1989, December). *Justice and disability: Final report.* Sacramento, CA: Author.

Caliso, J.A., & Milner, J.S. (1992). Childhood history of abuse and child abuse screening. *Child Abuse & Neglect, 16*(5), 647–659.

Cameron, D.E. (1956). Psychic driving. *American Journal of Psychiatry, 112*, 502–508.

Cameron, S.J., Dobson, L.A., & Day, D.M. (1991). Stress in parents of developmentally delayed and nondelayed school children. *Canada's Mental Health, 39*(1), 13–17.

Cameronchild, J. (1980). *An autobiography of violence.* In G.J. Williams & J. Money (Eds.), *Traumatic abuse and neglect of children* (pp. 21–32). Baltimore: Johns Hopkins University Press.

Canadians help rescue sick kids: Staff fled mental hospital. (1993, July 20). *Edmonton Journal*, p. A1.

Canter, F.M. (1963). The relationship between authoritarian attitudes, attitudes toward mental patients, and the effectiveness of clinical work with mental patients. *Journal of Clinical Psychology, 19*, 124–127.

Carlberg, C., & Kavale, K. (1980). The efficacy of special versus regular class placement for exceptional children: A meta-analysis. *Journal of Special Education, 14*, 295–309.

Carmody, M. (1991). Invisible victims: Sexual assault of people with an intellectual disability. *Australia and New Zealand Journal of Developmental Disabilities, 17*, 229–236.

Carney, I.H. (1991). Working with families. In F.P. Orelove & D. Sobsey, *Educating children with multiple disabilities: A transdisciplinary approach* (2nd ed., pp. 407–429). Baltimore: Paul H. Brookes Publishing Co.

Carroll, C.F., & Repucci, N.D. (1978). Meanings that professionals attach to labels of children. *Journal of Consulting and Clinical Psychology, 46*, 372–374.

Carroll, L. (1978). *Alice's adventures in wonderland and through the looking glass.* London: Methuen (Original work published 1872)

Carter, G., & Jancar, J. (1984). Sudden deaths in the mentally handicapped. *Psychological Medicine, 14*, 691–695.

Casanova, G.M., Domanic, J., McCanne, T.R., & Milner, J.S. (1992). Physiological responses to non-child-related stressors in mothers at risk for child abuse. *Child Abuse & Neglect, 16*(1), 31–44.

Caudill, W., & Frost, L. (1975). A comparison of maternal care and infant behavior in Japanese-American, American, and Japanese families. In U. Bronfenbrenner & M. Mahoney (Eds.), *Influences on human development* (pp. 329–342). Hinsdale, IL: Dryden Press.

Cauffiel, L. (1992). *Forever and five days.* New York: Zebra Books.

Center for Women's Policy Studies. (1984). Sexual exploitation and abuse of women with disabilities. *Response to Violence in the Family and Sexual Assault, 7,* 7–8.

Chamberlain, A., Ruah, J., Passer, A., McGrath, M., & Burkett, R. (1984). Issues in fertility control for mentally retarded female adolescents: I. Sexual activity, sexual abuse, and contraception. *Pediatrics, 73,* 445–450.

Champagne, M.P., & Walker-Hirsch, L.W. (1982). Circles: A self-organization system for teaching appropriate social/sexual behavior to mentally retarded/developmentally disabled persons. *Sexuality and Disability, 5*(3), 172–174.

Chandler, L.K., & Lubeck, R.C. (1989). The appropriateness and utility of a child-focused view of jeopardy: A family focused alternative. *Topics in Early Childhood Special Education, 9*(2), 101–116.

Chase, N.F. (1976). *A child is being beaten: Violence against children, an American tragedy.* New York: McGraw-Hill.

Child abuse by whiplash. (1984). *Emergency Medicine, 16*(15), 71–72.

Cirrin, F.M., & Rowland, C.M. (1985). Communicative assessment of nonverbal youths with severe/profound mental retardation. *Mental Retardation, 23,* 52–62.

Civil Rights Act of 1866, 42 U.S.C. § 1981 (1981).

Claster, D.S., & David, D.S. (1981). The resisting victim: Extending the concept of victim responsibility. In B. Gallaway & J. Hudson (Eds.), *Perspectives on crime victims* (pp. 183–188). St. Louis: C.V. Mosby.

Cohen, S., & Warren, R.D. (1990). The intersection of disability and child abuse in England and the United States. *Child Welfare, 69,* 253–262.

Cole, L. (1972). *Our children's keepers.* New York: Grossman Publishers.

Coles, W. (1990). Sexual abuse of persons with disabilities: A law enforcement perspective. *Developmental Disabilities Bulletin, 18*(2), 35–43.

Comfort, R.L. (1985). Sex, strangers and safety. *Child Welfare, 64,* 541–545.

Committee of the Board of Health to Study Venereal Diseases. (1922). *Appendices to the Journals of the House of Representatives* [New Zealand]. H-31-A, 11–12.

Committee of Inquiry into Mental Defectives and Sex Offenders (Hon. W.H. Triggs, Chairman). (1925). *Report of the Committee Inquiry into Mental Defectives and Sex Offenders.* Wellington, New Zealand: Government Printer.

Community Visitors (Intellectual Disabilities Services) Board. (1991). *Annual report of community visitors, 1991.* Melbourne, Australia: Office of the Public Advocate.

Condon, J.T. (1986). The spectrum of fetal abuse in pregnant women. *The Journal of Nervous and Mental Disease, 174,* 509–516.

Cooper, C. (1978). Symptoms, signs and diagnosis of physical abuse. In V. Carver (Ed.), *Child abuse: A study text* (pp. 52–70). New York: The Open University Press.

Cotter, L.H. (1967). Operant conditioning in a Vietnamese mental hospital. *American Journal of Psychiatry, 124,* 23–28.

Cotter, L.H. (1968). Dr. Cotter replies. *American Journal of Psychiatry, 124,* 1137.

Couston, T.A. (1954). Indifference to pain in low-grade mental defectives. *British Medical Journal, 1,* 1128–1129.

Coverman, S., & Sheley, J.F. (1986). Change in men's housework and child care time, 1965–1975. *Journal of Marriage and the Family, 48*, 413–422.

Craft, A., & Craft, M. (1978). *Sex and the mentally handicapped*. London: Routledge & Kegan Paul.

Craft, A., & Hitching, M. (1989). Keeping safe: Sex education and assertiveness skills. In H. Brown & A. Craft (Eds.), *Thinking the unthinkable: Papers on sexual abuse and people with learning difficulties* (pp. 29–38). London: Family Planning Association Education Unit.

Crossley, R. (1991). *Assessment of people with severe communication impairments*. Caulfield, Australia: DEAL Communication Centre.

Crossmaker, M. (1986). *Empowerment: A systems approach to preventing assaults against people with mental retardation and/or developmental disabilities*. Columbus, OH: The National Assault Prevention Center.

Crossmaker, M. (1991). Behind locked doors—Institutional sexual abuse. *Sexuality and Disability, 9*, 201–219.

Cruz, V.K., Price-Williams, D., & Andron, L. (1988). Developmentally disabled women who were molested as children. *Social Casework: The Journal of Contemporary Social Work, 69*(7), 411–419.

Cunningham, D. (1991, October 3–9). Social workers accused of Britain's worst child abuse: Sex case terror of children in care. *International Express*, pp. 1, 3.

Cushna, B., Szymanski, L.S., & Tanguay, P.E. (1980). Professional roles and unmet manpower needs. In L.S. Szymanski & P.E. Tanguay (Eds.), *Emotional disorders of mentally retarded persons: Assessment, treatment and consultation* (pp. 3–17). Baltimore: University Park Press.

Daly, M., & Wilson, M. (1988). *Homicide*. New York: Aldine de Gruyter.

Daro, D. (1991). Child sexual abuse prevention: Separating fact from fiction. *Child Abuse & Neglect, 15*(1–2), 1–4.

Davies, R.K. (1979). Incest and vulnerable children. *Science News, 116*, 244–245.

Davies, S. (1980, August 3–9). Staff reveal horrifying practices in state psychiatric hospital. *The National Times* [Australia], p. 3.

Denial of health care is contested. (1991, December). *N. Z. Disabled, 11*(6), p. 65.

Denno, D., & Cramer, J.A. (1976). The effect of victim characteristics on judicial decision making. In W.F. McDonald (Ed.), *Criminal justice and the victim* (pp. 215–226). Beverly Hills: Sage Publications.

Department of Justice Canada. (1993). *Amendments to the Criminal Code and the Canada Evidence Act with respect to persons with disabilities*. Ottawa, Canada: Author.

Deutsch, A. (1949). *The mentally ill in America: A history of their care and treatment from colonial times* (2nd ed.). New York: Columbia University Press.

Developmental Disablties Assistance and Bill of Rights Act of 1975, 42 U.S.C. §§ 6000–6081.

Diamond, G.W., & Cohen, H.J. (1992). Developmental disabilities in children with HIV infections. In A.C. Crocker, H.J. Cohen, & T.A. Kastner (Eds.), *HIV infection and developmental disabilities: A resource for service providers* (pp. 33–42). Baltimore: Paul H. Brookes Publishing Co.

Diamond, L.J., & Jaudes, P.K. (1983). Child abuse in a cerebral-palsied population. *Developmental Medicine and Child Neurology, 25*, 169–174.

Dickens, B.M. (1982). Retardation and sterilization. *International Journal of Law and Psychiatry, 5*, 295–318.

Dietrich, D., Berkowitz, L., Kadushin, A., & McGloin, J. (1990). Some factors influencing abusers' justification of their child abuse. *Child Abuse & Neglect, 14*, 337–345.

DiMaio, V.J.M., & Bernstein, C.G. (1974). A case of infanticide. *Journal of Forensic Sciences, 19*, 744–754.

Dinsmore, J. (1992). *Pregnant drug users: The debate over prosecution.* Alexandria, VA: National Center for the Prosecution of Child Abuse.

Dixon, R. (1988, June). Silent victims find a voice: The public advocate in Victoria. *Interaction: The Australian Magazine on Intellectual Disability, 2*(3), 5–8.

Doctors for Sexual Abuse Care. (1991). *Manual for medical management of child sexual abuse.* Auckland, New Zealand: Author.

Donnellan, A.M., Mirenda, P.L., Mesaros, R.A., & Fassbender, L.L. (1984). Analyzing communicative functions of aberrant behavior. *Journal of The Association for Persons with Severe Handicaps, 7*(1), 20–32.

Doob, A.N., & Ecker, B.P. (1970). Stigma and compliance. *Journal of Personality and Social Psychology, 14*, 302–304.

Doucette, J. (1986). *Violent acts against disabled women.* Toronto, Ontario, Canada: DisAbled Women's Network Canada.

Downes, M. (1982). Counseling women with developmental disabilities. *Women and Therapy, 1*(3), 101–109.

Dudley, J.R. (1983). *Living with stigma: The plight of people who we label as mentally retarded.* Springfield, IL: Charles C Thomas.

Duff, R.S., & Campbell, A.G.M. (1973). Moral and ethical dilemmas in the special care nursery. *The New England Journal of Medicine, 289*(17), 890–894.

Dunn, L.M. (1968). Special education for the mildly retarded—Is much of it justifiable? *Exceptional Children, 35*, 5–22.

Dunst, C.J., Cooper, C.S., & Bolick, F.A. (1987). Supporting families of handicapped children. In J. Garbarino, P.E. Brookhouser, K.J. Authier, & Associates (Eds.), *Special children—Special risks: The maltreatment of children with disabilities* (pp. 17–46). New York: Aldine de Gruyter, Inc.

Dunst, C.J., Jenkins, V., & Trivette, C.M. (1988). Family support scale. In C.J. Dunst, C.M. Trivette, & A. Deal (Eds.), *Enabling & empowering families: Principles & guidelines for practice* (p. 157). Cambridge, MA: Brookline Books.

Dunst, C.J., Trivette, C.M., & Deal, A. (1988). *Enabling & empowering families: Principles & guidelines for practice.* Cambridge, MA: Brookline Books.

Dupont, A., & Mortensen, P.B. (1990). Avoidable death in a cohort of severely mentally retarded. In W.I. Fraser (Ed.), *Key issues in mental retardation research* (pp. 28–36). London: Routledge.

Dybwad, R.F. (1990). *Perspectives on a parent movement: The revolt of parents of children with intellectual limitations.* Cambridge, MA: Brookline Books.

Dyer, K. (1993, January). Functional communication training: Review and future directions. *Behavior Therapist, 16*, 18–23.

Dziech, B.W., & Schudson, C.B. (1991). *On trial: America's courts and their treatment of sexually abused children.* Boston: Beacon Press.

Edgerton, R.B. (1970). *Mental retardation in nonwestern societies: Toward a cross-cultural perspective on incompetence.* Berkeley: University of California Press.

Edwards, J.P., & Elkins, T.E. (1988). *Just between us: A social sexual guide for parents and professionals with concerns for persons with developmental disabilities.* Portland, OR: Ednick Communications.

Egeland, B., & Vaughn, B. (1981). Failure of "bond formation" as a cause of abuse, neglect, and maltreatment. *American Journal of Orthopsychiatry, 51*, 78–84.

Egginton, J. (1989). *From cradle to grave: The short lives and strange deaths of Marybeth Tinning's nine children.* New York: William Morrow.

Elbow, M. (1977). Theoretical considerations in violent marriages. *Social Casework, 58,* 515–526.

Elkind, P. (1989). *Death shift: The true story of Genene Jones and the Texas baby murders.* New York: Onyx.

Elmer, E. (1977). A follow-up study of traumatized children. *Pediatrics, 59,* 273–279.

Elmer, E., & Gregg, G.S. (1967). Developmental characteristics of abused children. *Pediatrics, 40*(4, Part I), 596–602.

Elvik, S.L., Berkowitz, C.D., Nicholas, E., Lipman, J.L., & Inkelis, S.H. (1990). Sexual abuse in the developmentally disabled. Dilemmas of diagnosis. *Child Abuse & Neglect, 14,* 497–502.

Englade, K. (1988). *Cellar of horror: The true story.* New York: St. Martins Press.

Engman, K. (1992, June 17). Teens get probation for torture of handicapped man. *Edmonton Journal,* p. A1.

Engman, K., & Crockatt, J. (1992, June 18). Anger rises over youths' probation in fatal beating of handicapped man. *Edmonton Journal,* p. B1.

Engman, K., & Tanner, A. (1993, June 11). Jason's own mother isn't a saint, but was never cruel—relative. *Edmonton Journal,* pp. A1, A9.

Erikson, M.F., Egeland, B., & Pianta, R. (1989). Effects of maltreatment on the development of young children. In D. Crichetti & V. Carlson (Eds.), *Child maltreatment: Theory and research on causes and consequences of child abuse and neglect* (pp. 647–684). Cambridge, England: Cambridge University Press.

Euthanasia. (1942). *The American Journal of Psychiatry, 99,* 141–143.

Evans, I.M. (1990). Teaching personnel to use state of the art nonaversive alternatives for dealing with problem behavior. In A.P. Kaiser & C.M. McWhorter (Eds.), *Preparing personnel to work with persons with severe disabilities* (pp. 181–201). Baltimore: Paul H. Brookes Publishing Co.

Evenden, J.L. (1988). Issues in behavioral pharmacology: Implications for developmental disorders. In M.G. Aman & N.N. Singh (Eds.), *Psychopharmacology of the developmental disabilities* (pp. 216–238). New York: Springer-Verlag.

Feldman, M.P. (1977). *Criminal behavior: A psychological analysis.* New York: John Wiley & Sons.

Felske, A.W., & Barnes, H. (1992). *The law and your rights.* Edmonton, Alberta, Canada: The Alberta Association for Community Living.

Finger, P. (1990). [Sterilization of the mentally handicapped according to section 1905 of the German Civil Code in relation to developing a patient management regulation]. *Prax Kinderpsychol Kinderpsychiatr, 39*(4), 132–138.

Finkelhor, D. (1984). *Child sexual abuse: Theory and research.* New York: The Free Press.

Finkelhor, D., & Baron, L. (1986). High-risk children. In D. Finkelhor (Ed.), *A sourcebook on child sexual abuse* (pp. 60–88). Beverly Hills: Sage Publications.

Finkelhor, D., & Browne, A. (1985). The traumatic impact of childhood sexual abuse: A conceptualization. *American Journal of Orthopsychiatry, 55,* 530–541.

Fireside, H. (1979). *Soviet psychoprisons.* New York: W.W. Norton.

Firsten, T. (1990). *An exploration of the role of physical and sexual abuse in psychiatrically institutionalized women.* Toronto, Ontario, Canada: The Ontario Women's Directorate.

5 accused of sex attack on retarded girl. (1989, May 26). *Edmonton Journal* [Associated Press Wirestory], p. A15.

Floyd, F.J., & Phillippe, K.A. (1993). Parental interactions with children with and without mental retardation: Behavior management, coerciveness, and positive exchange. *American Journal on Mental Retardation, 97*(6), 673–684.

Flynt, S.W., & Wood, T.A. (1989). Stress and coping of mothers with children with moderate mental retardation. *American Journal on Mental Retardation, 94*, 278–283.

Foley, G.M. (1985). Emotional development of children with handicaps. Special Issue. The feeling child: Affective development reconsidered. *Journal of Children in Contemporary Society, 17*(4), 57–73.

Forest, M. (1991). It's about relationships. In L.H. Meyer, C.A. Peck, & L. Brown (Eds.), *Critical issues in the lives of people with severe disabilities* (pp. 399–407). Baltimore: Paul H. Brookes Publishing Co.

Former foster parents on ill-treatment charges. (1991, October 16). *Otago Daily Times*, p. 26.

Four found guilty in sexual assault of mentally retarded girl. (1993, March 16). Newark, NJ: Clarinews@clarinet.com (United Press International).

Foxx, R.M., & McMorrow, M.J. (1985). Teaching social skills to mentally retarded adults: Follow-up results from three studies. *Behavior Therapist, 8*(4), 77–78.

Frechette, A., & Rimsza, M.E. (1992). Stun gun injury: A new presentation of the battered child syndrome. *Pediatrics, 89*(5), 898–901.

Friedrich, W.N., & Boriskin, J.A. (1978). Primary prevention of child abuse. Focus on the special child. *Hospital and Community Psychiatry, 29*(4), 248–256.

Frisch, L.E., & Rhoads, F.A. (1982). Child abuse and neglect in children referred for learning evaluation. *Journal of Learning Disability, 15*(10), 538–541.

Frye v. United States, 293 F. 1013 (1923).

Fryer, G.E., Kraizer, S.K., & Miyoshi, T. (1987). Measuring the actual reduction of risk for child abuse: A new approach. *Child Abuse & Neglect, 11*, 173–179.

Fuller, P.R. (1949). Operant conditioning of a human vegetative organism. *American Journal of Psychology, 62*, 587–590.

Furey, E.M., & Haber, M. (1989). Protecting adults with mental retardation: A model statute. *Mental Retardation, 27*(3), 135–140.

Furniss, T. (1991). *The multi-professional handbook of child sexual abuse: Integrated management, therapy, & legal intervention*. London: Routledge.

Gadow, K.D., & Poling, A.G. (1988). *Pharmacotherapy and mental retardation*. Boston: Little, Brown.

Gahagan, S., & Rimsza, M.E. (1991). Child abuse or osteogenesis imperfecta: How can we tell? *Pediatrics, 88*(5), 987–992.

Garbarino, J. (1987). The abuse and neglect of special children: An introduction to the issues. In J. Garbarino, P.E. Brookhouser, & K.J. Authier (Eds.), *Special children—special risks: The maltreatment of children with disabilities* (pp. 3–14). New York: Aldine de Gruyter.

Garbarino, J., & Stocking, S.H. (1980). The social context of child maltreatment. In J. Garbarino & S.H. Stocking (Eds.), *Protecting children from abuse and neglect: Developing and maintaining support systems for families* (pp. 1–14). San Francisco: Jossey-Bass.

Gardner, J.F., & Chapman, M.S. (1985). *Staff development in mental retardation services: A practical handbook*. Baltimore: Paul H. Brookes Publishing Co.

Gelles, R.J. (1975, January). Violence in pregnancy: A note on the extent of the problem and the need for services. *The Family Coordinator*, 81–86.

Gennaro, S. (1991). Facilitating parenting of the neonatal intensive care unit graduate. *Journal of Perinatal and Neonatal Nursing, 4*(4), 55–61.

Gentles, I., & Cassidy, E. (1988). Child sexual abuse prevention programs and their evaluation: Implications for planning and programming. *Journal of Child Care, 3*(6), 81–83.

Geskie, M.A., & Salesek, J.L. (1988). Attitudes of health care personnel toward persons with disabilities. In H.E. Yuker (Ed.), *Attitudes toward persons with disabilities* (pp. 187–200). New York: Springer.

Gething, L. (1991). Generality vs. specificity of attitudes toward people with disabilities. *British Journal of Medical Psychology, 64*, 55–64.

Gil, D. (1970). *Violence against children: Physical child abuse.* Cambridge, MA: Harvard University Press.

Gil, E. (1979). *Handbook for understanding and preventing abuse and neglect of children in out of home care.* San Francisco: San Francico Child Abuse Council.

Gil, E. (1981). Protecting the rights of children in institutions. In National Legal Resource Center for Child Advocacy and Protection Staff (Eds.), *Protecting children through the legal system* (pp. 303–323). Washington, DC: American Bar Association.

Gil, E., & Baxter, K. (1979). Abuse of children in institutions. *Child Abuse & Neglect, 3*, 693–698.

Glasser, I. (1978). Prisoners of benevolence: Power versus liberty in the welfare state. In W. Gaylin, I. Glasser, S. Marcus, & D.J. Rothman (Eds.), *Doing good: The limits of benevolence* (pp. 99–168). New York: Pantheon Books.

Glick, P.S., Guyer, B., Burr, B.H., & Gorbach, I.E. (1983). Pediatric nursing homes: Implications of the Massachusetts experience for residential care of multiply handicapped children. *New England Journal of Medicine, 309*, 640–646.

Glidden, L.M. (1993). What we do *not* know about families with children who have developmental disabilities: Questionnaire on resources and stress as a case study. *American Journal on Mental Retardation, 97*, 481–495.

Goddard, H.H. (1919). *The psychology of the normal and subnormal.* New York: Dodd, Mead.

Godschalz, S.M. (1983). Mark: Psychotherapy with a developmentally disabled adult. *Image: The Journal of Nursing Scholarship, 15*(1), 12–16.

Goffman, E. (1961). *Asylums: Essays on the social situation of mental patients and other inmates.* New York: Doubleday.

Goffman, E. (1963). *Stigma: Notes on the management of spoiled identity.* Englewood Cliffs, NJ: Prentice Hall.

Goodman, G.S., Taub, E.P., Jones, P.H., England, P., Port, L.K., Rudy, L., & Prado, L. (1992). Testifying in criminal court. *Monographs of the Society for Research in Child Development, 57*(5), 1–142.

Goodwin, T.M., & Breen, M.T. (1990). Pregnancy outcome and fetomaternal hemorrhage after noncatastrophic trauma. *American Journal of Obstetrics and Gynecology, 188*, 665–671.

Gordon, S. (1979). *Sex education and the library: A basic bibliography for the general public with special resources for the librarian.* Syracuse, NY: ERIC Clearinghouse on Information Resources. (ERIC Document Reproduction Service No. ED 180 504)

Gould, M.J. (1993, June 1–5). *Positive contributions of persons with mental retardation in historic events.* Paper presented at the 117th meeting of the American Association on Mental Retardation, Washington, DC.

Gould,S.J. (1981). *The mismeasure of man*. New York: Norton.

Graber, B., Hartmann, K., Coffman, J.A., Huey, C.J., & Golden, C.J. (1982). Brain damage among mentally disordered sex offenders. *Journal of Forensic Sciences, 27*(1), 125–134.

Graziano, A.M., & Mills, J.R. (1992). Treatment for abused children: When is a partial solution acceptable? *Child Abuse & Neglect, 16*, 217–228.

Green, A.H., Gaines, R.W., & Sandgrund, A. (1974). Child abuse: Pathological syndrome of family interaction. *American Journal of Psychiatry, 131*, 882–886.

Green, A.H., & Schetky, D.H. (1988). True and false allegations of child sexual abuse. In D.H. Schetky & A.H. Green (Eds.), *Child sexual abuse: A handbook for health care and legal professionals* (pp. 104–124). New York: Brunner/Mazel.

Green, A.H., Voeller, K., Gaines, R.W., & Kubie, U. (1981). Neurological impairment in maltreated children. *Child Abuse & Neglect, 5*(2), 129–134.

Green, G. (1993). Controlled evaluation of facilitated communication. *Autism Research Review, 7*(1), p. 2.

Greenland, C. (1987). *Preventing CAN deaths: An international study of deaths due to child abuse and neglect*. London: Tavistock Publications.

Greenspan, S., & Budd, K.S. (1986). Research on mentally retarded parents. In J.J. Gallagher & P.M. Vietze (Eds.), *Families of handicapped persons: Research, programs, and policy issues* (pp. 115–127). Baltimore: Paul H. Brookes Publishing Co.

Gregory, V. (1983, July 6). Nurse knew dose lethal. *Edmonton Sun*, p. 2.

Griffith, J.L. (1988). The family systems of Münchausen syndrome by proxy. *Family Process, 27*, 423–437.

Griffiths, D.M., Hingsburger, D., & Christian, R. (1985). Treating developmentally handicapped sexual offenders: The York Behaviour Management Services Treatment Program. *Psychiatric Aspects of Mental Retardation Reviews, 4*(12), 49–52.

Griffiths, D.M., Quinsey, V.L., & Hingsburger, D. (1989). *Changing inappropriate sexual behavior: A community-based approach for persons with developmental disabilities*. Baltimore: Paul H. Brookes Publishing Co.

Gross, R.H., Cox, A., Taytrek, R., Polloway, M., & Barnes, W.A. (1983). Early management and decision making for the treatment of myelomeningocele. *Pediatrics, 72*(4), 450–458.

Groth, N. (1979). *Men who rape*. New York: Plenum Press.

Guess, D. (1990). Transmission of behavior management technologies from researchers to practioners: A need for professional self-evaluation. In A.C. Repp & N.N. Singh (Eds.), *Perspectives on the use of nonaversive and aversive interventions for persons with developmental disabilities* (pp. 158–172). Sycamore, IL: Sycamore Press.

Guess, D., Helmstetter, E., & Turnbull, H.R., III. (1987). *Use of aversive procedures with persons who are disabled: An historical review and critical analysis*. Seattle, WA: The Association for Persons with Severe Handicaps.

Gunn, M. (1989). Sexual abuse and adults with mental handicap: Can the law help? In H. Brown & A. Craft (Eds.), *Thinking the unthinkable: Papers on sexual abuse of people with disabilities* (pp. 51–73). London: Family Planning Association Education Unit.

Haddock, M.D., & McQueen, W.M. (1983). Assessing potentials for abuse. *Journal of Clinical Psychology, 39*, 1021–1029.

Halderman v. Pennhurst State School and Hospital, 446 I. Supp. 1295, 1314–1320 (E.D. Pa., 1977).

Haller, J., Jr. (1989). The role of physicians in America's sterilization movement, 1894–1925. *New York State Journal of Medicine, 89*(3), 169–179.

Hard, S. (1986). *Sexual abuse of the developmentally disabled: A case study.* Paper presented at the National Conference of Executives of Associations for Retarded Citizens, Omaha, Nebraska.

Harder, S.R., Kalachnik, J.E., Jensen, M.A., & Feltz, J. (1987). Psychotropic drug use with successful and unsuccessful community placed developmental disability groups. *Research in Developmental Disabilities, 8*, 191–202.

Harlow, H.F. (1959). Love in infant monkeys. *Scientific American, 200*, 68–74.

Hart, N.W. (1970). Frequently expressed feelings and reactions of parents toward their retarded children. In N.R. Bernstein (Ed.), *Diminished people: Problems in the care of the mentally retarded* (pp. 47–71). Boston: Little, Brown.

Harvey, W., & Watson-Russell, A. (1986). *So, you have to go to court.* Toronto, Ontario, Canada: Butterworths.

Hauerwas, S. (1986). Suffering the retarded: Should we prevent mental retardation? In P.R. Dokecki & R.M. Zaner (Eds.), *Ethics of dealing with persons with severe disabilities: Toward a research agenda* (pp. 53–70). Baltimore: Paul H. Brookes Publishing Co.

Hawking, S. (1988). *A brief history of time: From the big bang to black holes.* London: Bantam Press.

Hawkins, W.E., & Duncan, D.F. (1985). Children's illnesses as risk factors for child abuse. *Psychological Reports, 56*, p. 638.

Hayes, S.C., & Hayes, R. (1982). *Mental retardation: Law, policy and administration.* Sydney, Australia: The Law Book Company.

Heath, P. (1974). *The philosopher's Alice.* London: Academy Editions.

Hebert, P. (1986, August). Our justice system is lacking [Letter to the editor]. *Spokesman*, p. 4.

Heinrichs, P. (1992a). State "tortured" family. *The Sunday Age*, February 16, pp. 8–9.

Heinrichs, P. (1992b). "Tortured" family may call for probe on facilitated evidence. *The Sunday Age*, February 23, p. 8.

Heisler, G. (1974). Ways to deter law violations: Effects on levels of threat and vicarious punishment on cheating. *Journal of Consulting and Clinical Psychology, 42*, 577–582.

Helfer, R.E., & Kempe, R.S. (Eds.). (1987). *The battered child.* Chicago: The University of Chicago Press.

Helfer, R.E., Slovis, T.L., & Black, M. (1977). Injuries resulting when small children fall out of bed. *Pediatrics, 60*, 533–535.

Helmstetter, E., & Durand, M. (1991). Nonaversive interventions for severe behavior problems. In L.H. Meyer, C.A. Peck, & L. Brown (Eds.), *Critical issues in the lives of people with severe disabilities* (pp. 559–600). Baltimore: Paul H. Brookes Publishing Co.

Hendricks, S.E., Fitzpatrick, D.F., Hartmann, K., Quaife, M.A., Stratbucker, R.A., & Graber, B. (1988). Brain structure and function in sexual molesters of children and adolescents. *Journal of Clinical Psychiatry, 49*, 108–112.

Herbert, D. (1982). *The geography of urban crime.* New York: Longman.

Herr, S.S. (1984). *Issues in human rights: A guide for parents, professionals, policy makers and all those who are concerned about the rights of mentally retarded and developmentally disabled people.* New York: Young Adult Institute Press.

Herrenkohl, E.C., & Herrenkohl, R.C. (1981). *Explanations of child maltreatment: A preliminary appraisal.* Durham: New Hampshire University, Center for Social Research. National Conference for Family Violence Researchers.

Hickey, E.W. (1991). *Serial murderers and their victims*. Pacific Grove, CA: Brooks/Cole Publishing.

Hillard, P.J.A. (1985). Physical abuse in pregnancy. *Obstetrics & Gynecology, 66*, 185–190.

Hingsburger, D. (1990a). *I Contact: Sexuality and people with disabilities*. Mountville, PA: VIDA Publishing.

Hingsburger, D. (1990b). *i to I: Self concept and people with developmental disabilities*. Mountville, PA: VIDA Publishing.

Hirschbach, E. (1982). Children beyond reach? In R. Hanson (Ed.), *Institutional abuse of children and youth* (pp. 99–107). New York: Haworth Press.

Hitler, A. (1934). *Mein kampf* [My struggle]. Munich, Germany: Auflage.

Hochstadt, N.J., Jaudes, P.K., Zimo, D.A., & Schacter, J. (1987). The medical and psychosocial needs of children entering foster care. *Child Abuse & Neglect, 11*, 53–62.

Holmes, R.M. (1989). *Profiling violent crimes: An investigative tool*. Newbury Park, CA: Sage Publications.

Horejsi, C.R. (1979). Developmental disabilities: Opportunities for social workers. *Social Work, 24*, 40–43.

Horne, M.D. (1988). Modifying peer attitudes toward the handicapped. Procedures and research issues. In H.E. Yuker (Ed.), *Attitudes toward persons with disabilities* (pp. 203–213). New York: Springer.

Houston students expelled in sexual assault. (1992, October 7). UPI Wirestory.

Howard, J. (1929). *The state of prisons*. New York: E.P. Dutton.

Hughes, H.M., & DiBrezzo, R. (1987). Physical and emotional abuse and motor development: A preliminary investigation. *Perceptual and Motor Skills, 64*, 469–470.

Hume, J. (1991a, October). The unremembered holocaust [part 1]. *N.Z. Disabled, 11*(5), 61–63.

Hume, J. (1991b, December). The unremembered holocaust [part 2]. *N.Z. Disabled, 11*(6), 64–65.

Hunter, J.A., Stringer, M., & Watson, R.P. (1991). Intergroup violence and intergroup attributions. *British Journal of Social Psychology, 30*(3), 261–266.

Hutchinson, M. (1990). *The anatomy of sex and power. An investigation of the mind-body politics*. New York: William Morrow.

Hyman, B. (1993, March). *Group therapy: A treatment model for child sexual abuse survivors with disabilities*. Paper presented at the Ninth National Symposium on Child Sexual Abuse, Huntsville, AL.

Illich, I. (1992). *In the mirror of the past: Lectures and addresses*. New York: Marion Boyers.

Intellectual Disability Review Panel. (1989). *Investigation into the reliability and validity of the assisted communication technique*. Victoria, Australia: Department of Community Services.

Jacobson, A., & Richardson, B. (1987). Assault experiences of 100 psychiatric inpatients: Evidence for the need for routine inquiry. *American Journal of Psychiatry, 144*(7), 908–913.

Jimenez, M. (1993, July 22). No Canadian home for Bosnian kids, *The Edmonton Journal*, p. A4.

Johnson, A. (1903). A report of the committee on colonies for segregation of the defectives. *Proceedings of the National Conference on Charities and Correction*, 245–253.

Johnson, B., & Morse, H. (1968). Injured children and their parents. *Children, 15*, 147–152.

Johnson, D.W., & Johnson, R.T. (1989). Cooperative learning and mainstreaming. In R. Gaylord-Ross (Ed.), *Integration strategies for persons with handicaps* (pp. 233–248). Baltimore: Paul H. Brookes Publishing Co.

Johnson, W.R. (1975). *Sex education and counseling of special groups: The mentally and physically handicapped, ill and elderly.* Springfield, IL: Charles C Thomas.

Jones, D.N., Pickett, J., Oates, M.R., & Barbor, P.R.H. (1987). *Understanding child abuse* (2nd ed.). London: Macmillan Education.

Jones, D.P.H., & McGraw, J.M. (1987). Reliable and fictitious accounts of sexual abuse of children. *Journal of Interpersonal Violence, 2*, 27–45.

Judge, C. (1987). *Civilization and mental retardation.* Melbourne, Australia: Author.

Kahle, L.R. (1984). *Attitudes and social adaptation: A person-situation interaction approach.* New York: Pergamon Press.

Kanner, L. (1967). *A history of the care and study of the mentally retarded.* Springfield, IL: Charles C Thomas.

Karsten, R. (1932). *Indian tribes of the Argentine and Bolivian Chaco: Ethnological studies.* Helsingfors: Society Scientifica Fennica.

Kater, M.H. (1989). *Doctors under Hitler.* Chapel Hill: University of North Carolina Press.

Katz, I., Glass, D.C., Lucido, D.J., & Farber, J. (1977). Ambivalence, guilt, and the denigration of a physically handicapped victim. *Journal of Personality, 45*(3), 419–429.

Katz, I., Glass, D.C. Lucido, D., & Farber, J. (1979). Harm-doing and victim's racial or orthopedic stigma as determinants of helping behavior. *Journal of Personality, 47*(2), 340–364.

Katz, M.B. (1986). Child-saving. *History of Education Quarterly, 26*(3), 413–424.

Kehoe, B.P. (1993). *Zen and the art of the Internet.* Englewood Cliffs, NJ: Prentice Hall.

Keller, R.A., Cicchinelli, & Gardner, D.M. (1989). Characteristics of child sexual abuse treatment programs. *Child Abuse & Neglect, 13*, 361–368.

Kelley, S.J. (1986). Learned helplessness in the sexually abused child. *Issues in Comprehensive Pediatric Nursing, 9*(3), 193–207.

Kempe, C.H., Silverman, F.N., Steele, B.F., Droegemueller, W., & Silver, H.K. (1962). The battered child syndrome. *Journal of the American Medical Association, 181*, 17–24.

Kempe, R.S., & Kempe, C.H. (1978). *Child abuse.* Cambridge, MA: Harvard University Press.

Kempton, W. (1975). *Sex education for persons with disabilities that hinder learning: A teacher's guide.* Boston: Duxbury Press.

Kennedy, F. (1942). The problem of social control of the congenital defective: Education, sterilization, euthanasia. *The American Journal of Psychiatry, 99*, 13–18.

Kermani, E.J. (1991). The U.S. Supreme Court on victimized children: The constitutional rights of the defendant versus the best interests of the child. *Journal of the American Academy of Child and Adolescent Psychiatry, 30*(5), 839–841.

King, R.D., Raynes, N.V., & Tizzard, J. (1971). *Patterns of residential care: Sociological studies in institutions for handicapped children.* London: Routledge & Kegan Paul.

Knoll, J.A. (1990). Defining quality in residential services. In V.J. Bradley & H. Bersani (Eds.), *Quality assurance for individuals with developmental disabilities: It's everybody's business* (pp. 235–261). Baltimore: Paul H. Brookes Publishing Co.

Korbin, J.E. (1987). Child abuse and neglect: The cultural context. In R.E. Helfer & R.S. Kempe (Eds.), *The battered child* (pp. 23–41). Chicago: The University of Chicago Press.

Koss, M.P. (1988). Hidden rape: Sexual aggression and victimization in a national sample of students of higher education. In A.W. Burgess (Ed.), *Rape and sexual assault* (Vol. 2, pp. 3–25). New York: Garland.

Krauss, M.W. (1993). Child-related and parenting stress: Similarities and differences between mothers and fathers of children with disabilities. *American Journal on Mental Retardation, 97*, 393–404.

Krugman, R.D. (1985). Fatal child abuse: An analysis of 24 cases. *Pediatrician, 12*, 68–72.

Kwakman, A.M., Zuiker, F.A., Schippers, G.M., & de Wuffel, F.J. (1988). Drinking behavior, drinking attitudes, and attachment relationship of adolescents. *Journal of Youth and Adolescence, 17*(3), 247–253.

Lakin, K.C., & Bruininks, R.H. (Eds.). (1985). *Strategies for achieving community integration of developmentally disabled citizens*. Baltimore: Paul H. Brookes Publishing Co.

Lamb, M.E., Gaensbauer, T.J., Malkin, C.M., & Schultz, L.A. (1985). The effects of child maltreatment on security of infant–adult attachment. *Infant Behavior and Development, 8*(1), 35–45.

Langevin, R., Wright, P., & Handy, L. (1989). Characteristics of sex offenders who were sexually victimized as children. *Annals of Sex Research, 2*(3), 227–253.

Langlois, N.E., & Gresham, G.A. (1991). The ageing of bruises: a review and study of the colour changes with time. *Forensic Science International, 50*(2), 227–238.

Larmer, K.R., & Webb, L.C. (1989). Facilities development. In L.K. Webb (Ed.), *Planning and managing adult day care* (pp. 37–59). Owings Mills, MD: National Health Publishing.

Larson, S., & Lakin, C. (1989). *Deinstitutionalization of persons with mental retardation: The impact on daily living skills* (Policy Research Brief, Vol. 1, No. 1). Minneapolis: University of Minnesota, Institute on Community Integration, Research and Training Center on Community Living.

Laterza, P. (1979). An eclectic approach to group work with the mentally retarded. *Social Work with Groups, 2*(3), 235–245.

Lawmaker wants autopsies for kids under three who die unexpectedly. (1993, Feb. 18). Harrisburg, PA: Clarinews@clarinet.com (United Press International).

Leaning, J. (1993, February 6). German doctors and their secrets. *New York Times*, p. 121.

Lederer, S.E. (1992). Orphans as guinea pigs. In R. Cooter (Ed.), *In the name of the child: Health and welfare, 1890–1940*. London: Routledge.

LeGrand, C. (1984). Mental hospital regulation and the safe environment. *Law, Medicine & Health Care, 12*(6), 236–242.

Lehne, G.K. (1986). Brain damage and paraphilia: Treated with medroxyprogesterone acetate. *Sexuality and Disability, 7*(3/4), 145–158.

Leippe, M.R., Brigham, J.C., Cousins, C., & Romanczyk, A. (1989). The opinions and practices of criminal attorneys' regarding child eyewitnesses: A study. In S.J. Ceci, D.F. Ross, & M.P. Toglia (Eds.), *Perspectives on children's testimony* (pp. 110–130). New York: Springer-Verlag.

Levine, M. (1990). In K.M. Schwier (Ed.), *Speak-easy: People with mental handicaps talk about their lives in institutions and the community* (pp. 71–79). Austin, TX: PRO-ED.

Levy, L. (1968). Operant conditioning in Vietnam. *American Journal of Psychiatry, 124,* 1136.

Lewis, C.S. (1970). The humanitarian theory of punishment. In W. Hooper (Ed.), *God in the dock: Essays on theology and ethics* (pp. 287–300). Grand Rapids, MI: William B. Eerdmans.

Lewis, D.O., Pincus, J.H., Bard, B., Richarson, E., Prichep, L.S., Feldman, M., & Yeager, C. (1988). Neuropsychiatric, psychoeducational, and family characteristics of 14 juveniles condemned to death in the U.S. *American Journal of Psychiatry, 145,* 584–589.

Lightcap, J.L., Kurland, J.A., & Burgess, R.L. (1982). Child abuse: A test of some predictions from evolutionary theory. *Ethology and Sociobiology, 3*(2), 61–67.

Livneh, H. (1988). A dimensional perspective on the origin of negative attitudes toward persons with disabilities. In H.E. Yuker (Ed.), *Attitudes toward persons with disabilities* (pp. 35–46). New York: Springer.

Lloyd, D.W. (1992). Ritual child abuse: Definitions and assumptions. *Journal of Child Sexual Abuse, 1*(3), 1–14.

Loder, R.T., & Bookout, C. (1991). Fracture patterns in battered children. *Journal of Orthopedic Trauma, 5*(4), 428–433.

Long, S. (1987). *Death without dignity: The story of the first nursing home corporation indicted for murder.* Austin, TX: Texas Monthly Press.

Lorber, R., Felton, D.K., & Reid, J.B. (1984). A social learning approach to the reduction of coercive process in child abuse families: A molecular analysis. *Advances in Behavior Research & Therapy, 6,* 29–45.

Lord, J. (1991). *Lives in transition: The process of personal empowerment.* Kitchener, Ontario, Canada: Centre for Research & Education.

Lord, J., & Pedlar, A. (1991). Life in the community: Four years after the closure of an institution. *Mental Retardation, 2,* 81–86.

Lovett, H. (1985). *Cognitive counseling & persons with special needs: Adapting behavioral approaches to the social context.* New York: Praeger.

Luckasson, R. (1992). People with mental retardation as victims of crime. In R.W. Conley, R. Luckasson, & G.N. Bouthilet (Eds.), *The criminal justice system and mental retardation: Defendants and victims* (pp. 209–220). Baltimore: Paul H. Brookes Publishing Co.

Ludwig, S., & Hingsburger, D. (1993). *Being sexual: An illustrated series on sexuality and relationships. Unit 15: Sexual abuse.* East York, Ontario, Canada: Sex Information and Education Council of Canada.

Luiselli, J.K. (1990). Recent developments in nonaversive treatment: A review of rationale, methods, and recommendations. In A.C. Repp & N.N. Singh (Eds.), *Perspectives on the use of nonaversive and aversive interventions for persons with developmental disabilities* (pp. 73–86). Sycamore, IL: Sycamore Press.

Lujan, C., DeBruyn, L.M., May, P.A., & Bird, M.E. (1989). Profile of abused and neglected American Indian children in the Southwest. *Child Abuse & Neglect, 13,* 449–461.

Lusk, R., & Waterman, J. (1986). Effects of sexual abuse. In K. McFarlane & J. Waterman (Eds.), *Sexual abuse of young children: Evaluation and treatment* (pp. 101–118). New York: The Guilford Press.

Lusthaus, E. (1991). Drastic actions: The results of viewing people as less than human. *Developmental Disabilities Bulletin, 19,* 28–48.

Lutzker, J.R. (1990). "Damn it, Burris, I'm not a product of Walden Two," or Who's controlling the controllers? In A.C. Repp & N.N. Singh (Eds.), *Perspectives on the use of nonaversive and aversive interventions for persons with developmental disabilities* (pp. 495–501). Sycamore, IL: Sycamore Press.

Lutzker, J.R., & Rice, J.M. (1984). Project 12 Ways: Measuring outcome of a large in-home service for treatment and prevention of child abuse and neglect. *Child Abuse & Neglect, 8*, 141–155.

Lynch, M.A., & Roberts, J. (1977). Predicting child abuse: Signs of bonding failure in the maternity hospital. *British Medical Journal, 1*, 624–626.

Lynch, M.A., & Roberts, J. (1982). *Consequnces of child abuse.* London: Academic Press.

Lyons, M. (1991). Enabling or disabling? Students' attitudes toward persons with disabilities. *American Journal of Occupational Therapy, 45*(4), 311–316.

MacFadden, J.V. (1991). *The right to control what happens to your body.* Toronto, Ontario, Canada: The Roeher Institute.

MacNamara, R.D. (1988). *Freedom from abuse in organized care settings for the elderly and handicapped.* Springfield, IL: Charles C Thomas.

MacNamara, R.D. (1992). *Creating abuse free environments for children, the disabled, and the elderly: preparing, supervising, and managing caregivers for the emotional impact of their responsibilities.* Springfield, IL: Charles C Thomas.

Mansell, S., Sobsey, D., & Calder, P. (1992). Sexual abuse treatment for persons with developmental disability. *Professional Psychology: Research and Practice, 23*, 404–409.

Marchetti, A.G., & McCartney, J.R. (1990). Abuse of persons with mental retardation: Characteristics of the abused, the abusers, and the informers. *Mental Retardation, 6*, 367–371.

Margolin, L. (1991). Child abuse by mothers' boyfriends: Why the overrepresentation. *Child Abuse & Neglect, 16*, 541–551.

Mars, G. (1982). *Cheats at work. An anthology of workplace crime.* London: George Allen & Unwin.

Marshall, W.L., & Barrett, S. (1990). *Criminal neglect: Why sex offenders go free.* Toronto, Ontario, Canada: Doubleday Canada Ltd.

Martin, H.P. (1976). Neurologic status of abused children. In H.P. Martin (Ed.), *The abused child: A multidisciplinary approach to developmental issues and treatment* (pp. 67–82). Cambridge, MA: Ballinger Publishing Co.

Martin, H.P., Beezley, P., Conway, E.F., & Kempe, C.H. (1974). The development of abused children: A review of the literature and physical, neurologic, and intellectual findings. *Advances in Pediatrics, 21*, 25–73.

Marvasti, J. (1989). Play therapy with sexually abused children. In S.M. Sgroi (Ed.), *Vulnerable populations: Vol. 2. Sexual abuse treatment for children, adult survivors, offenders, and persons with mental retardation* (pp. 1–41). New York: Lexington Books.

Marx, G.T. (1981). Ironies of social control: Authorities as contributors to deviance through escalation, nonenforcement, and covert facilitation. *Social Problems, 28*, 221–246.

Masson, J. (1984). *The assault on truth: Freud's suppression of the seduction theory.* London: Faber.

May, M. [assisted by R. Gerzon]. (1989, December). Mavis May's story. *IH Review, 27*(4), 28–30.

McCall, R.B., & Gregory, T.C. (1987). Mass media issues. In J. Garbarino, P.E. Brookhouser, & K.J. Authier and Associates (Eds.), *Special children—Special risks: The maltreatment of children with disabilities* (pp. 211–227). New York: Aldine de Gruyter.

McCelland, C.O., Rekate, H., Kaufman, B., & Persse, L. (1980). Cerebral injury in child abuse: A changing profile. *Child's Brain, 7*(5), 225–235.

McCormick, H. (1992). *Expert evidence in child sexual abuse cases.* Toronto, Ontario, Canada: Institute for the Prevention of Child Sexual Abuse.

McFarlane, J. (1989). Battering during pregnancy: The tip of an iceberg revealed. *Women & Health, 15*, 69–84.

McGrath, T. (1991). Overcoming institutionalized child abuse: Creating a positive climate. *Journal of Child and Youth Care, 6*(4), 61–68.

McGregor, B.M.S., & Dutton, D.G. (1991). Child sexual abuse within populations that require health system intervention. In C.R. Bagley & R.J. Thomlinson (Eds.), *Child sexual abuse: Critical perspectives on prevention, intervention, and treatment* (pp. 135–156). Toronto, Ontario, Canada: Wall and Emerson.

McGuire, T.L., & Feldman, K.W. (1989). Psychologic morbidity of children subjected to Münchausen syndrome by proxy. *Pediatrics, 83*, 289–292.

McKnight, J. (1977). Professionalized service and disabling help. In I. Illich, I.K. Zola, J. McKnight, J. Caplan, & H. Shaiken (Eds.), *Disabling professions.* London: Marion Boyars.

McLaren, J., & Bryson, S.E. (1987). Review of recent epidemiological studies of mental retardation: Prevalence, associate disorders, and etiology. *American Journal on Mental Retardation, 92*, 243–254.

McPhedran, M. (1992). Investigating the sexual abuse of patients: The Ontario experience. *Health Law Review, 1*(3), 3–15.

Mead, J.J., & Westgate, D.L. (1992). *Child abuse wound identification.* Chino, CA: R.C. Law & Co.

Meadow, R. (1977). Münchausen syndrome by proxy: The hinterland of child abuse. *Lancet, 2*, 343–345.

Meadow, R. (1982). Münchausen syndrome by proxy. *Archives of Disease in Childhood, 57*, 92–98.

Medical discrimination against children with disabilities. (1989, September). Washington, DC: U.S. Commission on Civil Rights.

Medicine Hat Regional Association for the Mentally Handicapped. (1993). *Toward a better tomorrow.* Medicine Hat, Alberta, Canada: Author.

Medvedev, Z., & Medvedev, R. (1971). *A question of madness.* New York: Knopf.

Megargee, E.I. (1982). Psychological determinants and correlates of criminal violence. In M.E. Wolfgang & N.A. Weiner (Eds.), *Criminal violence* (pp. 81–170). Beverly Hills: Sage Publications.

Meier, J.H. (1978). *A multifactorial model of child abuse dynamics* (Monograph No. 3:4/83). Beaumont, CA: CHILDHELP USA/INTERNATIONAL, Research Division.

Melnick, B., & Hurley, J.R. (1969). Distinctive personality attributes of child abusing mothers. *Journal of Consulting and Clinical Psychology, 33*, 746–749.

Melton, G.B., & Garrison, E.G. (1987). Fear, prejudice, and neglect: Discrimination against mentally disabled persons. *American Psychologist, 42*(11), 1007–1026.

Mendelsberg, R.G. (Ed.). (1991). *Medical murderers.* New York: Pinnacle Books.

Mercer, S.O. (1983). Consequences of institutionalization of the aged. In J.I. Kosberg (Ed.), *Abuse and maltreatment of the elderly: Causes and interventions* (pp. 84–103). Boston: John Wright, PSG Inc.

Mertz, A.W. (1986). Sexual abuse of anesthesized patients. In A.W. Burgess (Ed.), *Sexual exploitation of patients by health professionals* (pp. 61–65). New York: Praeger.

Metha, M.N., Lokeshwar, M.R., Bhatt, S.S., Athavale, V.B., & Kulkarni, B.S. (1979). 'Rape' in children. *Child Abuse & Neglect, 3*, 671–677.

Meyer, L.M. (1973). Comparison of attitudes toward mental patients of junior and senior nursing students and their university peers. *Nursing Research, 22*, 242–245.

Meyers, C.E., & Blacher, J. (1987). Historical determinants of residential care. In S. Landesman & P. Vietze (Eds.), *Living environments and mental retardation* (pp. 3–16). Washington, DC: American Association on Mental Retardation.

Michaud, G., & Aynesworthy, H. (1989). *Ted Bundy: Conversations with a killer.* New York: Signet Books.

Miller, J.L., Rossi, P.H., & Simpson, J.E. (1986). Perceptions of justice: Race and gender differences in judgement of appropriate prison sentences. *Law & Society Review, 20*(3), 334.

Miller, T.R., Handal, P.J., Gilner, F.H., & Cross, J.F. (1991). The relationship between abuse and witnessing violence on the Child Abuse Potential Inventory with Black adolescents. *Journal of Family Violence, 6*(4), 351–363.

Miller, W.R., Rosellini, R.A., & Seligman, M.E.P. (1977). Learned helplessness and depression. In J.D. Maser & M.E.P. Seligman (Eds.), *Psychopathology: Experimental models* (pp. 104–130). San Francisco: W.H. Freeman and Co.

Milner, J.S. (1980). *Research perspectives on the prediction and identification of child abuse and neglect: The Child Abuse Potential Inventory.* Webster, NC: Psytec.

Milner, J.S. (1989). Applications of the Child Abuse Potential Inventory. *Journal of Clinical Psychology, 45*(3), 450–454.

Milner, J.S., Robertson, K.R., & Rogers, D.L. (1990). Childhood history of abuse and child abuse potential. *Journal of Family Violence, 5*(1), 15–34.

Mitchell, D.R. (1987). Parents' interactions with their developmentally disabled or at-risk infants: A focus for intervention. *Australia and New Zealand Journal of Developmental Disabilities, 13*(2), 73–81.

Monahan, J. (1990). The social and economic context of violent behavior. In L.J. Hertzberg, G.F. Ostrum, & J.R. Field (Eds.), *Violent behavior: Vol. I. Assessment & intervention* (pp. 125–150). Great Neck, NY: PMA.

Monahan, J., & Klassen, D. (1982). Situational approaches to understanding and predicting individual violent behavior. In M.E. Wolfgang & N.A. Weiner (Eds.), *Criminal violence* (pp. 292–319). Beverly Hills: Sage Publications.

Monat-Haller, R. (1992). *Understanding and expressing sexuality: Responsible choices for individuals with developmental disabilities.* Baltimore: Paul H. Brookes Publishing Co.

Monfils, M. (1983). Social work challenges: Meeting the mental health needs of mentally retarded young adults. In F.J. Menolascino & B.M. McCann (Eds.), *Mental health and mental retardation: Bridging the gap* (pp. 187–201). Baltimore: University Park Press.

Monfils, M. (1985). Theme-centered group work with the mentally retarded. *Social Casework: The Journal of Contemporary Social Work, 66*(3), 177–184.

Monfils, M., & Menolascino, F.J. (1984). Modified individual and group treatment approaches for the mentally retarded-mentally ill. In F.J. Menolascino & J.A. Stark (Eds.), *Handbook of mental illness in the mentally retarded* (pp. 155–169). New York: Plenum Press.

Moore, K., & Reed, D. (1988). *Deadly medicine*. New York: St. Martin's Press.

Moore, T., & Thompson, V. (1987). Elder abuse: A review of research, programmes and policy. *The Social Worker, 55*(3), 115–122.

Morey, M.A., Begleiter, M.L., & Harris, D.J. (1981, December 5). Profile of a battered fetus. *The Lancet*, pp. 1295–1296.

Morgan, S.R. (1987). *Abuse and neglect of handicapped children.* Boston: Little, Brown.

Morse, C.W., Sahler, O.Z., & Friedman, S.B. (1970). A three-year follow-up study of abused and neglected children. *American Journal of Diseases of Children, 120*, 439–446.

Mrazek, P.B. (1981). The nature of incest: A review of contributing factors. In P.B. Mrazek & C.H. Kempe (Eds.), *Sexually abused children and their families* (pp. 97–107). Oxford: Pergamon Press.

Mullins, J.B. (1986). The relationship between child abuse and handicapping conditions. *Journal of School Health, 56*(4), 134–136.

Murphy, J.M., Jellinek, M., Quinn, D., Smith, G., Poitrast, F.G., & Goshko, M. (1991). Substance abuse and serious child mistreatment: Prevalence, risk, and outcome in a court sample. *Child Abuse & Neglect, 15*(3), 197–211.

Murphy, S., Orkow, B., & Nicola, R.M. (1985). Prenatal prediction of child abuse and neglect: A prospective study. *Child Abuse & Neglect, 9*, 225–235.

Murphy, W.D., Coleman, M.A., & Haynes, M.R. (1983). Treatment and evaluation issues with the mentally retarded sex offender. In J.G. Greer & I.R. Stuart (Eds.), *The sexual aggressor* (pp. 22–41). New York: Van Nostrand Reinhold.

Murray, M., & Chambers, M. (1991). Effect of contact on nursing students' attitudes to patients. *Nursing Education Today, 11*(5), 363–367.

Musick, J.L. (1984). Patterns of institutional sexual assault. *Response to Violence in the Family and Sexual Assault, 7*(3), 1–2, 10–11.

The Nelson A. Rockefeller Institute of Government. (1983). *1983–84 New York State statistical yearbook* (10th ed.). Albany: State University of New York.

Neuffer, E. (1987, August 14). Body unearthed on S.I. is that of missing girl. *The New York Times*, p. B3.

Newberger, C.M., & Newberger, E.H. (1986). When the pediatrician is a pedophile. In A.W. Burgess (Ed.), *Sexual exploitation of patients by health professionals* (pp. 99–106). New York: Praeger.

Newlands, M., & Emery, J.S. (1991). Child abuse and cot deaths. *Child Abuse & Neglect, 15*(3), 275–278.

Newman, O. (1972). *Defensible space*. New York: Macmillan.

Newton, M. (1990a). *Hunting humans: An encyclopedia of modern serial killers*. Port Townsend, WA: Loompanics Unlimited.

Newton, M. (1990b). *Hunting humans: The encyclopedia of serial killers (Vol. 2)*. Port Townsend, WA: Avon Books.

Nibert, D., Cooper, S., & Crossmaker, M. (1989). Assaults against residents of a psychiatric institution: Residents' history of abuse. *Journal of Interpersonal Violence, 4*(3), 342–349.

Nirje, B. (1969). The normalization principle and its human management implications. In R. Kugel & W. Wolfensberger (Eds.), *Changing patterns of residential services for the mentally retarded* (pp. 179–185). Washington, DC: President's Committee on Mental Retardation.

No private right of action under CRIPA. (1989). *Mental and Physical Disability Law Reporter, 13*(5), 471.

Nova Scotia, Department of Attorney General and Department of Solicitor General. (1991). *Protocol for investigation and prosecution of cases involving persons with special communication needs.* Halifax, Nova Scotia: Author.

Nunno, M.A., & Motz, J.K. (1988). The development of an effective response to the abuse of children in out-of-home care. *Child Abuse & Neglect, 12,* 521–528.

Oates, K., & Peacock, A. (1984). Intellectual development of battered children. *Australia and New Zealand Journal of Developmental Disabilities, 10*(1), 27–29.

O'Brien, J., O'Brien, C., & Schwartz, D. (Eds.). (1990). *What can we count on to make and keep people safe?* Syracuse, NY: Human Policy Press.

O'Day, B. (1983). *Preventing sexual abuse of persons with disabilities.* St. Paul: Minnesota Department of Corrections, Program for Victims of Sexual Assault.

Ojanen, M. (1992). *The International Journal of Social Psychiatry, 38*(2), 120–130.

Oliver, J.E. (1985). Successive generations of child maltreatment: Social and medical disorders in the parents. *British Journal of Psychiatry, 147,* 484–490.

Ombudsman of British Columbia. (April, 1987). *The use of criminal record checks to screen individuals working with vulnerable people* (Public Report No. 5). Vancouver, Canada: Ombudsman of British Columbia.

O'Neill, J., Brown, M., Gordon, W., & Schonhorn, R. (1985). The impact of deinstitutionalization on activities and skills of severely/profoundly mentally retarded multiply-handicapped adults. *Applied Research in Mental Retardation, 6,* 361–371.

Orelove, F.P., & Sobsey, D. (1991). *Educating children with multiple disabilities: A transdisciplinary approach* (2nd ed.). Baltimore: Paul H. Brookes Publishing Co.

O'Sullivan, C.M. (1989). Alcoholism and abuse: The twin family secrets. In G.W. Lawson & A.W. Lawson (Eds.), *Alcoholism & substance abuse in special populations* (pp. 273–303). Rockville, MD: Aspen Publishers.

Oswin, M. (1979). The neglect of children in long stay hospitals. *Child Abuse & Neglect, 3,* 89–92.

The Oxford English Dictionary, Compact Edition, Vol. 1. (1971). Oxford University Press.

Packard, E. (1973). *Modern persecution. Insane asylums unveiled.* New York: Arno Press.

Page, A.C. (1991). Teaching developmentally disabled people self-regulation in sexual behavior. *Australia and New Zealand Journal of Developmental Disabilities, 17*(1), 81–88.

Parker, H., & Parker, S. (1986). Father daughter sexual abuse: An emerging perspective. *American Journal of Orthopsychiatry, 56,* 531–539.

Parton, N. (1985). *The politics of child abuse.* London: Macmillan.

Patterson, O. (1982). *Slavery and social death: A comparative study.* Cambridge, MA: Harvard University Press.

Payne, J., & Patton, J. (1984). *Mental retardation.* Columbus, OH: Charles E. Merrill.

Pearpoint, J., Forest, M., & Snow, J. (Eds.). (1992). *The inclusion papers: Strategies to make inclusion work.* Toronto, Ontario, Canada: Inclusion Press.

Pecora, P.J., Whittaker, J.K., & Maluccio, A.N. (1992). *The child welfare challenge: Policy, practice, research.* New York: Aldine de Gruyter.

Perlman, N., & Ericson, K. (1992). Interviewing developmentally handicapped persons: The ability of developmentally handicapped individuals to accurately report on witnessed events. In J. Casselman (Ed.), *Law and mental health* (pp. 202–206). Brussels: Leuven.

Perry, N.W., & Wrightsman, L.S. (1991). *The child witness: Legal issues and dilemmas.* Newbury Park, CA: Sage Publications.

Perske, R. (1972). The dignity of risk and the mentally retarded. *Mental Retardation, 10*(10), 24–27.

Perske, R. (1991). *Unequal justice? What can happen when persons with retardation or other developmental disabilities encounter the criminal justice system.* Nashville: Abingdon Press.

Peters, S.D., Wyatt, G.E., & Finkelhor, D. (1986). Prevalence. In D. Finkelhor (Ed.), *A sourcebook on child sexual abuse* (pp. 15–59). Beverly Hills: Sage Publications.

Peterson, D. (Ed.). (1982). *A mad people's history of madness.* Pittsburgh: University of Pittsburgh Press.

Pillemer, K. (1985). The dangers of dependency: New findings on the domestic violence against the elderly. *Social Problems, 33*, 146–158.

Pillemer, K., & Finkelhor, D. (1989). Causes of elder abuse: Caregiver stress versus problem relatives. *American Journal of Orthopsychiatry, 59*, 179–187.

Pincus, A., & Minahan, A. (1973). *Social work practice: Model and method.* Itasca, IL: F.E. Peacock.

Polansky, N.A., Gaudin, J.M., Ammons, P.W., & Davis, K.B. (1985). The psychological ecology of the neglectful mother. *Child Abuse & Neglect, 9,* 265–275.

Pontius, A.A. (1988). Introduction to biological issues, with neuropathological case illustrations. In R.A. Prenky & V.L. Quinsey (Eds.), *Human sexual aggression: Current perspectives* (pp. 148–153). New York: The New York Academy of Sciences.

Pope, K.S., Keith-Spiegel, P., & Tabachnick, B.G. (1986). Sexual attraction to clients: The human therapist and the (sometimes) inhuman training system. *American Psychologist, 41*, 147–158.

Porter, F.S., Blick, L.C., & Sgroi, S.M. (1982). Treatment of the sexually abused child. In S.M. Sgroi (Ed.), *Handbook of clinical intervention in child sexual abuse* (pp. 109–145). Lexington, MA: Lexington Books.

Powers, J.L., Mooney, A., & Nunno, M. (1990). Institutional abuse: A review of the literature. *Journal of Child and Youth Care, 4*, 81–95.

Prescott, J.W. (1990). Affectional bonding for the prevention of violent behaviors: Neurobiological, psychological, and religious/spiritual determinants. In L.J. Hertzberg, G.F. Ostrum, & J.R. Field (Eds.), *Violent behavior: Vol. I. Assessment & intervention* (pp. 95–124). Great Neck, NY: PMA.

Project concern in Romania. (1991, Nov.–Dec.). *News & Notes: Newsletter of the American Association on Mental Retardation*, p. 6.

Protection and Advocacy for Mentally Ill Individuals Act of 1986, 42 U.S.C. § 1081 (1986).

Proverbs 23: 13–14. Holy Bible.

Radford, J.P., & Tipper, A. (1988). *Starcross: Out of the mainstream.* Toronto, Ontario, Canada: The G. Allan Roeher Institute.

Rainforth, B., York, J., & Macdonald, C. (1992). *Collaborative teams for students with severe disabilities.* Baltimore: Paul H. Brookes Publishing Co.

Rees, L.M., Spreen, O., & Harnadek, M. (1991). Do attitudes toward persons with handicaps really shift over time? Comparison between 1975 and 1988. *Mental Retardation, 2*, 81–86.

Reichle, J., York, J., & Sigafoos, J. (1991). *Implementing augmentative and alternative communication: Strategies for learners with severe disabilities.* Baltimore: Paul H. Brookes Publishing Co.

Reid, J.G.S. (1992). Abuse: A sad world tour. *International League of Societies for Persons with Mental Handicap News, 13,* 5–6.

Reiger, H. (1972). *Too many teachers: Fact or fiction.* Bloomington, IN: Phi Delta Kappa.

Reinart, M.A. (1987). Sexually abused boys. *Child Abuse & Neglect, 11,* 229–235.

Repp, A.C., & Singh, N.N. (Eds.). (1990). *Perspectives on the use of nonaversive and aversive interventions for persons with developmental disabilities.* Sycamore, IL: Sycamore Press.

Reppucci, N.D., & Aber, M.S. (1992). Child maltreatment prevention and the legal system. In D.J. Willis, E.W. Holden, & M. Rosenberg (Eds.), *Prevention of child maltreatment: Developmental and ecological perspectives* (pp. 249–266). New York: John Wiley & Sons.

Reskin, B.F., & Visher, C.A. (1986). The impact of evidence and extralegal factors in jurors' decisions. *Law & Society Review, 20*(3), 423–438.

Resnick, P.J. (1980). Murder of the newborn: A psychiatric review of neonaticide. In G.J. Williams & J. Money (Eds.), *Traumatic abuse and neglect of children* (pp. 143–153). Baltimore: Johns Hopkins University Press.

Ricci, L.R. (1991). Photographing the physically abused child. Principles and practice. *American Journal of Diseases of Children, 145*(3), 275–281.

Richards, I.A. (1980). *The portable Coleridge.* New York: Penguin Books.

Richwald, G.A., & McClusky, T.C. (1985). Family violence during pregnancy. In D.B. Jelliffe & E.F.P. Jelliffe (Eds.), *Advances in international maternal and child health* (pp. 87–96). Oxford, England: Clarendon Press.

Ridington, J. (1989). *Who do we think we are? Self-image and women with disabilities.* Toronto, Ontario, Canada: DisAbled Women's Network Canada.

Riemer, J.W. (1977). Varieties of naturalistic research. *Urban Life and Culture, 5,* 467–478.

Riffenburgh, R.S., & Sathyavagiswaran, L. (1991). Ocular findings at autopsy of child abuse victims. *Ophthalmology, 98*(10), 1519–1524.

Rindfleisch, N. (1984, September 18–19). *Factors which influence the severity of adverse events in residential facilities.* Paper presented at the international Congress on Child Abuse and Neglect, Montreal, Canada.

Rindfleisch, N., & Bean, G.J. (1988). Willingness to report abuse and neglect in residential facilities. *Child Abuse & Neglect, 12,* 509–520.

Rindfleisch, N., & Rabb, J. (1984). How much of a problem is resident mistreatment in child welfare institutions? *Child Abuse & Neglect, 8,* 33–40.

Rinear, E.E. (1985). Sexual assault and the handicapped victim. In A.W. Burgess (Ed.), *Rape and sexual assault* (pp. 139–145). New York: Garland.

Ritchie, J., & Ritchie, J. (1981). Childrearing and child abuse: The Polynesian context. In J.E. Korbin (Ed.), *Child abuse and neglect: Crosscultural perspectives* (pp. 186–204). Berkeley: University of California Press.

Rivera, G. (1972). *Willowbrook: A report on how it is and why it doesn't have to be that way.* New York: Vintage Books.

Robb, J.C. (1992). *The disadvantaged witness.* Edmonton, Alberta, Canada: Alberta Law Reform Institute.

Robertson, C.M.T., & Etches, P.C. (1988). Decreased incidence of neurological disability among neonates of high risk born between 1975 and 1984 in Alberta. *Canadian Medical Association Journal, 139,* 225–229.

Rodning, C., Beckwith, L., & Howard, J. (1989). Prenatal exposure to drugs and its influence on attachment. Conference of the Behavioral Teratology Society, the National Institute on Drug Abuse, and the New York Academy of Sciences: Prenatal abuse of licit and illicit drugs (1988, Bethesda, Maryland). *Annals of the New York Academy of Sciences, 562,* 352–354.

Rodriguez, D., & Hignett, W.M. (1976). Guidelines for selection of home-based day providers. *Child Welfare, 55*(1), 20–26.

Roe, J.M., Feldman, S.S., & Drivas, A. (1988). Interactions with three-month-old infants: A comparison between Greek mothers and institutional caregivers. *International Journal of Behavioral Development, 11,* 359–367.

Roeher Institute. (1993). *Answering the call: The police response to family and caregiver violence against people with disabilities.* North York, Ontario, Canada: Author.

Rose, E., & Hardman, M.L. (1981). The abused mentally retarded child. *Education and Training of the Mentally Retarded Child, 16*(2), 114–118.

Rosenberg, D.A. (1987). Web of deceit: A literature review of Münchausen syndrome by proxy. *Child Abuse & Neglect, 11,* 547–563.

Rosenberg, D.A. (1988). Recent issues in child mistreatment. In D.C. Bross, R.D. Krugman, M.R. Lenherr, D.A. Rosenberg, & B.D. Schmidt (Eds.), *The new child protection team handbook* (pp. 113–125). New York: Farland.

Rosenhan, D.L. (1973, January 19). On being sane in insane places. *Science, 179,* 250–258.

Rosenthal, J.A., Motz, J.K., Edmonson, D.A., & Groze, V. (1991). A descriptive study of abuse and neglect in out-of-home-placement. *Child Abuse & Neglect, 15,* 249–260.

Ross, A.L., & Grenier, G.L. (1990). Moving beyond the evil empire of institutional abuse—may the organizational force be with you. *Journal of Child and Youth Care, 4*(6), 23–33.

Rothman, D. (1984). *The Willowbrook wars.* New York: Harper & Row.

Rousso, M. (1982). Special considerations in counseling clients with cerebral palsy. *Sexuality and Disability, 5*(2), 78–88.

Rubin, R.L. (1983). Bridging the gap through individual counseling and psychotherapy with mentally retarded people. In F.J. Menolascino & B.M. McCann (Eds.), *Mental health and mental retardation: Bridging the gap* (pp. 119–128). Baltimore: University Park Press.

Rusch, R.G., Hall, J.C., & Griffin, H.C. (1986). Abuse-provoking characteristics of institutionalized mentally retarded individuals. *American Journal of Mental Deficiency, 90*(6), 618–624.

Rutter, M. (1989). Intergenerational continuities and discontinuities in serious parenting difficulties. In D. Crichetti & V. Carlson (Eds.), *Child maltreatment: Theory and research on causes and consequences of child abuse and neglect* (pp. 317–348). Cambridge, England: Cambridge University Press.

Rutter, P. (1989). *Sex in the forbidden zone.* Los Angeles: Jeremy P. Tarcher.

Ryan, J., & Thomas, F. (1987). *The politics of mental handicap* (revised edition). London: Free Association Books.

Ryan, R. (1992). Post traumatic stress syndrome: Assessing and treating the aftermath of sexual assault. *Crossing new borders: Proceedings of the Ninth Annual Conference of The National Association for the Dually Diagnosed,* 8–11.

Ryder, D. (1992). *Breaking the circle of satanic and ritual abuse: Recognizing and recovering from the hidden trauma.* Minneapolis, MN: CompCare.

Sales, B.D., Powell, D.M., & Van Duizend, R. (1982). *Disabled persons and the law: State legislative issues.* New York: Plenum Press.

Samuels, M.P., McClaughlin, W., Jacobson, R.R., Poets, C.F., & Southall, D.P.

(1992). Fourteen cases of imposed upper airway obstruction. *Archives of Diseases of Children, 67*(2), 162–170.

Sandgrund, A., Gaines, R.W., & Green, A.H. (1974). Child abuse and mental retardation: A problem of cause and effect. *American Journal of Mental Deficiency, 79*(3), 327–330.

Sanik, M.M. (1990). Parents' time use. A 1967–1986 comparison. *Lifestyles: Family and Economic Issues, 11,* 299–316.

Schaffer, J., & Sobsey, D. (1991). A dialogue on medical responsibility. In L.H. Meyer, C.A. Peck, & L. Brown (Eds.), *Critical issues in the lives of people with severe disabilities* (pp. 601–606). Baltimore: Paul H. Brookes Publishing Co.

Schanberg, S.H. (1992, November 6). These youths disgraced themselves. *Long Island Newsday.*

Scharfetter, C. (1984). Ein Anliegen der Menschheitserziehung: Delegierte Destruktivatat [An objective of education of mankind: Delegated destructiveness]. *Schweizer Archiv fur Neurologie, Neurochirurgie und Psychiatrie, 134*(2), 279–293.

Scheerenberger, R.C. (1983). *A history of mental retardation.* Baltimore: Paul H. Brookes Publishing Co.

Schei, B., Samuelson, S.O., & Bakketeig, L.S. (1991). Does spousal physical abuse affect the outcome of pregnancy? *Scandinavian Journal of Social Medicine, 19,* 26–31.

Schilit, J. (1979). The mentally retarded offender and criminal justice personnel. *Exceptional Children, 46,* 16–22.

Schilling, R.F., Kirkham, M.A., & Schinke, S.P. (1985). *Coping, social support, and prevention of maltreatment of handicapped children: Final report.* Seattle: Washington University, Child Development & Mental Retardation Center.

Schilling, R.F., Kirkham, M.A., & Schinke, S.P. (1986). Do child protection services neglect developmentally disabled children? *Education and Training of the Mentally Retarded, 21,* 21–26.

Schlapp, M.G. (1915). Available field for research and prevention in mental defect. *Proceedings of the National Conference on Charities and Correction,* 320–328.

Schutter, L.S., & Brinker, R.P. (1992). Conjuring a new category of disability from prenatal cocaine exposure: Are the infants unique biological or caretaking casualties? *Topics in Early Childhood Special Education, 11*(4), 84–111.

Schwartz, D. (1990). Quality assurance in the asylum. In J. O'Brien, C.L. O'Brien, & D.B. Schwartz (Eds.), *What can we count on to make and keep people safe?* Lithonia, GA: Responsive Systems Associates. (EDRS No. 336 922)

Schwier, K.M. (1990). *Speak-easy: People with mental handicaps talk about their lives in institutions and the community.* Austin, TX: PRO-ED.

Seagull, E.A.W., & Scheurer, S.L. (1986). Neglected and abused children of mentally retarded parents. *Child Abuse & Neglect, 10,* 493–500.

Segrave, K. (1992). *Women serial and mass murderers: A worldwide reference, 1580–1990.* Jefferson, NC: McFarland.

Seligman, M., & Darling, R.B. (1989). *Ordinary families, special children: A systems approach to childhood disability.* New York: Guilford Press.

Sengstock, W.L., Magerhans-Hurley, H., & Sprotte, A. (1990). The role of special education in the Third Reich. *Education and Training in Mental Retardation, 25,* 225–236.

Senn, C.Y. (1988). *Vulnerable: Sexual abuse and people with an intellectual handicap.* Downsview, Ontario, Canada: G. Allan Roeher Institute.

Sereny, G. (1974). *Into the darkness: From mercy killing to mass murder.* London:

Andre Deutsch.

Settlement in case alleging abuse of special education students. (1991, July–August). *Youth Law News*, p. 23.

Sexual assault; transportation; sovereign immunity; expert. (1993). *Mental & Physical Disability Law Reporter, 17*(2), 193.

Sgroi, S.M. (1989). Evaluation and treatment of sexual offense behavior in persons with mental retardation. In S.M. Sgroi (Ed.), *Vulnerable populations: Vol. 2. Sexual abuse treatment for children, adult survivors, offenders, and persons with mental retardation* (pp. 245–281). New York: Lexington Books.

The shame of Fojnica. (1993, July 22). *The Edmonton Journal*, p. A14.

Sigal, M.D., Altmark, D., & Carmel, I. (1986). Münchausen syndrome by proxy: A perpetrator using two adults. *The Journal of Nervous and Mental Disease, 174*, 696–698.

Sigurdson, E., Marginet, C., & Onysko, R. (1991). A child abuse risk index: Annotated bibliography. In C.R. Bagley & R.J. Thomlinson (Eds.), *Child sexual abuse: Critical perspectives on prevention, intervention, and treatment* (pp. 49–78). Toronto, Ontario, Canada: Wall and Emerson.

Silver, J.M., Yudofsky, S.C., & Hales, R.E. (1987). Neuropsychiatric aspects of traumatic brain injury. In R. Hales & S. Yudofsky (Eds.), *Textbook of neuropsychiatry* (pp. 179–190). The American Psychiatric Press.

Sinason, V. (1990). Individual psychoanalytical psychotherapy with severely and profoundly handicapped patients. In A. Dosen, A. Van Gennep, & G.J. Zwanikken (Eds.), *Treatment of mental illness and behavioral disorders in the mentally retarded* (pp. 71–80). Amsterdam: Logon Publications.

Sinason, V. (1992). *Mental handicap and the human condition: New approaches from the Tavistock*. London: Free Association Books.

Singer, G.H.S., & Irvin, L.K. (1991). Supporting persons with severe disabilities: Emerging findings, practices, and questions. In L.H. Meyer, C.A. Peck, & L. Brown (Eds.), *Critical issues in the lives of people with severe disabilities* (pp. 271–312). Baltimore: Paul H. Brookes Publishing Co.

Skoog, D.M., & O'Sullivan, S.P. (1993). *Police training and family violence: A foundation for the future*. Ottawa, Canada: Solicitor General of Canada and Canadian Association of Chiefs of Police.

Smith, D. (1992). Speaking out: One woman's experience. In M. Ticoll (Ed.), *No more victims: A manual to guide families and friends in preventing the sexual abuse of people with a mental handicap* (pp. 11–13). North York, Ontario, Canada: The Roeher Institute.

Smith, S.L. (1984). Significant research findings in the etiology of child abuse. *Social Casework, 65*(6), 337–346.

Sobsey, D. (1983). Reinstitutionalization: An alternative descriptor for current practices. *The Association for Persons with Severe Handicaps Newsletter, 9*(3), 3.

Sobsey, D. (1988). Research on sexual abuse: Are we asking the right questions? *Newsletter of the American Association on Mental Retardation, 1*(4), 2, 8.

Sobsey, D. (1989a). Are we preventing mental retardation? *Newsletter of the American Association on Mental Retardation, 2*(2), 2, 8.

Sobsey, D. (1989b). Whiplash shaking syndrome. *Newsletter of the American Association on Mental Retardation, 2*(6), 2, 8.

Sobsey, D. (1990a). Modifying the behavior of behavior modifiers: Arguments for countercontrol against aversive procedures. In A.C. Repp & N.N. Singh (Eds.), *Perspectives on the use of nonaversive and aversive interventions for persons with developmental disabilities* (pp. 422–433). Sycamore, IL: Sycamore Press.

Sobsey, D. (1990b, December). *Patterns of sexual offenses against people with severe disabilities*. Paper presented at The Annual Conference of The Association for Persons with Severe Handicaps, Chicago, IL.

Sobsey, D. (1990c). Too much stress on stress? Abuse & the family stress factor. *Newsletter of the American Association on Mental Retardation, 3*(1), 2, 8.

Sobsey, D. (1992). Liberty, equality, community. *Network, 2*(1), 26–34.

Sobsey, D. (1993). Responding to the needs of sexually abused children with disabilities: Program criteria. *Journal of Child Sexual Abuse, 2*(2), 131–133.

Sobsey, D. (in press). Crime prevention and personal safety skills. In M. Agran, N.E. Marchand-Martella, & R.C. Martella (Eds.), *Promoting health and safety: Skills for independent living*. Baltimore: Paul H. Brookes Publishing Co.

Sobsey, D., & Cox, A. (1991). Integrating health care and educational programs. In F.P. Orelove & D. Sobsey (Eds.), *Educating children with multiple disabilities: A transdisciplinary approach* (2nd ed., pp. 155–185). Baltimore: Paul H. Brookes Publishing Co.

Sobsey, D., & Doe, T. (1991). Patterns of sexual abuse and assault. *Journal of Sexuality and Disability, 9*(3), 243–259.

Sobsey, D., Gray, S., Wells, D., Pyper, D., & Reimer-Heck, B. (1991). *Disability, sexuality, & abuse: An annotated bibliography*. Baltimore: Paul H. Brookes Publishing Co.

Sobsey, D., & Mansell, S. (1990). The prevention of sexual abuse of people with developmental disabilities. *Developmental Disabilities Bulletin, 18*(2), 51–66.

Sobsey, D., & Mansell, S. (1992). Teaching people with disabilities to be abused and exploited: Part I. Blaming the victim. *Active Treatment Solutions, 3*(4), 1, 7–11.

Sobsey, D., Mansell, S., & Wells, D. (1991). *Sexual abuse of children with disabilities and sexual assault of adults with disabilities: Prevention strategies*. Manuscript submitted for publication.

Sobsey, D., & Varnhagen, C. (1989). Sexual abuse of people with disabilities. In M. Csapo & L. Gougen (Eds.), *Special education across Canada: Challenges for the 90s* (pp. 199–218). Vancouver, Canada: Centre for Human Development & Research.

Sobsey, D., & Varnhagen, C. (1991). Sexual abuse, assault, and exploitation of individuals with disabilities. In C. Bagley & R.J. Thomlinson (Eds.), *Child sexual abuse: Critical perspectives on prevention, intervention, and treatment* (pp. 203–216). Toronto, Ontario, Canada: Wall and Emerson.

Social prejudice linked with mental handicap in Africa. (1992). The ILSMH addresses the general assembly of the United Nations. *International League of Societies for Persons with Mental Handicap News, 14*, 16.

Söder, M. (1990). Prejudice or ambivalence? Attitudes toward people with disabilities. *Disability, Handicap & Society, 5*, 227–241.

Souther, M. (1984). Developmentally disabled abused and neglected children: A high risk/high need population. In National Center on Child Abuse and Neglect (Ed.), *Perspectives on child maltreatment in the mid '80s* (DHHS Publication No. [OHDS]84-30338). Washington, DC: U.S. Department of Health and Human Services.

Sovner, R., & Hurley, A.D. (1982). Psychotropic drug side effects presenting as behavior disorders. *Psychiatric Aspects of Mental Retardation Newsletter, 1*(12), 45–48.

Spackman, R., Grigel, M., & MacFarlane, C. (1990). Individual counseling and therapy for the mentally handicapped. *Alberta Psychology, 19*(5), 14–18.

Spitz, R.A. (1945). Hospitalism: An inquiry into the genesis of psychiatric conditions in early childhood. Part 1. *Psychoanalytic Studies of the Child, 1*, 53–74.

Spradley, J.P. (1980). *Participant observation.* New York: Holt, Rinehart and Winston.

Stagg, V., & Catron, T. (1986). Networks of social supports for parents of handicapped children. In R.R. Fewell & P.F. Vadasy (Eds.), *Families of handicapped children: Needs and supports across the lifespan* (pp. 279–296). Austin, TX: PRO-ED.

Starr, R., Dietrich, K.N., Fischhoff, J., Ceresnie, S., & Zweier, D. (1984). The contribution of handicapping conditions to child abuse. *Topics in Early Childhood Special Education, 4*(1), 55–69.

Stedman, T.L. (1990). *Stedman's medical dictionary* (25th ed.). Baltimore: Williams and Wilkins.

Steege, M.W., Wacker, D.P., Berg, W.K., Cigrand, K.K., & Cooper, L.J. (1989). The use of behavioral assessment to prescribe and evaluate treatments for severely handicapped children. *Journal of Applied Behavior Analysis, 22*, 23–34.

Steinmetz, S. (1983). Dependency, stress, and violence between middle-aged caregivers and their elderly parents. In J.I. Kosberg (Ed.), *Abuse and maltreatment of the elderly: Causes and interventions* (pp. 134–149). Boston: John Wright PSG Inc.

Stenson, P., & Anderson, C. (1987). Treating juvenile sex offenders and preventing the cycle of abuse. *Journal of Child Care, 3*(2), 91–102.

Stevenson, R.D., & Alexander, R. (1990). Münchausen syndrome by proxy presenting as a developmental disability. *Developmental and Behavioral Pediatrics, 11*, 262–264.

Stimpson, L., & Best, M.C. (1991). *Courage above all: Sexual assault against women with disabilities.* Toronto, Ontario, Canada: DisAbled Women's Network Canada.

Sullivan, P.M. (1993). Sexual abuse therapy for special children. *Journal of Child Sexual Abuse, 2*(2), 117–125.

Sullivan, P.M., Brookhouser, P.E., Scanlan, J.M., Knutson, J.F., & Schulte, L.E. (1991). Patterns of physical and sexual abuse of communicatively handicapped children. *Annals of Otology, Rhinology, and Laryngology, 100*(3), 188–194.

Sullivan, P.M., Scanlan, J.M., Knutson, J.F., Brookhouser, P.E., & Schulte, L.E. (1992). The effects of psychotherapy on behavior problems of sexually abused deaf children. *Child Abuse & Neglect, 16*(2), 297–307.

Sullivan, P.M., Vernon, M., & Scanlan, J.M. (1987). Sexual abuse of deaf youth. *American Annals of the Deaf, 132*(4), 256–262.

Sumarah, J., Maksym, D., & Goudge, J. (1988). The effects of a staff training program on attitudes and knowledge of staff toward the sexuality of persons with intellectual handicaps. *Canadian Journal of Rehabilitation, 1*(3), 127–136.

Summit, R.C. (1988). Hidden victims, hidden pain: Societal avoidance of child sexual abuse. In G.E. Wyatt & G.J. Powell (Eds.), *Lasting effects of child sexual abuse* (pp. 39–60). Newbury Park, CA: Sage Publications.

Summit, R.C. (1993, March 10–13). *McMartin children vindicated: Archaeologist confirms tunnel stories.* Paper presented at the Ninth Annual Symposium on Child Sexual Abuse, Huntsville, AL.

Sundberg, S.L., Barbaree, H.E., & Marshall, W.L. (1991). Victim blame and the disinhibition of sexual arousal to rape vignettes. *Violence Victimology, 6*(2), 103–120.

Sundram, C.J. (1984). Obstacles to reducing patient abuse in public institutions. *Hospital and Community Psychiatry, 35*(3), 238–243.

Sundram, C.J. (1986). Strategies to prevent patient abuse in public institutions. *New England Journal of Human Services, 6,* 20–25.

Susser, M. (1988). The quantification of risk factors in major neurodevelopmental disorders. In F. Kulbi, N. Patel, W. Schmidt, & O. Linderkamp (Eds.), *Perinatal events and brain damage in surviving children* (pp. 12–27). New York: Springer-Verlag.

Suzuki, D.T., Griffiths, A.J.F., & Lewontin, R.C. (1981). *An introduction to genetic analysis* (2nd ed.). San Francisco: Freeman.

Szymanski, L.S. (1980). Individual psychotherapy with retarded persons. In L.S. Szymanski & P.E. Tanguay (Eds.), *Emotional disorders of mentally retarded persons: Assessments, treatment and consultation* (pp. 131–147). Baltimore: University Park Press.

Szymanski, L.S., & Rosefsky, Q.B. (1980). Group psychotherapy with retarded persons. In L.S. Szymanski & P.E. Tanguay (Eds.), *Emotional disorders of mentally retarded persons: Assessments, treatment and consultation* (pp. 173–194). Baltimore: University Park Press.

Talbot, Y., & Shaul, R. (1987). Medical students learn about attitudes and handicaps. *Entourage, 2*(3), 6–11.

Tanguay, P.E., & Szymanski, L.S. (1980). Training of mental health professionals in mental retardation. In L.S. Szymanski & P.E. Tanguay (Eds.), *Emotional disorders of mentally retarded persons: Assessments, treatment and consultation* (pp. 19–28). Baltimore: University Park Press.

Taylor, S.J., & Bogdan, R. (1992). Defending illusions: The institutions struggle for survival. In P.M. Ferguson, D.L. Ferguson, & S.J. Taylor (Eds.), *Interpreting disability: A qualitative reader* (pp. 78–98). New York: Teacher's College Press.

Taylor, S.J., Bogdan, R., & Racino, J.A. (1991). Introduction. In S.J. Taylor, R. Bogdan, & J.A. Racino (Eds.), *Life in the community: Case studies of organizations supporting people with disabilities* (pp. 1–13). Baltimore: Paul H. Brookes Publishing Co.

Terman, L.M. (1916). *The measurement of intelligence.* Boston: Houghton Mifflin.

Tharinger, D., Horton, C.B., & Millea, S. (1990). Sexual abuse and exploitation of children and adults with mental retardation and other handicaps. *Child Abuse & Neglect, 14,* 301–312.

Thomas, G. (1988). *Journey into madness.* London: Corgi Books.

Thomlison, R.J. (1991). A review of child sexual abuse outcome research. In C. Bagley & R.J. Thomlinson (Eds.), *Child sexual abuse: Critical perspectives on prevention, intervention, and treatment* (pp. 181–202). Toronto, Ontario, Canada: Wall & Emerson.

Ticoll, M. (1992a). *No more victims: A manual to guide counsellors and social workers in addressing the sexual abuse of people with a mental handicap.* North York, Ontario, Canada: The Roeher Institute.

Ticoll, M. (1992b). *No more victims: A manual to guide families and friends in preventing the sexual abuse of people with a mental handicap.* North York, Ontario, Canada: The Roeher Institute.

Ticoll, M. (1992c). *No more victims: A manual to guide police in addressing the sexual abuse of people with a mental handicap.* North York, Ontario, Canada: The Roeher Institute.

Tinkham v. Groveport-Madison Local School District, 602 N.E.2d 256 (Ohio Court of Appeals, 1991).

Tomasulo, D. (1990). *Group counseling for people with mild to moderate mental retardation and developmental disabilities: An interactive-behavioral model.* New York: Young Adult Institute.

Tower, C.C. (1989). *Understanding child abuse and neglect.* Boston: Allyn and Bacon.

Trojanowicz, R.C., Trojanowicz, J.M., & Moss, F.M. (1975). *Community based crime prevention.* Pacific Palisades, CA: Goodyear Publishing Co.

Trute, B., Teft, B., & Segall, A. (1989). Social rejection of the mentally ill: A replication study of public attitude. *Social Psychiatry and Psychiatric Epidemiology, 24,* 69–76.

Tully, K. (1986). *Improving residential life for disabled people.* Melbourne, Australia: Churchill Livingstone.

Turk, V., & Brown, H. (1992, August 5–7). *Sexual abuse of adults with learning disabilities.* Paper presented at the Conference of the International Association for Scientific Study of Mental Deficiency, Brisbane, Australia.

Tymchuk, A.J., & Andron, L. (1990). Mothers with mental retardation who do or do not abuse or neglect their children. *Child Abuse & Neglect, 14,* 313–323.

Uditsky, B. (1993). Natural pathways to friendships. In A.N. Amado (Ed.), *Friendships and community connections between people with and without developmental disabilities* (pp. 85–95). Baltimore: Paul H. Brookes Publishing Co.

Ulicny, G.R., White, G.W., Bradford, B., & Mathews, R.M. (1990). Consumer exploitation by attendants: How often does it happen and can anything be done about it? *Rehabilitation Counselling Bulletin, 33*(3), 240–246.

Underwood, N. (1989, October 30). Sex and scandal: An inquiry hears graphic allegations of abuse. *Macleans, 102,* 84.

United Nations Convention on the Rights of the Child of 1989, 28 I.L.M. 1456. (1989).

United Nations Declaration on the Rights of Disabled Persons of 1975, V.N. G.A. Res. 3447, U.N. GAOR, 30th Sess., Supp. No. 34, U.N. Doc. A/10034 (1975).

United States v. Kozminski, 108 S. Ct. 2751 (1988).

Untalan, F.F., & Mills, C.S. (1992). Multidisciplinary approaches in child abuse and neglect. In F.F. Untalan & C.S. Mills (Eds.), *Interdisciplinary perspectives in child abuse and neglect* (pp. 1–15). New York: Praeger.

van der Kolk, B., Perry, J.C., & Herman, J.L. (1991). Childhood origins of self-destructive behavior. *American Journal of Psychiatry, 148*(12), 1665–1671.

VanDusen, L. (1987). We just want the truth. *Macleans, 100*(44), 56, 58.

Vogel, P.A. (1982). Treating lower-functioning institutionalized mentally handicapped with severe behavior problems: An emphasis on language. *Tidsskrift-for-Norsk-Psychologforening, 19*(12), 601–608.

von Hentig, H. (1967). *The criminal and his victims.* Hamden, CT: Archon Books.

Walter, B. (1993). *In need of protection: Children and youth in Alberta: Child welfare review.* Edmondton, Alberta, Canada: Children's Advocate/The Queen's Printer.

Wambold, H. (1990). Oral history. In M. Crossmaker & D. Merry (Eds.), *Stigma: Stereotypes and scapegoats* (pp. 53–56). Columbus, OH: Ohio Legal Rights Society.

Wang, M.C., Anderson, K.A., & Bram, P.J. (1985). *Toward an empirical data base on mainstreaming: A research synthesis of program implementation and effects.* Pittsburgh: University of Pittsburgh, Learning Research and Development Center.

Warren, S.F., & Reichle, J. (Eds.). (1992). *Causes and effects in communication and language intervention*. Baltimore: Paul H. Brookes Publishing Co.

Wasserman, G.A., Lennon, M.C., Allen, R., & Shilansky, M. (1987). Contributors to attachment in normal and physically handicapped infants. *Journal of the American Academy of Child and Adolescent Psychiatry, 26*(1), 9–15.

Wasson, D.K. (1984). *Community-based preventive policing: A review 1984–1990*. Ottawa, Canada: Programs Branch Secretariat, Ministry of the Solicitor General.

Waterman, J., & Lusk, R. (1986). Scope of the problem. In K. McFarlane & J. Waterman (Eds.), *Sexual abuse of young children: Evaluation and treatment* (pp. 3–14). New York: The Guilford Press.

Waxman, B.F. (1991). Hatred—The unacknowledged dimension in violence against disabled people. *Journal of Sexuality and Disability, 9*(3), 185–199.

Webber, L. (1993, May 10). Convicted of raping a retarded adult: A video tape and hearsay evidence clinches the case. *Alberta Report*, p. 27.

Weber, M. (1992). Collaboration does not mean consorting with the enemy. *Protecting Children, 9*(2), 3–9.

Webster's New World Dictionary of American English (3rd college ed.). (1988). New York: Simon & Schuster.

Webster's Ninth New Collegiate Dictionary. (1989). Springfield, MA: Merriam-Webster.

Weicker, L. (1987). Federal response to institutional abuse and neglect: The Protection and Advocacy for Mentally Ill Individuals Act. *American Psychologist, 42*(1), 1027–1028.

Weiss, R.S. (Ed.). (1973). *Loneliness: The experience of emotional and social isolation*. Cambridge, MA: Massachusetts Institute of Technology Press.

Werry, J.S. (1988). Conclusions. In M.G. Aman & N.N. Singh (Eds.), *Psychopharmacology of the developmental disabilities* (pp. 239–245). New York: Springer-Verlag.

West, M.A., Richardson, M., LeConte, J., Crimi, C., & Stuart, S. (1992). Identification of developmental disabilities and health problems among individuals under child protective services. *Mental Retardation, 30*, 221–225.

Westcott, H. (1991). The abuse of disabled children: A review of the literature. *Child Care, Health and Development, 17*, 243–258.

Westcott, H. (1992). The 1991 Criminal Justice Act: Research on children's testimony. *Adoption & Fostering, 16*(3), 7–12.

Westcott, H. (1993). *Abuse of children and adults with disabilities*. London: National Society for Prevention of Cruelty to Children.

Wetherow, D. (Ed.). (1992). *The whole community catalog: Welcoming people with disabilities into the heart of community life*. Manchester, CT: Communitas.

Wheeler, R.J., & Berliner, L. (1988). Treating the effects of sexual abuse on children. In G.E. Wyatt & G.J. Powell (Eds.), *Lasting effects of child sexual abuse* (pp. 227–247). Newbury Park, CA: Sage Publications.

Whitcomb, D. (1992). *When the victim is a child* (2nd ed.). Washington, DC: National Institute of Justice.

Whitfield, C.L. (1990). Alcoholism, other drug misuse, and violence: An overview. In L.J. Hertzberg, G.F. Ostrum, & J.R. Field (Eds.), *Violent behavior: Vol. I. Assessment & intervention* (pp. 201–225). Great Neck, NY: PMA.

Whitney, C.R. (1993, Jan. 15). Top German doctor admits SS past. *New York Times*, p. 13.

Wildin, S.R., Williamson, W.D., & Wilson, G.S. (1991). Children of battered women: Developmental and learning profiles. *Clinical Pediatrics, 30*(5), 299–304.

Wilgosh, L. (1990). Sexual assault and abuse of people with disabilities: Parents' concerns. *Developmental Disabilities Bulletin, 18*(2), 44–50.

Williams, K.M. (1976). The effect of victim characteristics on the disposition of violent crimes. In W.F. McDonald (Ed.), *Criminal justice and the victim* (pp. 177–213). Beverly Hills: Sage Publications.

Wilson, C., & Brewer, N. (1992). The incidence of criminal victimization of individuals with an intellectual disability. *Australian Psychologist, 2*, 114–117.

Winett, R.W., & Winkler, R.C. (1972). Current behavior modification in the classroom: Be still, be quiet, be docile. *Journal of Applied Behavior Analysis, 5*, 499–504.

Wolfe, D.A., Sandler, J., & Kaufman, K. (1981). A competency-based parent training program for child abusers. *Journal of Consulting and Clinical Psychology, 49*, 633–640.

Wolfensberger, W. (1972). *Normalization: The principle of normalization in human services*. Toronto, Ontario, Canada: National Institute on Mental Retardation.

Wolfensberger, W. (1975). *The origin and nature of our institutional models*. Syracuse, NY: Human Policy Press.

Wolfensberger, W. (1980). The definition of normalization: Update, problems, disagreements, and misunderstandings. In R. Flynn & K. Nitsch (Eds.), *Normalization, social integration, and community services* (pp. 71–115). Baltimore: University Park Press.

Wolfensberger, W. (1981). The extermination of handicapped people in World War II Germany. *Mental Retardation, 19*, 1–7.

Wolfensberger, W. (1991). Historical account of a "wolf-child." *Disability Rag, 13*(1), [Electronic edition].

Wooley, P.V., Jr., & Evans, W.A., Jr. (1955). Significance of skeletal lesions in infants resembling those of traumatic origin. *Journal of the American Medical Association, 181*, 17–24.

Workers at mental health center charged with abusing patients. (1986, November 21). *The New York Times*, p. B5.

Wyndham, J. (1955). *The chrysalids*. New York: Penguin Books.

Yoder, P.J., Davies, B., & Bishop, K. (1992). Getting children with developmental disabilities to talk to adults. In S.F. Warren & J. Reichle (Eds.), *Causes and effects in communication and language intervention* (pp. 255–275). Baltimore: Paul H. Brookes Publishing Co.

Youngblade, L.M., & Belsky, J. (1989). Child maltreatment, infant–parent attachment security, and dysfunctional peer relationships in toddlerhood. *Topics in Early Childhood Special Education, 9*(2), 1–15.

Yuker, H.E. (1986). Disability and the law: Attitudes of police, lawyers, and mental health professionals. *Rehabilitation Psychology, 31*(1), 13–25.

Yuker, H.E. (1988). The effects of contact on attitudes toward disabled persons: Some empirical generalizations. In H.E. Yuker (Ed.), *Attitudes toward persons with disabilities* (pp. 262–274). New York: Springer.

Zantal-Weiner, K. (1987). *Child abuse and the handicapped child*. Reston, VA: CEC. (ERIC Document Reproduction Service No. 446)

Zellman, G.L. (1991). The impact of case characteristics on child abuse reporting decisions. *Child Abuse & Neglect, 16*(1), 57–74.

Zigler, E., & Hall, N.W. (1989). Physical child abuse in America: Past, present and future. In D. Cicchetti & V. Carlson (Eds.), *Child maltreatment: Theory and research on the causes and consequences of child abuse and neglect* (pp. 38–75). New York: Cambridge University Press.

Zimbardo, P.G., & Leippe, M.R. (1991). *The psychology of attitude change and social influence*. New York: McGraw-Hill.

Zirpoli, T.J., Snell, M.E., & Loyd, B.H. (1987). Characteristics of persons with mental retardation who have been abused by caregivers. *The Journal of Special Education, 21*(2), 31–41.

Zola, I.K. (1992). Any distinguishing features? The portrayal of disability in the crime-mystery genre. In P.M. Ferguson, D.L. Ferguson, S.J. Taylor (Eds.), *Interpreting disability: A qualitative reader* (pp. 233–250). New York: Teacher's College Press.

Index